Stress, Attitudes, and Decisions

Centennial Psychology Series
Charles D. Spielberger, *General Editor*

Anne Anastasi   *Contributions to Differential Psychology*

William K. Estes   *Models of Learning, Memory, and Choice*

Hans J. Eysenck   *Personality, Genetics, and Behavior*

Irving L. Janis   *Stress, Attitudes, and Decisions*

Neal Miller   *Bridges Between Laboratory and Clinic*

Brenda Milner   *Brain Function and Cognition*

O. Hobart Mowrer   *Leaves from Many Seasons*

Charles E. Osgood   *Psycholinguistics, Cross-Cultural Universals, and Prospects for Mankind*

Julian B. Rotter   *The Development and Applications of Social Learning Theory*

Seymour B. Sarason   *Psychology and Social Action*

Benton J. Underwood   *Studies in Learning and Memory*

Stress, Attitudes, and Decisions

Selected Papers

Irving L. Janis

PRAEGER

PRAEGER SPECIAL STUDIES • PRAEGER SCIENTIFIC

Library of Congress Cataloging in Publication Data

Janis, Irving Lester, 1918–
  Stress, attitudes, and decisions.

  (Centennial psychology series)
  Bibliography: p.
  Includes index.
  1. Stress (Psychology)—Addresses, essays, lectures.
  2. Attitude change—Addresses, essays, lectures.
  3. Decision-making—Addresses, essays, lectures.
  I. Title. II. Series. [DNLM: 1. Stress, Psychological
  —Collected works. 2. Attitude—Collected works.
  3. Decision making—Collected works. WM 172 J33s]
  BF575.S75J33 1982   150   82-9007
  ISBN 0-03-059036-1   AACR2

Published in 1982 by Praeger Publishers
CBS Educational and Professional Publishing
a Division of CBS Inc.
521 Fifth Avenue, New York, New York 10175, U.S.A.

3456789 052 98765432

Printed in the United States of America

Contents

Author's Preface — vii

Editor's Introduction — ix

1   Introduction: Theoretical Models and Research Orientation (1982) — 1

2   Control of Fear: Studies of Combat Infantrymen and Air Crews (1949) — 11

3   Aftermath of the Atomic Disasters (1951) — 25

4   Reactions to Air War: Fear and Coping Mechanisms (1951) — 39

5   Psychological Effects of Warnings (1962) — 57

6   Group Identification under Conditions of External Danger (1963) — 93

7   Attitude Change via Role Playing (1968) — 113

8   Adaptive Personality Changes Resulting from Stressful Episodes (1969) — 127

9   Coping with Decisional Conflict: An Analysis of How Stress Affects Decision-Making Suggests Interventions to Improve the Process (1976) [with Leon Mann] — 147

10   The Influence of Television on Personal Decision-Making (1980) — 167

11   Psychological and Sociological Ambivalence: An Analysis of Nonadherence to Courses of Action Prescribed by Health-Care Professionals (1980) — 193

12   Effective Interventions in Decision Counseling:
     Implications of the Findings from Twenty-three Field
     Experiments (1982)   217

13   Stress Inoculation in Health Care: Theory and
     Research (1982)   259

14   Counteracting the Adverse Effects of Concurrence-
     Seeking in Policy-Planning Groups: Theory and
     Research Perspectives (1982)   291

15   Postscript: Improving Research Strategies (1982) 309

     Biographical Sketch (1982)   319

     Publications: A Comprehensive Bibliography   324

     Author Index   333

     Subject Index   341

Author's Preface

In selecting papers for this book, I have given priority to those that combine a discussion of research findings with theoretical analysis. Instead of selecting research reports that present only a single social psychological investigation, I have chosen synthesizing papers; each of them contains a relatively comprehensive discussion that summarizes a number of interrelated studies bearing on the same set of general hypotheses or the same theoretical model. For readers who might be interested in technical details about the methods used and the data analysis of any particular study, references are cited to each of the published research reports.

At first, I thought it might be possible to organize the book into separate sections for each of the three main topics—stress, attitudes, and decisions. But it soon became apparent that there were too many papers that would fit into all three categories. Throughout my writings the three topics are closely interrelated. For example, in the papers on warnings about health hazards such as lung cancer, certain types of *stress* stimuli are described as inducing changes in *attitudes* concerning personal vulnerability, which in turn lead to corresponding changes in *decisions* about taking protective action. In other papers, such as those dealing with stress inoculation, the three are linked in the reverse causal sequence—that is, prior *attitudes* and *decisions* are treated as antecedent causes of the magnitude of perceived *stress* and of its disruptive effects. Hence I have given up attempting to sort the papers into the three categories; instead, I simply present them in chronological order. This arrangement may have some advantages for those readers interested in seeing how the later phases of my theory and research on decision making evolved from my earlier survey work on the stresses of wartime or peacetime disasters and also from my experimental studies of atttude changes induced by warning communications.

The papers in this book are essentially unchanged from the way they were originally published. The few changes that have been made consist of deletions of nonessential or redundant material. Whenever there is a discussion of the same specific subtopic in two different papers, I have retained the one that seems most clear and eliminated the other, marking the deletion in the conventional way with three ellipsis dots and giving a cross-reference. In a few chapters I have also added cross-references to other chapters in the present book where subsidiary material on related subtopics can be found.

For aid in making decisions pertaining to the editing of this volume, I wish to express my special thanks to Professor Charles D. Spielberger.

Editor's Introduction

The founding of Wilhelm Wundt's laboratory at Leipzig in 1879 is widely acclaimed as the landmark event that provided the initial impetus for the development of psychology as an experimental science. To commemorate scientific psychology's one-hundredth anniversary, Praeger Publishers commissioned the Centennial Psychology Series. The general goals of the Series are to present, in both historical and contemporary perspective, the most important papers of distinguished contributors to psychological theory and research.

As psychology begins its second century, the Centennial Series proposes to examine the foundation on which scientific psychology is built. Each volume provides a unique opportunity for the reader to witness the emerging theoretical insights of eminent psychologists whose seminal work has served to define and shape their respective fields, and to share with them the excitement associated with the discovery of new scientific knowledge.

The selection of the Series authors was an extremely difficult task. Indexes of scientific citations and rosters of the recipients of prestigious awards for research contributions were examined. Nominations were invited from leading authorities in various fields of psychology. The opinions of experienced teachers of psychology and recent graduates of doctoral programs were solicited. There was, in addition, a self-selection factor: a few of the distinguished senior psychologists invited to participate in the Series were not able to do so, most often because of demanding commitments or ill health.

Each Series author was invited to develop a volume comprising five major parts: (1) an original introductory chapter; (2) previously published articles and original papers selected by the author; (3) a concluding chapter; (4) a brief autobiography; and (5) a complete bibliography of the author's publications. The main content of each volume consists of articles and papers especially selected for this Series by the author. These papers trace the historical development of the author's work over a period of forty to fifty years. Each volume also provides a cogent presentation of the author's current research and theoretical viewpoints.

In their introductory chapters, Series authors were asked to describe the intellectual climate that prevailed at the beginning of their scientific careers, and to examine the evolution of the ideas that led them from one study to another. They were also invited to comment on significant factors—both scientific and personal—that stimulated and motivated them to embark on their research programs and to consider special opportunities or constraints that influenced their work, including experimental failures and blind alleys only rarely reported in the literature.

In order to preserve the historical record, most of the articles reprinted in the Series volumes have been reproduced exactly as they appeared when they were first published. In some cases, however, the authors have abridged their original papers (but not altered the content), so that redundant materials could be eliminated and more papers could be included.

In the concluding chapters, the Series authors were asked to comment on their selected papers, to describe representative studies on which they are currently working, and to evaluate the current status of their research. They were also asked to discuss major methodological issues encountered in their respective fields of interest and to identify contemporary trends that were considered most promising for future scientific investigation.

The biographical sketch that is included in each Series volume supplements the autobiographical information contained in the original and concluding chapters. Perhaps the most difficult task faced by the Series authors was selecting a limited number of papers that they considered most representative from the comprehensive bibliography of the author's life work that appears at the end of each volume.

Janis's Contributions

Although general guidelines were suggested for each Centennial volume, the authors were encouraged to adapt the Series format to meet their individual needs. For this book, Professor Janis has selected thirteen papers that report some of his most important contributions to the research literature' on psychological stress, attitude change, and decisional conflict. Most of these papers provide a comprehensive and integrated account of a series of studies and the theoretical hypotheses that were tested.

In his introductory chapter, Professor Janis describes three theoretical models that have guided his research on psychological trauma, attitude change, and decision making. He also discusses the significant professional and personal experiences that influenced his early work on analyzing Nazi propaganda and investigating stress among combat infantrymen and air crews during World War II, and his postwar research on peacetime disasters and on stress and anxiety in medical and surgical patients who undergo painful treatment. Acknowledging his debts to Freud, Lewin, Klineberg, Lasswell, Stouffer, and especially Carl I. Hovland, Janis discusses the specific research strategies he has evolved as his investigations progressed from survey research and laboratory studies to controlled field experiments. His preference for carefully controlled field studies grows out of a strong conviction that psychological theory must ultimately be evaluated in terms of its potential for helping people to "avoid psychological trauma, obtain their goals, or improve the quality of their lives" (p. 8).

Spanning a period of more than thirty years, the thirteen selected papers are presented in chronological order. The first four papers (Chapters 2–5) report the results of early survey research on psychological stress in combat settings and postwar investigations of maladaptive attitude changes in civilians exposed to war- or peacetime disasters. The selected papers also include articles based on participant observation and laboratory and field investigations of the psychological effects of warnings and role playing on attitude change. Over the past two decades, Professor Janis's research has focused on complex decision-making processes, with a corresponding emphasis on controlled field experiments. His highly original theoretical insights and innovative methodology are matched by his research productivity. Of the six papers in this book that are centrally concerned with personal decision making and "groupthink" (Chapters 9–14), five were written during the past three years and three will be published for the first time during the current year.

In the final chapter, Professor Janis suggests a number of prescriptive rules for improving research methods and strategies in psychological investigations. In order to draw meaningful conclusions about cause-effect relationships, Professor Janis cautions that the variables that are investigated should represent important behaviors in their own right, with high generality for embracing a wide range of relevant social phenomena. Consistent with these convictions, Janis describes how he transformed his social psychology laboratory at Yale into a community weight-reduction clinic for conducting research on personal decisions. The magnitude of weight loss provides an objective, socially relevant measure of the behavioral consequences of dieting decisions.

In recognition of his many significant theoretical and empirical contributions to scientific psychology, the American Psychological Association presented its Distinguished Scientific Contributions Award to Professor Janis in August 1981. The citation that accompanied this award provides an excellent summary of his outstanding contributions to psychological science:

> For his contributions to the understanding of conflict and its resolution. Equally at home in the laboratory and the field, his groundbreaking experiments and astute observations have illuminated both intra-individual stress and inter-group tensions. His distinguished research on persuasion and on decision-making are landmark contributions. His pioneering work on stress and his continuing interest in self-regulation are basic to the emerging field of health psychology. His analysis of groupthink has clarified the pervasive distortions that can mark political decision-making. His accomplishments have provided a broad theoretical and empirical foundation not only for psychology but for all the social sciences.

Acknowledgements

The interest and enthusiasm of all with whom we have consulted concerning the establishment of the Series have been most gratifying, but I am especially grateful to Professors Anne Anastasi, Hans J. Eysenck, and Irving L. Janis for their many helpful comments and suggestions and for their early agreement to contribute to the Series. For his invaluable advice and consultation in the conception and planning of the Series, and for his dedicated and effective work in making it a reality, I am deeply indebted to Dr. George Zimmar, psychology editor for Praeger Publishers.

The Series was initiated while I was a Fellow-In-Residence at the Netherlands Institute for Advanced Study, and I would like to express my appreciation to the director and staff of the Institute and to my NIAS colleagues for their stimulation, encouragement, and strong support of this endeavor.

Charles D. Spielberger

Stress, Attitudes, and Decisions

1

Introduction: Theoretical Models and Research Orientation (1982)

This chapter will describe the theoretical and methodological orientations that run through the research studies discussed in the papers selected for this book. I shall also try to indicate how my research interests in certain substantive problems and my preferences for a certain research style evolved. First, in order to convey the theoretical context of the studies reported in the selected papers, I shall give a brief account of the main theoretical models that I have been trying to develop. Next comes a discussion of the strategies that guided my early research on stress and attitude change. Finally, I shall mention the reasons for focusing my later work directly on decision making and for giving priority to field experiments on the effects of interventions that are intended to help people avoid making impulsive or erroneous choices that they subsequently regret.

THEORETICAL MODELS

In the thirteen papers that follow, a number of miniature and middle-range theories are discussed. Some of them are only roughly sketched out, whereas others are more fully developed, evaluated, and modified in light of the available evidence. In the latter category are three theoretical models dealing with somewhat different ranges of phenomena that overlap a bit since all of them are concerned with certain aspects of psychological stress. Probably all three of these middle-level theories will someday be integrated and improved by an astute behavioral scientist who will come up with a good overarching theory that provides explanations for a much broader range of phenomena. For the present, however, I am resigned to working with them separately because whenever I try to subsume any two of them under a common set of more general propositions, they lose their predictive power.

It seems to me that the overarching propositions proposed so far by other behavioral scientists suffer from the same fatal defect. The so-called integrative concepts—whether formulated in terms of learning principles, information processing, or systems analysis—become so vague that they offer little more than another vocabulary for saying what we already know. They provide facile explanations for all research outcomes no matter how mutually contradictory, which means that they explain nothing at all. Hence I find it necessary to accept the relatively narrow scope of each of the models in order to gain the advantages of generating testable predictions, including some that I probably would not have thought of without the theory.

Psychological Trauma

One of the three models attempts to explain the severe psychological disturbances observed among disaster victims. My reformulations and extensions of MacCurdy's (1943) concepts of "near-miss" versus "remote-miss" experiences provide the rudiments of a theory that may account for the disruptive emotional impact of all sorts of disasters in terms of the shattering of the victim's feelings of personal invulnerability (Chapters 4 and 5). The theory applies to a wide variety of extreme stress situations that sometimes have traumatizing effects, including surgical operations.

The additional concepts that I introduce pertaining to "the work of worrying" and "emotional inoculation" (or "stress inoculation") help explain how psychological trauma and maladaptive behavior can be prevented by the provision of appropriate warnings and other preparatory communications before the onset of severely stressful events (Chapters 8 and 13). What I say about the work of worrying is strongly influenced by Freud, whose writings especially on anxiety, depression, and mechanisms of defense I studied intensively during postdoctoral training at the New York Psychoanalytic Institute, where I participated in the seminars of Heinz Hartmann, Ernst Kris, Edith Jacobson, and other leading Freudian psychoanalysts.

Coping with Decisional Conflict

Much more applicable to everyday life is the theoretical model that specifies the conditions under which a person will succeed or fail to go through the essential steps for arriving at sound decisions (Chapter 9 by Janis & Mann). By sound decisions we mean ones that are likely to attain the person's objectives and that are unlikely to give rise to disappointment, regret, or failure to live up to commitments. The model is based on observations of the causes and consequences of ineffective coping patterns (such as hypervigilance and defensive avoidance) in contrast to an effective coping pattern (vigilance), all of which occur under certain conditions in situations of severe danger when people have to make emergency decisions.

A key assumption in our analysis of decision making is that everyone's repertoire includes the same coping patterns for responding to any challenging threat or opportunity that generates the stress of decisional conflict. Accordingly, the model is generalized to apply to all consequential decisions, including those affecting the decision maker's career, personal finances, love life, and health (see Janis, 1977, 2; Janis, 1980, 5). The theory is also applicable to policymaking when the decision maker is a member of an executive committee; it helps to explain governmental fiascos resulting from groupthink (Chapter 14).

Social Influence of Change Agents

The third model (Chapters 11 and 12) deals with the social influence of professional counselors and others who function as change agents in the lives of normal people. Although the observations on which it is based come from case studies of psychotherapy and counseling, it is intended to be broadly applicable to all sorts of interpersonal contacts in which one person exerts an influence on others to commit themselves to a new course of action. The theory specifies the conditions under which people will internalize the norms conveyed by an adviser or change agent as a result of becoming temporarily dependent on that individual for maintaining self-esteem.

EARLY RESEARCH ON ATTITUDES AND STRESS

My first published research study (Janis, 1943, 3) was carried out with a fellow graduate student in 1941 when both of us were in a seminar on experimental psychology conducted by Robert S. Woodworth at Columbia University. This study initiated a series of systematic investigations on the causes and consequences of attitudes. My interest in attitude change and related topics in social psychology was stimulated in a graduate seminar at Columbia University with Otto Klineberg. These interests were strongly reinforced by wartime experiences.

During the early years of World War II, I had the opportunity to work as a research associate with Harold D. Lasswell, analyzing Nazi and native fascist propaganda by developing and using systematic content analysis techniques (see Janis, 1943, 1, 2, 4; 1949, 4, 5). Then, for the next three years, starting when I was drafted into the U.S. Army in the fall of 1943, I worked as a military research psychologist under the supervision of Carl I. Hovland and Samuel A. Stouffer in the Research Branch of the Information and Education Division of the War Department. Our mission was to carry out surveys and field experiments on factors influencing morale attitudes. After the war these studies were published with extensive commentaries in *The American Soldier* by Stouffer and a number of co-authors, including Arthur A. Lumsdaine, Robin M. Williams, Jr., M. Brewster Smith, and myself (see Janis, 1949, 1, 2, 3).

As I carried out the studies of military morale, my psychological horizons broadened to include a wide range of problems in the area of psychological stress. At the outset of my military service, I learned that stress experiences were closely linked with attitude changes. This was the main theme of a report on my participant observations of adjustment mechanisms of draftees undergoing the stresses of rigorous military training (Janis, 1945). Later on, I participated in systematic research on various aspects of psychological stress among infantrymen and air crews (see Chapter 2). In all these studies I noticed that exposure to stress appeared to be a major source of attitude change among military personnel, sometimes stimulating them to pursue adaptive courses of action, sometimes, conversely, creating demoralization or defeatism.

A major determinant of adaptive versus maladaptive behavior in response to threats of injury or death in combat appeared to be the formal and informal communications to which soldiers were exposed during their military training. These communications influenced the soldiers' attitudes concerning the nature of the danger and their own capabilities for dealing with it. From my analysis of morale survey data indicating that certain precombat training experiences might be related to changes in self-confidence and fear in combat, I came to realize that attitude changes should be studied as causes as well as consequences of psychological stress.

After the war I continued to investigate the two-way interaction between stress and attitudes in a variety of settings. These studies are represented in papers on adaptive and maladaptive attitude changes in civilians exposed to wartime or peacetime disasters (Chapters 3, 4, and 5), and in patients undergoing painful medical treatments or surgery (Chapters 8 and 13). The interaction of stress and attitudes was also investigated in students and middle-aged people exposed to fear-arousing appeals in public health communications that were intended to influence attitudes and decisions about counteracting such hazards as tooth decay from inadequate toothbrushing and lung cancer from cigarette smoking (Janis, 1967).

RESEARCH ON ATTITUDE CHANGE

The studies of attitude change were carried out mainly during the late 1940s and the 1950s, when I was one of the main participants in the Yale research project on attitudes and communications, under the direction of Carl I. Hovland (see Janis, 1953, 2). My research on this project was not confined to investigating the effects of fear-arousing appeals. Other attitude-change problems that I investigated during the 1950s and early 1960s included individual differences in responsiveness to persuasive communications (Janis, 1959, 3), effectiveness of different sequences of pro and con arguments (Janis, 1957, 3), facilitating effects of situational rewards (Janis, 1965, 3, 6); and the effects of role playing on internalization (see Chapter 7).

During the many years I worked collaboratively with Hovland, from 1944 until his untimely death in 1961, I learned a great deal about research methods. Under his influence I became strongly committed to carrying out systematic investigations designed to test hypotheses derived from explanatory theories. In pursuing this style of research, I came to prize most highly those studies that have theory as both input and output—research that starts and ends with a theory, but not exactly the same one. That is to say, the most exciting and rewarding investigations are those designed not only to test a hypothesis derived from theory but also to look into the limiting conditions under which the hypothesis does and does not hold true, so as to identify the effects of interacting variables. Such studies are likely to suggest modifications of the original theory, which then form the basis for the next investigation in the series. When successful, the subsequent studies on interaction effects can clear up the confusion created when the results of one well-designed study fail to confirm predictions from a hypothesis that seems to have been confirmed by other well-designed studies.

Hovland also encouraged a predilection I had acquired from intensive reading of Kurt Lewin's (1948, 1951) major contributions to social psychology. From Lewin and Hovland I learned to distrust the conclusions drawn from any single study designed to test a general hypothesis, and to remain highly skeptical until confirmatory evidence becomes available from investigations using a variety of research methods, all of which provide conceptual replications that converge in supporting the same hypothesis. From both Hovland and Lewin I acquired a chronic sensitivity to the problems of external as well as internal validity, taking account of the fact that every research method has its strengths and weaknesses.

In a classic paper published in 1959 on the problems posed by conflicting results from experimental and survey studies of attitude change, Hovland pointed out that the two approaches need to be used conjointly so as to obtain the advantages of their respective virtues. The rigorous control of the laboratory experimental method enhances internal validity, but at the cost of potential errors in generalizing to the real world outside the laboratory. The conceptual breadth and the focus on real-life variables of surveys and other field-research methods enhance external validity of observed relationships; but this gain is at the cost of potential errors in identifying the probable causes of the observed effects. Since the two approaches have some nonoverlapping virtues and defects, we need to use both to test the same hypotheses. Otherwise we can have little hope of arriving at dependable conclusions with sufficient generality in the real world to make it worthwhile to expend time and energy on social-psychological research. In short, we must aggregate and integrate the findings from studies using different methods. This is the approach that I have used most explicitly in *Decision Making* (1977, 2), written collaboratively with Leon Mann, and in a number of papers dealing with the same topic—for example, Chapter 9.

RESEARCH ON DECISION MAKING

In the late 1950s I started to redirect my research toward problems of decision making. Like many other social psychologists, I had become disillusioned with attitude-change research that relied exclusively on changes in verbal responses obtained in questionnaires or interviews. My disillusionment became acute as more and more evidence accumulated on demand characteristics and other artifacts that distort the verbalizations elicited in seemingly well-controlled experiments. There was also unsettling evidence that could not be ignored from field studies showing gross discrepancies between expressed attitudes and overt social behavior.

I came to realize that the only attitude-change studies I could take seriously were those dealing with a person's behavioral intentions that have direct implications for action and that could be assessed independently of what the person says he or she thinks is the best thing to do. My research gradually changed in the direction of investigating real-life personal decisions, such as giving up smoking or going on a low-calorie diet, with priority given to those decisions for which behavioral measures of changes in action could be obtained. Nevertheless, I retained my interest in observing changes in verbalized attitudes as indicators of mediating processes that might help to account for adherence or nonadherence to a new course of action to which the decision maker is committed.

Recently social psychologists have become extremely suspicious of verbal indicators, partly because of an influential paper by Nisbett and Wilson (1977) in which they point to impressive divergences between what experimental subjects retrospectively report they were thinking about and what they actually did during the experiment. Nisbett and Wilson take the position that the subjects' accounts are not worth very much for elucidating the thoughts that mediate their judgments and decisions. This view is challenged by Ericsson and Simon (1980), who argue that worthwhile verbal data can be obtained from subjects' verbal accounts of their subjective thoughts if investigators go about collecting such data in the right way. These authors cite impressive theoretical reasons, supported by some research findings, for specifying the conditions that must be met to obtain trustworthy verbal reports that could be useful in studying mediating processes. These conditions include the following: (1) eliciting verbalizations while the subject is making a decision or only a few minutes afterward; (2) asking each subject to describe what he or she is thinking about, rather than asking the subject to try to explain why he or she behaved in a certain way; and (3) limiting the questions to information that the subject is likely to be aware of at least briefly (that is, has stored in short-term memory), which avoids forcing the subject to infer rather than remember his or her mental processes.

My own research experience bears out Ericsson and Simon's position. In the research on personal decision making, I have found that verbalized attitudes obtained while the individual is making a decision are especially helpful for getting clues for evaluating theoretical assumptions that might explain the effects of information about the consequences of alternatives, social support, and other variables that affect subsequent adherence. However, because all such verbal evidence is subject to many sources of distortion, I relegate it to a secondary role.

FIELD EXPERIMENTS

Although the validity of any theoretically oriented hypothesis can be ascertained only when there is a convergence of evidence from studies using different research methods, there is one particular method that in my opinion is less subject to error than any other. Controlled field experimentation is the method on which I rely most heavily for testing social-psychological hypotheses because, when properly used, it can combine the main virtues of laboratory experiments with those of social surveys and other nonexperimental methods of field research. (The advantages are discussed more fully in Chapter 15.)

The controlled field experiment is the method most often used in my research during the past twelve years, and the findings obtained from such experiments are the ones to which I give the most weight in testing predictions from any theory. Despite this preference, however, some of the problems that interest me cannot be investigated by means of controlled experiments in field settings; at least, I have not been able to find any feasible way of doing so. Some papers in this book feature studies employing survey research (Chapters 2, 3, 4, 5, and 10); others, which are purely exploratory, feature participant observations or intensive case studies (Chapters 6, 11, and 14). Nevertheless, I prefer data from field experiments, as is well illustrated by my synthesis (Chapter 12) of the research that I and my collaborators carried out to test the theoretical model of the influence of helping relationships on stressful personal decisions. That same preference can also be seen in papers in which I review evidence bearing on other theoretical models (Chapters 9 and 13).

THE ACID TEST

The three theoretical models described at the beginning of this chapter have generated research on basic processes that mediate stress reactions, attitude change, and decision making. They also have led to the development of new interventions, some of which have been systematically investigated and found to have practical value. Like many other behavioral scientists, I do not believe a definite line can or should be drawn between basic and applied research. I consider the following question an acid test for any basic theory that purports to explain how emotion-arousing communications or actual stressful events influence attitudes and decisions: Does the theory generate any interventions that are effective for helping people avoid psychological trauma, attain their goals, or improve the quality of their lives?

REFERENCES

Ericsson, K. A., & Simon, H. A. Verbal reports as data. *Psychological Review,* 1980, *87,* 215-251.

Hovland, C. I. Reconciling conflicting results derived from experimental and survey studies of attitude change. *American Psychologist,* 1959, *14,* 8-17.

Lewin, K. *Resolving social conflicts.* New York: Harper, 1948.

Lewin, K. *Field theory in social science.* New York: Harper, 1951.

MacCurdy, J. *The structure of morale.* New York: Macmillan, 1943.

Nisbett, R. E., & Wilson, T. D. Telling more than we can know: Verbal reports on mental processes. *Psychological Review,* 1977, *84,* 231-259.

2

Control of Fear: Studies of Combat Infantrymen and Air Crews (1949)

INTRODUCTION

In the preceding chapters [of *The American Soldier*, Vol. II, 1949], the overall combat situation has been described and the variety of intense psychological stresses engendered in combat have been discussed. In this chapter the focus will be narrowed down to concentrate on a number of problems arising from reactions to one primary source of stress in combat—physical danger.

From the standpoint of the individual soldier, it is primarily the danger of death or injury which makes the combat situation so harassing an experience. The intense emotional strains of actual battle are to a large extent rooted in the inescapable fear and anxiety

Janis, I. L. Problems related to the control of fear in combat. In S. A. Stouffer et al., *The American soldier: Combat and its aftermath.* Princeton, N.J.: Princeton University Press, 1949, 1977. Pp. 192, 193, 220–231.

Janis, I. L. Objective factors related to morale attitudes in the aerial combat situation. In Stouffer et al., *The American soldier.* Pp. 378–384.

This chapter contains excerpts from certain sections (Chapters 4 and 8) written by Irving L. Janis in *The American Soldier*, Vol. II of Studies in Social Psychology in World War II, which was edited under the auspices of the Social Science Research Council. The findings that are discussed are from several studies bearing on fear control carried out by the Research Branch of the Information and Education Division in the War Department during World War II. The introduction in this chapter comes from pages 192 and 193; the section on precombat training comes from pages 220-231; the final section on anxiety symptoms in members of combat air crews comes from pages 378-384. The final section is partly based on a draft prepared by Robin M. Williams, Jr. The data in Figures 2.3 and 2.4 come from studies in the Eighth Air Force, which were designed and analyzed by Arthur A. Lumsdaine and Marion Harper Lumsdaine. The principal credit for compiling and analyzing the objective data in Figure 2.5 goes to A. J. Jaffe.

Reprinted by permission of Princeton University Press.

reactions continually aroused by ever-present stimuli which signify objective threats of danger. The threats of being maimed, of undergoing unbearable pain, and of being completely annihilated elicit intense fear reactions which may severely interfere with successful performances. If soldiers are given no preparation for dealing with danger situations and if special techniques for controlling fear reactions are not utilized, many men are likely to react to combat in a way which would be catastrophic to themselves and to their military organization.

There is always the possibility, when men are exposed to the objective dangers of combat, that they will react by fleeing in panic or that they will be immobilized by uncontrollable terror. Even if these extreme reactions are averted, there is still the danger that many men will become so disorganized by fear that they will fail to carry out their military mission adequately. The preceding chapters describe some of the general institutional patterns of the Army which serve to impel soldiers to withstand the harassing conditions of combat so that they carry out the complex integrated activities of engaging the enemy. In this chapter we shall discuss some of the major practices of the [U.S. military forces] during World War II which were designed either entirely or partially to minimize the potential damage of disruptive fear reactions in soldiers exposed to the objective dangers of combat. . . .

PRECOMBAT TRAINING ACTIVITIES RELATED TO FEAR CONTROL

In a sense, all aspects of the Army training program which develop effective combat skills serve to reduce the disruptive effects of fear reactions in combat, in so far as they provide soldiers with a set of habitual responses which are adaptive in danger situations. There are two major aspects of training, however, which are most directly related to the control of fear in combat: training which prepared men to cope with specific kinds of danger situations and exposure to intense battle stimuli.

In their precombat training, the troops were given considerable practice in performing specific acts which would be adaptive in the face of specific dangers. They were taught to disperse and "hit the dirt" when subjected to a sudden strafing attack by enemy aircraft; to crawl under machine gun fire; to roll away when confronted by an approaching tank; to "freeze" when a flare was set off at night; to dig a hasty slit trench from a prone position when pinned down under fire; to advance in rushes, running zigzag in a crouched position toward an obstacle which provided cover when required to advance under fire; to "hit the dirt" at the sound of an approaching shell.

In some cases the men were drilled over and over again on certain act sequences which they were required to execute promptly and in a stereotyped way whenever the danger cue was given. Gas-mask drill, for example, was practiced in this way; whenever a leader shouted the single word "gas," no matter what activity was in progress, the men were required to go through a highly routinized act sequence of putting on the gas mask. Drill of this type, when repeated sufficiently so that the response is "overlearned," tends to build up an automatic adaptive response to a source of combat danger.

Acquisition of an automatic habitual response to a danger cue is probably effective, to some extent, in counteracting the disruptive effects of fear in combat. It is a plausible hypothesis that, as a result of such training, the correct act would tend to be performed as soon as the specific danger cue was given despite the competing response tendencies aroused by fear-eliciting stimuli. Before the man had "time to think about it" he would automatically make the correct response, whereas if he had not been drilled in the habit, in his excited emotional state he might react in a maladaptive way.

Although repetitive drill designed to build up automatic reactions to specific danger cues may contribute to reducing the disruptive effects of fear, there are serious limitations upon the usefulness of this type of training for combat. There are very few routine act sequences which would be generally adaptive, whenever a given kind of danger was encountered. Most types of danger situations in combat require varying responses, depending upon the particular mission the man is assigned to carry out, the protective resources which happen to be available in his immediate vicinity, and other highly specific characteristics of the particular situation in which the danger occurs.

Most of the Army training for combat was designed to build up a repertoire of specific combat skills which the individual soldier could draw upon whenever they were needed in combat. Rather than attempting to develop automatic reactions to combat dangers, training was designed to teach men to count on instructions from superiors or, if necessary, to exercise their own judgment about the best response to make when confronted by a given type of danger; it was also designed to provide practice in combat skills which were likely to be needed in order to react efficiently in danger situations, once the man knew what action he was going to take. This type of preparation for combat would serve to reduce fear in combat in two major ways: (1) the general level of anxiety in combat would tend to be reduced in so far as the men derived from their training a high degree of self-confidence about their ability to take care of themselves and to handle almost any contingency that might threaten them with sudden danger; and (2) the intensity of fear reactions in specific danger situations would tend to be reduced once the man began to carry out a plan of action in a skilled manner. The major problem in this type of training, from the standpoint of fear control, is the danger that when the men are actually in battle and are confronted with a situation for which they have been trained, they will be unable to apply their training because of their excited emotional state. Fear reactions are apt to interfere so seriously that the men are unable to exercise good judgment or to carry out skillfully an action which they have been trained to perform. The major solution to this problem probably lies in training men to carry out combat activities under conditions which closely parallel those encountered in battle. During the war, the Army introduced a number of "battle inoculation" features into the training program. By 1943, almost all men in basic training were being put through an infiltration course which required crawling over rough ground for about eighty yards under live machine-gun fire. From time to time Infantry troops were exposed to the sounds of near-by artillery fire and took part in maneuvers which introduced realistic battle stimuli. This was done especially in combat training which troops received overseas during preinvasion periods.

There are a number of ways in which exposure to battle stimuli during training would be expected to reduce the disruptive effects of fear in battle: (1) a certain amount of adaptation to the extremely loud noises and other intense stimuli probably takes place with repeated exposures so that when the stimuli are encountered in battle they elicit less fear; (2) exposure to battle conditions during training enables the men to develop a realistic expectation of what combat is like, which would tend to increase motivation to acquire combat skills and would also tend to reduce anxiety about combat in those men who, having heard a great deal about the horrors of war, grossly overestimate the psychological shock of being exposed to battle conditions; (3) in so far as the men obtain practice in making decisions and in carrying out skilled activities (such as firing at moving targets) in the presence of stimuli which elicit fear reactions, this experience decreases the probability that fear reactions will interfere with successful performance in combat; (4) the experience of being exposed to stimuli which elicit fear tends to mobilize the psychological defenses of the individual and as a result he may develop some personal techniques for coping with his emotional reactions—such as focusing his attention upon the details of his own combat mission as a form of distraction, frequently asserting to himself that he can take it, or some other type of action or verbalization which reduces anxiety.[1]

It is difficult to estimate the extent to which American troops were exposed to battle stimuli during their precombat training. It is probable that the majority of men who were sent into combat had been given relatively little exposure to battle stimuli other than small arms fire. Later in this chapter some research results will be presented which suggest that there may have been insufficient exposure to intense battle stimuli during precombat training. . . .

It would be extremely valuable to know the extent to which each of the aspects of precombat training which were discussed in the preceding section contributed to the control of fear in combat. Systematic studies of the effectiveness of those Army training activities designed to reduce the disruptive effects of fear in combat would undoubtedly have furnished many useful insights into the conditions under which this type of psychological preparation for danger is of maximum effectiveness. In the absence of systematic research on these important aspects of fear control, it may be of some value to examine certain attitude data which bear indirectly upon these problems.

A cross-section survey of combat veterans in an Infantry division in the Southwest Pacific area provides some indirect evidence of a relationship between the intensity of fear reactions to combat and self-confidence in ability to perform well in combat. It was found that those men who reported the largest number of physiological symptoms of fear tended to show less confidence in their ability to perform successfully in combat, as indicated by their self-ratings on degree of self-confidence prior to going into combat for the first time, changes in self-confidence as a result of combat experience, and self-confidence about ability to take charge of a squad on a combat mission. The relationship between degree of fear[2] in combat and

---

[1] Exposure to fear-eliciting stimuli during training may also have some detrimental effects which would tend to increase fears and anxieties in combat. Plans were made by the Research Branch for research studies to test hypotheses about the conditions under which exposure to battle stimuli is most effective. But the projected studies were not carried out.

[2] The scores on the index of fear symptoms were determined by the number of physiological fear symptoms each man reported having experienced "sometimes" or "often." Ten symptoms were included in the fear symptoms questionnaire: "violent pounding of the heart," "shaking or trembling all over," "sinking feeling in the stomach," "feeling sick at the stomach," "cold sweat," "feeling of weakness or feeling faint," "feeling of stiffness," "vomiting," "losing control of bowels," and "urinating in pants."

each of the three indicators of self-confidence is shown graphically in Figure 2.1.

From the type of correlational data presented in Figure 2.1, it is unsafe to make any inferences about causal factors.[3] It may be useful, however, to point out some of the alternative hypotheses suggested by these results, since they have implications for further research on the problems of fear control.

1. First of all there is the possibility that lowered self-confidence is a consequence of having experienced intense fear reactions in combat; this hypothesis would be difficult to test and, although it would have practical implications for the treatment of men who had undergone intense fear experiences, it would have little direct bearing on the problems of precombat training.

2. A second possibility is that the relationship reflects some relatively persistent personality characteristic. In other words, both intense fear reactions to danger and self-confidence about one's ability may be a function of some personality variable which had not undergone any pronounced change in the course of Army experience. It is unnecessary to speculate upon the nature of the underlying personality trait that may be involved because in any case there is the implication that attitude items dealing with self-confidence may serve as an indicator of some factor which is predictive of fear reactions in danger situations. This suggests that it may be worth while to test the usefulness of such attitude items for the prediction of subsequent reactions to danger. If it were found that a low degree of self-confidence expressed during the precombat training period was predictive of intense fear reactions to combat, it would be possible to utilize this finding in the selection of personnel for important combat assignments or for leadership positions in combat units.

3. A third possible interpretation of the relationship shown in Figure 2.1 is that it reflects a dynamic relationship between level of self-confidence prior to entering combat and fear reactions in combat. This would mean that by increasing the men's self-confidence about their abilities to perform well in combat, their subsequent fear reactions to combat would be reduced. If this hypothesis should

---

[3] It should be recognized that the data in Figure 2.1 not only fail to indicate the causal sequence but are also of limited value as evidence of a correlation between fear reaction and self-confidence. There is always the possibility that some extraneous attitude may have colored both the way in which fear reactions in combat were recalled and reported, and questionnaire responses to items on self-confidence. For example, the correlation might simply reflect some factor like candidness in reporting about oneself, unwillingness for further service, or high anxiety originating from current personal problems other than those involved in facing combat danger.

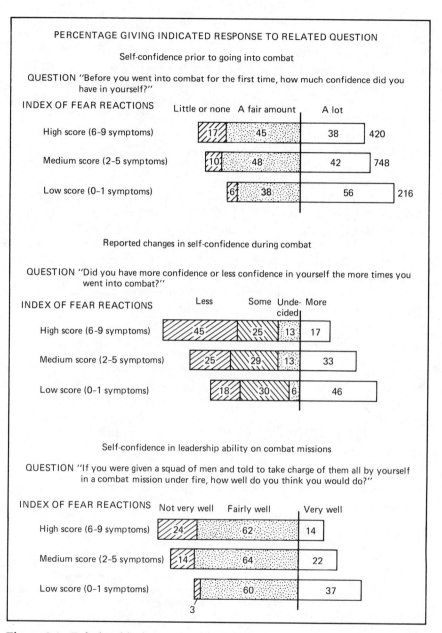

Figure 2.1 Relationship between self-confidence and fear reactions to combat (based on questionnaire responses of 1,350 men in a combat division in the Southwest Pacific, January 1944)

prove to be true, it would have very direct implications for precombat training since it would point up the need for utilizing every available means for building up the men's self-confidence in their own abilities to perform their combat jobs. In evaluating whether or not a given unit needed more precombat training and in designing the training program itself, it would be necessary to take account not only of the men's performance with respect to necessary combat skills but also their *attitudes* with respect to the adequacy of their preparation for combat.

It is interesting to note at this point that from the survey of combat veterans in an Infantry division in the Southwest Pacific we find a relationship between self-ratings on the adequacy of training for the combat job and the index of fear reactions to combat.[4] The data are shown in Figure 2.2. This finding is consistent with the hypothesis which we have been discussing; it suggests that fear reactions in combat may be due, in part, to an attitudinal factor—the feeling that one has not had sufficient training for one's combat job. It should be recognized, however, that not very much weight can be given to the results in Figure 2.2 as *evidence* for the hypothesis since alternative interpretations of the relationship cannot be excluded. . . .

One indication of the importance of exposing men to fear-eliciting battle stimuli during precombat training is provided by the criticisms and suggestions for training made by combat veterans, on the basis of their own experience in combat. From a number of attitude surveys there is evidence that combat veterans, in evaluating their own preparation for combat, felt that . . . exposure to battle stimuli prior to entering combat was one of the major deficiencies in their own training for combat. . . .

---

[4] The following question on adequacy of training was used in this study: When you were first sent into combat, were you assigned to a job or duty for which

—You were thoroughly trained
—You had some, but not enough training
—You had no training

In the chart, the category "not enough training" combines the second and third choices. This was done because less than 6 per cent of the men checked the third choice ("You had no training"). The scores on the index of fear in combat were determined by the number of symptoms which the men reported having experienced "sometimes" or "often," such as "violent pounding of the heart," "shaking and trembling all over," etc. . . . In obtaining the data for the correlation, all cases where no answer was given to one or the other question were omitted. Several hundred cases in the original total sample were therefore excluded from the correlation table because they had failed to answer at least one of the parts to the fear symptom question and hence an accurate score could not be assigned to them. The "no answer" group on fear symptoms tended to respond to the question on training in the same way as the high score on fear symptoms group. This is not an unusual finding; it has been found in a number of Research Branch studies, on the basis of independent criteria, that it is the more emotionally disturbed men who tend to omit answering questions about fear or anxiety symptoms.

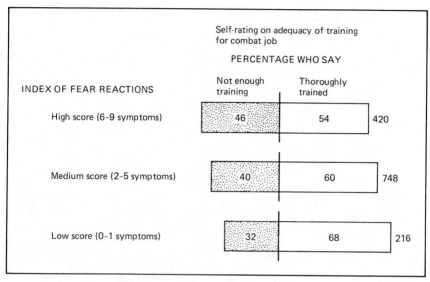

Figure 2.2   Relationship between self-rating on adequacy of training and fear reactions to combat (based on questionnaire responses of combat veterans in an infantry division in the Southwest Pacific, January 1944)

In [a later] section, on fear of enemy weapons, we . . . present some findings which suggest that with increased exposure to actual combat conditions, the men's ratings of the dangerousness of weapons tended to correspond more closely to the actual effectiveness of the weapons and exaggerated fears of enemy weapons tended to be reduced. It is likely that this type of adjustment to sources of objective danger is one of the ways in which exposure to realistic battle stimuli serves to prepare men psychologically for combat. . . .

ANXIETY SYMPTOMS IN MEMBERS OF COMBAT AIR CREWS

. . . The findings presented . . . [earlier] on the decrease in willingness for combat with increased number of combat missions flown are borne out by the results shown in Figure 2.3. Men with combat flying experience were less likely to express willingness for combat flying than those with no combat flying experience.

The June 1944 survey of combat flying personnel in the European theater included . . . [a] single questionnaire item requiring self-ratings of general physical condition. [The results, shown in

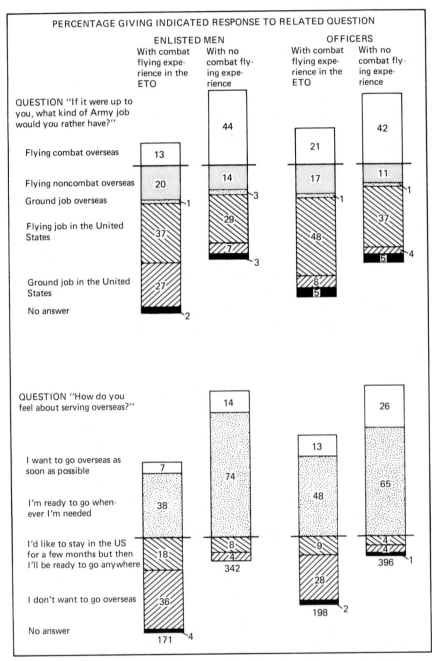

Figure 2.3 Responses of flying personnel with and without combat flying experience on items indicative of willingness for future combat flying (based on a survey of officer and enlisted air crew members in one very heavy bombardment, B-29, wing in training in the United States, May 1945)

Figure 2.4, indicate] . . . that with increased number of combat missions flown there was a decrease in the proportion reporting "good" or "very good" physical condition.

To some extent, of course, the men's estimates of their own physical condition reflect the physiological fatigue engendered by repeated combat activity. But self-ratings of physical condition have been found to be correlated with NSA scores based on psychosomatic complaints and other items [that] are predictive of psychoneurotic tendencies. Hence the increased concern about health, shown in Figure 2.4, may be interpreted as symptomatic of an increase in anxiety reactions.

According to Hastings, Wright and Glueck (1949) symptoms of anxiety—such as nausea and vomiting, headache and dizziness, rapid heart rate and palpitations, weakness and easy fatigability—occur in only a small percentage of combat air crew members during the early missions of the tour of duty. But, during the latter part of the combat tour, a wide variety of anxiety symptoms develop in many men as a

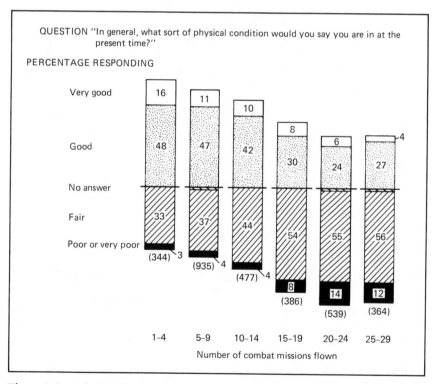

Figure 2.4 Relationship between amount of combat experience and self-rating of physical condition (based on a survey of heavy bomber crews in the European theater, June 1944)

result of the stresses of combat flying duty. Hastings et al. report on the basis of a psychiatric study that among a group of 150 heavy bomber crew members who had successfully completed their tour of duty, 95 per cent had developed definite symptoms of "operational fatigue," which is characterized by a group of behavioral symptoms: tenseness, irritability, hyperaggressiveness, impairment of motor dexterity due to fine or gross tremors, depression, and slowing of mental processes.

Among medium bomber crews surveyed by the Research Branch the proportion of men reporting "good" or "very good" physical condition declines steadily with increased number of missions, from 73 per cent among those with less than 10 combat missions to 41 per cent among men who had flown 40-49 missions, and to 25 per cent among men who had flown 60-69 missions. A similar, though less marked, decline occurs among light bomber crews: from 70 per cent among men with less than 10 missions to 52 per cent among those with 40-49 missions.

In the case of fighter pilots, there is a steady decline from 84 per cent who report "good" or "very good" physical condition among pilots who had flown less than 50 combat hours to 55 per cent among pilots who had flown 200-249 hours.

For heavy bomber crews certain data were obtained through the Office of the Air Surgeon which give a basis for appraising the men's actual behavior with respect to their subjective concern about physical condition. The data, presented in Figure 2.5, show that the proportion of combat crew members who requested medical examination (the sick-call rate) decreased after the first few missions, and then remained fairly stable until 30 missions had been flown. After 30 missions, there was an abrupt rise in the sick-call rate and an even sharper increase in the percentage of men removed from flying duty on medical recommendation. [Thirty missions was the minimum required to complete their tour of duty.]

The results on sick-call rates shown in Figure 2.5 cover the same time period (early June 1944) as the cross-section attitude data presented in Figure 2.4. It is readily seen that the trend in Figure 2.5, which indicates the men's actual *behavior* with respect to physical symptoms, differs markedly from the trend in Figure 2.4, which indicates the men's *attitudes* toward their own physical condition. The discrepancies between the trends in the two charts provide some suggestive insights into the motivations of combat flyers.

During the early stages of the tour of combat duty, self-evaluation of physical condition deteriorated markedly. In so far as this attitude change reflects an increase in subjective concern about health

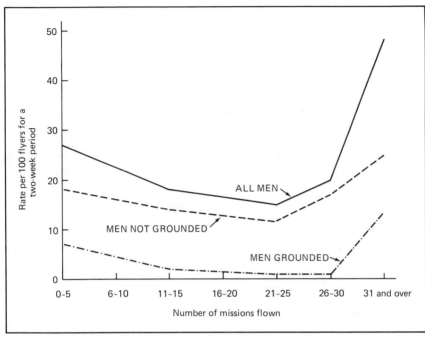

Figure 2.5 Relationship between sick-call rate and number of combat missions flown among heavy bomber crews

and specific physical symptoms, it would be expected that a larger proportion of men would voluntarily present themselves for medical attention. But, instead, as shown in Figure 2.5, the sick-call rate decreased slightly during this stage. Moreover, toward the end of the tour of combat duty, there appears to be a fairly stable attitude toward physical condition, i.e., there is little difference between those who flew 20–25 missions and those who flew 25–29 missions. If we were to extrapolate from this finding, we would expect little change in self-evaluations of physical condition after 20–24 missions. But Figure 2.5 shows that after 25 missions there is a gradual rise in the sick-call rate followed by a very sharp increase after 30 missions.

These findings suggest that the behavior of men in heavy bomber crews was strongly oriented toward the goal of completing the number of missions which constituted the tour of combat duty. To some extent sick call was avoided while the 30 missions were in progress, despite the increasing concern about health. Under normal conditions men with physical complaints had nothing to lose, in general, by bringing their health problems to the attention of medical officers.

But for men in heavy bomber crews, temporary or permanent removal from flying status might be the consequence, and this would
seriously interfere with achieving the goal of completing the tour of
combat duty and being rotated back to the United States.

Identification with the combat crew undoubtedly gave rise to
another powerful motivation [that] reinforced the avoidance of reporting physical complaints, which might result in interference with
the normal sequence of combat missions. Results have been cited . . .
earlier which indicate that almost all men in heavy bomber crews
preferred to fly with their own crews. If a man were to be grounded
for a temporary physical disability, he might have to face the prospect of finishing his tour of combat duty later on as an isolated
"black sheep" in a strange crew, separated from the original crew
with whom strong bonds of friendship and loyalty had developed.

Under these conditions it is understandable that combat crew
members would be reluctant to go on sick call while their tour of
duty was in progress, despite increased concern about health. The
contrast between the trend in Figure 2.5 (sick-call rate) and the trend
in Figure 2.4 (self-rating of physical condition) probably reflects
the fact that there was a strong tendency to save up physical complaints until the tour of 30 combat missions was completed.

3

Aftermath of the
Atomic Disasters (1951)

INTRODUCTION

The study of reactions to disaster may prove to have important implications for general behavior theory by illuminating basic processes of human adjustment that occur under conditions of severe environmental stress. Moreover, sound information about the psychological impact of wartime catastrophes is a fundamental requirement . . . for appraising the political, social, and moral consequences of atomic warfare.

Although a considerable amount of information is available on "conventional" air warfare, there is a dearth of relevant material on atomic warfare. Very little psychological research has been carried out among the tens of thousands of Japanese survivors who lived through the disasters at Hiroshima and Nagasaki.

In [this] Part [of *Air War and Emotional Stress*] , all the available observations on reactions of survivors are brought together in an attempt to arrive at a comprehensive description of the psychological impact resulting from the atomic-bombing disasters. Whenever possible, an effort is made to discern similarities and differences between atomic and other types of bombing, with a view to exploring the question of whether atomic weapons might have unique psychological effects. . . .

There has been only one systematic study of a cross section of A-bombed survivors: a small sample survey by the Morale Division of

Janis, I. L. *Air war and emotional stress.* New York: McGraw-Hill, 1951. Pp. 1-2, 41-43, Chapter 3. Except for the introduction, this chapter consists of Chapter 3 of *Air War and Emotional Stress*. The introduction is from pages 1-2 and pages 41-43 of the same book. Reprinted with the permission of the Rand Corporation.

the United States Strategic Bombing Survey,[1] conducted about three
months after the A-bombs were dropped.[2]

In the USSBS survey, the standard interview was focused mainly
on questions of morale. Consequently, there is a fair amount of
empirical data on postdisaster attitudes. Only a small part of the
interview, however, was devoted to personal experience of the bombing; among the standard set of questions there were none which dealt
directly with overt behavior, subjective feelings, or emotional tension
during the crisis phases of the disaster. Nevertheless, many of the
interviews contain spontaneous comments that tell us something
about the emotional impact resulting from the A-bombing.

In order to make as full use as possible of this unique source of
information, the original protocols of the interviews (which are now
available for the use of research scholars in the National Archives at
Washington, D.C.) were examined and analyzed. The reanalysis of
the interviews provides new information which supplements the
findings published in the USSBS report on Japanese morale.[3] In
addition to the USSBS interviews and the case studies published by
Hersey,[4] there are a few eyewitness reports which are also used as
source materials.

To understand the aftermath, it is necessary to take account of
the *immediate* psychological impact of the A-bomb attack. The following summary is based on the available evidence (discussed in
Chapter 2 of *Air War and Emotional Stress*) concerning how people
reacted during the first few hours following the A-bomb explosion:

1. At both Hiroshima and Nagasaki the populace was caught
completely by surprise. The absence of warning and the generally
unprepared state of the population probably augmented the emotional effects of the A-bomb disasters.

2. Practically all survivors in the target cities experienced personal exposure to physical danger, accompanied by sudden, sharp
awareness of the threat to personal survival. The incidence of
"narrow-escape" experiences was extremely high.

3. A large proportion of the survivors initially believed that it
was their own houses or their own immediate neighborhoods that
had been directly hit by a bomb. In most cases, there was no realization of the magnitude of the disaster until after various escape
actions had been taken.

4. There were three outstanding disaster events which were perceived by the vast majority of survivors: the flash of the explosion,
the blast effects, and the presence of large numbers of casualties.

5. A substantial proportion of the survivors reacted automatically
to the brilliant flash as a danger signal. Some who were not located
near ground zero took prompt action, such as falling to a prone

position, which minimized exposure to the blast and secondary heat waves. In other cases, the opportunity to minimize the danger was missed because the individual remained fixed or because the action which was taken proved to be inappropriate.

6. Severe blast effects probably played a primary role as the danger stimuli evoking strong emotional excitement. In this respect the traumatic impact resulting from the atomic explosion does not appear to differ from that of other types of explosions and bombings.

7. The perception of large numbers of burned, cut, and maimed bodies was a major source of emotional trauma. Many survivors located only a short distance from the center of the explosion appear to have undergone a double emotional shock—the first, from the physical impact of the explosion and, the second, after they ran out into the streets and saw large numbers of casualties. Among those at the periphery who escaped the full physical violence of the explosion, the initial emotional impact seems to have occurred when they saw the streams of injured victims pouring out of the destroyed areas. Apparently it was not simply the large numbers of casualties, but also the specific character of the injuries, particularly the grossly altered physical appearance of persons who suffered severe burns, that produced emotional disturbances among those who witnessed them.

8. Acute fear was a dominant reaction among the survivors during the crisis phase of the atomic disasters. At least in a small percentage of cases, the emotional excitement reached such a high level that there was temporary loss of inhibitory control over primitive, automatic manifestations of acute anxiety. In some cases, the emotional disturbance took the form of acute depressive reactions. In general, however, the acute symptoms among the A-bombed survivors do not appear to differ from those observed among the British, Germans, and Japanese subjected to exceptionally severe air attacks.

9. There was at least one incident of overt panic behavior among a sizeable crowd of survivors. In addition, at least a small proportion of terrified survivors behaved impulsively, and perhaps irrationally, for a brief period of time. But the meager, fragmentary evidence available on overt behavior does not provide substantial support for claims that overt panic, disorganized activity, or antisocial behavior occurred on a mass scale during the two A-bomb disasters.

KEY QUESTIONS

Does an atomic disaster give rise to delayed psychological effects that are qualitatively different from those caused by other types of wartime disasters? Are there any unusual syndromes—comparable to the delayed biological effects—that characterize the psychological state of the survivors after an atomic explosion? The material on postdisaster reactions to be presented in this chapter provides an empirical basis for formulating some tentative answers to these questions.

. . . We have seen that there was relatively little that was unique about the immediate reactions of the A-bombed survivors. It was noted that there was an exceptionally high incidence of narrow-escape experiences and of disturbing perceptions of the casualties; nevertheless, the emotional effects of such exposures do not appear to differ from those seen in persons exposed to heavy bombardment or incendiary attacks. The symptoms of acute emotional shock observed in a small proportion of the A-bombed survivors apparently were the same as those seen in other types of disasters. The widespread feelings of fear and apprehensiveness seem to have been typical "objective" anxiety reactions of the sort to be expected whenever people are exposed to sudden danger. From the fragmentary evidence, it seems that overt panic was not of frequent occurrence and was probably evoked only when survivors were trapped in the presence of rapidly approaching fires or were caught in other special circumstances where they were helpless in the face of imminent danger.

The possibility remains, however, that there may have been some unique postdisaster reactions. Insidious, delayed effects might have shown up in the form of unusually persistent anxiety reactions, prolonged apathy, or other sustained symptoms that are indicative of a failure to re-establish normal emotional equilibrium. Conceivably, the exceptionally intense stress of an atomic disaster might even have had the effect of weakening psychological stamina to the point where acute psychoses, traumatic neuroses, or other forms of chronic mental disorder would be prevalent. Or perhaps the atomic disasters had a profoundly demoralizing effect, giving rise to extreme changes in the social and political attitudes of the survivors.

Such possibilities will be examined in our survey of the observations on postdisaster reactions. As will be seen, the evidence points to some fairly severe psychological sequelae; but, again, none of the effects appears to differ from those which have been noted among the English, German and Japanese people who were exposed to "conventional" air attacks.

SUSTAINED FEAR REACTIONS

After the acute danger phases of the atomic disasters had come to an end, the sources of emotional stress had by no means subsided. The

A-bomb shattered the normal pattern of community life and left the survivors in an extremely deprived state. For many days there was practically no medical aid for the tens of thousands suffering from acute burns, lacerations, and other severe injuries. Injured and uninjured alike were homeless, without adequate clothing or shelter. Food was in such scarce supply that starvation and malnutrition became widely prevalent.[5]

In addition to the extreme physical deprivations, there were many other sources of emotional stress. With the economic and social life of their community so completely disrupted, the survivors faced a bleak and insecure future. Moreover, during the postdisaster period most survivors experienced grief over the death of relatives or close friends and many were continually worried about those who were missing, seriously injured, or unexpectedly afflicted with radiation sickness. Under such conditions, emotional recovery from the traumatic events of the disaster could hardly be expected to proceed rapidly.

Various sources of information indicate that severe anxiety persisted among some of the survivors for many days and possibly weeks after the bombings. One of the most frequent types of sustained emotional disturbances appears to have been a phobic-like fear of exposure to another traumatic disaster. This reaction consisted in strong feelings of apprehensiveness accompanied by exaggerated efforts to ward off new threats.

A vivid description of anxiety states evoked by minimal signs of potential danger has been given by Dr. T. Hagashi, a physician in Hiroshima, who was one of the special informants on postdisaster reactions interviewed by USSBS investigators:

> Whenever a plane was seen after that, people would rush into their shelters. They went in and out so much that they did not have time to eat. They were so nervous they could not work. . . .
> . . . Most of the people were very, very uneasy and afraid that another bomb would be dropped. They lived in that condition for days and days.[6]

. . . Further indications of sustained apprehensiveness among the populace comes from the anxiety-laden rumors which are reported to have been widely circulated during the postdisaster period. Both Siemes[7] and Hersey[8] state that there were rumors that American parachutists had landed in the vicinity of Hiroshima shortly after the A-bomb attack. The latter author also reports that several weeks after the disaster stories were circulating to the effect that "the atomic bomb had deposited some sort of poison on Hiroshima which

would give off deadly emanations for seven years; nobody could go
there all that time." Brues[9] reports similar exaggerated fears of
lingering danger at Nagasaki. He states that there was a widely circulated rumor that Nagasaki would remain uninhabitable for years to
come and that this rumor was still creating concern when his party of
investigators visited the city several months after the disaster. . . .

To some extent, fear rumors may have been touched off or reinforced by the unexpected appearance of many cases of radiation
sickness.[10] During the weeks following the atomic explosion numerous unusual signs of organic pathology began to appear among survivors: loss of hair, high fever, excessive fatigue, hemorrhagic spots
under the skin, and other severe symptoms of radiation sickness.[11] A
number of the morale interviews contain references to the surprising
occurrence of severe illness and sudden death among the ranks of
seemingly intact survivors. For example: . . .

> Some of the folks when they came seemed normal. But about one month
> later their hair all dropped off and they died. . . .

From descriptions such as these, it is apparent that over a long
period of time the survivors were likely to see the human damage
caused by the violent release of nuclear energy; such experiences
probably augmented the sustained emotional disturbances created
by the disaster.

With respect to overt avoidance behavior, there is one well-
established fact from which some inferences can be made. Within
twenty-four hours after the mass flight from Hiroshima, thousands of
refugees came streaming back into the destroyed city. According to
one of the USSBS reports, road blocks had to be set up along all
routes leading into the city because there were so many people who
wanted to search for missing relatives or to inspect the damage. . . .

Although both Hiroshima and Nagasaki required almost complete
rebuilding and lacked an adequate food supply, the inhabitants gradually returned to live in improvised shacks. Within three months the
population in each city was back to about 140,000.[12]

The fairly prompt return of large numbers of survivors to the
target cities is itself a noteworthy postdisaster reaction. This behavior
points up the obvious fact that despite whatever potential radiation
hazards might persist after an atomic explosion, there are no immediate, impressive signs of lingering danger that impel people to stay
away. . . . Apparently there were strong "approach" motives among
the survivors: to search for the missing, to salvage possessions, or to
satisfy curiosity. Of central importance to our present inquiry is the

inference that such motives were capable of overriding reluctance to return to the scene of the disaster. From the material presented earlier, we know that apprehensiveness about another attack may have been prevalent immediately after the disaster and, later on, fear of contamination may have developed; but evidently such fears were generally not so intense as to prevent resettlement in the target cities. In any case, the fact that such large numbers of survivors returned to the target cities during the days and weeks following the disasters implies that the A-bomb did not produce a unique mass avoidance of the disaster locale.

DEPRESSION AND APATHY

Among some of the survivors, severe reactions of guilt and depression are known to have occurred during the postdisaster period. Dr. Nagai gives a vivid description of his own guilt feelings.[13] Despite being injured, he had worked assiduously during the disaster rescuing people and rendering medical aid until he collapsed from loss of blood and utter fatigue. Nevertheless, he blamed himself for numerous shortcomings: by remaining at the hospital with the members of his first-aid squad, he was neglecting his own wife and children, as well as his injured neighbors who were expecting him to care for them; while devoting himself to directing the rescue work of patients, he was aware of the "selfish" motive of wanting to achieve social recognition for his heroism; several nurses who subsequently succumbed to radiation sickness had complained to him of feeling weak, but, not recognizing the early symptoms, he had forced them to keep going; later on, while lying ill and exhausted, he experienced intense fear of another bomb attack and could not get up the nerve to cut across the shelterless wastes to the ruins of his neighborhood, where his wife lay dead.

In the context of reporting his personal reactions, Nagai develops the general thesis that practically all survivors were affected in the same way:

> We of Nagasaki, who survive, cannot escape the heart-rending, remorseful memories. . . .
> We carry deep in our hearts, every one of us, stubborn, unhealing wounds. When we are alone we brood upon them, and when we see our neighbors we are again reminded of them; theirs as well as ours.

Nagai believes that persistent "survivor-guilt" is an inevitable consequence of atomic bombing, because most survivors could not avoid behaving negligently in one way or another: people who were in the heart of the city were able to survive only by running away from the fires without stopping to rescue others; people who were in a position to give aid could not simultaneously perform all the duties and obligations of rescuing the wounded, rushing to their own families, assisting neighbors, carrying out their civil defense assignment, saving valuable materials at the office or factory where they worked, preserving treasured household articles, etc.

Although there are independent observations which indicate that some survivors experienced temporary guilt reactions following the A-bombings, there is no satisfactory evidence to support the claim that such reactions persisted in large numbers of survivors or that, four years after the war, the "rents in the ties of friendship and love . . . seem to be getting wider and deeper." . . .

Other sources of information provide no substantial basis for concluding that persistent guilt or depressive reactions were an inordinately frequent consequence of the atomic bombings.

Some of the evidence cited [earlier] indicates that at least a small percentage of the survivors felt depressed during or immediately after the disaster. But in the entire sample of USSBS morale interviews, there were found only a few cases who made comments suggesting that they had experienced feelings of guilt, sadness, hopelessness, or apathy during the postdisaster period. . . .

The claim that there was widespread apathy or lethargy among the A-bombed survivors is evidently based solely on the fact that the restoration of housing, public utilities, and hospital facilities had proceeded at a very slow rate.[14] However, when a city has been almost totally destroyed, with over half its population killed or injured, the rate of restoration probably is not an adequate indicator of the motivational state of the remainder of the city's population. Restoration would undoubtedly depend to a large extent on the amount of aid received from the rest of the country.

It should also be borne in mind that apathy and absence of cooperative activity have been reported by the USSBS Morale Division as characteristic of the entire Japanese nation after the war was terminated by the unexpected surrender, which came shortly after the A-bomb attacks.[15] . . .

When the factors mentioned . . . above . . . are taken into account, together with the other findings from the morale surveys, it appears unwarranted to conclude that the A-bombs produced an exceptionally high degree of apathy or depression among those who survived at Hiroshima and Nagasaki.

PSYCHIATRIC CASUALTIES

In [a later] chapter . . . it will be seen that chronic psychopathological disorders were rarely produced by heavy bombing attacks, although emotional shock reactions occurred with considerable frequency among those who had undergone direct personal involvement. Does this conclusion apply equally to atomic bombings? Or are there indications that the severe stress of an atomic disaster gives rise to psychiatric effects which are different in some ways from those produced by other types of wartime disaster?

It has already been mentioned that typical symptoms of acute emotional shock—anxiety states, apathy, depression—occurred temporarily in A-bombed survivors immediately after the destructive impact of the explosion. From the fact that large numbers of survivors had undergone harrowing danger experiences and had suffered direct personal loss, it might be predicted that in many people the emotional disturbances would persist for months after the disaster. The scanty observations described in preceding sections indicate that symptoms of acute emotional disturbance probably persisted for several days, and perhaps for a number of weeks in some cases. But the information is too incomplete to permit an adequate estimate of the incidence of such reactions. The available evidence serves only to exclude extreme possibilities: it indicates that postdisaster disturbances were neither wholly absent nor inordinately widespread.

[In the 6 years since the attacks] . . . no psychiatric studies of the A-bombed survivors have been reported. . . .

In the absence of any other information, it is worthwhile to look into the morale interviews for whatever psychiatric leads they may contain. After examining the interviews from Hiroshima and Nagasaki, one is left with the impression that there were at least a few cases who suffered from sustained neurotic symptoms which were caused or precipitated by atomic-disaster experiences. This impression, however, is based only on very fragmentary indications of the following sort:

Case 1. A fifty-year old carpenter in Nagasaki alluded to difficulties which suggest a neurotic fatigue reaction. He reported that he had been uninjured during the disaster and had been extremely energetic in his attempts to save his three children, all of whom subsequently died. Although more than three months had elapsed since the disaster, he complained that he was still excessively fatigued: "I have not regained my energy yet."

Case 2. A twenty-seven-year-old housewife in Nagasaki described a symptom which suggests conversion hysteria. In a highly emotionalized account of her disaster experiences she mentioned that she was "not hurt" by the bombing but a few days later certain parts of her body had felt sore and stiff. During the months that followed she was free from any such complaints. Then two days before the interview, the symptom reappeared: the soreness and stiffness returned in exactly the same regions of her body that had previously been affected.

Case 3. Another housewife in Nagasaki, forty-five years of age, evidently experienced an unusually severe anxiety attack during the disaster and thereafter appears to have developed a persistent phobia. More than three months later, according to her statements, she could not stand the sight of any of the damaged areas in the bombed city.

It should be emphasized that these three cases represent the most extreme instances of postdisaster disturbances culled from more than 100 interviews. Very few respondents made any explicit reference to suffering from emotional upset, and none mentioned being incapacitated in any way because of psychological symptoms. Altogether, there were only a handful of cases who referred to complaints that could be construed as possible signs of neurosis or psychosomatic illness.

In evaluating the interview evidence, it is necessary to take account of possible selective factors affecting the morale-survey sample: Very severe psychiatric casualties, by virtue of their incapacities, might have been excluded from the group of survivors who were interviewed. Nevertheless, if the incidence of gross psychopathology were extremely high, one would expect signs of behavioral disturbance to appear in any group of 100 survivors, particularly when the group had been selected according to sampling criteria designed to provide a cross section of the bombed population. . . .

The tentative conclusions to be drawn from the interview data tend to support the generalizations derived from other types of wartime disasters. The most severe types of psychiatric disorder appear to have been of rare occurrence following the A-bomb attacks. While there are no signs of psychosis or of grossly incapacitating neurosis among the survivors, there are some indications that a few individuals may have developed minor neurotic symptoms, such as excessive fatigue, recurrent bodily complaints, and persistent phobias. The more transient symptoms of emotional shock described earlier probably were the predominant psychiatric effects of the atomic disasters.

MORALE EFFECTS AMONG THE SURVIVORS

It is to be expected that such a shattering event as an A-bomb disaster would have a powerful effect on morale. Study of beliefs, expectations, and morale attitudes of the survivors indicates that pronounced changes occurred as a result of the atomic bombings. Nevertheless, the A-bombs did not give rise to any different kind of morale effects than those produced by other types of heavy air attack. This is the conclusion reached by USSBS investigators in Japan, on the basis of their extensive morale survey.[16]

The morale of the people in and around Hiroshima and Nagasaki did not fall below that of the rest of Japan. For example, only 27 per cent of the respondents in the A-bombed areas reported that before the surrender they had felt victory was impossible; the corresponding figure for the rest of Japan was 26 per cent. On other indicators of wartime morale ("personal willingness to continue the war" and "confidence in victory"), a significantly *larger* percentage of people in the A-bombed areas expressed high morale.

In general, the amount of defeatism at Hiroshima and Nagasaki was less than in other Japanese cities. When compared with respondents elsewhere in Japan, the attitudes of the A-bombed population were found to resemble those of people in the lightly bombed and unbombed cities rather than in the heavily bombed cities. Of the sixty cities and towns in which the USSBS morale survey was conducted, Nagasaki ranked tenth highest on an over-all morale index and Hiroshima ranked thirty-second highest. . . .

From the USSBS data, it appears to be very probable that the same factors found to be responsible for lowering morale among civilians exposed to "conventional" air attacks apply equally to the effects of the A-bomb. The inverse relationship between personal involvement and morale, which will be discussed in [a later chapter,] has been found to hold for the A-bombed population:

> Hiroshima and Nagasaki respondents were divided into two groups on the basis of having been physically affected by the bomb. In the first group were placed all those who were knocked down, injured, or wounded in any way by the bomb. In the second were placed those who merely saw the effects of the bomb. The two groups were significantly different in respect to several indices of morale.
>
> In a group of questions designed to measure confidence in victory, the physically affected group was much lower in morale than the unaffected group. . . .
>
> In the Morale Index, thirty-one per cent of the physically unaffected group fell into the highest of the four morale index categories, while seventeen per cent of the affected group fell into this category.[17]

In this connection, it is worth noting that certainty of defeat and other attitudes indicative of low morale were more prevalent at Hiroshima, where the area of devastation and the casualties were greater, than at Nagasaki. . . .

SUMMARY

1. Fear reactions persisted among a sizeable proportion of the population for many days and possibly weeks after the atomic bombings. One of the most frequent types of emotional disturbance noted during the postdisaster period consisted in sustained feelings of apprehensiveness accompanied by exaggerated efforts to ward off new exposures to danger.

2. During the weeks following the atomic disasters, the distressing symptoms and sudden deaths from radiation sickness, as well as the presence of people suffering from intractable burns and other sustained, visible injuries, produced strong emotional reactions among some of the survivors and may have augmented or reinforced the emotional disturbances evoked by the original disaster experience.

3. Anxiety-laden rumors circulated among the survivors during the postdisaster period. In both target cities, there were rumors which exaggerated the lingering dangers of contamination.

4. Although apprehensiveness about another attack and fears of contamination may have been fairly frequent, such fears evidently were not so intense as to prevent resettlement in the target cities. From the fact that very large numbers of survivors promptly returned to the destroyed areas, it appears that avoidance of the disaster locale did *not* occur on a mass scale.

5. Among a small percentage of the survivors, there were sustained reactions of depression during the postdisaster period. But the available evidence does not support the claim that the A-bomb produced an unusually high incidence of severe guilt feelings or of apathy among those who survived at Hiroshima and Nagasaki.

6. Although no adequate psychiatric observations are available, some highly tentative conclusions emerge from indirect sources of information which tend to bear out the findings from other types of wartime disasters. Psychoses, traumatic neuroses, and other severe psychiatric disorders appear to have been a rare occurrence following the A-bomb attacks. A small percentage of survivors probably developed some minor neurotic symptoms that were evoked or precipitated by disaster experiences, such as, excessive fatigue, recurrent bodily complaints, and persistent phobias. Although most cases of reproductive disorders following the atomic bombings are probably attributable to the physiological effects of gamma radiation, there is some possibility that the high incidence of menstrual difficulties and miscarriages among female survivors may have been due, in part, to emotional stress engendered by atomic-disaster experiences. In general, the more transient symptoms of acute emotional shock seem to have been the predominant psychiatric effect of the atomic disasters.

7. The morale of the people in and around the target cities did not fall below that of the rest of Japan. Apparently the A-bombing at Hiroshima and at Nagasaki produced no greater drop in morale than would be expected from a single raid of the type carried out during the massed B-29 campaign against other Japanese cities.

8. Relatively little sustained hostility against the United States was observed among survivors of the A-bomb attacks.

9. Some of the residents of Hiroshima and Nagasaki subsequently blamed their own war leaders for the bombing of Japan, but this reaction did not occur to a greater extent than in other Japanese cities. In Nagasaki, there appears to have been some resentment toward the Japanese government for withholding information about the Hiroshima disaster and for failing to prepare the population for the A-bomb attack.

10. The inverse relationship between personal involvement and postdisaster morale, observed following other types of air attack, was also found to hold for the A-bomb attacks.

11. Outside the target areas, the A-bombs had very little effect on the morale of the Japanese population. The absence of publicity about the bomb, the rapid termination of the war, and other special factors probably prevented the demoralizing potentialities of the atomic weapon from materializing in the rest of Japan.

NOTES

1. Throughout this book, the United States Strategic Bombing Survey will be referred to by the initials USSBS.
2. USSBS Report, *The Effects of Strategic Bombing on Japanese Morale,* U.S. Government Printing Office, Washington, D.C., 1947.
3. *Ibid.*
4. John Hersey, *Hiroshima,* Alfred A. Knopf, New York, 1946.
5. USSBS Report, *The Effects of Atomic Bombs on Health and Medical Services in Hiroshima and Nagasaki,* U.S. Government Printing Office, Washington, D.C., 1947.
6. These quotations and similar ones are taken from the original protocols of the USSBS interviews in Hiroshima, Nagasaki, and the towns surrounding those two cities.
7. Father Siemes, "Hiroshima—August 6, 1945," *Bull. Atomic Scientists,* Vol. 1, May, 1946, pp. 2–6.
8. John Hersey, *Hiroshima,* Alfred A. Knopf, New York, 1946.
9. A. M. Brues, "With the Atomic Bomb Casualty Commission in Japan," *Bull. Atomic Scientists,* Vol. 3, June, 1947, pp. 143–144.
10. T. Nagai, *We of Nagasaki: The Story of Survivors in an Atomic Wasteland,* Duell, Sloan and Pearce, Inc., New York, 1951.

11. Los Alamos Scientific Laboratory, *The Effects of Atomic Weapons*, U.S. Government Printing Office, Washington, D.C., 1950; USSBS, *The Effects of Atomic Bombs on Health and Medical Services in Hiroshima and Nagasaki.*

12. Report of British Mission to Japan, *The Effects of the Atomic Bombs at Hiroshima and Nagasaki*, His Majesty's Stationery Office, London, 1946.

13. Nagai, *op. cit.*

14. USSBS, *The Effects of Atomic Bombs on Health and Medical Services in Hiroshima and Nagasaki.*

15. USSBS, *The Effects of Strategic Bombing on Japanese Morale.*

16. *Ibid.*

17. *Ibid.*

4

Reactions to Air War:
Fear and Coping Mechanisms (1951)

CHARACTERISTIC FEAR REACTIONS

. . . The evidence from psychiatric studies [reviewed in Chapter 5 of *Air War and Emotional Stress*] indicates that the air attacks to which civilians were exposed during World War II produced only a very slight increase in psychoses, chronic traumatic neuroses, and other sustained psychopathological disorders in adults and in children. The most common psychiatric casualties were temporary cases of emotional shock, with symptoms of acute anxiety and mild depression. Most of these psychiatric casualties recovered within a few days up to several weeks following a bombing disaster.

Much more widespread are the severe fear reactions that do not result in obvious maladjustment. Schmideberg,[1] in describing the reactions of British civilians, claims that "When it was said of someone that he was not afraid of the raids, what was meant as a rule was that he got over the fright in a few minutes or hours, usually by the next morning." The same point is emphasized by Fraser, Leslie, and Phelps,[2] and is based on their interviews of approximately one thousand British civilians who were exposed to the air blitz. According to these authors, the usual reaction was acute fear with somatic symptoms of emotional tension. This "normal" reaction, however, was

Janis, I. L. *Air war and emotional stress.* New York: McGraw-Hill, 1951. Chapters 6, 8; pp. 96, 97. This chapter contains extensive excerpts from two chapters in *Air War and Emotional Stress.* Chapter 6 on fear and emotional adaptation deals with the descriptive evidence, and Chapter 8 on adjustment mechanisms introduces explanatory concepts and additional observations bearing on mediating processes that help us to interpret the descriptive evidence. The second paragraph was added, with slight changes, from pages 96 and 97 of the same book in order to specify the general conclusions to which the opening paragraph alludes. Reprinted with the permission of the Rand Corporation.

39

characterized by a high degree of *appropriateness to the danger situation*. Usually the symptoms were elicited only by signs of immediate danger, such as the sound of bombs exploding. Although the warning signal of planes overhead frequently evoked apprehensiveness, the somatic symptoms of fear usually did not build up if there was merely a "quiet" alert. Whenever a dangerous raid occurred, however, acute symptoms developed and persisted throughout the period of danger, generally subsiding within one-quarter of an hour after the end of the bombing attack. . . .

THE MAGNITUDE OF THE AIR ATTACK

From the preceding discussion, it is clear that when we speak of "fear reactions" we are referring to many different correlated variables, including both subjective and overt forms of emotional behavior: (1) feelings of apprehensiveness; (2) excited and disorganized action during the period of danger; (3) persistent emotional upset after the danger has subsided; (4) impairment of postdanger adjustment by startle responses or by incapacitating anxiety symptoms; or (5) reduced capacity for controlling emotional responses upon subsequent exposures to danger; etc. For purposes of formulating and evaluating general hypotheses on the conditions under which a high incidence of such reactions occur, it appears to be useful to retain the term "fear reactions" to designate this entire set of intercorrelated response variables. We should recognize, however, that ultimately, as our knowledge of reactions to danger increases, our hypotheses will require more precise formulation. The evidence to be presented in this chapter deals primarily with subjective feelings of fear (type 1). Only insofar as strong reactions of this type may be assumed to be *indicators* of each of the other types, is one justified in inferring that the conclusions will apply to all types of fear reactions.

Rarely does one find in the literature on air attacks an explicit discussion of the central problem upon which our inquiry will be focused: under what conditions is an air raid most likely to evoke severe fear reactions on a mass scale? One obvious condition has previously been alluded to a number of times; namely, the *physical magnitude of the air raid*. We have already noted that emotional-shock reactions are most likely to occur following a heavy air raid. (By a heavy air raid is meant one which produces relatively high casualties and extensive destruction.) Not only does a greater proportion of the population suffer from incapacitating emotional disorders in heavier air attacks, but, among the majority who escape being psychiatric casualties, the subjective fear reactions are more severe.[3] This is, of course, precisely what one would expect on the basis of the popularly accepted principle that the greater the danger, the greater the fear. A more detailed inquiry into the specific factors involved in heavy raids will lead us to some less obvious determinants of intense fear reactions.

The experience of undergoing an air attack is one in which a person is exposed to a large number of unusual and complex stimuli, evoking a wide variety of "meanings"; it is in their unique sequences, combinations, and patternings that the stimuli produce intense emotional responses. Nevertheless, for purposes of predicting mass reactions, it is necessary to discover *which variables* play the most important role in augmenting fear.

Early in the war, Harrisson observed at first hand the widespread fear among people living in "blitztowns" and he speculated that:

> . . . the most upsetting factor is *uncertainty*. . . . First, you never know what night the raid is going to come. Secondly, you never know which plane noise or other noise is the noise which may mean your end.[4]

It is undoubtedly true that some degree of emotional tension is aroused when an air attack is anticipated. If one becomes aware of the fact that a heavy raid has begun and that the danger may be very great, tension is likely to mount. Fear increases markedly during the suspenseful period when one has not yet been affected, but the bomb explosions or incendiary fires occurring nearby clearly indicate that the threat of impending danger is rapidly materializing. Nevertheless, the available evidence from many observers does not confirm Harrisson's hypothesis that such "uncertainties" constitute "the most upsetting factor" in connection with heavy raids. The experiences involved in anticipating a heavy attack—being aware that a dangerous raid has begun and undergoing the suspense entailed by perceiving the danger approach closer and closer—probably evoke acute fear symptoms in a relatively small number of predisposed personalities. Such experiences appear to be of the type which people in Britain and in other countries were able to "take" and to which they typically became emotionally adapted (described later in this chapter).

THE "NEAR-MISS" FACTOR

There is another type of experience which has been singled out by MacCurdy[5] as the most critical factor in the emotional impact of bombing: the experience of suddenly facing danger in the immediate vicinity. After discussing MacCurdy's hypotheses we shall examine the available evidence. It will be seen that by and large his views are well supported.

When a high explosive hits a person's house or shelter and the walls come crashing down all about him; when the blast from a powerful explosion hurls him to the ground; when the incendiary fires suddenly flare up and a member of his family is burned to death—situations of this kind, according to MacCurdy, arouse the most acute and persistent fear symptoms. Emotional-shock reactions, ranging from a dazed stupor to jumpiness and preoccupation with the horrors of the air raid, occur primarily among the "near-misses"—people who undergo direct exposure to actual danger. This may involve a narrow escape from death, being wounded, witnessing the destruction of persons close by, or suffering the loss of a loved one.

In contrast to the powerful reinforcement of fear among the near-misses, there is likely to be a reduction of fear among those who do not directly experience the destructive impact of the air attack. The "remote-misses," as MacCurdy calls them, often experience considerable tension when they perceive danger cues, e.g., a warning siren, enemy planes overhead, bombs exploding somewhere not far off. But when a raid is over, there is immense relief, a feeling that "It has happened and I'm safe." Under these conditions the experience is one of *successful escape*. Previous fearful anticipations of personal loss and destruction tend to be replaced by feelings of optimism and confidence. This benign effect is especially likely if, upon visiting scenes of destruction, the damage is found to be circumscribed and the bodies have already been removed. Hence, ". . . the proportion of fear to courage in the population will correspond to the relative sizes of the near- and remote-miss groups."[6]

The heavier the raid, the higher the proportion of the population in the community who will be near-misses. It is this simple relationship which MacCurdy singles out to explain the fact that a heavy raid, as against a light raid, will produce a marked increase in the incidence of emotional shock and other severe fear reactions. He applies this explanation to the morale of the community as well:

> If the remote-miss person has more courage after a raid than before it, if courage, like fear, is contagious, and if the near-miss group in any community is small, it follows that a light, a "token" bombing must improve morale in that community. Innumerable Home Security reports attest the truth of this conclusion as I have been told.[7]

MacCurdy's emphasis upon *the degree of personal involvement* as the major determinant of severe fear reactions was presumably based on his own clinical experience as well as on impressionistic observations of air-raid victims. There are many independent observations which, when considered together, definitely tend to support this hypothesis. . . .

A report by the Military Mobilization Committee of the American Psychiatric Association summarizes the available material on British reactions during the early war years. This report asserts that at the beginning of the war, psychoneurotic manifestations occurred primarily among highly educated persons in positions of responsibility; whereas, during the period of the air blitz, such reactions appeared mainly among people who had been in actual danger, had been knocked down by blasts, or had been in houses wrecked by high explosives.[8]

Supporting data on the importance of the personal involvement factor are provided by Fraser, Leslie, and Phelps.[9] These investigators obtained the names of all uninjured persons admitted to First-Aid Posts in one (unspecified) English city during a period of heavy bombing. This group is assumed to be fairly representative of all of those who had undergone severe personal involvement during the air raids, since it was the usual practice for A.R.P. workers to send all such cases to one of the Posts for a routine examination in order to check on possible physical injury. All traceable cases were followed up and interviewed ten months after they had been examined in the First-Aid Post. There was a small group of thirty-five people who had experienced severe personal involvement—buried beneath debris for over an hour because of a bomb explosion in the immediate vicinity. Of this group, 66 per cent developed temporary or persistent neurotic symptoms; in 40 per cent, the emotional disorder resulted in absence from work for three weeks or longer. A larger group (94 cases), which comprised all persons who had experienced direct blast effects, also showed a high incidence of neurotic symptoms, the most frequent being anxiety states and depression. The high incidence for these groups is in marked contrast to the low incidence of neurotic symptoms noted among the general population of the bombed city.

A direct comparison was made between those First-Aid-Post cases who developed clear-cut neurotic symptoms (61 cases) and those who did not (33 cases). The nonneurotic group was found to have suffered slightly less severe danger experiences than the neurotic group. Furthermore, close to 50 per cent of the neurotic group had experienced a definite personal loss from the air attack (destruction of the home or death of a close friend); whereas, among the non-neurotic group, such loss was experienced by only 4 per cent. From these and other findings, the investigators conclude that "neurosis is likely to follow severe personal air-raid experiences, which at the time upset the individual emotionally, or produced a serious upset in the pattern of his living by destroying a much-esteemed home or a close friend. . . ." Formerly stable personalities as well as those with personality defects were found to have developed neurotic symptoms following direct personal involvement. Among the latter, the symptoms were likely to persist for many months, whereas, among the former, recovery usually occurred within a few weeks.

Reports on German civilians who were exposed to extremely heavy air raids also tend to support the hypothesis that severe fear reactions occur primarily under conditions of direct personal involvement. Seydewitz, for example, gives the following impressionistic description of the aftermath of the devastating attack against Hamburg (summer of 1943), where practically all the survivors were near-misses:

> For weeks eyewitnesses were unable to report without succumbing to their nerves and weeping hysterically. They would try to speak, then would break down and cry: "I can't stand seeing it again; I can't stand it!"[10]

. . . There is some quantitative evidence based on interviews of a cross section of German civilians which indicates the importance of the personal involvement factor. The increase in fear, as well as the deterioration in morale resulting from increased bomb tonnage, was found to be "produced" principally by the amount of personal involvement incident to the bombing.

> When personal involvement, in terms of casualties in the immediate family or property loss, is taken as a measure of the severity of raids, there is a marked decline in morale as the degree of involvement increases. There is little evidence of diminishing returns and no tendency for morale to improve at the level of greatest personal involvement. Personal involvement is clearly the most sensitive measure of the severity of raids for the individual, and is more closely related to changes in morale than the other measures reported.[11]

Thus the evidence from the USSBS Morale Survey of German civilians definitely tends to bear out MacCurdy's assertion that morale deteriorates chiefly in the near-miss group. In the above quotation from the USSBS report, the term "morale" is used in a very broad sense to include fear reactions as well as war weariness, defeatism, and other unfavorable wartime attitudes. Among the "indices of morale" referred to were the interview responses to questions dealing with (1) fear experienced during the first big raid; (2) increased fear with successive raids; (3) anxiety about future raids; and (4) apathy and fatigue experienced under conditions of continuing raids. Presumably these four variables were found to be related to personal involvement. Unfortunately, the quantitative data on the *degree* of relationship between personal involvement and severity of fear reactions are not presented in the USSBS report. Nevertheless, the evidence reported does lend considerable weight to the general proposition that the psychological impact of heavy air raids is determined to a large extent by the proportion of people in the community who undergo a high degree of personal involvement. . . .

The findings from the large-scale survey of German civilians, when combined with the reports by independent British observers, provide a fairly substantial empirical basis for accepting MacCurdy's near-miss factor as a critical one in determining the high incidence of severe fear reactions produced by the heaviest air raids. Apparently, it is those survivors who directly experience the physical impact of the air attack who are most likely to exhibit severe and prolonged fear reactions.

EMOTIONAL ADAPTATION TO AIR RAIDS

MacCurdy's theory is not limited merely to the proposition that fear reactions are augmented by undergoing a near-miss experience. In describing the remote-miss reaction pattern he makes the assumption that the level of fear is actually *diminished* by exposure to an air raid in which one does not directly experience a narrow escape. In other words, MacCurdy assumes that people who are exposed to a series of air raids will tend to show increased capacity to withstand the emotional stress of subsequent air attacks provided that they do not have a near-miss experience. The available evidence on emotional adaptation tends to bear out this assumption, and it raises a number of important theoretical issues in connection with personal adjustment to objective threats of danger. . . .[12]

There was a definite decline in overt fear reactions as the air blitz continued, even though the raids became heavier and more destructive.[13] With successive dangerous raids, the bombed population displayed more and more indifference toward air attacks. Warning signals tended to be disregarded unless attacking planes were overhead. . . .

The British observations on widespread emotional adaptation to heavy air attacks, when considered together with the observations cited in the preceding section on the occurrence of severe emotional reactions following direct personal involvement, definitely tend to support MacCurdy's theory that fears are extinguished by remote-miss experiences and are reinforced by near-miss experiences.

USSBS reports indicate that emotional adaptation to heavy air attacks occurred among at least a substantial minority of the bombed populations of Japan and Germany. According to the report on Japanese morale:

> Urban people who experienced more continuous bombing and therefore represent the better test on the question of adaptation, clearly indicate that they became better adapted as their bombing experience increased, while rural people, who had less direct and less frequent experience, became more afraid.[14]

Among the Germans, 36 per cent of a cross section of the bombed population reported that they had felt less afraid with successive air attacks; 30 per cent reported no change; and 28 per cent reported increased fear.[15] The fact that a sizeable proportion of Germans reported having experienced emotional adaptation, even though they were subjected to far more destructive attacks than were the British, is consistent with the hypothesis that among a population exposed to severe air attacks fear reactions will be reinforced among some persons but extinguished among others, depending on the personal experiences they have during the raids. In this connection, it is important to note that one of the items which was correlated with direct personal involvement among bombed German civilians was the question dealing with emotional adaptation to successive air attacks.[16] Apparently, those who were *not directly involved in danger,* despite exposure to extremely heavy air attacks, were the ones who were most likely to feel *less afraid* as the raids continued. (This statement is implied by the material presented in the USSBS morale report, although the specific data are not reported.)

From the various sources of evidence, it seems fairly safe to conclude that a sizeable proportion of the civilian population exposed to successive air attacks during World War II displayed a gradual decline in fear reactions. Insofar as the air attacks represent typical situations of external danger, the findings carry the obvious implication that among people in our culture there may be a general tendency toward emotional adaptation under conditions of repeated danger exposures. This implication is likely to be grossly misleading, however, unless one takes into account other reaction tendencies that are also evoked by recurrent danger experiences—tendencies which would operate in the direction of counteracting or preventing the development of emotional adaptation.

Of critical importance is the decline in the individual's capacity to withstand emotional stress as a consequence of near-miss experiences. There are also other factors associated with prolonged stress which might produce a similar impairment in protective "ego" functions. Numerous studies have been made among military personnel who were repeatedly exposed to combat situations that were comparable in some important respects to the recurrent air attacks to which civilian populations were subjected. From such studies, it is apparent that emotional adaptation is by no means the dominant tendency when there is a high degree of personal involvement. Morale surveys of combat ground troops in the United States Army show that with increased duration of front-line duty, there is a marked rise in the incidence of anxiety symptoms.[17] Similarly, among combat flying personnel there is a definite increase in symptoms of chronic tension and anxiety as the number of missions flown are increased.[18]

. . . Obviously, when a population is exposed to recurrent danger, widespread manifestations of emotional adaptation can be expected *only if there is a relatively low incidence of near-miss experiences.* The gradual loss of fear reactions and the decline in conformity to protective measures noted among the civilians in bombed communities were probably consequences of the remote-miss character of their air-raid experiences.

Emotional adaptation would probably be a rare occurrence in a target city subjected to atomic bombing or to a series of "conventional" attacks that entailed a high incidence of direct personal involvement. Under such conditions, an increase in fear reactions rather than a decrease would be the expected trend. Probably there would also be a progressive increase in fear reactions insofar as the danger exposures give rise to severe deprivations, unremitting fatigue, and other cumulative stresses of the sort which weaken the psychological stamina of combat troops. Consequently, emotional adaptation cannot be regarded in any sense as the "typical" reaction to successive air attacks. Rather, it is a reaction tendency that can easily be submerged or counteracted, becoming a dominant trend in a community only under relatively limited disaster conditions.

DETERMINANTS OF PSYCHOLOGICAL STRESS

From the discussion of the differential effects of near-miss and remote-miss experiences, it is possible to single out certain specific features of an air attack which are likely to be major determinants of the emotional impact upon the bombed community. Of primary importance in predicting the incidence of severe fear reactions is the number of persons who become directly involved in immediate danger. Typical indices of this factor might be the number of non-fatal casualties, the number of public air-raid shelters damaged, and the number of homes and buildings damaged in neighborhoods where public shelters were lacking or were not used.

A second predictive factor is the number of persons who suffered some degree of personal loss, whether or not they had been directly involved in personal danger. The number of families in which one or more fatalities occurred, the number of persons made homeless, and a variety of similar indicators might be used to estimate the incidence of personal loss. A third factor is exposure to the sight of the dead, the dying, and the wounded. The extent to which the population witnesses such disturbing sights is determined by the total number of casualties in the community and by the promptness with which casualties are removed to emergency centers before large numbers of people emerge from their homes or shelters. . . .

FEELINGS OF INVULNERABILITY

[Earlier in this chapter we saw] that much of the available evidence tends to support MacCurdy's theory: It is primarily the experience of being a near-miss that produces emotional disturbance, and, in the absence of such an experience, fear reactions tend to diminish during a series of air attacks.[19] As yet there is little empirical evidence that helps to explain the dynamics of near-miss and remote-miss reactions.

It is probable that when a near-miss experience involves exposure to primary fear-eliciting stimuli, such as sharp pain, sudden loss of physical support, or excessively loud noises, conditioned fear reactions are acquired in the same way that such reactions are produced in experimental studies of emotional conditioning. In other words, certain of the intense and terrifying stimuli occurring during a near-miss experience may act as powerful reinforcements for building up a conditioned fear response to previously neutral air-raid cues. When the latter stimuli occur during safe (remote-miss) experiences, on the other hand, emotional relief would tend to become the prepotent reaction and fear would be extinguished.

In addition to the simple (nonverbal) conditioned response mechanism, complex symbolic processes may also be involved. Thoughts, expectations, and fantasies play an important role in determining the amount of anxiety experienced, even without any exposure to real danger. When intense fear reactions are acquired, they are not at all limited to situations containing specific cues which were temporally contiguous with the terrifying stimuli, but are manifested in a variety of situations which do not necessarily resemble the original danger episode.

The writings of clinical psychoanalysts contain some suggestive material on mediating processes. Although based to some extent on interviews with a small number of persons who were studied intensively, their hypotheses are somewhat speculative in character. Nevertheless, they call attention to certain basic features of emotional adaptation which may help to explain some of the main phenomena of personal adjustment to wartime dangers.

According to numerous independent clinical observers, persons who face the prospect of recurrent air raids tend to develop sponteneously a variety of psychological defenses, all of which have the effect of reducing anticipatory anxieties. In preceding sections, reliance on talismans, magical rituals to ward off the danger, and other common adjustment mechanisms have been described. In addition to these, a variety of less overt personal defenses against anxiety is likely to develop. Complete denial of the impending danger, implicit trust in the protectiveness of the authorities, reversion to an infantile belief in personal omnipotence—these and other unconscious or partially conscious defense mechanisms have been described as typical modes of adjustment during a period of impending air attack.[20] Irrespective of the particular modes of defense a person employs, however, the net effect may be an illusion of personal invulnerability. According to Rado,[21] this is a "general human tendency" in situations of potential danger.

This hypothesis is consistent with the views of MacCurdy, who emphasizes the reinforcement of the feeling of invulnerability which occurs among the remote-miss group. He cites the following illustrative testimony as an extreme instance of the typical belief in personal invulnerability which counteracts fearful anticipations of personal destruction:

"When the first siren sounded I took my children to our dugout in the garden and I was quite certain we were all going to be killed. Then the all-clear went without anything having happened. Ever since we came out of the dugout I have felt sure nothing would ever hurt us."[22]

The remote-miss survivor, after emerging unscathed from an air raid, may be able to reduce his anxieties by saying to himself, "God protects me" or "So long as I go to the shelter in the basement I am completely safe," or by reassuring himself with a variety of similar self-promulgated promises of security against subsequent danger. Some of these reassurances may be realistic and others may be purely magical. But so long as no real danger is encountered, this entire set of symbolic responses may be highly effective in evoking expectations of personal safety despite danger, which is essentially what is referred to by the term "feelings of invulnerability."

The unique emotional consequences of near-miss experiences immediately become apparent if one assumes that large numbers of civilians manage to control their fears of death, of injury, and of personal loss from air attacks primarily by developing, to varying degrees of inner conviction, a feeling of personal invulnerability. If this assumption is correct, it would be expected that one of the most critical sources of prolonged anxiety reactions and of reduced capacity for controlling emotional responses in subsequent air raids would be those narrow-escape experiences during which people feel that they are no longer protected from the impact of danger. It is only among the remote-miss group that Kris's hypothesis would be expected to hold true: "Real danger is, on the average, faced better than vague apprehensions; the fantastic or imaginary elements of anxiety are deflated by the impact of the concrete situation."[23] Among the near-miss group, on the other hand, latent anticipatory fears would be strongly reinforced because the experience of being unprotected from danger would tend to break down feelings of invulnerability which had previously been effective.

This is essentially the hypothesis that Schmideberg presents in her comprehensive report on psychoanalytic observations of individual reactions to air raids:

> A person's conviction that nothing can happen to him is sometimes painfully shattered if something actually *does* happen to him. In that case the shock of being hurt or losing his property will be intensified by the shock of realizing his vulnerability.[24]

Probably it is not so much the awareness of facing immediate danger as the feeling of helplessness which is the critical psychological factor. Having once had the experience of being powerless to avert the direct physical impact of an explosion, the survivor may no longer be able to convince himself that he will be safe in subsequent raids because he is unable to dispel from his fantasies, and from his image of future raids, the memory of that harrowing experience in which he was helpless.

. . . there are two quite separable factors involved in the making of a danger into a "narrow escape." The first is that the immediate, unreflective action taken in the emergency is effective or ineffective. In the former case the emergency ends and the incident is closed without any emotional reaction and, probably, leaves no memory behind it except perhaps for a few minutes. In the latter case the ineffective action lingers in the memory and there are thoughts about what would have happened if the final scramble had been unsuccessful. So, for the production of fear there must be not merely danger but ineffective action to it. . . .[25]

Clinical case studies of combat personnel who developed diffuse anxiety symptoms also call attention to the loss of feelings of invulnerability once a person has experienced the reality of being powerless in the face of actual danger. Quantitative data relevant to the relationship between combat neurosis and feelings of invulnerability were obtained from a study of fliers.[26] A questionnaire was administered to 284 aircrew officers, all of whom had developed acute neurotic symptoms during or immediately after their tour of combat duty. Their responses were compared with those of a control group of 260 aircrew officers who had undergone similar combat experiences but without developing symptoms. To a direct question about feelings of invulnerability ("Did you feel that while others might be hurt or killed it couldn't happen to you?"), positive responses were given by only a small percentage of the patient group, as compared with the control group. The statistically significant difference between the two groups, as well as subgroup comparisons, indicates that neurotic breakdown under conditions of danger is associated with the absence or loss of feelings of invulnerability.

Further research along these lines, with more refined methods, is needed in order to explain why some people are able to undergo harrowing danger experiences without any pronounced effect, whereas others develop neurotic symptoms. The *kind* of invulnerability defense that a person builds up during the period preceding exposure to danger may have important consequences. For example, one of the unfavorable effects of relying on magical beliefs, according to Rickman, is that when danger is actually experienced, "the magical remedy against danger may be suddenly doubted."[27] Perhaps those people who develop an illusion of invulnerability based on total denial of impending danger ("nothing at all unpleasant will happen to me") are more likely to be traumatized than those who develop a more limited sense of invulnerability, keyed to the reality of the threat ("I might be bombed out, but I will survive"). Qualitative differences of this kind might be due to personality predispositions or to situational factors, such as official communications which predict that there will be or will not be any real danger.

Although some psychological defenses may prove to be "healthier" in the long run than others, there may nevertheless be a general tendency for all of them to be impaired, to some degree, as a result of any experience which makes the person sharply aware of his personal vulnerability. If this type of awareness is assumed to be a critical psychological factor in breaking down a person's emotional resistance, it would be expected that certain other types of disaster experiences, in addition to direct personal involvement, would have the general effect of producing severe and persistent fear reactions. Loss of loved ones and loss of other objects with which the person feels identified, even when the destruction has occurred while he was far off, may have the effect of destroying his feelings of invulnerability. The discovery that the air attack has killed or injured a close relative or friend or that it has destroyed his home may produce a degree of disturbance which goes far beyond the usual emotional response to such loss. By making him consciously realize, for the first time, that he might be overwhelmed by a similar fate, such experiences may reduce the person's capacity for defending himself against air-raid anxiety. Witnessing unexpected, extensive destruction and seeing maimed bodies after the raid is over may have a similar effect upon many persons.

> An Air Raid Warden told me that for a time he did not mind the raids, but that when he had seen the dead bodies of the victims and witnessed some gruesome incidents he visualized the reality of the situation and became thoroughly alarmed. The majority of the population only saw damaged buildings and bomb-craters, heard of people being killed or injured but did not actually see the casualties. Thus many lived through the blitz without fully appreciating the realities of the situation.[28]

Thus, a strong reinforcement of fear reactions would tend to occur not only among those who experience a narrow escape, but also among those who lose members of their families, whose homes or property has been destroyed, or who happen to observe, after the raid is over, the carnage it produced.

The importance of these additional factors in eliciting profound emotional disturbances is also implied by psychoanalytic hypotheses on guilt reactions, which may be reformulated as follows. Perception of damage and injury to others may evoke a feeling of profound relief: "I'm glad it happened to him and not to me." This initial response may be followed by feelings of guilt and fear of punishment for having permitted oneself to indulge in such a narcissistic thought. If the person toward whom the invidious contrast is directed has been a friend or a member of the family, and particularly if there had been strongly ambivalent feelings toward him, the survivor's guilt reaction may be reinforced by regressive thought processes, e.g., "because I was glad it happened, I am responsible for it." The heightened guilt may increase the survivor's fear of punishment, giving rise to the apprehensive feeling that "next time it will be my turn." Hence, in some cases, the spontaneous reaction to the perception of damage to others may produce guilt feelings which, in turn, may form the basis for heightened air-raid anxiety. In others who experience this type of reaction, the predominant feeling may be that "I deserve to be punished." This subjective response may be responsible, in part, for the excessive docility, apathy, and other depressive symptoms observed among air-raid victims.[29]

None of the hypotheses which have been discussed precludes the possibility that some persons who are burdened with strong guilt feelings might react to the punishment of a near-miss experience with a decrease in emotional tension. From the available observations, however, it appears that the guilt-relief reaction occurred relatively infrequently among air-raid victims. Although Vernon[30] and Harrisson[31] report that there were some people who seemed to think that after one narrow escape they had "had their share" and would be safe in the future, there is no indication in the literature that optimistic reactions, relief, or elation occurred among any sizeable proportion of near-miss survivors. . . .

SUMMARY

1. The incidence of severe fear reactions tends to increase with increased physical magnitude of the air raid. In heavier air attacks there is not only a higher incidence of incapacitating symptoms of anxiety or depression, but there is also a higher incidence of intense fear reactions among those who do not become psychiatric casualties.

2. Severe and prolonged fear reactions are most likely to occur among those who undergo near-miss experiences, i.e., direct exposure to the physical impact of the air attack (knocked down by blast, injured, home destroyed, etc.). It is primarily because a higher proportion of the population undergoes direct personal involvement that a very heavy raid, as against a light raid, produces a marked increase in the incidence of severe emotional reactions.

3. In contrast to the powerful reinforcement of fear reactions which occurs among those who are near-misses, the level of fear is *diminished* among the remote-misses, i.e., those who are exposed to

an air raid in which they do not directly experience a narrow escape or direct personal loss. People who are exposed to a series of air raids tend to show increased capacity to withstand the emotional stress of subsequent air attacks, provided they do not have a near-miss experience.

4. The high degree of uncertainty and suspense characteristic of periods when air attacks are expected probably elicits acute fear symptoms in only a relatively small proportion of the population. The fact that emotional adaptation occurred in the vast majority of remote-misses implies that, in the long run, such factors are not generally effective in producing intense and prolonged fear reactions.

5. When a population is exposed to a series of *false alarms or light raids* in which there is little or no objective danger, fear responses tend to extinguish and air-raid precautions are generally ignored. From the experience of the British, it appears that two major factors may be involved in the emotional adaptation which occurs when there are successive exposures to relatively nondangerous alerts: (*a*) a change in the "meaning" of air-raid alerts so that terrifying expectations of danger tend to be eliminated and (*b*) psychophysical adaptation to the intense auditory stimulus used as a warning signal.

6. When a population is exposed to a series of *heavy and relatively dangerous* raids, fear responses again subside and precautionary measures tend to be gradually disregarded (except when near-miss experiences counteract emotional adaptation). . . .

7. Many of the personal defenses that minimize or deny the threat of real danger appear to be effective in reducing anxiety primarily because they serve to build up an illusion of personal invulnerability. This hypothesis provides a plausible basis for explaining the dynamics of remote-miss and near-miss reactions. The critical disaster experiences which give rise to acute and persistent anxiety reactions are probably those which evoke a feeling of being powerless to avert actual danger. Narrow escapes from danger, loss of persons or objects with whom one feels identified, and witnessing maimed bodies may have the effect of shattering the entire set of psychological defenses (anxiety-reducing symbolic responses) involved in maintaining the expectation of personal invulnerability.

NOTES

1. M. Schmideberg, "Some Observations on Individual Reactions to Air Raids," *International J. Psychoanal.*, Vol. 23, 1942, pp. 146–176.

2. R. Fraser, I. M. Leslie, and D. Phelps, "Psychiatric Effects of Severe Personal Experiences during Bombing," *Proc. Roy. Soc. Med.*, Vol. 36, 1943, pp. 119-123.

3. E. Glover, "Notes on the Psychological Effects of War Conditions on the Civilian Population," Part III, "The Blitz," *International J. Psychoanal.*, Vol. 23, 1942, pp. 17-37; J. Langdon-Davies, *Air Raid*, George Routledge & Sons, Ltd., London, 1938; *op cit.*; J. Stern, *The Hidden Damage*, Harcourt, Brace and Company, Inc., New York, 1947; USSBS, *The Effects of Strategic Bombing on German Morale*, Vol. 1; P. E. Vernon, "Psychological Effects of Air Raids," *J. Abnorm. Soc. Psychol.*, Vol. 36, 1941, pp. 457-476.

4. T. Harrisson, "Obscure Nervous Effects of Air Raids," *Brit. Med. J.*, Vol. 1, 1941, pp. 573-574 and 832.

5. J. T. MacCurdy, *The Structure of Morale*, The Macmillan Company, New York, 1943.

6. *Ibid.*

7. *Ibid.*

8. Military Mobilization Committee of the American Psychiatric Association, *Psychiatric Aspects of Civilian Morale*, Family Welfare Assoc. of America, New York, 1942.

9. *Loc. cit.*

10. M. Seydewitz, *Civil Life in Wartime Germany*. The Viking Press, Inc., New York, 1945.

11. USSBS, *The Effects of Strategic Bombing on German Morale*, Vol. 1.

12. E. Klein, "The Influence of Teachers' and Parents' Attitudes and Behavior upon Children in Wartime," *Mental Hygiene*, Vol. 26, New York, 1942, pp. 434-445; MacCurdy, *op. cit.*; "Mass Observation," Schmideberg, *loc. cit.* Glover, *loc. cit.*; MacCurdy, *op. cit.*; Harrisson and Madge (eds.), *War Begins at Home*, Chatto & Windus, London, 1940; Schmideberg, *loc. cit.*; Vernon, *loc. cit.*; Glover, *loc. cit.*; MacCurdy, *op. cit.*; I. Matte, "Observations of the English in Wartime," *J. Nervous Ment. Disease*, Vol. 97, 1943, pp. 447-463; Schmideberg, *loc. cit.*; R. M. Titmuss, *Problems of Social Policy*, His Majesty's Stationery Office, London, 1950; Vernon, *loc. cit.*

13. R. D. Gillespie, "Résumé of His Addresses before the New York Academy of Medicine," *So. J. Med.*, Vol. 41, 1941; pp. 2346-2349; MacCurdy, *op. cit.*; J. M. Mackintosh, *The War and Mental Health in England*, Commonwealth Fund, Division of Publication, New York, 1944; Matte, *loc. cit.*; Schmideberg, *loc. cit.*

14. USSBS, *The Effects of Strategic Bombing on Japanese Morale.*

15. USSBS, *The Effects of Strategic Bombing on German Morale*, Vol. 1.

16. *Ibid.*

17. R. M. Williams and M. B. Smith, "General Characteristics of Ground Combat," Chap. 2 in S. Stouffer, *et al.*, *The American Soldier: Combat and Its Aftermath*, Vol. 2, Princeton University Press, Princeton, N.J., 1949.

18. I. L. Janis, "Objective Factors Related to Morale Attitudes in the Aerial Combat Situation," Chap. 8 in *ibid.*

19. MacCurdy, *op. cit.*

20. Glover, *loc. cit.*; MacCurdy, *op. cit.*; J. Rickman, "Panic and Air-raid Precautions," *Lancet*, Vol. 1, 1938, pp. 1291-1295; Schmideberg, *loc. cit.*
21. S. Rado, "Pathodynamics and Treatment of Traumatic War Neurosis (Traumataphobia)," *Psychosomat. Med.*, Vol. 43, 1942, pp. 362-368.
22. MacCurdy, *op. cit.*
23. E. Kris, "Morale in Germany," *Am J. Sociology*, Vol. 47, 1941, pp. 452-461.
24. Schmideberg, *loc. cit.*
25. MacCurdy, *op. cit.*
26. R. R. Grinker, *et al.*, "A Study of Psychological Predisposition to the Development of Operational Fatigue," *Am. J. Orthopsychiat.*, Vol. 16, 1946, pp. 191-214.
27. Rickman, *loc. cit.*
28. Schmideberg, *loc. cit.*
29. Glover, *loc. cit.*; T. Harrisson, "Obscure Nervous Effects of Air Raids," *Brit. Med. J.*, Vol. 1, 1941, pp. 573-574 and 832; A. M. Meerloo, *Aftermath of Peace*, International Universities Press, New York, 1946; Schmideberg, *loc. cit.*; USSBS Report, *The Effect of Bombing on Health and Medical Care in Germany*, U.S. Government Printing Office, Washington, D.C., 1945; USSBS Report, *The Effects of Bombing on Health and Medical Services in Japan*, U.S. Government Printing Office, Washington, D.C., 1947; Vernon, *loc. cit.*
30. *Loc. cit.*
31. *Loc. cit.*

5

Psychological Effects
of Warnings (1962)

In analyzing disaster behavior it is essential to determine the conditions under which warnings are taken seriously and whether they evoke adaptive or maladaptive responses. Earlier reports by the author and his collaborators have presented experimental evidence bearing on the effects of different dosages of fear-arousing material in warning communications (Hovland, Janis, and Kelley, 1953; Janis, 1958a; Janis and Feshbach, 1953) and have shown how personality predispositions are related to high and low responsiveness to mass media communications (Hovland and Janis, 1959; Janis and Feshbach, 1954). This chapter will analyze the pertinent evidence from field studies of large-scale disasters in order to obtain some new leads bearing on the psychology of warnings.

A set of hypotheses will be presented which provide some tentative answers to the following questions:

1. When signs of potential danger and informative communications about an impending disaster are presented, what factors determine whether they will instigate *effective preparatory behavior,* enhancing the recipients' ability to cope with subsequent adversity?

2. Under what conditions do warnings and informative communications about potential unfavorable events produce *emotional sensitization,* increasing the likelihood that maladaptive behavior will occur as a consequence of overwhelming anxiety, obsessional fear, or demoralization?

3. What are the main factors that promote *underreactions* to warnings—apathy, indifference, wishful thinking, and various forms of denial which interfere with successful preparation?

Janis, I. L. Psychological effects of warnings. In G. W. Baker and D. W. Chapman (Eds.), *Man and society in disaster.* New York: Basic Books, 1962. Reprinted by permission.

Despite obvious shortcomings of the available observations, numerous bits of available evidence can be pieced together to obtain clues concerning the key variables that are likely to influence the way people will respond to disaster warnings. . . .

REACTIONS TO WARNINGS DURING
A POISON LIQUOR EPISODE

To illustrate the various types of reactions to which the theoretical constructs and empirical generalizations are intended to apply, let us examine what happened when people were given warnings about the threat of being blinded or killed by poison liquor during a toxicological disaster in a large American city. J. W. Powell's observations on this crisis (1953, pp. 87–103) provide some statistical data on the incidence of extreme emotional disturbances evoked by warning communications and, at the same time, call attention to various types of inappropriate actions that created serious problems for the civil and medical authorities who were attempting to control the danger.

In October 1951 nearly 300 gallons of illegally distilled whiskey, containing lethal doses of methyl alcohol, were distributed in various sections of Atlanta, Georgia. Within one week, 39 people were killed, 9 were totally blinded, and over 100 others were suffering from one or more symptoms of methanol poisoning—stomach cramps, severe vomiting, impairment of vision, dizziness, breathing difficulties. A few victims were white, but the majority were black. Shortly after the first victims arrived at the emergency ward of the local black hospital, warnings were disseminated throughout the city, especially in those black sections where the poisoned whiskey was known to have been distributed.

As more and more warning messages came to public attention, hundreds of apprehensive persons asked for medical attention because they thought they might have been poisoned. According to Powell, the symptoms of many people who asked to be examined were purely psychological. Records from the medical staff of Emory University's Grady Hospital indicated that 433 clinic interviews were conducted with persons who thought they had been poisoned. Altogether, 183 cases (42 per cent) were found to be negative on standard medical tests and completely asymptomatic. These persons were suffering from nothing more than extreme apprehensiveness in response to the alarming warnings and rumors that spread throughout the city. Of the remaining cases, 75 reported definite physical symptoms which were found to be negative on the medical tests. These people had apparently developed hysterical reactions which mimic the symptoms of methanol poisoning. Thus, it is estimated that only 40 per cent of those examined at the emergency clinic proved to be genuine casualties. As J. W. Powell puts it, "Of every ten people who took up the doctors' time during those five crucial days, four had had no poison or showed no symptoms, two more had had no poison and did report symptoms; and only four had actually had the poison and did require treatment" (1953, p. 91).[1]

Other types of psychological problems were also encountered in the Atlanta poisoning disaster. At the opposite extreme from the hypervigilant, apprehensive people who unnecessarily overloaded the emergency medical facilities were the disaster victims who, despite clear-cut physical symptoms, ignored the warnings concerning the need for prompt medical attention and did not come to the clinic. An illustrative example of a denial reaction in response to repeated warnings is to be found in one of J. W. Powell's (1951) intensive interviews. Mrs. F., a forty-year-old black waitress, spent one evening sharing a bottle of bootleg whiskey with a woman friend, Louise, and her brother. Early the following morning, Louise awoke Mrs. F. with excited complaints of being unable to see anything and of feeling terribly sick. Within fifteen minutes, while Mrs. F. was phoning for a doctor, Louise died. Shortly thereafter, Louise's brother, who slept in the same house, developed the same symptoms of blindness and nausea. With Mrs. F.'s help, he was rushed to the hospital by ambulance. This was followed by a visit from a police detective who examined Mrs. F.'s liquor bottles, told her about the poison whiskey that had been sold in Atlanta, and informed her that her friends were victims of methanol poisoning. Up to this time, Mrs. F. had assumed her woman friend died of a heart attack and had remained puzzled about the similar symptoms of her friend's brother. But now, despite the clear-cut warning information given by the detective, Mrs. F. did not think of herself as needing medical help. A few hours later, when she developed her first symptom of poisoning, she merely took a home remedy to alleviate gastric distress.

A short time later, Mrs. F. suddenly became "blind as a bat"

---

[1] The incidence of apprehensive and hysterical reactions found in this study may be extraordinarily high, but the lack of systematic data from other disasters precludes comparative assessment. In any case, one cannot rely upon the estimates obtained from this study for predicting the incidence of emotional overreactions in other disasters because there are two special features of the Atlanta poisoning episode that could augment the occurrence of such reactions: (1) The threat of poisoning seems to be especially potent in eliciting hysterical conversion symptoms; (2) Most of the people directly affected were southern blacks of a low educational level—. . . .

and felt "scared to death." Only then did she begin to think of getting medical attention. In accounting for her failure to take adequate account of the series of warning events, Mrs. F. gave some indication of the latent fears that lay behind her maladaptive attempts to deny the danger.

> *Interviewer:* "You said before that perhaps you were so busy worrying about the others rather than yourself."
> *Mrs. F.:* "Yeah, I think if I would of ever thought that it could have happened to me, I would of had a heart attack or something would have happened to me."

Denial reactions in the Atlanta disaster resulted not only in delay of treatment, as in the case of Mrs. F., but also in failure to follow other urgent medical recommendations. Powell reports that a sizable number of clinic patients ignored the physician's instructions to carry out the prescribed self-treatment for preventing symptoms from growing worse, with the result that they were brought back to the hospital in critical condition. Another serious form of under-reaction to the official warnings was noted in a few recorded cases treated for minor symptoms at the clinic, who, after returning home, evidently drank more of the poisoned whiskey. Some of these victims may have failed to comprehend the warnings or, later on, may have denied the danger as a result of the temporary psychotic state induced by methanol poisoning.

In contrast to the maladaptive behavior of those who overreacted or underreacted to the warnings, some of the potential victims reacted with discriminative vigilance, watching themselves carefully for possible symptoms, checking on the liquor they had recently drunk, and seeking further medical information about the danger. Adaptive reactions of this type may have occurred in some of the nonpoisoned cases who came to the clinic, especially in those who were uncertain as to whether minor symptoms of gastric upset might be the prelude to more serious symptoms of methanol poisoning. The mood of cautious watchfulness also led some of the high-status members of the black community to check on rumors that black victims were being sent to the morgue before they were dead and were being mistreated in the medical clinic. According to Powell, these rumors gained credence from local beliefs about the past history of police brutality and from earlier stories of drunken blacks who had been beaten to death but were listed by the authorities as having died from poison whiskey. Vigilance reactions occurred in a number of well-educated blacks affiliated with the local university. Some of them surreptitiously entered the morgue and the hospital wards to see for themselves whether the rumors were true. Their eyewitness testimony evidently helped to alleviate suspicion and to counteract the spread of disruptive rumors.

Studies of other community disasters, and of psychological stress engendered in individuals facing the threats of ill-health or surgery, call attention to essentially the same varieties of reactions to warning communications as were seen in the Atlanta toxicological disaster. On the one hand, there are many people who respond to an external threat by becoming vigilant in a highly discriminative way, watching for signs of oncoming danger, seeking for information about how to cope with the crisis, and getting set to carry out protective actions. On the other hand, there are people who behave in a maladaptive way. Some overreact to warnings by becoming excessively excited or by developing acute psychoneurotic symptoms; others underreact by denying the threat and by failing to take essential precautions (cf., Diggory, 1956; Janis, 1958b; Wolfenstein, 1957).

FUNCTIONAL PROPERTIES OF REFLECTIVE FEAR

Many psychologists have followed Freud in distinguishing between "normal fear" (or "objective anxiety") occurring when a person is aware of a known danger, and "neurotic anxiety" arising from inner dangers linked with the person's unconscious impulses. Freud recognized, however, that the question of whether or not the person is aware of an external danger is not an entirely dependable criterion, inasmuch as the same external conditions that elicit normal fear can also elicit neurotic anxiety (see Freud, 1936, p. 148). Detailed studies of people facing objective danger situations bear out Freud's observations that reality-oriented fears are sometimes heavily overlaid with neurotic anxiety or neurotic guilt, so that criteria other than the eliciting stimulus must be used to differentiate nonneurotic from neurotic reactions (see Janis, 1958b, pp. 107-125). In the following discussion, I shall attempt to describe the criteria that enable a consistent distinction to be made. In doing so, I shall attempt to make explicit a number of functional properties of reality-oriented fear that Freud alluded to implicitly but did not specify in his writings on anxiety. Since the construct will be somewhat redefined, I shall give it a distinctive label in order to avoid confusion: "reflective fear." (The adjective "reflective" is used both in the sense of deliberative or thoughtful and in the sense of reflecting the realities of the external danger situation.) . . . This construct can be anchored to empirical observations by positing the following functional properties:

1. Influence of Environmental Cues

The arousal of reflective fear is assumed to depend upon perceptions of actual threat stimuli, warning communications, and other environmental cues that convey information about impending danger. Thus, for example, in a pre-disaster situation, a person's level of reflective fear will increase or decrease depending upon whether he receives new warnings about the imminence of catastrophe or new reassurances from the community authorities. This functional property is in direct contrast to the relatively unmodifiable character of neurotic fear or anxiety.

2. Arousal of Need for Vigilance

A major behavioral consequence of reflective fear is a strong need for vigilance. The manifestations of this need include a broad class of observable changes which can be generally described as increased attentiveness to environmental events and readiness to take protective action in response to any cue perceived as indicating the onset of danger. Adopting a vigilance set involves cognitive as well as action changes—scanning the environment for signs of danger, attending to information pertinent to the danger, planning alternative courses of action for dealing with emergency contingencies, and the like. On the action side, a vigilance set involves a lower threshold for executing plans involving precautionary measures, heightened muscular tension, and increased gross motor activity oriented toward avoiding the anticipated danger. In the Atlanta poison liquor episode, some of the dominant forms of vigilant activity consisted in paying close attention to feelings of physical discomfort and coming to a medical clinic to be checked by a physician.

3. Arousal of Need for Reassurance

Another consequence of reflective fear is a strong need for alleviating emotional tension by obtaining convincing reassurances. Like "vigilance," the "need for reassurance" is a dispositional construct; we assume it is positively correlated with the level of reflective fear and entails changes in both the cognitive and action aspects of behavior. For example, an increase in the need for reassurance is manifested by selective attention to and recall of communications that minimize the danger or play up the protective resources available for coping with it. Heightened need for reassurance is also manifested by changes in beliefs and attitudes—the adoption of a fatalistic outlook or a greater faith in divine protection, the use of magical or superstitious practices for warding off bad luck, and the acceptance of rationalizations for continuing on a business-as-usual basis (see Hovland *et al.*, 1953, pp. 60–89). Corresponding changes in action include overt efforts to avoid exposure to danger warnings and greater adherence to conventional morality in an effort to avoid offending the "powers that be."

The most extreme forms of reassurance are those involving anticipations of total invulnerability: the person feels convinced either that the danger will never materialize in his vicinity ("It can't happen here") or that, if it does, he will be completely protected from it ("Others may suffer, but we shall be safe"). Such extreme anticipations, referred to as "blanket reassurances," may dominate completely over vigilance tendencies, as was seen in those victims of the Atlanta toxicological disaster who ignored the warnings and failed to seek medical aid even though suffering from obvious symptoms of poisoning.

4. Development of Compromise Formations Involving Discriminative Vigilance and Reassurance

On the one hand, vigilance and reassurance are potentially conflicting tendencies, in that they can impel a person toward incompatible cognitions or actions. ("I must watch out because something dangerous is likely to happen at any moment," *versus* "I can relax and forget about it because the danger will not affect me.") On the other hand, the two tendencies do not *necessarily* conflict every time both are aroused. It is possible to develop *compromise formations* which combine vigilance (anticipating danger, seeking information about it, remaining alert to signs of threat) and reassurance (expecting to be able to cope successfully with the danger or to be helped by others if the danger becomes extreme). In the Atlanta study, the examples given of well-educated members of the black community becoming agitated by scare rumors about maltreatment of fellow blacks and then checking the reliability of the rumors by visiting the local hospital wards and the morgue, clearly represent such compromise formations. Presumably these persons obtained emotional relief when their investigations failed to confirm the rumors.

A common type of compromise formation among men in hazardous occupations involves *danger-contingent* reassurances: The person

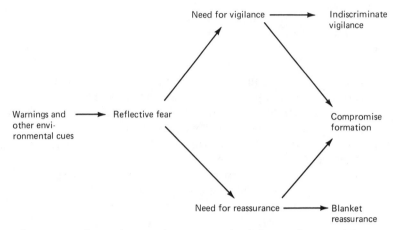

Figure 5.1 Alternative reactions to perceived threat of external danger

acknowledges vulnerability to the potential disaster and makes plans
for carrying out protective actions that can be relied upon to enable
him to survive *if* one or another form of danger actually arises. Such
an attitude, combining discriminative vigilance with discriminative
reassurance, is likely to be much more adaptive than an attitude of
either blanket reassurance or indiscriminate vigilance. Thus, the
development of compromise formations is conceived as one of three
alternative modes of responding to threat situations which arouse
reflective fear.

The diagram in Figure 5.1 shows the three alternatives specified
in the foregoing assumptions about the functional properties of reflective fear. The likelihood that a person will develop one or another
of the three modes of defense is assumed to depend upon a large
number of situational as well as predispositional variables, some of
which will be described in later sections of this chapter.

The capacity for adopting a sustained vigilance set presupposes a
relatively high level of development of the "ego" functions essential
for testing reality, since it requires the person to forgo an immediate
gratification—the warding off of dysphoric feelings—in exchange for
an anticipated reward—greater safety in the future. Evidently children learn only gradually to bear the emotional tension that goes
along with vigilance. Even many adults find it extremely difficult to
adopt a set of watchfulness, alertness, and readiness to take protective action in the face of known danger. Whenever they are not exposed to constant reminders of the danger, they seem disposed to
abandon this vigilance set in favor of a more comfortable attitude of
blanket reassurance. But if danger signs are present, vigilance tends to

be aroused. Later on we shall see that discriminative vigilant reactions will be fostered if fear does not mount to a high level. If it does mount, however, the person may make impulsive decisions and display "panic" reactions that objectively increase the danger.

BASIC REACTION PATTERNS EVOKED BY WARNINGS

Figure 5.2 . . . indicates the main causal sequences implied by the foregoing discussion of reflective fear. Five main sequences are represented here, and these appear to be consistent with the available empirical findings concerning the varieties of pre-disaster reactions displayed by normal personalities. . . .

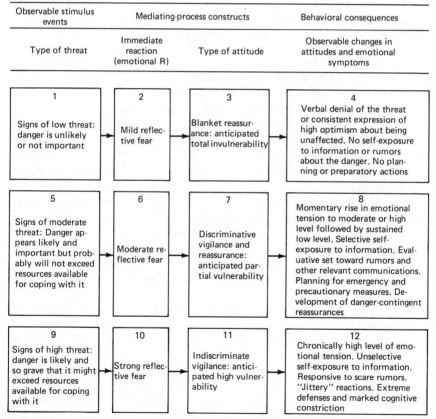

Observable stimulus events	Mediating-process constructs		Behavioral consequences
Type of threat	Immediate reaction (emotional R)	Type of attitude	Observable changes in attitudes and emotional symptoms
1 Signs of low threat: danger is unlikely or not important	**2** Mild reflective fear	**3** Blanket reassurance: anticipated total invulnerability	**4** Verbal denial of the threat or consistent expression of high optimism about being unaffected. No self-exposure to information or rumors about the danger. No planning or preparatory actions
5 Signs of moderate threat: Danger appears likely and important but probably will not exceed resources available for coping with it	**6** Moderate reflective fear	**7** Discriminative vigilance and reassurance: anticipated partial vulnerability	**8** Momentary rise in emotional tension to moderate or high level followed by sustained low level. Selective self-exposure to information. Evaluative set toward rumors and other relevant communications. Planning for emergency and precautionary measures. Development of danger-contingent reassurances
9 Signs of high threat: danger is likely and so grave that it might exceed resources available for coping with it	**10** Strong reflective fear	**11** Indiscriminate vigilance: anticipated high vulnerability	**12** Chronically high level of emotional tension. Unselective self-exposure to information. Responsive to scare rumors. "Jittery" reactions. Extreme defenses and marked cognitive constriction

Figure 5.2 Schematic summary of "normal" psychological changes evoked by warnings or signs of external danger

1. Normal Reaction to Low Threat

The first normal sequence in Figure 5.2 (1→2→3→4) usually occurs in response to warnings about potential dangers or losses that the community generally regards as relatively unimportant or improbable. In response to such threats, clinically normal people tend to react with *mild* reflective fear, which is promptly reduced by means of blanket reassurance, with the consequence that behavior remains essentially unaffected by the warning. If the initial estimates prove to be correct (i.e., either the danger does not materialize at all or, if it does, it entails little suffering and only minor losses), such reactions can be said to have adaptive value in that the person avoids wasting time and energy on useless preparation and conserves his resources for more important tasks. Few people will suffer adverse consequences from ignoring low-threat warnings in a community where such warnings generally predict external events accurately. If serious dangers were to materialize, however, this sequence would prove to be just as maladaptive as Number 5 below.

2. Hypervigilant Reaction to Low Threat

Occasionally, signs of low threat are grossly misinterpreted by clinically normal persons, who consequently anticipate being victimized or possibly annihilated by the impending danger. This exaggerated fear reaction can give rise to either of the following subsequences: 1→6→7→8, or 1→10→11→12. Examples of the latter sequence, which can have markedly disruptive effects on the community, were observed in a few people who thought that the huge, mushroomlike cloud following an industrial explosion in South Amboy, N.J., had been caused by an atomic bomb (see Green and Logan, 1950).

3. Normal Reactions to Moderate or High Threat

When warnings of moderate or high threats occur, the normal sequence of reaction is assumed to be 5→6→7→8. Thus, in clinically normal persons the arousal of reflective fear is expected to lead to reality-oriented compromise formations which satisfy both vigilance and reassurance needs in a discriminative way, with corresponding changes in attitudes and behavior. This sequence generally is adaptive in that the person is better prepared to cope with the danger situation if it subsequently materializes.

4. Hypervigilant Reaction to Moderate or High Threat

When a warning of serious danger occurs, hypervigilance is assumed to be a maladaptive type of overreaction that does not necessarily imply neurotic anxiety, the sequence being 5 or 9→10→11→12. The crucial feature of this pattern is that reflective fear becomes so strong that it prevents compromise formation. Any normal person, whether or not he is hypersensitive to a given threat, is assumed to be capable of indiscriminate vigilance if he apperceives an impending danger as far greater than his limited resources for coping with it. Because this sequence is likely to result in impulsive or inefficient behavior if serious danger actually materializes, it is regarded as maladaptive.

5. Hypovigilant Reaction to Moderate or High Threat

A different type of maladaptive outcome results from extreme underreaction to a serious threat, as represented by the sequence 5 or 9→2→3→4. This reaction pattern, which resembles the denial symptoms encountered in some psychotics, does not necessarily imply pre-existing emotional disorder, since it occurs in clinically normal persons under special environmental conditions. (The environmental conditions which promote this type of underreaction will be discussed in the next section.) If the danger does not materialize, hypovigilant reactions have no specially negative consequences; but if the danger does materialize, maladaptive behavior and sustained symptoms of psychological trauma are likely to occur. Studies of surgical patients and observations of soldiers' and civilians' reactions to wartime dangers indicate that when warnings arouse a moderate degree of reflective fear prior to the occurrence of a stressful life situation, they will function as a form of "emotional inoculation" (Janis, 1958b). . . .

CONDITIONS FOSTERING VIGILANCE VERSUS REASSURANCE TENDENCIES

From the foregoing analysis, it is apparent that one central research problem is to determine the environmental conditions which foster high vigilance *versus* high reassurance needs when people are warned of impending dangers. During the pre-impact phase of a disaster,

clinically normal personalities are capable of the extreme complacency accompanying an attitude of blanket reassurance or the
extreme hypervigilance characterizing states of acute panic. What
types of information about the danger foster vigilance and what
types foster reassurance? When pertinent information about the
danger is held constant, what additional factors need to be taken into
account in order to predict overreactions and underreactions to
warnings? What types of events and communications promote adaptive compromise formations?

The remainder of this chapter will present tentative hypotheses
concerning situational factors which appear to affect significantly the
probability that people will react one way or another when a warning
is issued. Some of the hypotheses are based on assumptions about
the origins of vigilance and reassurance tendencies, which are assumed to develop early in each person's life history, as a joint product of personal learning in fear-arousing situations, and social training
in those norms of the community that prescribe where, when, and
how one should take account of various types of anticipated dangers.
Additional hypotheses are suggested by empirical findings from
disaster studies which deal with reactions during the pre-impact
phase. Each hypothesis will be discussed briefly without attempting
to review all the pertinent findings, but references will be made to a
few cogent disaster studies.

EFFECTS OF DIFFERENT TYPES
OF INFORMATION

The level of reflective fear induced by a warning stimulus determines
to a large extent whether the person will adopt a discriminate or indiscriminate reaction. One main assumption is that when a very low
degree of reflective fear is aroused by unambiguous warnings dealing
with remote, improbable, or relatively trivial dangers, the average
person will tend to ignore the warnings ("Nothing will happen to me,
I don't need to worry about it"). As fear mounts, however, blanket
reassurances become less and less successful in suppressing awareness
of danger; at the same time, previously acquired habits of vigilance
become increasingly prepotent. The probability of developing discriminative compromise formations appears to be greatest when reflective fear is at a moderate level (see Hovland *et al.*, 1953, pp. 66-
88). When reflective fear reaches a very high level, there is an increase
in indiscriminate vigilance reactions, manifested by reduced mental
efficiency and a predominance of regressive thought processes involv-

ing poor discrimination between safe and unsafe features of the environment (see Janis, 1958b).

Thus, we expect a curvilinear relationship between the level of reflective fear and the probability of discriminative reactions to warnings. At the low end of the fear continuum, reassurance tendencies are likely to predominate; in the middle range, both reassurance and vigilance tendencies will be aroused to a moderate degree; at the upper end, vigilance tendencies will tend to dominate the person's behavior. The information factors that determine the person's level of reflective fear are therefore assumed to have a marked influence on his mode of defense.

The arousal of reflective fear is assumed to depend upon two types of information. One type, which tends to increase reflective fear, consists of unambiguous information about the magnitude of oncoming danger. The second type, which tends to reduce reflective fear, consists of unambiguous information about the magnitude of personal and community resources for coping with the danger. The first type also includes information indicating that the danger has a high probability of occurrence. Similarly, the second type includes information indicating that a given resource for coping with the danger will be available and effective at the time it will be needed. The highest level of reflective fear, and hence the greatest likelihood of indiscriminate vigilance, will occur when there is a great deal of information of the first type and none of the second type.

Thus, for example, when an urban population has been alerted to signs of an impending flood or tornado, the average person tends to show an increase in reflective fear if subsequent warnings issued by a credible source assert any one of the following four themes: (1) the potential disaster, if it happens to hit here, can cause more destruction or more casualties than had previously been predicted; (2) the chances of being hit here are now substantially greater than had previously been predicted; (3) our rescue teams, fire fighters, first-aid units, or other disaster-control organizations do not have enough manpower or equipment to cope with the potential disaster as effectively as most people hope; or (4) our disaster-control personnel cannot be mobilized in an emergency as quickly as people expect, or cannot be of much help until after the initial destructive impact. Conversely, the level of reflective fear and the probability of vigilance reactions tend to be lowered if subsequent communications reverse the content in any of the four categories. (The term "reassurances" is used to refer to any assertion to the effect that the potential disaster will cause less destruction, or is less likely to materialize, or can be more effectively dealt with than had been expected; we shall continue to designate as "warnings" those communications and physical signs that convey any of the four types of themes that heighten awareness of vulnerability to danger.)

Only when unambiguous information about impending danger is available to the warned population can we apply the rather obvious propositions presented in the preceding paragraphs. But what happens if the information available during the pre-disaster period is so inadequate or confusing that people cannot obtain a clear-cut conception of what is in store for them? Especially when the threat is an unfamiliar one, involving a nonrecurrent type of personal or community disaster, people may be confronted with an abundance of vague folklore, uneducated guesses, and conflicting rumors (see Allport and Postman, 1947).

From a survey of existing studies of ambiguous threats, the following hypothesis is suggested: *Under conditions where a serious warning has aroused fear to a moderate or high level, the recipient's vigilance tendencies will tend to be increased by any subsequent communication or physical sign that he perceives as containing ambiguous information about his vulnerability.*

This "ambiguity" hypothesis is intended to apply whenever the significance of a verbal message or physical event is obscure or equivocal. In the case of verbal communications, ambiguity is usually due to imprecise wording. Ambiguity can also arise from the use of highly precise technical language with which members of the audience are partially or wholly unfamiliar, so that for them parts of the message become equivalent to double-talk. Similarly, when a person is unfamiliar with the nature of the danger or with the environmental setting in which the danger cues occur, he will often be puzzled and wonder what is happening. Thus, ignorance can endow purely neutral events with ambiguous status, whereupon they may be interpreted as mysterious or potentially ominous signs.

The "ambiguity" hypothesis, it will be noted, does not refer to instances of low-threat warnings. When the initial warning arouses only a slight degree of fear, we would expect subsequent items of ambiguous information either to be ignored or to be interpreted as confirming the recipient's low-threat expectations, thus reinforcing an attitude of blanket reassurance. There are numerous indications in the disaster literature that ambiguous signs and communications pertaining to oncoming danger do, in fact, foster complacency if the threat is initially regarded as unimportant (Fritz and Marks, 1954; Wolfenstein, 1957). Perhaps the most widely observed instances occur in flood disasters; examples will be cited in a later section on factors that give rise to hypovigilance. . . .

It seems likely, therefore, that ambiguous signs and communications are capable of increasing or decreasing vigilance, depending on whether the level of fear aroused by antecedent warnings is high or low. Withey (1962) . . . has suggested that there is a general tendency to assimilate any new information as reinforcement for whatever psychological set is dominant at the time of the exposure. He points out that when a person is not expecting disaster, any threat cues will tend to be interpreted "as unthreatening until such interpretation can no longer be made" (p. 113). But when a person is set to expect disaster, he tends to become so oversensitive that even a minor suggestion of possible threat will be capable of stimulating emergency reactions.

Withey's assumptions are essentially the same as those presented here, except that we add a further assumption which makes explicit the importance of the ambiguity factor: unambiguous information about impending dangers will evoke marked changes in the level of fear and there will be little or no assimilation; but the more ambiguous the cues, the more likely that they will be assimilated into the pre-existing psychological set. . . .

One implication of the foregoing assumptions is that a marked shift from extreme hypovigilance to extreme hypervigilance is to be expected whenever: (1) highly ambiguous threat signs appear at a time when people are not expecting any danger at all, and then (2) the signs persist or reappear after one or more additional warning signs have induced awareness that a serious, albeit unknown, threat is actually present. . . .

SITUATIONAL FACTORS INFLUENCING ACTIONAL READINESS

We shall now examine some implications of our earlier assumption that vigilance tendencies will be increased by any verbal or physical signs that lower the person's appraisal of his own or his community's resources for coping with an anticipated disaster, even though his appraisal of the magnitude of the external danger remains essentially unchanged. A series of four hypotheses will be presented which specify situational factors that change a person's self-appraisal and thereby influence his readiness to take action. Like the ones presented earlier, these hypotheses have not yet been adequately tested but appear to be plausible in the light of existing evidence from disaster research.

1. Anticipated Unacessibility of Existing Escape Routes

*Under conditions where a personal or community disaster is antici-
pated, the strength of vigilance tendencies will be increased by any
warning communication or physical sign interpreted by the perceiver
as indicating that a currently available escape route will become inac-
cessible to him once the danger materializes.*

The term *escape route* in this hypothesis refers, broadly speaking,
to any behavioral sequence or course of action that will lead to
avoidance or mitigation of the danger stimuli. Anticipated inaccessi-
bility may involve expectations about deficiencies in the physical or
social environment (e.g., "Roads will be so overcrowded that they
will be useless to us") or in one's own skills (e.g., "I might become
too excited to be able to drive my car"). Regardless of the perceived
source of the deficiency, the net result is that the person anticipates
a loss in his power to cope with mounting danger if the emergency
situation should arise. In a summary statement on the problem of
panic prepared for the National Research Council (Janis, Chapman,
Gillin, and Spiegel, 1955), it was pointed out that the most extreme
forms of indiscriminate vigilance occur at times when people expect
great danger to be imminent and, at the same time, perceive the last
remaining escape routes to be rapidly closing. Studies of the effects
of pre-disaster warnings suggest that even when a threat is perceived
as entailing a relatively low magnitude of danger, the strength of vigilance tendencies will increase if new information is received about
the closing of escape routes (see Danzig, *et al.*, 1958). Hence the
hypothesis has been formulated in such a way as to include low- as
well as high-threat situations.

On the assumption that the relationship specified by the hypothesis is mediated by a change in the anticipated degree of victimization, we would expect the following complementary hypothesis to
hold: Vigilance reactions will be diminished by any communication
or physical sign interpreted by the perceivers as indicating that existing escape routes will become more accessible to them or that new
ones will be opened up if an anticipated threat materializes. Some of
the observed effects of reassuring communications appear to be consistent with this hypothesis (see Janis, 1958a, 1958b).

2. Anticipated Need for Self-Initiated Action

*The strength of a person's vigilance tendencies will be high or low,
depending on whether the available verbal information and physical
signs lead him to expect that, if the anticipated danger materializes,*

his own actions will have high or low importance with respect to mitigating danger. Vigilance increases when the person is exposed to signs indicating that adequate protection for himself and his family will require self-initiated action; vigilance decreases when the person is exposed to signs indicating that he can rely on others to protect him and his family.

The individual's expectations concerning the importance of his own actions determine whether or not the anticipated danger is in the category of those events for which the person acknowledges a sense of responsibility. There are numerous indications in the disaster literature that a marked lowering of vigilance activity is produced among the residents of a potential disaster area by authoritative communications which convey that community leaders or specialists in disaster control can be expected to carry out whatever protective measures are required (Janis, 1951). The reassuring effects produced by such communications may stem partly from a reactivation of childhood attitudes of trust in the protective powers of the parents. But we would expect that, as a result of social training and distressing life experiences, the individual learns to discriminate between danger situations in which other people can be relied upon to protect him and those in which his safety is partly or wholly his own responsibility.

3. Anticipated Restriction of Activity

Under any conditions of threat, including those in which a person does not expect his own activity to play a significant role in reducing his chances of being victimized, the strength of his vigilance tendencies will be increased whenever he is exposed to communications or physical signs indicating that at the time of danger impact his own activity will be restricted.

This proposition applies to restrictions of perceptual as well as cognitive and motor activity. For example, during World War II both combat troops and civilians became more agitated when air-raid warnings came at night rather than during the day (Garner, 1945; Glover, 1942; Janis, 1951; U.S. Strategic Bombing Survey, 1947a and 1947b). Reflective fear may be more readily aroused at night partly because people expect that poor visibility will interfere with their ability to find and use escape routes. Many Japanese civilians reported that they were especially fearful of night raids because they knew it would be more difficult to escape from fires and collapsing buildings when they could not see clearly (U.S. Strategic Bombing Survey, 1947b). Such instances of anticipated restriction are equivalent to anticipated interference with escape opportunities and hence can be subsumed under the hypothesis concerning the effects of the anticipated closing of escape routes (pp. 74-75). But in many instances the heightening of vigilance seems to occur even when the person believes that the limitation will not alter his chances of survival. A surgical patient is likely to become extraordinarily jittery and hypervigilant when the cues he receives in the operating room make him realize that the physicians will impose severe restrictions upon his perceptual, cognitive, and motor activity, despite his conscious knowledge that such restrictions will reduce rather than augment the danger (Janis, 1958b). In such cases, expectations of enforced passivity may arouse reflective fear to a disproportionately high degree because of a reactivation of childhood situations of passive helplessness. Similar instances of irrational heightening of vigilance evidently occur during the pre-impact phase of large-scale disasters (Glover, 1942; Sullivan, 1941; Wolfenstein, 1957).

4. Anticipated Restriction of Social Contacts

The strength of vigilance tendencies will be increased whenever a person is exposed to communications or physical signs indicating that during a period of oncoming danger he will be out of contact with authority figures, members of his primary group, or other significant persons upon whom he is emotionally dependent.

There is considerable evidence of a striking increase in affiliative needs under conditions of external threat (Glover, 1942; Janis, 1951; Schachter, 1959; Wolfenstein, 1957). Reliance on parent surrogates and primary groups evidently constitutes a major source of reassurance, alleviating fears of abandonment and annihilation derived from childhood separation experiences, which are reactivated by threat situations in adult life.

When a person knows that authority figures, friends, or members of his family are nearby he feels reassured and his vigilance reactions tend to be lower than if he knows such persons are absent. But the net effect of the *actual* presence of a significant person depends partly on what that person says and how he says it. For example, if he makes dire predictions or displays acute emotional symptoms, a group leader will transmit fear, thus heightening vigilance rather than lowering it (Hudson, 1954). . . .

The hypothesis under discussion, however, refers to *anticipated* rather than to actual separation from authority figures or other significant persons. Heightened vigilance has been observed among soldiers when they expect to be required to remain alone for a long period in foxholes, and among civilians when they perceive signs indicating the possibility of becoming socially isolated at a time of impending disaster. High vigilance is also to be expected when an individual is not physically isolated but separated by a great *social distance* from the people with whom he is in contact. Extreme instances of hypervigilant reactions have been noted, for example, when refugees were exposed to the threat of air raids in a foreign country or when wartime evacuees found themselves among people of a markedly different ethnic or social class background (Janis, 1951).

Cues evoking anticipated psychological separation are sometimes obtained from the *absence of communications* on the part of authority figures from whom information or reassurance is expected. When civic leaders and trusted news services fail to issue bulletins about what is going on during a large-scale community disaster, many people begin to lose confidence in them; they become increasingly preoccupied with signs of threat and display more and more hypervigilant reactions, such as accepting and spreading exaggerated rumors about the terrible things that are going to happen (see Glover, 1940).

There are, of course, many different signs that arouse vigilance by creating anticipations of psychological separation from significant persons. Such anticipations can readily be evoked by an impressive news story or exposé propaganda which describes the authorities in an unfavorable manner, making them appear to be untrustworthy, indifferent, or hostile toward the recipients. Similar effects are likely to be produced by authoritative communications containing weak or vague statements which generate doubts as to whether the authorities really intend to be helpful (see Janis, 1958b, pp. 134-138, 170-172, 302-325).

ADAPTATION AND SENSITIZATION EFFECTS PRODUCED BY ANTECEDENT WARNINGS

A major implication of the assumptions about reflective fear introduced at the beginning of this chapter is that the way a person reacts to any given warning will depend partly upon the type of information he has received from antecedent warnings. The available evidence, as we shall see shortly, indicates that in a pre-disaster situation a series of preliminary warnings can induce an "emotional adaptation" effect, decreasing the probability that any new emergency warning will evoke vigilance reactions. But other observations indicate that the opposite outcome can also occur: under certain conditions, a series of preliminary warnings can produce a "sensitizing" effect, with the result that the probability of vigilant reactions to a new emergency warning is increased rather than decreased. In the sections that follow, we shall attempt to differentiate between the conditions fostering adaptation and those fostering sensitization. First we shall examine some comparative findings bearing on the differences between "nonprecipitant" and "precipitant" disasters, which contain important leads concerning the conditions under which emotional adaptation is likely to occur. Then we shall scrutinize additional observations concerning the features of those predisaster situations in which preliminary warnings appear to have a sensitizing effect.

NONPRECIPITANT VERSUS PRECIPITANT DISASTERS

A report by a disaster research team at the University of Oklahoma Research Institute (1952) refers to disaster situations which build up slowly as "nonprecipitant" or "crescive." In this report, the characteristic reactions to warnings in nonprecipitant disasters are illustrated by a case study of the great Kansas City flood and fire of 1951, which damaged or destroyed the homes of nearly 20,000 residents. During the hour or so immediately before the city was inundated, the city's officials issued strong warnings of the imminent danger together with urgent orders to evacuate without delay. Despite these warnings, the majority of residents did not leave. The people who failed to respond remained skeptical that the flood waters would overcome the powerful systems of dikes. Most of them did not attempt to leave the stricken area until they actually saw the water coming into their homes, by which time the only way to escape was to climb to the roof and remain there until rescued by boat. From their interviews with flood victims and disaster control personnel, the authors conclude that a major factor contributing to the population's nonvigilant reaction to the final urgent warning was the series of preliminary communications, issued during the days preceding the actual crisis, warning the residents that the area might be endangered. "The very fact that it was possible to issue warnings long before the danger was immediate made possible a gradual, easy adaptation to the approaching danger, but, at the same time, rendered the warnings less effective" (University of Oklahoma Research Institute, 1952, p. 18).

Hudson (1954, p. 57) reports similar observations in the town of Miami, Oklahoma, when the same flood waters reached there after having inundated Kansas City. Reports concerning reactions to many other floods in the United States and in other countries point to the tendency to ignore urgent last-minute warnings when they occur in a nonprecipitant type of disaster (Ballach *et al.*, 1953; Clifford, 1956; Spiegel, 1957).

Reactions to other kinds of nonprecipitant disasters are also characterized by indifference to last-minute emergency warnings. Logan and his collaborators have reported that in Pitcher, Oklahoma, a large number of residents refused to accept warnings by officials during 1950 that the long-standing threat of cave-ins from former mining operations had become so great as to endanger the life of everyone who did not immediately evacuate.

> It is evident that living on the dangerously unstable roof of a mine had become part of the normal existence of these people. Rumblings due to blasting in the mines almost every afternoon had become a familiar part of their lives, as had periodic warnings that they were living in an area which might suddenly sink. Hence, when the company issued a new warning, even one accompanied by an order to evacuate, they did not perceive this as a threat but as a normal, familiar event. They even made jokes about it. The day following the issuing of the evacuation order, one man brought a parachute to a Lions Club meeting! (Logan, Killian, and Marrs, 1952, p. 94).

Similar reactions of indifference to serious dangers were observed toward the end of the air war in Britain among residents of London who had been extremely vigilant during the first air raids but then had gradually become more and more emotionally adapted to the recurrent threat (Janis, 1951, pp. 109–116).

In contrast, the reactions to emergency warnings issued in precipitant disasters differ markedly. Typical findings were reported in a study of the tornado at Leedy, Oklahoma, in 1958. During the half-hour before the tornado struck, official radio bulletins warned of the approaching storm and advised the residents to enter storm cellars. The warnings were heeded to such an extent that "almost the total population was in storm cellars when the tornado struck" (Tornado Warning, 1948).

In this case, the vigilant behavior evoked by the warning was of an adaptive character. But inappropriate vigilant activity sometimes results when an emergency warning is given without having been preceded by any preliminary warning. Fritz and Marks (1954) present some comparative data from an Arkansas tornado in 1951 which suggest that a last-minute warning in a precipitant disaster can evoke maladaptive behavior to such an extent that the population might be better off with no warning at all. Their evidence indicates that the incidence of casualties bears a curvilinear relationship to forewarning time (i.e., time interval between warning and disaster impact). Death loss and injury loss (to the respondent or his immediate family) were found to be higher for the group that received a warning less than one minute before impact than for either (1) the group with longer forewarning time or (2) the group with no forewarning at all. After calling attention to various uncontrolled factors that make it necessary to regard the apparent relationship with considerable skepticism, the authors present the following tentative conclusion: ". . . comparisons of actions taken with losses sustained would suggest that people who had only brief forewarning took action with a protective *intent,* but that the actions taken may have actually increased their danger or they may have been caught unprotected during the process of taking [inappropriate] protective action" (Fritz and Marks, 1954, p. 38). In other words, the people who recevied a forewarning of one minute or less may have become so excited that they exercised poor judgment or acted in an inefficient manner which increased their chances of becoming casualties.

The various studies mentioned above provide preliminary support for the generalization that *emergency warnings are less likely to induce vigilant reactions in nonprecipitant disasters than in precipitant disasters.* This proposition might be explained on the basis of a number of alternative hypotheses, all of which are compatible with the theoretical assumptions stated earlier concerning the nature of reflective fear:

1. Signs of urgency and imminence are more likely to be present in precipitant than in nonprecipitant disasters. The more imminent the disaster is perceived to be, the greater the likelihood that vigilance will be aroused.

2. Precipitant disasters may be regarded by most people as more dangerous and more difficult to escape than nonprecipitant disasters. If so, the propositions presented earlier concerning the anticipated magnitude of danger and the availability of escape routes could help to explain the higher incidence of vigilance behavior in precipitant disasters, since the warnings issued in such a disaster would tend to generate a higher level of reflective fear, which, in turn, would give rise to a higher degree of vigilance.

3. In nonprecipitant disasters numerous antecedent warnings are likely to be issued before the final emergency warning is given; whereas in precipitant disasters there is little or no opportunity to

issue any warnings prior to the emergency warning. Any emergency warning will be less likely to evoke vigilant reactions if it comes relatively late in a sequence of warnings about familiar dangers insofar as people tend to become emotionally adapted to the threat.

THEORETICAL IMPLICATIONS CONCERNING ADAPTATION AND SENSITIZATION

The third hypothesis just presented has implications that go beyond the question of why nonprecipitant disasters evoke less vigilance than precipitant disasters. In its most general form, the "emotional adaptation" hypothesis asserts that *the vigilance tendencies aroused by any warning concerning a familiar source of danger will be dampened if the recipients have previously been exposed to one or more warnings pertaining to the same threat, provided that the warnings do not add any new information about increased vulnerability to the danger.* Little experimental evidence is available as yet, but field studies of disaster behavior provide some preliminary support for this hypothesis (see Janis, 1951; Janis, 1959, pp. 227–229; MacCurdy, 1943).

From our earlier theoretical assumptions, we would expect the level of reflective fear to decrease if preliminary warnings present new information about decreased vulnerability (e.g., convincing arguments to the effect that the danger is much less serious than had been thought). The adaptation hypothesis asserts that fear will also decrease if the antecedent warnings have conveyed no new information at all about vulnerability but merely have made the recipient realize that a known source of danger might materialize in the foreseeable future.

From what has just been said it is apparent that sensitization effects are likely only if antecedent warnings communicate that vulnerability is greater than had previously been anticipated. The following hypothesis seems to be consistent with the existing evidence from disaster studies: *when preliminary warnings provide information that heightens awareness of potential vulnerability to an impending disaster, the recipients will become more sensitized to new warnings, as manifested by a general increase in their fear reactions to all relevant threat cues and a corresponding increase in vigilance reactions to subsequent emergency warnings about the imminent onset of the danger.*

This "sensitization" hypothesis is intended to apply whether the source of danger is initially familiar or unfamiliar. It is also applicable to implicit or explicit warnings, no matter how slight the danger is perceived to be. But, of course, the over-all adaptive value of sensitization would be different for high- versus low-threat situations. If the final emergency warning refers to a *severe* threat, we would expect an antecedent sensitizing warning to increase *hypervigilant* behavior. But if the final emergency warning is perceived as referring to a very *mild* threat that can be safely ignored, the sensitization effect would promote *adaptive compromise formations.* When reflective fear has been heightened by a strong preliminary warning, a subsequent mild warning will be more likely to evoke discriminative vigilance reactions that lead the person to become alert to the danger and to seek for ways of mitigating it.

These generalizations concerning the conditions under which adaptation and sensitization will occur and the differential consequences that will ensue for high- versus low-threat warnings could be tested by carefully designed experiments or by systematic controlled comparisons. But, once again, when we look for pertinent evidence we must make use of studies that bear only indirectly on the hypotheses under discussion. . . .

SENSITIZING EFFECTS OF FALSE ALARMS

A marked increase in vigilance would be expected to follow any false alarm which interferes with expectations of blanket immunity ("It *can* happen to me—and it almost did"). Unconfirmed warnings of dire disaster do not invariably produce the outcome described in the popular "wolf-wolf" story. This is indicated by Killian's study (1954) of reactions to a series of hurricane warnings. In September 1953 the residents of Panama City, Florida, were informed by newspaper, radio, and other media that Hurricane Florence was approaching the Gulf coast and would probably hit them with the worst storm in Florida's history. The two local radio stations broadcasted hourly an official warning advising all people near the coast to move to inland shelters. An estimated 10,000 residents followed this advice. But the hurricane suddenly changed its course. Instead of hitting Panama City with its full force, the storm center crossed the coast about 100 miles away, so that Panama City experienced a relatively mild windstorm which produced only slight damage. It became apparent to everyone in the area that the people who had ignored the evacuation warnings lost nothing by doing so and were much less inconvenienced than those who had taken the trouble to go to shelters or to leave town.

In a series of intensive interviews, Killian investigated how people who had accepted the official evacuation advice felt about it after-ward. He found that few of the evacuees complained about having been misled by the false alarm; the vast majority said they would evacuate again under the same circumstances. If their interview state-ments can be accepted as valid, these people remained as ready as ever to take emergency action in response to any new hurricane warnings.

Commitment to a decision concerning protective action is one of the factors that may foster the continuation of an attitude of vigi-lance. Having once decided to take the action recommended in the warning communications, those who did leave may have become motivated to reduce cognitive dissonance or to minimize postdeci-sional conflict by thinking up good reasons for what they did (see Festinger, 1957; Janis, 1959). Perhaps discussions of the potential disaster among fellow evacuees provided the opportunity to "pool" good arguments and rationalizations as well as to receive social sup-port when it became apparent that the protective action had been unnecessary.

In the false alarm investigated by Killian, the commitment factor might have contributed to the outcome, but does not in itself pro-vide an adequate explanation for all the pertinent findings. Killian noted that sensitivity to the hurricane threat was not restricted to those respondents who had decided to evacuate but also occurred in a sizable minority of those who had decided not to do so. Forty per cent of the latter stated unequivocally that they would evacuate in response to a new hurricane warning, even though they did not do so the first time. These people seemed to regret having rejected the evacuation warning despite the fact that it proved to be a false alarm. They made no attempt to bolster their decision even though it would have been quite easy for them to do so. Rather, they seem to have increased cognitive dissonance by adopting a new position which was not compatible with their recent decision. Evidently some addi-tional information was obtained from the false alarm and its after-math which induced them to regret their decision and to adopt a new attitude toward the threat.

It is important to take account of the fact that although the evacuation proved to be unnecessary, the alarm was only partially falsified. The residents' direct observations of the windstorm in their own area were reinforced by news reports which described the enormous damage wreaked by the 160-mile-an-hour hurricane in areas less than 100 miles away. Under such circumstances, many who remained in their homes may have been induced to think about what the full force of a hurricane would be like and to imagine what might have happened if they had not been lucky compared with others. Those near the waterfront, for example, could not help noticing the enormously high tide, which perhaps made some of them realize, for the first time, what a hurricane could do to a city like theirs, situated only fourteen feet above sea level. Had nothing at all happened, they might not have been stimulated to think about the potential dangers of being pounded by flood waters nor to notice the inadequate protection afforded by their homes in the event of a much stronger windstorm than the one they experienced.

Returning to the sensitization hypothesis, we must note that although the Panama City findings are consistent with it, alternative interpretations cannot be excluded. Perhaps it would be most accurate to say that the sensitization hypothesis offers a basis for understanding those instances where false alarms do not result in any lowering of vigilance. If a warning evokes vigilant reactions that subsequently prove to be unnecessary, as when the center of Hurricane Florence failed to hit Panama City, the net effect of the false alarm experience will depend upon the type of information conveyed about the threat. If no new information is obtained, or if the new information shows the threat to be less dangerous than had been supposed, a marked lowering of vigilance is to be expected, as occurred following the false alarms in British towns during the early days of the air blitz of 1941 (Glover, 1942; Janis, 1951; Vernon, 1941). But if new information is obtained which points up their personal vulnerability, people will react by becoming more vigilant than before the false alarm occurred. When such information has been conveyed, we can expect increased vigilance in those who had ignored the unnecessary warnings as well as in those who had become alarmed, although, as was suggested earlier, the effect might conceivably be more pronounced in those who had committed themselves to some form of protective action in response to the false alarm.

A REINTERPRETATION OF "NEAR-MISS" REACTIONS

The sensitization outcome is much more likely to occur, of course, when a preliminary warning does *not* turn out to be a false alarm. As soon as it becomes apparent that an earlier warning should have been taken seriously, people are likely to regret their foolishness in having risked endangering themselves, and thereafter will become all the more responsive to future warnings (see Wolfenstein, 1957). Thus, whenever a warning is confirmed by subsequent disaster events, the intact survivors who ignored the warning would be expected to show a greater increase in vigilance than those who took it seriously (holding constant the degree of victimization entailed by the physical impact of the disaster).

A study of the Texas City disaster (Logan, Killian, and Marrs, 1952) provides examples of extreme sensitization to fire alarms after a series of devastating explosions demonstrated to the entire population that earlier warning signs should have been heeded. Similar changes in readiness to respond to warning signals have also been observed as a consequence of direct experience with other danger stimuli. Formerly unnoticed storm clouds and the sounds of rising wind come to evoke strong fear reactions in the survivors of tornado disasters, producing sleeplessness, obsessional watchfulness, and other post-traumatic reactions that can be properly described as hypervigilant in character (Fritz and Marks, 1954; National Opinion Research Center, 1953). Such traumatizing events have been described as "near-miss" experiences, in contrast to "remote-miss" experiences in which warning signs occur without being accompanied by any distressing danger impact (MacCurdy, 1943). Studies of wartime and peacetime disasters indicate that acute emotional shock, traumatic neurosis, and various transient forms of emotional disturbance are most likely to occur among those persons who undergo narrow escapes or who are actually victimized by the disaster (Fraser, Leslie, and Phelps, 1943; Glover, 1942; Janis, 1951; MacCurdy, 1943; Moore, 1958; Wolfenstein, 1957). But these studies also indicate that remote-miss experiences sometimes induce sustained apprehensiveness accompanied by extreme vigilance reactions of the type ordinarily associated with near-miss experiences. Under what conditions does this exceptional type of remote-miss reaction occur? Are there also some exceptional near-miss experiences that have benign rather than traumatic effects, and, if so, under what conditions do they occur?

In a number of instances already cited, direct personal involvement in a disaster gave rise to discriminative vigilant reactions which had adaptive value. Many people who had been victimized by tornadoes, for example, developed apprehensive alertness to signs of a possible recurrence of the disaster, listening regularly to weather forecasts on the radio, watching carefully any unusual cloud formations, and preparing storm shelters. Moore (1958) reports that after the 1953 tornado in San Angelo, Texas, which destroyed or damaged practically every home in the entire town, over one third of the surviving families built storm cellars, which were put to good use when another severe storm hit the town a year later. In many such instances the near-miss episode can be characterized as having a benign effect, inducing awareness of *partial* vulnerability and leading to adaptive compromise formations.

Thus, the distinction between remote-miss and near-miss experiences cannot be regarded as a basic one for explaining adaptive as against maladaptive reactions, even though there is some evidence indicating that the use of these concepts enables us to make better-than-chance predictions (see Janis, 1951). Accordingly, we shall reexamine the concepts briefly in the light of our theoretical analysis of reflective fear, focusing on the conditions under which danger episodes give rise to indiscriminate vigilance as against compromise formations.

In line with earlier discussions of the dynamics of near-miss reactions, our initial assumption is that attitudes of hypervigilance are produced by danger episodes in which anticipations of personal invulnerability are so completely shattered that the person is no longer able to ward off strong reflective fear when he encounters new danger cues. In contrast, the more benign type of near-miss experiences can be regarded as mildly admonitory in character, merely breaking down blanket-immunity reassurances, inducing the person to become aware of his potential vulnerability but without rendering him incapable of evolving new danger-contingent reassurances. Some of the people at San Angelo seemed to be referring to this type of change in self-concept when they described themselves as having "learned a lesson from the tornado," and when they spoke about their newly acquired desire to have storm shelters ready before there were any more tornado warnings (Moore, 1958).

Martha Wolfenstein cites numerous examples of disaster victims who express a need to avoid repeating their mistaken disregard of warnings and to protect themselves from again being taken by surprise (e.g., "I'm not going to let them [storm clouds] slip up on me like that"). She points out that an attitude of alert watchfulness can satisfy the need for reassurance, by counteracting feelings of passivity and helplessness.

> One pictures oneself in action rather than overwhelmed by distress. The image of oneself as a rescuer pushes aside that of one's being a victim. . . . Confidence in know-how, with the image of oneself as doing skillful and useful things, strengthens the feeling one can remain in control in a danger situation (Wolfenstein, 1957, pp. 42–43).

At first, the vigilant reactions following a disaster are likely to accompany a moderate or high state of fear. But, later on, we would expect emotional adaptation gradually to set in, as the person builds up confidence in new precautionary measures and acquires various other new compromise formations that function as effective sources of reassurance. After the San Angelo tornado, for example, one woman stated that "a cellar helps your nerves a lot in any storm. . . . I just couldn't stay by myself at nighttime until the cellar was finished, if [there] was a cloud." Another spoke about the calming effect of being in contact with friends and neighbors in their big storm cellar: ". . . We have had as many as twenty-seven in there at one time. . . . When we're down there we just talk and laugh. We have a club meeting down there. . . . Kiddoes named it our 'Tornado Club'" (Moore, 1958, pp. 271-272).

A similar development of new fear-reducing habits has been noted after many other disasters. In the final stage the person is ordinarily free from fear in his everyday life but is, nevertheless, in a habitual state of readiness to become vigilant if clear-cut warning signals occur. Taking account of the concepts introduced earlier in the discussion of "reflective fear" . . . , we can view the learning effects of a near-miss experience as resulting in a set of discriminatory habits such that (1) in the normal course of events, when no warning signal is present, the person's level of fear remains very low, with blanket reassurance as the dominant reaction; and (2) when clear-cut warnings are perceived, the person's fear mounts to a moderate level that falls well above the threshold for discriminatory vigilance but below the threshold for hypervigilance. In contrast, when a person has been emotionally shocked by a near-miss experience, his level of fear will fall above the latter threshold and he will display hypervigilant reactions. If such reactions occur only at times when a person perceives clear-cut warning signals, his life adjustment may not be seriously impaired, but if they are also evoked at times when only very mild threat cues are present, the hypervigilance is much more disruptive and may be classified as a severe traumatic neurosis.

Using "near-miss" and "remote-miss" as purely descriptive terms to designate, respectively, a high *versus* low degree of victimization sustained in a disaster, we can say that the former is more likely to produce hypervigilance, whereas the latter is more likely to produce an attitude of blanket reassurance. Despite these differential tendencies, however, the effects of near-miss and remote-miss experiences can overlap to a considerable degree, and both types are capable of giving rise to adaptive compromise formations. In short, the sustained effects of any given disaster episode, whether near-miss or remote-miss in character, can range over the entire continuum, motivating the development of blanket reassurances or compromise formations or hypervigilance. The question of which type of outcome will ensue depends upon the two main factors discussed earlier in this chapter: (1) the type of information conveyed by the disaster experience, and (2) the person's level of fear in response to the threat stimuli (prior to the occurrence of the disaster episode). When the information conveyed by the episode is of the type specified by the sensitization hypothesis, . . . the predicted postdisaster reaction to any recurrence of the threat will be: (1) maladaptive hypervigilance if the person's fear level initially was moderate or high, and (2) adaptive compromise formations if the person's fear level initially was low. On the other hand, if the information conveyed by the episode is of the type specified by the adaptation hypothesis, . . . the predicted postdisaster outcome will be: (1) blanket reassurance if the person's fear level initially was low, and (2) compromise formation if the person's fear level initially was moderate or high.

These propositions serve to link the psychological impact of direct disaster experiences with the impact of purely verbal warnings. We assume continuity between the two types of situations in that the same type of emotional learning occurs in both and is influenced by the same basic factors. Direct disaster experiences, of course, are generally much more impressive than verbal messages, since one cannot easily ignore the relevant danger cues. In addition, direct exposure to danger stimuli entails more powerful rewards and punishments. Consequently, we would expect that more drastic changes in habitual reactions to threat stimuli will be produced by near-miss or remote-miss disaster experiences than by verbal descriptions or predictions about oncoming dangers. It is only in this respect that near-miss and remote-miss experiences take on special psychological significance, particularly when we are attempting to explain extreme changes such as those observed in cases of severe traumatic neurosis.

The assumption that the same principles of perception and learning operate whether people are exposed to actual danger events or to purely verbal messages about them, leads us to expect that when the appropriate conditions are present the latter can produce the same dramatic changes in emotionality as the former. That a purely verbal warning occasionally does so is a well-known fact to physicians who have the responsibility of communicating positive findings obtained from X-rays and medical tests to patients diagnosed as suffering from cancer or some other serious disease. When patients are told the truth by their physician, or learn it inadvertently from members of the family, they sometimes become as chronically hypervigilant as people who have been traumatized in a physical disaster or as depressed as those who have actually been bereaved (Bernstein and Small, 1951;

Janis, 1958b; Lindemann, 1941; Wittkower, 1949 and 1952). In such instances, since the person is initially familiar with the nature of the threat, a terse authoritative communication is sufficient to make him perceive himself as seriously endangered. But when the source of danger is relatively unfamiliar, sustained emotional changes are not likely to occur unless vivid communications are presented which familiarize the person with the magnitude of the danger and stimulate him to imagine himself as being threatened by it.

In certain types of disasters, such as virus epidemics and mass poisoning episodes, where the source of the danger is known only to experts, the psychological effect on large numbers of potential victims is determined almost entirely by verbal communications. For example, when an explosion of radioactive thorium unexpectedly occurred at the Sylvania Laboratories in Queens, New York, the official messages communicated to the firemen, newspaper reporters, and others who came to the site of the disaster resulted in a drastic change in their anticipations of vulnerability to danger, transforming their perceptions of themselves as unaffected bystanders into potential victims of radiation disease (National Analysts, Inc., 1956). Similarly, the sporadic outbreaks of illness and blindness in the black sections of Atlanta during the poison liquor episode were not recognized by the residents as signs of threat until verbal communications were issued explaining that poison liquor was causing the casualties (J. W. Powell, 1953, pp. 87–103). In both disasters the information conveyed by warning communications was sufficient to induce a marked increase in vigilance, leading to cautious, protective behavior of an adaptive character in some people and excited, inefficient overreactions of a maladaptive character in others. Although sensitization-inducing information is especially likely to occur during a near-miss disaster episode, such information can also occur and have the same effect during a pre-disaster warning period, during a remote-miss experience, or during a false alarm episode.

ADDITIONAL DETERMINANTS

The factors singled out for discussion in this chapter are those that appear to be most plausible as determinants of alternative modes of response to warning stimuli. Among the numerous other factors mentioned in disaster studies are a few which at first seemed to be promising candidates but which, on further scrutiny, were excluded because of contradictory observations, indicating the need for further investigation in order to specify limiting conditions. One such equivocal candidate, of sufficient potential importance to warrant brief discussion here, is the factor of *role assignment*. Some investigators claim that this factor operates in the direction of preventing disorganized hypervigilant behavior. In a study of the excellent performance of firemen on a variety of disaster-control tasks carried out under the extraordinarily hazardous conditions of the Kansas City flood and fire of 1951, a major conclusion is that ". . . established role-conceptions, sustained and enforced by reference-group norms, enabled the firemen to keep going in the face of threat and danger" (University of Oklahoma Research Institute, 1952, p. 34). Other writers on disaster behavior also assert that emotional control is facilitated by assignment to a social role entailing some degree of responsibility for the welfare of others (Form and Nosow, 1958; Logan *et al.*, 1952).

One can readily surmise how a role assignment might counteract some of the negative effects of several hypervigilance-producing factors discussed earlier—e.g., by reducing ambiguity about what should be done in a confused disaster situation, by fostering group identification with others in the same role, by providing a form of anticipated (symbolic) contact, or actual telephone communication, with the authority figures who issue orders. But despite these and other possible advantages, the responsibilities attached to a role assignment sometimes interfere with emotional equanimity in an emergency by giving rise to intense role conflicts and new sources of anxiety (Glover, 1942; Janis, 1951; Killian, 1952; Schmideberg, 1942; Spiegel, 1953). Commenting on British reactions to the great North Sea flood, Spiegel (1953) points out that some men placed in a position to make decisions about what should be done to protect the community became obsessionally concerned about their responsibilities, devoted themselves to examining reconnaissance information, repeatedly checked on what was happening, and thereby deferred action. As a result, many lives were lost that could otherwise have been saved. Obviously, much more needs to be known about the conditions under which the advantages outweigh the disadvantages before we shall be able to state exactly which types of role assignment, if any, should be included among the vigilance-reducing or vigilance-enhancing factors.

Role assignment is but one example of the numerous additional factors that await systematic investigation. The various informational, situational, and sequential factors discussed in this chapter should not be regarded as an exhaustive list of all the pertinent variables mentioned in the extensive social psychological literature bearing on reactions to warnings. Nor are any of the hypotheses concerning the effects of the various factors firmly established as yet by systematic research data. Rather, they should be regarded as a highly selected set of descriptive and explanatory hypotheses which, in the light of the existing evidence, offer promising leads concerning the environmental conditions under which warnings will foster indiscriminate vigilance, compromise formation, or blanket reassurance.

REFERENCES

Allport, G. W., & Postman, L. *The psychology of rumor.* New York: Holt, 1947.

Balloch, J., Braswell, L. R., Rayner, Jeannette F., & Killian, L. M. Studies of military assistance in civilian disasters: England and the United States. Unpublished report, Committee on Disaster Studies, National Academy of Sciences–National Research Council, 1953.

Bernstein, S., & Small, S. Psychodynamic factors in surgery. *J. Mt. Sinai Hosp.,* 1951, *17*, 938–958.

Clifford, R. A. *The Rio Grande flood: A comparative study of border communities in disaster.* Disaster Study Number 7. Washington: National Academy of Sciences–National Research Council, 1956.

Danzig, E. R., Thayer, P. W., & Galanter, Lila R. *The effects of a threatening rumor on a disaster-stricken community.* Disaster Study Number 10. Washington: National Academy of Sciences–National Research Council, 1958.

Diggory, J. C. Some consequences of proximity to disease threat. *Sociometry,* 1956, *19*, 47–53.

Festinger, L. *A theory of cognitive dissonance.* Evanston, Ill.: Row, Peterson, 1957.

Form, W. H., & Nosow, S. *Community in disaster.* New York: Harper, 1958.

Fraser, R., Leslie, I., & Phelps, D. Psychiatric effects of severe personal experiences during bombing. *Proc. Royal Soc. Med.,* 1943, *36*, 119–123.

Freud, S. *The problem of anxiety.* Trans. by H. A. Bunker. New York: Norton, 1936.

Fritz, C. E., & Marks, E. S. The NORC studies of human behavior in disaster. *J. soc. Issues,* 1954, *10*, 26–41.

Garner, H. Psychiatric casualties in combat. *War Med.,* 1945, *8*, 343–357.

Glover, E. *The psychology of fear and courage.* New York: Penguin, 1940.

Glover, E. Notes on the psychological effects of war conditions on the civil population: Part III, the blitz. *Int. J. Psycho-anal.,* 1942, *23*, 17–37.

Green, J. B., & Logan, L. *The South Amboy disaster.* Chevy Chase, Md.: Operations Research Office, 1950.

Hovland, C. I., & Janis, I. L. (eds.), *Personality and persuasibility.* New Haven, Conn.: Yale University Press, 1959.

Hovland, C. I., Janis, I. L., & Kelley, H. H. *Communication and persuasion.* New Haven, Conn.: Yale University Press, 1953.

Hudson, B. B. Anxiety in response to the unfamiliar. *J. soc. Issues,* 1954, *10,* 53–60.

Janis, I. L. *Air war and emotional stress: Psychological studies of bombing and civilian defense.* New York: McGraw-Hill, 1951.

Janis, I. L. Emotional inoculation: Theory and research on effects of preparatory communications. In W. Muensterberger & S. Axelrod (eds.), *Psychoanalysis and the social sciences,* Vol. 5. New York: International Universities Press, 1958. (a)

Janis, I. L. *Psychological stress.* New York: Wiley, 1958. (b)

Janis, I. L. Psychological aspects of decisional conflicts. In M. Jones (ed.), *Nebraska symposium on motivation* 1959. Lincoln: University of Nebraska Press, 1959.

Janis, I. L., Chapman, D. W., Gillin, J. P., & Spiegel, J. P. *The problem of panic.* Washington: Fed. Civil Defense Admin. Bull. TB-19-2, 1955.

Janis, I. L., & Feshbach, S. Effects of fear-arousing communications. *J. abnorm. soc. Psychol.,* 1953, *48,* 78–92.

Janis, I. L., & Feshbach, S. Personality differences associated with responsiveness to fear-arousing communications. *J. Pers.,* 1954, *23,* 154–166.

Killian, L. M. The significance of multiple-group membership in disaster. *Amer. J. Sociol.,* 1952, *57,* 309–314.

Killian, L. M. *Evacuation of Panama City before Hurricane Florence.* Washington: National Academy of Sciences–National Research Council, Committee on Disaster Studies, 1954.

Lindemann, E. Observations on psychiatric sequelae to surgical operations in women. *Amer. J. Psychiat.,* 1941, *98,* 132–139.

Logan, L., Killian, L. M., & Marrs, W. *A study of the effect of catastrophe on social disorganization.* Chevy Chase, Md.: Operations Research Office, 1952.

MacCurdy, J. T. *The structure of morale.* New York: Macmillan, 1943.

Moore, H. E. *Tornadoes over Texas.* Austin: University of Texas Press, 1958.

National Analysts, Inc. *Study of public reactions to the explosion at Sylvania Laboratories in Queens, New York.* Washington: National Academy of Sciences–National Research Council, Committee on Disaster Studies, 1956.

National Opinion Research Center. An airplane crash in Flagler, Colorado. In *Conference on field studies of reactions to disasters.* Chicago: National Opinion Research Center, 1953.

Powell, J. W. Interview protocols of victims of the toxicological disaster in Atlanta, 1951. Unpublished. Disaster Research Group, National Academy of Sciences–National Research Council, 1951.

Powell, J. W. A poison liquor episode in Atlanta, Georgia. In *Conference on field studies of reactions to disasters.* Chicago: National Opinion Research Center, 1953.

Schachter, S. *The psychology of affiliation.* Stanford: Stanford University Press, 1959.

Schmideberg, M. Some observations on individual reactions to air raids. *Int. J. Psycho-Anal.,* 1942, *23,* 146–176.

Spiegel, J. P. Psychological transactions in situations of acute stress. In *Symposium on stress* (16–18 March 1953). Washington: Walter Reed Army Medical Center, Army Medical Service Graduate School, 1953.

Spiegel, J. P. The English flood of 1953. *Hum. Organization,* 1957, *16,* 3–5.

Sullivan, H. S. Psychiatric aspects of morale. *Amer. J. Sociol.,* 1941, *47,* 227–301.

Tornado warning. *Disaster,* February, 1948, 2, 5.

U.S. Strategic Bombing Survey. *The effects of strategic bombing on German morale.* (2 vols). Washington: U.S. Government Printing Office, 1947. (a)

U.S. Strategic Bombing Survey. *The effects of strategic bombing on Japanese morale.* Washington: U.S. Government Printing Office, 1947. (b)

University of Oklahoma Research Institute. *The Kansas City flood and fire of 1951.* Chevy Chase, Md.: Operations Research Office, 1952.

Vernon, P. E. Psychological effects of air raids. *J. abnorm. soc. Psychol.,* 1941, *36,* 457–476.

Withey, S. B. Reaction to uncertain threat. In G. W. Baker & D. W. Chapman (eds.), *Man and society in disaster.* New York: Basic Books, 1962.

Wittkower, E. *A psychiatrist looks at tuberculosis.* London: National Association for the Prevention of Tuberculosis, 1949.

Wittkower, E. Psychological aspects of physical illness. *Canad. Med. Assoc. J.,* 1952, *66,* 220–224.

Wolfenstein, Martha. *Disaster: A psychological essay.* Glencoe, Ill.: Free Press, 1957.

6

Group Identification under Conditions of External Danger (1963)

It has long been known that when people are exposed to external danger they show a remarkable increase in group solidarity. That is, they manifest increased motivation to retain affiliation with a face-to-face group and to avoid actions that deviate from its norms. The importance of primary group factors among soldiers was not fully appreciated until converging observations were made by psychiatrists, psychologists, and sociologists during World War II. These observations indicated that the average combat soldier's willingness to engage in hazardous combat duty depended largely on group identification. The term "group identification," although not rigorously defined, has been used to designate a set of conscious, preconscious, and unconscious attitudes which incline each member to apperceive the group as an extension of himself and impel him to remain in direct contact with the other members and to adhere to the group's standards.

In the present paper, I shall focus on a set of intriguing theoretical problems concerning the causes and consequences of group identification—problems which can be illuminated by examining situations of extreme danger. Why is it that exposure to external danger has such a marked effect on the solidarity of a face-to-face group? What are the preconscious and unconscious mechanisms that underlie the strengthening of group ties under conditions of danger? What are the favorable and unfavorable consequences of group identification?

My interest in these problems dates back to the last months of

Janis, I. L. Group identification under conditions of external danger. *British Journal of Medical Psychology*, 1963, *36*, 227–238. Reprinted in D. Cartwright and A. Zander (Eds.), *Group dynamics: Research and theory.* New York: Harper and Row, 1968. Reprinted by permission.

World War II. As psychologists in a morale research organization of the U.S. Army, my colleagues and I conducted a large number of intensive interviews with American combat soldiers in the European Theater. Time and again we encountered instances when a man failed to act in accordance with his own self-interests in order to ward off separation fears or guilt about "letting the other guys down." For example, soldiers who had performed well in combat sometimes refused to accept a promotion if it entailed being shifted to another group. Men who were physically ill, or suffering from acute anxiety symptoms, avoided going on sick call and struggled against being withdrawn from combat because they did not want to be separated from their unit. Severe casualty cases, after being sent to a hospital in the rear, developed intense guilt feelings concerning their comrades at the front and sometimes went A.W.O.L. from the hospital or replacement depot in order to return to the front in an attempt to rejoin their comrades.

During the year and a half following the end of the war, the opportunity arose to check my observations against the findings from a variety of other sources of morale data, while working on a large social psychological study of World War II, in collaboration with Samuel Stouffer and others. This collaborative work, which was subsequently published in a volume entitled *The American Soldier: Combat and Its Aftermath* (14) is one of the main sources of empirical data on the behavior of combat groups used in preparing the present paper. I have also examined carefully the extensive psychiatric literature bearing on emotional aspects of the behavior of combat soldiers, including some reports about those in the British Army and German Army as well as the American Army.

In formulating hypotheses about the causes and consequences of group identification, I have also taken into account parallel phenomena on group solidarity encountered in my research investigations on the way people react when they are facing objective threats of body damage and annihilation. One investigation, reported in a book on *Air War and Emotional Stress* (8), involved surveying the existing evidence on civilian reactions to wartime dangers during World War II. A more recent series of studies published a few years ago in a book on *Psychological Stress* (9) was focused on psychological aspects of *surgery* and was based on my psychoanalytic observations as well as behavioral studies of surgical patients.

My formulations and illustrations concerning group identification in the present paper are based mainly on the studies of surgical patients and the studies of wartime danger situations. However, most, if not all, of the hypotheses seem to be applicable to *any* face-to-face group that is exposed to *any* common source of external stress. One of the values of concentrating on group behavior under the conditions of extreme physical danger is that we can sometimes see quite clearly the manifestations of basic psychological process. The same processes may occur in a much more subtle form in the group behavior of people who face the common threats of everyday social life, such as loss of esteem from fellow workers or friends, disapproval from one's employer, and all the various signs of potential failure, humiliation, and loss of status that typically give rise to social anxiety in clinically normal people.

Most of the hypotheses to be presented are based on psychoanalytic theory and make use of concepts derived from clinical psychoanalytic observations. Scattered throughout the extensive psychoanalytic literature on ego ideals, super-ego functions, object relations, and related topics, there are numerous case study observations that seem relevant for specifying the unconscious determinants of group behavior in normal, as well as neurotic, adults. Major sources for such material are Freud's classical contributions to group psychology, Flugel's monograph on *Man, Morals, and Society* (3) and Fritz Redl's studies of antisocial adolescent gangs (10, 11).

The hypotheses I have singled out are ones that appear to be highly plausible in the light of the existing evidence. But, since the observations come primarily from studies of extreme danger situations, it must be emphasized from the outset that we cannot be at all certain about how far these hypotheses can be generalized. Perhaps some of them apply only when there is actual danger of annihilation combined with a host of severe deprivations of the type seldom encountered by anyone except in wartime. All such questions concerning the verification and generality of the hypotheses obviously must remain open until more systematic evidence becomes available from further research.

TRANSFERENCE REACTIONS

According to Freud's (5) theory of group behavior, much of the motivation for group solidarity comes from the strong emotional bonds established between each member and the leader. Freud speaks of "transference" reactions toward the idealized leader who, as a parent surrogate, provides the main impetus to a group for sharing common ideals and standards of conduct.

Certain regressive features of unconscious transference reactions toward authority figures become quite apparent whenever one observes people who are exposed to severe reality dangers, especially when there is a threat of mutilation or annihilation. I have been strongly impressed by manifestations of unconscious dependency needs not only among combat soldiers but also among civilians when they are exposed to the warnings of wartime bombing attacks or peacetime disasters or to the more personalized threats of illness and surgery. One of the main hypothetical constructs which seems to be useful in accounting for the upsurge of these dependency reactions is the *reactivation of separation anxiety.* We know, of course, that exaggerated fears of being abandoned by the parents arise early in life, especially on occasions when the child feels ill, injured, or unable to escape from threatened pain. Such fears persist in latent form in adulthood and underlie the characteristic changes in the social behavior of persons exposed to danger: they show increased interest in establishing close affiliation with any available primary group and they *seek to be reassured that the significant persons in their lives will not leave them or break preexisting affectionate ties.* This fear-ridden type of dependency is likely to develop toward any authority figures who are perceived to be in a position to increase or decrease their chances of warding off the danger. I refer to such persons as "danger-control authorities." These authorities tend to be over-idealized and misperceived in a variety of ways, under the influence of deep-seated attitudes and expectations derived from early life experiences. Here I refer mainly to those experiences in which one or both parents had been perceived by the child as being responsible for the onset and termination of suffering and pain.

The manifestations of transference on the part of normal adults who face serious external dangers are remarkably parallel to those shown by psychoneurotic patients undergoing psychoanalysis, especially during critical periods of treatment when the analyst becomes momentarily an authority figure to whom the patient's own superego functions have been assigned (**12**, **156–158**). Persons in both types of situations overestimate the power of the authority figure and become preoccupied about whether his intentions are good or bad. They also become extraordinarily sensitive to his demands, continually attempting to do and say things that will please him, reacting with bitter disappointment at any apparent slights, and becoming depressed or aggrieved whenever they are not in communication with him.

In addition to the foregoing dependency phenomenon induced by reality threats, the propensity to develop affectionate ties with an authority figure and with comrades is probably augmented whenever a group is socially isolated. For example, soldiers in combat are far removed from their parents, siblings, and all those other persons back home who may have played a significant role in satisfying their emotional needs. Similarly, patients in a surgical ward are separated from their families and friends except for rather brief visits. Transference reactions, under these conditions, become a matter of psychological *replacement,* an unconscious means of enabling the missing family members to become symbolically present. Thus, the company commander or the surgeon is likely to become a symbolic representative of the father, and a fellow soldier or fellow patient may become a substitute for an older or younger brother. The individual will then unconsciously respond to the parent substitute and the sibling substitute in some of the same ways that he used to respond to the original family members.

If this unconscious substitutive process occurs at a time when external dangers foster strong dependency needs, the individual is especially likely to undergo a partial regression in his dealings with the surrogate persons. This entails what Erik Erikson has described as a "blurring of an adult-relationship through the transfer upon it of infantile loves and hates, dependencies, and impotent rages" (1, 94).

Perhaps the most essential feature of transference from the standpoint of group dynamics is the tendency to overestimate the power of the surrogate person, which heightens sensitivity to his expressions of approval and disapproval. When a conscientious officer is unconsciously regarded as a father surrogate, the men under his command will be strongly motivated to accept his orders and to adhere to the group standards, if only to maintain the approval of a man who is now endowed with the attributes of a significant authority figure from the past.

REASSURANCE NEEDS

Next we shall consider additional *needs for reassurance* that are directly stimulated by external danger and that are satisfied through interaction with fellow members of the primary group. Studies of combat soldiers provide exceptionally rich material on this aspect of group psychology.

In morale surveys during World War II, we found that many soldiers said they would not want to be shifted to any other unit because they felt *safer* with their own group. For example, a wounded veteran of combat in North Africa said: "The fellows don't want to leave when they're sick. They're afraid to leave their own men—the men they know. Your own outfit—they're the men you have confidence in. It gives you more guts to be with them."

Now when a soldier says that "it gives you more guts" to be with the men in your own outfit, it is not merely because of the increase in actual protection he consciously anticipates. External threats foster increased reliance on the group by arousing a variety of basic psychological needs for reassurance, some of which are, of course, preconscious, or unconscious.

At least temporary emotional relief seems to be obtained not merely from the occasional serious discussions in which the men implicitly promise to "stick by" each other in the event of injury or dire need. They also tell each other jokes and tall stories about how badly things are going; they exchange banter concerning their poor chances of survival; and they engage in many other forms of "kidding around" that are heavily tinged with gallows humor.

Whether serious or humorous, these informal interchanges among members of a combat team probably touch off a number of different reassurance mechanisms, all of which can contribute to the alleviation of fear.

1. From the affective expressions as well as the content of his team-mate's comments, the individual soldier can quickly come to realize that they must be suffering from essentially the same worries, longings, and conflicts as himself. The damage to a man's self-esteem is minimized by the opportunity to perceive that other men are equally frightened—that they too have strong wishes to escape from hazardous assignments and are equally unsure of their own capacity to live up to the masculine ideals of not being a "sissy."

2. By openly expressing his private fears and confessing his weaknesses to one or more empathic listeners, the individual may gain emotional rapport similar to that occurring in the early sessions of psychotherapy. Here the crucial factor may be the permissive social atmosphere of the work group, which provides an opportunity for mutual self-revelations with relatively little danger of being censured or humiliated.

3. When a man airs his private fears and grievances he will sometimes elicit comments from others which have a corrective effect on his appraisals of the external dangers. The more experienced combat veterans, despite their general proclivity for conveying a very black picture, would often "wisen up" the green replacements in their units. For example, many men entered combat with vague paranoid-like fears about the possibility of being shot by their own military authorities, partly because they thought this would be the prescribed

punishment if they were to fail to carry out a suicidal mission ordered by an uninformed or inhuman commander. But combat soldiers in the U.S. Army gradually came to realize that in actual practice offenders were not executed. The popular notion that American combat men were facing a choice of possible death from the enemy versus certain death if they refused to fight was a grossly unsubstantiated myth. Informal group discussions between fresh replacements and the more experienced members of the combat team probably served a reality-testing function, exploding such myths and correcting other exaggerated notions about the dire consequences of deviating from military regulations, as well as clearing up misconceptions about the strength of the enemy and about the devastating power of the enemy's weapons.

4. When a soldier knows that his group is facing severe danger and that his own life as well as the lives of his comrades are at stake, he becomes extremely sensitive to being treated impersonally, as a mere cog in a machine. In military service, however, it frequently happens that the men in operational units are subjected to seemingly arbitrary and impersonal treatment by officers in higher headquarters. During World War II, for example, a high percentage of combat men, after having spent weeks or months in overcrowded replacement depots, felt they had been badly "kicked around" by the military organization and were acutely aware of being treated as an expendable item. By becoming an accepted comrade the individual soldier can counteract, to some extent, the disturbing perception of himself as a *passive victim* at the disposal of an impersonal military organization whose high officers can make drastic decisions with little or no regard for the value of his life. The attractiveness of the local work group becomes greatly enhanced as the individual encounters the first acts of friendship on the part of his team-mates and immediate superiors, which reassure him that he *still counts as a person*. Moreover, once the men begin sharing their feelings about the Army organization, they soon acquire the illusion that the work group has the power to see to it that its members will not be neglected or maltreated by higher headquarters.

In so far as the soldier's needs for reassurance are satisfied by interpersonal relationships with his comrades, he becomes strongly dependent upon his work group to counteract his dysphoria. Thus the individual becomes strongly motivated to behave in such a way that the others will continue to accept him as a member in good standing. The threat of the group's disapproval or rejection, therefore, becomes all the more effective in suppressing any inclinations to deviate from the group norms.

The "sharing of fear" in combat units—in the many different forms which have just been described—probably enables many soldiers to adapt to severe stresses that they otherwise might not be able to withstand. In *Psychological Stress* (9), I have reported similar phenomena from studies of surgical patients. The evidence from these studies strongly suggests the following general proposition: when a person's anticipatory fears have been stimulated to a *moderate* degree before being exposed to actual stress stimuli, there is less likelihood of his being overwhelmed, or becoming resentful toward danger-control authorities, than if his anticipatory fears have *not been at all stimulated* during the precrisis period. For the purpose of conceptualizing the normal processes of inner psychological preparation, I have introduced the term "work of worrying," as a construct analogous to the "work of mourning." The work of mourning usually begins *after* object loss has occurred, whereas the work of worrying starts *before* a blow strikes, as soon as a person becomes convinced that he is facing a potential danger or loss.

The same book contains a detailed account of various situational factors (such as exposure to accurate warning information from an authority figure) that help a person to go through all the steps involved in completing the work of worrying and a number of hypotheses are presented concerning the ways in which this type of inner preparation can enable a person to adapt more adequately to a painful reality situation. For the present, it will suffice to call attention to the likelihood that the opportunity to talk about one's fears in a permissive group setting—and the opportunity to hear the members of the group verbalize fears similar to one's own—may have a long-range prophylactic effect. In other words, sharing one's fears with others may facilitate the development of adaptive defences and thereby reduce the chances of being traumatized if one is subsequently exposed to the actual harassments of severe danger.

MOURNING AND INTROJECTION

We turn now to a major source of military stress, which sets in after the emotional ties to the leader and to other members of the face-to-face group have become firmly established—namely, the repeated loss of buddies and of a succession of leaders who are members of the combat soldier's "family circle."

When a combat unit sustains casualties, a number of readjustive mechanisms can be discerned among the survivors, which appear to counteract group demoralization. One such mechanism involves unconscious identification with the men who had become casualties. As is frequently observed in psychoanalytic studies of civilian cases, the mourning soldier uses the mechanism of "introjection" to build up a substitute object within himself. In one way or another he changes his behavior to resemble the lost person. The characteristics taken over by the mourner, of course, include moral standards and ego ideals as well as physical characteristics. Fenichel (2) asserts that this process of introjection is a normal component of mourning, becoming a pathological depression only when it involves a prolonged period of "regression to orality," with a predominance of sadomasochistic tendencies that go beyond an attempt merely to undo the loss. (I shall return to the problem of pathological mourning later on.)

Psychoanalytic studies of "normal" reactions to the loss of a father figure indicate that the post-bereavement identification entails much more compulsive conformity with the standards of the man after he is dead than when he was alive. Flugel (3) points out that a live parent figure can be influenced by the individual into giving his approval to new patterns of behavior, and thus the internalized code need not be inflexible when new circumstances are encountered; but, when he is no longer alive, he cannot be persuaded or cajoled into giving his approval, nor can he offer forgiveness for minor deviations from his standards. Flugel says: "What psychoanalysts have sometimes called 'postponed obedience' to dead parents may be a harder discipline than obedience to a living parent" (3, 188).

In a closely knit combat group, the same type of "postponed obedience" seems to occur following the loss of a leader or comrade. An unconscious form of attitude change occurs which has the effect of markedly increasing adherence to all those group norms which were manifestly valued by the dead man. To a lesser extent, the same type of compensatory attitude change is to be expected when a leader or comrade has been removed from the unit because of a promotion to a new position of greater responsibility.

The foregoing comments about mourning reactions suggest that the blood price paid by units in active combat may contribute a powerful unconscious source of motivation to group conformity. However, there is a compulsive quality that characterizes the conformity behavior arising from introjection, which might sometimes interfere with the effectiveness of group performances. It is necessary, therefore, to examine the unfavorable as well as the favorable consequences of introjection and to attempt to predict the conditions under which the alternative consequences are likely to occur.

REACTIVE DEPRESSION AND THE
"OLD SERGEANT" SYNDROME

One clear-cut type of adverse reaction which has been repeatedly reported pertains to the small percentage of combat personnel who developed a pathological form of depression. Like the normal mourner, the depressed soldier seems to be attempting to undo the loss and to keep the missing person symbolically present; but he becomes almost exclusively preoccupied with these efforts, showing little or no interest in any aspect of his daily life. There is a well-known set of incapacitating symptoms of anxiety-mixed-with-depression which has been labelled the "old sergeant" syndrome. (This name was used because the most striking cases occurred among non-commissioned officers who were old in combat experience.) The syndrome consists of a progressive deterioration in attitudes and performance, including a gradual decrease in mental efficiency, loss of self-confidence in ability to cope with danger, withdrawal from current social activities, apathy, and intense guilt feelings. According to Sobel (13), who has given the classical account of it, this syndrome occurred during World War II in "well-motivated, previously efficient soldiers, as a result of the chronic and progressive breakdown of their normal defenses against anxiety in long periods of combat." The same syndrome was observed in a high percentage of psychiatric casualties in combat divisions fighting in Korea during 1950-51 (6).

The symptoms comprising this syndrome usually do not appear during the first month or two of combat, which is the period when group identification becomes intensified. However, as the subsequent months go by, and as casualties mount, friendships become sharply restricted to a few "old timers" who started out together in the original unit. This restriction in the formation of friendship ties evidently arises because the battle veteran fears a repetition of the painful reactions he has repeatedly experienced when he lost his closest friends in combat. It is during this later phase that symptoms of chronic anxiety and depression make their appearance, insidiously developing into the "old sergeant" syndrome. As more and more members of the original group become casualties, the survivors become more and more inhibited with respect to forming new attachments, precisely because they have developed an attitude of defensive *detachment* toward the here-and-now combat group. The old sergeant no longer perceives himself as an integral part of the entire fighting group, although he may retain a sense of identification with a few of its original members. The latter, however, are men who, like himself, have become apathetic, inefficient, and "beat up." As a result, his conception of the group no longer serves to bolster his self-confidence.

The fact that these men develop the classical symptoms of depression suggests that an unconscious process has occurred whereby they regress from object relations to a pathological form of incorporation. In order to account for this process, it is necessary to emphasize one aspect of the normal work of mourning that is often neglected, namely, the process of seeking for and finding *substitute persons in reality* who will replace the lost persons.

In *Mourning and Melancholia*, Freud (4) alludes to this process. When describing the pathological features of melancholia, he mentions in passing that *normal* adaptation to the loss of a cherished person involves not merely the withdrawal of cathexis from the lost loved one but also the *transference of cathexis to a new person*. This he regards as the normal pathway that is abandoned by the depressed patient, who reacts solely by incorporating the lost loved one into his own ego.

At the beginning of this paper, I introduced the assumption that the soldier's attachment to his leader and to others in his work group comes about partly as a result of the normal type of transference that enables him to replace his own absent family members and other loved persons he reluctantly had to leave behind. During the first few months of combat, this normal type of transference continues to take place to the surviving members of the group and leads to a heightened cathexis of the existing group. That is, the love and affection that had formerly been attached to the lost comrades is transferred to newcomers and to others in the existing combat group. Evidently, in order for this re-cathexis of the existing group to occur, the mourner must be able to seek and accept *substitute* persons in reality who will enable him to compensate for the lost gratifications and the lost emotional ties. But then the substitutes, in turn, are lost—often at a time when the work of mourning for the first lost comrade is not yet complete—and so a new painful loss is added to the original one. The mourner then seems to become wary of finding any new substitutes and begins to show a self-preoccupying process of identification with the dead.

This pathogenic development seems to involve a regressive process that could be considered as a form of *reactive narcissism*. I suspect that two sources contribute to this reaction. First, the loss of comrades through injury and death may be unconsciously equated to being *abandoned* by them at a time when they are sorely needed. Case studies of surgical patients strongly suggest that, in a situation of prolonged stress, the absence of any affectionate person (no matter how legitimate or excusable his or her absence is known to be at the conscious level) will unconsciously tend to reactivate childhood episodes of profound grief in which the parent's temporary absence during a period of illness or suffering was experienced by the child as an abandonment. Secondly, the longer the duration of suffering and deprivation, the greater the likelihood that the leader and other members of the group will be unconsciously perceived as failing to use their power to terminate the suffering. In effect, like a small child, the sufferer gradually becomes more and more angry at those he feels are supposed to protect him from harm because they haven't yet made the enemy—or any of the other bad things—go away. These two factors—the repeated *loss* of members of the group combined with prolonged *continuation* of danger and suffering—give rise to an aggrievement reaction. This reaction heightens the intensity of the individual's ambivalence toward the remaining members of the protective group, which probably sets in motion the regressive process, fostering the more pathological form of introjection that we see in the "old sergeant" syndrome. As Freud puts it, "the conflict due to ambivalence gives a pathological cast to mourning and forces it to express itself in the form of self-reproaches to the effect that the mourner himself is to blame for the loss of the loved object, i.e. that he had willed it" (4, 251).

DELINQUENT BEHAVIOR

The remainder of this paper will be devoted to another type of unfavorable consequence of group identification—mutual support for delinquent behavior. Freud and other psychoanalysts have pointed out that war conditions tend to create a "war superego" in soldiers, which is a type of auxiliary super-ego that permits the men to express a variety of impulses ordinarily held in check, thus overriding the "normal peace ego." In his book on *Group Psychology,* Freud states (5, 85):

> For the moment it [the group] replaces the whole of human society, which is the wielder of authority, whose punishments the individual fears, and for whose sake he has submitted to so many inhibitions. It is clearly perilous for him to put himself in opposition to it, and it will be safer to follow the example of those around him and perhaps even "hunt with the pack." In obedience to the new authority he may put his former "conscience" out of action, and so surrender to the attraction of the increased pleasure that is certainly obtained from the removal of inhibitions.

We know that the members of a highly cohesive group sometimes support each other in ignoring authoritative demands from outside the group and participate in delinquent actions without experiencing the intense feelings of social anxiety and guilt that would obviously develop if each man were alone. Redl and Wineman (11) have specified the following factors as necessary conditions for the "contagious effect" of delinquent or countermores behavior in a peer group: (*a*) an initiator must openly "act out" in such a way that he obviously gratifies an impulse that the rest of the members have been inhibiting; (*b*) the initiator must display a lack of anxiety or guilt; (*c*) the other members who perceive the initiator's actions must have been undergoing for some time an intense conflict with respect to performing the forbidden act; i.e., they must have such a strong urge to commit the act that they were just barely able to inhibit its release prior to the initiator's demonstration. Thus, according to Redl and Wineman (11) it is the sudden perception of fearless and guiltless enjoyment of what they have been longing to do that sways the members of a group to become psychologically infected by a delinquency-carrier.

While caught up in a group epidemic of delinquency, the members will commit sadistic and narcissistic acts that later on, after the atmosphere of shared excitement has subsided, evoke feelings of remorse, apprehension, and loss of self-esteem. Following any single episode of wayward group behavior, the intensity of an individual member's dysphoric reaction and the degree to which his inhibitory controls are re-established will depend partly on what the other members of the group do and say about it.

Psychoanalytic observers have called attention to the numerous ways in which the members of a cohesive group *share the guilt* so as to ward off or minimize their dysphoric reactions. "Sharing the guilt" refers to a complex set of mechanisms whereby internalized standards are temporarily set aside or modified as a consequence of interaction with others in a primary group. Each member of the group experiences some relief from knowing that "I am not the only one who did it." Fenichel (2) assumes that this relief occurs as a result of a "quasi-projection" mechanism: a guilty person who places the blame on his entire group is displaying an attenuated form of projection ("all of us did it, not just me"). This involves much less distortion of reality than the more extreme projections in which the blame is placed entirely on other people ("they are responsible, I had nothing to do with it").

In addition to a quasi-projection mechanism, it seems to me that there are other psychological processes which also enter into the sharing of guilt:

1. Denial of dysphoric affect and reaction formations against guilt are probably facilitated when the group members openly communicate to each other a manifest attitude of tough-minded indifference concerning immorality, especially when everyone continues to act as though he accepts at face value the carefree manner with which moral scruples are being ignored.

2. In a group atmosphere where the members are speaking nonchalantly about the morally objectionable things they have done, there are frequent opportunities for a surreptitious form of confession, for those who are seeking to unburden themselves of unacknowledged guilt.

3. Seeing and hearing others in the group talk unembarrassedly about participation in a collective spree can also have the effect of reinforcing an illusory belief of ethical validity ("it must be O.K. if everyone else admits doing it"). And, at the same time, it also fosters an illusory sense of being protected against the power of the punitive authorities ("we're all in this together, so they can't punish any of us").

4. After collectively committing serious acts of violence, the members' retrospective accounts to each other may help them to arrive at a convincing set of rationalizations to exculpate themselves. For example, they can excuse the damage they created by agreeing that "it was an accident." Or they can justify themselves for maltreating innocent victims by developing the shared belief that "they had it coming to them." A major type of guilt-evading rationalization that seems to be especially common both in military units and in adolescent gangs is the belief that one's own offenses are excused if some other person was the initiator of the forbidden behavior: "We didn't start it so we're not responsible."

From what has already been said it is apparent that intra-group communications can facilitate the formation of rationalizations in two ways: first, since the members share a common need for finding excuses for the offense, they can *pool their inventive resources* to arrive at a much better case for themselves than any one person would be able to think up himself; secondly, when all members show signs of accepting any alleged explanation for the offense, their *unanimity lends authenticity* to the excuse, furnishing the same type of consensual validation that is commonly accepted by most people as grounds for believing explanations about impressive events in their daily lives ("if everyone says so, it must be true").

In this connection, it is important to note that the same group influences that enable scrupulous men to overcome their inhibitions and become "good" soldiers may, later on, lead to their becoming "bad" soldiers and "bad" citizens.

The combat soldier is required to overcome his internal restraints against violent acts and, in order to do so, he relies more and more upon the support of the combat group. As inner controls based on personal conscience become partially replaced by outer controls based on signs of group approval or disapproval, the members are likely to support each other not only in connection with the release of hostility toward the enemy but with respect to other forms of gratification as well. For example, if the members adopt an informal code of regularly maltreating captured soldiers, and share the same rationalizations for warding off the accompanying guilt feelings, it becomes an easy step to accept and rationalize similar maltreatment of enemy *civilians* ("They have it coming to them for all the atrocities their side has committed against our side"). The least inhibited member of the military group then feels quite safe in initiating new forms of countermores activity in captured towns—such as looting private homes, misusing military food supplies to force old people to give up their jewelry or other hidden possessions, and applying pressure on young women to submit sexually. A contagious effect is then likely to occur among the other men in the unit, who have also been longing to obtain the same types of gratification during the long periods of extreme privation. As each man participates in more and more antisocial behavior, an acculturation process takes place, so that the inhibitory power of his former moral scruples is increasingly weakened.

The military group, then, serves an *initiating* function, in that it provides powerful incentives for releasing forbidden impulses, inducing the soldier to try out formerly inhibited acts which he originally regarded as morally repugnant. In addition, the military group furnishes a social milieu which *facilitates the unlearning of inhibitions*. It is especially in connection with the latter function that the various mechanisms of sharing the guilt enter in. With the help of the other men in his unit, the soldier who is burdened with guilt following a first violation will gradually take over the group-sanctioned rationalizations, projections, and reaction formations that enable his guilt to subside to a relatively low level.

FACTORS FOSTERING A DEVIANT INFORMAL CODE

When we examine the various documented instances of military violations on the part of local units, we obtain some clues pertinent to the following general question, which has considerable practical as well as theoretical implications: *Under what conditions will a cohesive local group provide mutual support for violations of the norms of the superordinate organization with which it is affiliated and develop an informal code of its own that opposes the organization's code?*

One major factor that must be taken into account was implied in my earlier statements about transference, namely, the attitudes conveyed by the local leader. Obviously, when a primary work group has a leader who openly opposes the demands of the organization, the chances are greater that the group will develop an informal code that deviates from the organizational norms. However, it is unwarranted to assume that a group of soldiers is wholly passive with respect to accepting a local leader's influence. If an officer encourages his men to perform acts that are extreme violations of the rules of the military organization—for example, shirking a dangerous assignment, engaging in looting, or selling military supplies on the black market—the group members may reject his demands and spontaneously turn to an informal leader who induces much less conflict. Thus, it is essential to examine the influence of a local leader with anti-army attitudes in relation to other factors that also enter into the picture when the members of a local unit undergo a conflict of the type under discussion.

Taking account of observations bearing on dissident behavior in industrial and political organizations, as well as the military studies already cited, I shall now attempt to draw some inferences concerning the conditions under which the members of a local group will mutually support each other in repeatedly violating the organization's norms. A number of important factors can be discerned, which appear to be major determinants of delinquent behavior in situations where the members of a military unit mutually support each other in taking advantage of opportunities for shirking their duties, for seeking personal aggrandizement, and for indulging in antisocial sexual exploits.

The following four conditions seem to be the most obvious antecedents of persistently deviant behavior on the part of a local unit: (*a*) most men in the unit have specific grievances against the superordinate organization, and feel resentful toward the top leadership for neglecting their needs, for inflicting unnecessary deprivations or for imposing extraordinarily harsh demands which menace their personal welfare; (*b*) the members perceive their group as having no channel open for communicating their grievances to the top levels of the hierarchy or are convinced that such communications would be wholly ineffective in inducing any favorable changes; (c) the organization is perceived as having little or no opportunity for detecting the deviant behavior in question; and (d) one or more central persons in the local unit communicates disaffiliative sentiments to the others and sets an example, either by personally acting in a way that is contrary to the organization's norms or by failing to use his power to prevent someone else in the same group from doing so.

The psychological conditions just described could be seen quite clearly among American occupation troops stationed in disorganized German cities at the end of World War II. I encountered a series of extreme examples in a study (7) conducted among American infantrymen stationed in Berlin during the summer of 1945, at a time when the entire population was suffering from an acute food shortage. Both the interviews and direct observations indicated that a very high percentage of the men were violating military regulations (and the moral code of their society) in taking advantage of their economic power over the starving Berliners. Most of the American soldiers were regularly profiteering on the black market (e.g., exchanging a few candy bars for a Leica camera) and were openly purchasing sexual partners (e.g., soliciting girls at public places by holding up a can of C-rations or a candy bar). The men who had been stationed in Berlin for less than ten days appeared to express more guilt feelings about exploiting the hungry civilians than the men who had been on occupation duty in Berlin for a longer period of time. At night in the barracks there were bull sessions in which they were "sharing the guilt." In their group discussions, the men encouraged each other to continue seeking out the rare opportunities afforded by being stationed in the starving city and spoke about the "reasons" why the German people deserved to be mistreated and why much of the blame for their exploitation could be placed on the Russian occupying forces, whose mistreatment of the Berliners in the eastern zone was said to be far worse than the Americans'.

Much of the exploitative behavior was instigated by combat veterans, who felt that they had already done more than their share and were resentful about not being sent back to the United States promptly. Furthermore, the men perceived themselves as being isolated to an unusual degree from the main headquarters of the U.S. Armed Forces in Europe (especially since they knew that the western sector of Berlin was only a small island in Russian-controlled territory). The social disorganization that characterized the entire city was such that most American soldiers felt there was little chance of being detected in black marketeering or in other illegal activities by the Berlin police, by the U.S. military police, or by any authorities in the U.S. Army. It is not known to what extent the leaders of the local units actually encouraged the men to indulge in illegal activities, but there is little question that the non-commissioned officers, and to some extent the commissioned officers, actively participated in such activities themselves. Thus, it seems likely that all four conditions were present and contributed to the development of an informal code such that the men felt relatively free to give in to the temptation to exploit the starving German population, thereby violating not only the policies of the U.S. Army, but also the humanitarian ethical norms of the western democratic nations.

In conclusion, I wish to state once again my expectation that the hypotheses concerning the conditions under which group identification will lead to "sharing the guilt" and the development of a deviant group code of behavior will prove to be applicable to many non-military groups in civilian life. I have the same expectation with respect to the potential applicability of the other hypotheses I have presented concerning transference toward the leader, the reassurances gained by group members from sharing their fears, and the heightened cathexis of the group that results from mourning for lost members. Essentially the same psychological processes that we see in *extreme form* in combat groups may occur in groups of factory employees, white collar workers, and professional men at times when they are facing the external dangers of financial insecurity or social censure. All of us can think of well-known examples of how outstanding artists, composers, writers, and scientists, before they gained recognition, have banded together and mutually supported each other against the scorn and derision of their community. We sometimes discern comparable instances of mutual support occurring in ordinary work groups, friendship cliques, and families at times of stress or bereavement.

Perhaps the main value of formulating hypotheses about the processes of group identification in extreme danger situations, as I stated at the outset, is that we become alerted to look for similar processes, which may be manifested in much less obvious ways, in our subsequent observations and research on other primary groups.

REFERENCES

1. Erikson, E. H. The first psychoanalyst. In B. Nelson (Ed.), *Freud and the twentieth century.* New York: Meridian, 1957, Pp. 79–101.
2. Fenichel, O. *The psychoanalytic theory of neurosis.* New York: Norton, 1945.

3. Flugel, J. *Man, morals, and society.* New York: International Universities Press, 1945.
4. Freud, S. *Mourning and melancholia.* London: Hogarth, 1917.
5. Freud, S. *Group psychology and the analysis of the ego.* London: Hogarth, 1922.
6. Glass, A. J. Psychotherapy in the combat zone. *American Journal of Psychiatry,* 1954, **110**, 725–731.
7. Janis, I. L. Morale attitudes and social behavior of American soldiers in post-war Berlin. Unpublished memorandum for the European Theater of Operations, Information and Education Division, Research Branch, 1945.
8. Janis, I. L. *Air war and emotional stress.* New York: McGraw-Hill, 1951.
9. Janis, I. L. *Psychological stress.* New York: Wiley, 1958.
10. Redl, F. Group emotion and leadership. *Psychiatry,* 1942, **5**, 573–596.
11. Redl, F., & Wineman, D. *The aggressive child.* Glencoe, Ill.: Free Press, 1957.
12. Sandler, J. On the concept of super-ego. *The psychoanalytic study of the child.* Vol. 15. New York: International Universities Press, 1960.
13. Sobel, R. The "old sergeant" syndrome. *Psychiatry,* 1947, **10**, 315–321.
14. Stouffer, S., et al. *The American soldier.* Vol. 2. *Combat and its aftermath.* Princeton, N.J.: Princeton Univ. Press, 1949.

7

Attitude Change via Role Playing (1968)

Role playing, although only recently brought into the experimental social psychology laboratory, frequently occurs in daily life and may be one of the main ways in which people encounter cognitive inconsistencies that lead them to decide to adopt new courses of action. Social scientists have long taken account of the strong social pressures that are exerted on men and women to live up to the demands of prescribed norms whenever they enter a new occupational role, advance to a more responsible position in an organizational hierarchy, or acquire a new social status in the community. It has been observed that many people, when complying with role demands, express the prescribed attitudes and values even though they do not privately accept them. A transformation from outer to inner compliance seems to be a central feature of role adaptation—a gradual change whereby the person comes to accept privately the beliefs and value judgments that he has expressed publicly while playing the expected social role.

A number of experimental studies have presented systematic evidence concerning the effects of role playing on attitude change. Janis and King (1954; King & Janis, 1956) found that when college students were induced to improvise a talk in order to fulfill the demands of a public-speaking task requiring them to express opinions that differed from their private beliefs, they showed more opinion change than an equivalent control group exposed to the same informational content. Kelman (1953) found a similar increase in opinion change when school children were given a mild incentive to write

Janis, I. L. Attitude change via role playing. In R. Abelson, E. Aronson, W. J. McGuire, T. M. Newcomb, M. J. Rosenberg, and P. H. Tannenbaum (Eds.), *Theories of cognitive consistency: A sourcebook.* Chicago: Rand McNally, 1968. Reprinted by permission.

essays in support of an arbitrarily assigned position; but he observed no such gain in an equivalent group of children put under strong pressure to conform with the role-playing task, many of whom showed signs of constriction, resentment, and negativism.

A "conflict" model can be used as a theoretical basis for a "self-persuasion" hypothesis to explain role-playing effects (Janis, 1959; Janis & Mann, 1968). Decisional conflicts are conceptualized in terms of a balance sheet containing weighted positive and negative values corresponding to the potential gains (positive incentives) and potential losses (negative incentives) that are anticipated by the decision maker when he evaluates each alternative open to him.

Janis and Gilmore (1965) point out that this theoretical approach specifies several conditions for inducing maximal attitude change via role playing that are quite different from those specified by cognitive dissonance theory:

> . . . when a person accepts the task of improvising arguments in favor of a point of view at variance with his own personal convictions, he becomes temporarily motivated to think up all the good positive arguments he can, and at the same time, suppresses thoughts about the negative arguments which are supposedly irrelevant to the assigned task. This "biased scanning" increases the salience of the positive arguments and therefore increases the chances of acceptance of the new attitude position. A gain in attitude change would not be expected, however, if resentment or other interfering affective reactions were aroused by *negative* incentives in the role-playing situation. Among the obvious instances of negative incentives would be information that lowers the prestige of the sponsor or that leads to his being perceived as a manipulative person who is trying to influence people for his own personal aggrandizement or for other alien purposes. Any signs of exploitative intentions in the behavior of the sponsor would also be expected to operate as negative incentives, evoking responses that conflict with the positive incentive value of improvising arguments in support of the conclusion assigned by the sponsor.

According to conflict theory, the amount of attitude change will depend largely on the degree to which the role player is induced to engage in intensive "biased scanning" of genuine positive incentives that he can accept into his own personal balance sheet. The role player will change his attitude only if he makes the following two types of verbal responses while carrying out the role-playing task: (a) recalling or inventing arguments that are capable of functioning as positive incentives for accepting a new attitude position, and (b) appraising the recalled or improvised arguments with a psychological set that fosters open-minded cognitive exploration of their positive incentive value, rather than a negativistic set of the type engendered by the arousal of hostility, resentment, or suspicion (Elms & Janis, 1965). If the first type of response is made, but not the second, no attitude change would be expected from a role-playing performance. For example, many intelligent American soldiers who were captured by the Chinese Communists during the Korean War could comply with the role-playing demands of their despised 'brain-washing' captors and nevertheless remain uninfluenced: While verbalizing 'good' pro-Communist arguments, the prisoners could privately label all the improvised arguments with negative epithets or could think of counterarguments to refute the statements they were overtly verbalizing (see Lifton, 1961; Schein, 1956).

It should also be noted that role playing would not be expected to bring about attitude change unless the new incentives that emerge when the subjects engage in biased scanning are powerful enough to create a challenge to their present position (Stage 1 in the model of decision-making stages; see Janis, 1959). A case in point is the study of Stanley and Klausmeir (1957) in which midwestern isolationists complied with the role-playing instructions to give short talks advocating world government, but showed no evidence of attitude change. It would be extremely improbable that, merely by engaging in a bit of biased scanning in a single experimental session, the subjects would generate a new set of incentives sufficiently powerful not only to seriously challenge their present position in favor of U.S. national autonomy but to reject it in favor of the new alternative. On the other hand, when experimenters set up the necessary conditions for bringing about sufficient challenge to induce at least a slight amount of attitude change (e.g., by selecting a less deeply held attitude or by first introducing an effective persuasive message) the use of the role-playing technique can alter each subject's personal balance sheet of positive and negative incentives sufficiently to produce a much greater amount of attitude change in the role players than in equated control subjects who are passively exposed to the same informational inputs.

The effectiveness of a role-playing procedure would also be expected to depend upon the type of arguments the person is asked to give. For example, if he is instructed to play the role of a person with whom he has little in common, and argues in terms of values and goals that are not his own, he will engage in very little biased scanning of incentives that enter into his own private balance sheet, with the result that none of his anticipations of gains or losses will be altered. In contrast, if the subject is instructed to play the role of someone who shares his values and to make up good arguments that would be convincing to persons like himself, the chances are greatly increased that some new incentives will enter into his private balance sheet and give rise to a change in his position on the issue.

Two specific variables can be singled out which enable predictions to be made that are opposite to those made by cognitive dissonance theorists:

1. The amount of attitude change produced by role playing, according to conflict theory, will be a positive function of the degree to which subjects engage in *overt* role playing by verbalizing arguments in support of the assigned position on the issue. Mere *commitment* to play the role could, of course, induce some degree of attitude change (particularly if the subjects engage in implicit role playing in anticipation of executing the task); but actually carrying out the task of verbalizing new arguments in support of the objectionable position would elicit more biased scanning and increase the salience of new incentives, thus increasing the likelihood of attitude change— provided that no strong interfering responses are evoked by unfavorable sponsorship or by other unfavorable conditions. According to a dissonance-theory analysis by Brehm and Cohen (1962), the mere fact that a person commits himself to play any such role, before he executes it, "should be sufficient to produce the attitude-changing dissonance" (pp. 254–255). They cite evidence from a study in which no difference was found between two groups, one of which wrote essays in which the dissonant position was overtly verbalized while the other merely agreed to write the essays (Rabbie, Brehm, & Cohen, 1959).

2. Role playing will be more successful in inducing attitude changes, according to conflict theory, if the sponsor is perceived as someone whose affiliations are benign and whose intentions are public-spirited than if he is perceived as someone whose affiliations and purposes are commercial, exploitative, or immoral. The opposite prediction would be made by a dissonance-theory explanation of role-playing effects, which postulates that "dissonance [among cognitive elements] gives rise to pressures to reduce the dissonance and to avoid increases in dissonance" (Festinger, 1957, p. 31). According to this theory, the crucial factor in role playing is that it creates dissonance between the person's private opinion and his awareness of what he is overtly saying and doing when he conforms with the sponsor's demands; "the changes in private opinion which ensue are the end result of a process of attempting to reduce or eliminate this dissonance" (Festinger, 1957, p. 112). The total magnitude of dissonance is assumed to decrease as the number and importance of the pressures and justifications which induce the person to say things he

does not privately believe are increased (see Brehm & Cohen, 1962, pp. 252–255). Consequently, the prediction would be that more dissonance and therefore more attitude change will result from role playing if the sponsor is perceived as having objectionable affiliations or purposes than if he is perceived as having goals consonant with the subjects' own values—provided, of course, that the subjects can be induced to conform to his role-playing instructions.

For the purpose of testing the opposing predictions from conflict theory and from dissonance theory, two experiements were carried out (Janis & Gilmore, 1965; Elms & Janis, 1965). In both experiments we compared the effects of a positive sponsorship condition that was consonant with the subjects' values with a negative sponsorship condition that was relatively dissonant. We also included, as a matter of secondary interest, the effects of large vs. small monetary payments for the role-playing performance, taking account of the controversial evidence on this variable from the experiments by Festinger and Carlsmith (1959), Brehm and Cohen (1962), and Rosenberg (1965). The third variable investigated was overt role playing vs. implicit role playing.

In order to include the third variable, we ran into a technical problem concerning the use of 'priming' questions as part of the overt role-playing procedure. During extensive pretesting, we noted that subjects had some difficulty in carrying out the role-playing task, which involved writing an essay as an advocate of a new policy with which they personally disagreed. We found it necessary to use some neutral 'priming' questions to get them thinking about what issues they might discuss. Without these neutral questions most of the essays were devoid of content and the overt role-playing variable we were trying to investigate obviously was not being successfully manipulated. Some brief checks indicated that these neutral questions alone had no effect on attitudes and hence we did not consider them as persuasive communications. We also tried out some priming questions with subjects in the non-overt role-playing condition (who were given the role-playing instructions and then, before carrying out the task, were given the attitude questionnaire). Here we ran into trouble because when the priming questions were combined with the role-playing instructions, we found that the subjects immediately began thinking up good arguments, even though we gave them no chance to write them down, and this threatened to make the differences between the overt and non-overt role-playing conditions so slight that this variable might not be well represented in the experiment. Accordingly, we arrived at the following compromise: In one of the experiments (Janis & Gilmore, 1965) we decided to avoid the risk of failing to manipulate the overt vs. covert role-playing variable by allowing the priming questions to be confounded with the overt role-playing condition and so we withheld the priming questions from the non-overt role players. (It should be noted here that dissonance theorists have argued that this confounding may have introduced a differential amount of new persuasive material and thus might account for the negative findings concerning dissonance theory predictions.) In the other experiment (Elms & Janis, 1965), we avoided the risks associated with differentially introducing the priming questions by giving the priming questions in exactly the same way in both the overt and non-overt conditions, at the risk of losing the opportunity to study the effects of overt vs. non-overt role playing.

For both experiments, a three dimensional factorial design was used in order to test the hypotheses about attitude change as a function of (a) unfavorable vs. favorable sponsorship of the role-playing task; (b) small vs. large monetary rewards (paid in advance, before carrying out the task); and (c) overt vs. non-overt role playing. The two experiments, however, used different topics and different instances of positive and negative sponsorship.

In the Janis and Gilmore experiment, the subjects wrote essays in favor of an unpopular educational policy (that of requiring all college undergraduates in the United States to have additional courses in mathematics and science). Less personal approval of the role-played position was found under Unfavorable Sponsorship conditions (E presenting himself as a representative of a commercial company that was hiring Ss to help prepare advertising copy to promote the sale of science textbooks) than under Favorable Sponsorship conditions (E presenting himself as a representative of a public welfare organization that was hiring Ss to help prepare for a nationwide educational survey). These findings tend to support conflict theory and contradict dissonance theory since they show that overt role playing was more effective when the sponsors' affiliations and goals were regarded by Ss as consonant with their own values than when they were regarded as being relatively dissonant. Additional findings from the same experiment showed that (a) under Favorable Sponsorship conditions, *overt* role playing (actually writing an essay in which S improvises arguments in favor of an opposed point of view) was more effective in inducing attitude change than *non-overt* role playing (merely agreeing to write such an essay without actually having the opportunity to do so); and (b) there were no significant differences between role players who were paid $20 in advance and those paid $1 in advance for writing the essays (although the maximum amount of attitude change occurred in the subgroup given the larger amount of money under Favorable Sponsorship conditions).

In the Elms and Janis experiment, college students were asked to invent arguments in favor of a counter-norm proposal, allegedly put forth by the Soviet Union, to allow American students to go to Russia for their entire four-year college education. In the Unfavorable Sponsorship condition, Ss were informed by the interviewer that the Soviet government had hired his firm to collect the materials needed to produce a pamphlet which representatives of the Soviet Union would distribute to all U.S. college campuses, presenting arguments in favor of the proposed program that would be appealing and convincing to American students. The Ss in the Favorable Sponsorship condition, after being given exactly the same background information, were told that the interviewer's firm had a contract with the U.S. State Department to carry out a survey of the attitudes of American students toward the program; relevant arguments were now being collected as a first step toward preparing survey questions, which would ask students whether they agreed or disagreed.

Analysis of variance of attitude-change scores showed a significant triple interaction effect: a high degree of acceptance of the counter-norm proposal occurred only under conditions of *overt* role playing when *acceptable* justification and *large* rewards were given. The largest amount of attitude change thus occurred in the overt role-playing group that was exposed to the *least dissonant* condition, i.e., favorable sponsorship with large monetary reward.

The results from the two experiments are similar in that the findings from both indicate that when role-playing conditions are relatively consonant with the subjects' values, they show more attitude change than when the conditions are dissonant. In the Elms and Janis study the sponsorship variable alone was found to have a positive effect on the amount of attitude change among the overt role-playing groups, but this effect was subordinate to the interaction of favorable sponsorship with the large monetary reward. This outcome, although somewhat different from that of the other experiment, bears out the prediction that a large monetary reward will have a positive effect on attitude change only when the role-playing task is sponsored by an acceptable group and is oriented toward a goal perceived by S as being consonant with his own; but the same large reward will tend to create suspicion, guilt, or other interfering responses that make for less attitude change when the role-playing task is sponsored by a distrusted sponsor and is perceived as having a purpose antithetical to one's own values.

Although the findings from the two experiments just described support conflict theory rather than dissonance theory, there is in the literature a great deal of seemingly contradictory evidence from other role-playing experiments concerning the effects of large vs. small monetary inducements, which appear to support dissonance theory. Alternative explanations in terms of conflict theory have been suggested elsewhere (Elms & Janis, 1965; Elms 1967) to account for the findings that appear to show dissonance effects (e.g., large payments may have unfavorable incentive effects when E is regarded by the subjects with suspicion after he asks them to lie to a fellow student). But this is a long story that requires detailed analysis of the incentive conditions employed in each relevant experiment. Suffice to say that relatively large monetary inducements evoke so many mixed reactions that this may be an unproductive type of incentive variable to continue investigating. As McGuire (1966) puts it, research on this variable has burgeoned into a widespread "twenty-dollar misunderstanding."

Conflict theory, along with other theories of cognitive inconsistency, can be expected to add its two-cents worth to the twenty-dollar questions. Some of the important questions that need to be answered by analytic experiments pertain to the crucial conditions under which relatively strong inducements for role playing will have negative rather than positive effects on attitude change. One obvious prediction from conflict theory has already been alluded to: We would expect that when people are uncertain about the covert intentions of someone who is trying to induce them to advocate a new policy, their suspicion that they are being manipulated will be aroused and will interfere with their open-minded exploration of the cognitions that might lend support to the new policy. Under these conditions, a strong inducement—whether in the form of money, social pressure, or the threat of a penalty—would be relatively ineffective; whereas a milder inducement, which makes for more open-minded exploration of new considerations, could result in more gain from biased scanning and hence produce more attitude change.

There are also more subtle interacting factors suggested by a conflict-resolution model, some of which could be used to extend and modify the promising hypothesis put forth by McGuire (1966) in an attempt to reconcile the conflict theory explanation of role-playing effects with the dissonance explanation. McGuire's hypothesis is that when role playing is actually carried out, the more reward the person is given for advocating a new point of view, the more adequate his performance will be and hence the greater the chances of self-persuasion; but when the person has merely committed himself to perform the role-playing task and has not yet executed it, his sense of commitment will be greater if he is given only a relatively small reward, which will incline him to justify himself by internalizing the new attitude position, as dissonance theory predicts.

One of the implications of this hypothesis is that whenever a person complies with a request to advocate a new attitude he does not personally accept, he will acquire a new incentive to accept that new attitude insofar as he has the *illusion* that he has committed himself voluntarily to comply with the request. It seems likely that this new incentive, which mainly involves anticipated social disapproval for subsequent reversal of the apparent commitment, would sometimes play a *determining* role, under certain very restricted conditions. One important condition specified by McGuire is that the committed role player has not yet been given the opportunity to carry out the role-playing performance. But even when the role-playing performance has already been carried out, the illusion of commitment to the new position could still play a determining role if certain other conditions were present, such as the following:

1. *Low interest in the issue:* If the decision, attitude, or judgment has little inherent interest to the person because it does not implicate any potential gains or losses that would make for ego involvement, the person is unlikely to think up any new relevant incentives no matter how conscientiously he tries to execute the role-playing task. Strong inducements to perform a role-playing task conscientiously can increase the degree of self-persuasion only when the role player can draw upon a cognitive repertoire to produce relevant arguments and appeals. There will be little or no self-persuasion when the role player is asked to advocate a counterattitudinal position on an issue for which he has only a meager cognitive repertoire, as is the case when he cannot see any ramifications related to his social values, his personal goals, or his previously acquired knowledge. For example, if the role player is instructed to tell others that it was enjoyable to work on a dull experimental task (that is now over and done with) he can easily comply by saying that he liked it, but he is likely to think up relatively few self-convincing arguments. Consequently, at the end of the role-playing session, the role player's personal balance sheet would not change very much from self-persuasion, whether or not he had been strongly motivated to try to think up good arguments. The main source of attitude change to be expected from this type of role playing would be that resulting from the new incentive added by the illusion of commitment, which requires a low pressure inducement.

The lower the subject's interest and ego involvement in the issue, the more likely that any attitude changes observed following a role-playing performance will be based on the illusion of commitment and not on the salience of self-persuading arguments. Thus an inter-action effect would be predicted such that when initial interest in the attitude issue is low, small rewards and weak justifications will be relatively more effective than stronger inducements; whereas, when initial interest is high, large rewards and strong positive justifi-cations will be relatively more effective than weaker inducements—provided, of course, that a significant amount of attitude change can be produced by the role-playing procedure (which must be unusually effective in order to overcome all the sources of resistance that make it difficult to change highly ego-involving attitudes).

2. *Low opportunity for genuine contemplation of the issue dur-ing the role-playing performance:* If the role-playing procedure is one that gives the person little time to think about the issue or introduces a source of distraction that prevents him from evaluating the arguments he is mouthing, no new incentives would be intro-duced into the person's internal balance sheet from self-persuasion. Under these restrictive conditions, the only way that a role-playing performance could give rise to attitude change would be by creating the illusion of commitment, which is fostered when the subject is offered very small rewards and weak justifications for complying. But we would expect strong inducements for performing consci-entiously to be relatively more effective whenever the procedures allow the role player ample opportunity to draw upon his cognitive repertoire to think up good arguments in support of the counter-attitudinal position he is advocating. Under these nonrestrictive con-ditions, biased scanning of self-persuading arguments can be a powerful impetus to attitude change, whether or not the subject acquires the illusory belief that he has publicly committed himself to the new position. Thus, here again an interaction effect is predicted: mild inducements will be more effective than strong ones when the role-playing task offers little opportunity for genuine contemplation of the issue; but strong positive inducements will be relatively more effective than mild ones when the task entails little distraction and allows the role players sufficient time to think up supporting argu-ments. The latter difference is especially likely to emerge when the role-playing performance does not involve public commitment (as when the role player is guaranteed anonymity or is assured that no one outside the research team will know what he said in his written essay or in his tape-recorded speech) since under these conditions there is little opportunity to develop an illusion of commitment.

The two hypotheses concerning variables that interact with large vs. small rewards could readily explain the apparent dissonance effects in the Festinger and Carlsmith (1959) experiment and in several others that used similar attitude issues of meager personal relevance for the subjects. They might also furnish an explanation for the double outcome in the Carlsmith, Collins, and Helmreich (1966) experiment, which showed that low payments were more effective than higher payments when subjects had to tell fellow students face-to-face that a dull experimental task was interesting, whereas the high payments were more effective than low payments when the subjects had to write anonymous essays (which probably gave them more opportunity to think up one or two arguments and created little social commitment).

In role-playing experiments that ask subjects to think up good arguments in the counterattitudinal direction on more interesting ego-involving issues, the gains from self-persuasion (fostered by large rewards and strong positive justifications) would tend to outweigh the gains from creating an illusion of commitment (fostered by small rewards and weak justifications). Thus, when students are asked to write essays on moderately ego-involving topics—such as whether American students should be permitted to go to the Soviet Union for their college education (Elms & Janis, 1965) or whether their victorious college football team should be prohibited from playing in the Rose Bowl game (Rosenberg, 1965)—we would expect that strong positive inducements for writing good essays will lead to more attitude change than weak ones, just as the results of these experiments show.

Some additional experiments will obviously be necessary to see if the type of issue (ego-involving vs. non-ego-involving) and the type of role-playing procedure (low vs. high opportunity for thinking up effective new arguments) influence the outcome as interacting variables and thus make a crucial difference on the effects of weak vs. strong inducements. It will also be relevant to investigate similar interactions of these two variables with active participation (improvised role playing) vs. passive participation (merely reciting someone else's arguments) since the same explanatory hypotheses might also account for the apparent inconsistencies in experimental findings on this variable (Janis & King, 1954; Jansen & Stolorow, 1962; King & Janis, 1956; McGuire, 1966; Zimbardo, 1965).

If the various interaction effects predicted from the conflict-theory analysis of counterattitudinal role playing are confirmed, we shall be able to conclude that attitude changes are fostered by strong inducements when the role-playing task allows opportunities for self-persuasion and that the dissonance outcome is limited to the special conditions where the only dominant incentive for attitude change is the illusion of voluntary commitment. But if the predicted interactions are not confirmed, the negative evidence will greatly reduce the presumption that conflict theory will account for all types of attitude change. In the meantime, considerable controversy is to be expected, especially since some of the experimental results already reported by dissonance theorists (e.g., Cohen's experiment described in Brehm & Cohen, 1962, pp. 73-78) remain quite recalcitrant both to the reconciliatory hypothesis offered by McGuire and the above elaborations of it based on the conflict model.

REFERENCES

Brehm, J. W., & Cohen, A. R. *Explorations in cognitive dissonance.* New York: Wiley, 1962.

Carlsmith, J. M., Collins, B. E., & Helmreich, R. L. Studies in forced compliance: I. The effect of pressure for compliance on attitude change produced by face-to-face role playing and anonymous essay writing. *Journal of Personality and Social Psychology,* 1966, *4,* 1-13.

Elms, A. C. Role playing, incentive, and dissonance. *Psychological Bulletin,* 1967, *68,* 132-148.

Elms, A. C., & Janis, I. L. Counter-norm attitudes induced by consonant versus dissonant conditions of role-playing. *Journal of Experimental Research in Personality,* 1965, *1,* 50-60.

Festinger, L. *A theory of cognitive dissonance.* Evanston, Ill.: Row, Peterson, 1957.

Festinger, L., & Carlsmith, J. M. Cognitive consequences of forced compliance. *Journal of Abnormal and Social Psychology,* 1959, *58,* 203-210.

Janis, I. L. Motivational factors in the resolution of decisional conflicts. In M. R. Jones (Ed.), *Nebraska symposium on motivation, 1959.* Lincoln, Nebraska: University of Nebraska Press, 1959. Pp. 198-231.

Janis, I. L., & Gilmore, J. B. The influence of incentive conditions on the success of role playing in modifying attitudes. *Journal of Personality and Social Psychology,* 1965, *1,* 17-27.

Janis, I. L., & King, B. T. The influence of role playing on opinion-change. *Journal of Abnormal and Social Psychology,* 1954, *49,* 211-218.

Janis, I. L., & Mann, L. A. A conflict-theory approach to attitude change and decision making. In A. Greenwald, T. Brock, & T. Ostrom (Eds.), *Psychological foundations of attitudes.* New York: Academic Press, 1968.

Jansen, M. J., & Stolorow, L. M. An experimental study in role playing. *Psychological Monographs,* 1962, *76,* No. 31.

Kelman, H. C. Attitude change as a function of response restriction. *Human Relations,* 1953, *6,* 185-214.

King, B. T., & Janis, I. L. Comparison of the effectiveness of improvised vs. non-improvised role playing in producing opinion changes. *Human Relations,* 1956, *9,* 177-186.

Lifton, R. J. *Thought reform and the psychology of totalism: A study of "brainwashing" in China*. New York: Norton, 1961.

McGuire, W. J. Attitudes and opinions. *Annual Review of Psychology*, 1966, *17*, 475–514.

Rabbie, J. M., Brehm, J. W., & Cohen, A. R. Verbalization and reactions to cognitive dissonance. *Journal of Personality*, 1959, *27*, 407–417.

Rosenberg, M. J. When dissonance fails: On eliminating evaluation apprehension from attitude measurement. *Journal of Personality and Social Psychology*, 1965, *1*, 28–42.

Schein, E. H. The Chinese indoctrination program for prisoners of war: A study of attempted "brainwashing". *Psychiatry*, 1956, *19*, 149–172.

Stanley, J. C., & Klausmeir, H. J. Opinion constancy after formal role playing. *Journal of Social Psychology*, 1957, *47*, 11–18.

Zimbardo, P. G. The effect of effort and improvisation on self-persuasion produced by role-playing. *Journal of Experimental Social Psychology*, 1965, *1*, 103–120.

8

Adaptive Personality Changes Resulting From Stressful Episodes (1969)

I have lain in prison for nearly two years. . . . I have passed through every possible mood of suffering. . . . I could not bear [my sufferings] to be without meaning. Now I find hidden somewhere away in my nature something that tells me that nothing in the whole world is meaningless, and suffering least of all. That something hidden away in my nature, like a treasure in a field, is humility.

It is the last thing left in me, and the best: the ultimate discovery at which I have arrived, the starting-point for a fresh development.

Oscar Wilde, *De Profundis*

We have been concentrating on the disruptive effects of danger, examining the temporary and persistent changes in personality functioning that prevent the individual from coping adequately with life stresses. But sometimes a stressful episode brings about a *positive* change, making the individual more responsive to relevant warnings, causing him to plan realistically for future emergencies, and even helping him to develop greater emotional control in dealing with similar dangers. And, as Oscar Wilde suggests in his autobiographical essay, written when he was in prison, a man is inclined to find in his suffering some meaning that enables him to feel he can correct the weaknesses that led to his misery. In this chapter we shall examine the conditions under which experiences of threat and danger lead to

Janis, I. L. Adaptive personality changes resulting from stressful episodes. In I. L. Janis, G. Mahl, J. Kagan, and R. R. Holt, *Personality: Dynamics, development, and assessment* (Part I): *Stress and frustration.* New York: Harcourt, Brace, and World, 1969. Copyright © 1969 by Harcourt Brace Jovanovich, Inc. Reprinted and reproduced by permission of the publisher.

adaptive changes that enable a person to cope more effectively with stress.

EMOTIONAL ADAPTATION IN SPORTS PARACHUTISTS

Suggestive evidence concerning adaptive changes comes from certain observations made by Epstein and Fenz (1965) in their research on sports parachutists. These investigators compared a group of highly experienced sports parachutists, all of whom had made more than 100 jumps, with relatively inexperienced men who had made from one to five jumps. They found marked differences in emotional reactions, which suggest that with increased experience the men became *de*sensitized; that is, after making a large number of jumps the men showed only a mild emotional reaction, in contrast to the intense emotional reaction they may have had earlier in the series. This type of change with increased exposure to a threat situation is referred to as *emotional adaptation*.

A special questionnaire was given to both the experienced and the inexperienced men immediately after they completed a jump. Each man was asked to rate the strength of his fear at 14 different time points leading up to the completion of his jump; he was told to give a rating of 10 to the point of strongest feelings of fear and a rating of 1 to the point of weakest feelings. As shown in Figure 8.1, the inexperienced jumpers reported becoming more and more fearful as the time for their next jump approached. Fear apparently reaches its maximum when the novice jumper, aloft in the airplane, receives the "ready" signal. He then goes out the open door onto the step above the wheel to wait for the final signal to jump. Once outside the plane, the man has reached the point of no return; at this crucial moment, fear begins to decrease. It continues to decrease during the free fall, which is actually the time of greatest danger. The investigators interpret these findings as indicating that maximum fear usually occurs when the novice realizes he is about to commit himself irrevocably to the dangerous action: As soon as the final decision is made, fear declines.

A quite different type of curve was obtained from experienced parachutists; this curve is also shown in Figure 8.1. The curve for the experienced jumpers shows the highest level of fear on the morning of the jump. Afterward the amount of fear decreases steadily up to the point where the final hazardous action occurs (the free fall before the parachute opens). It is only after this point of greatest

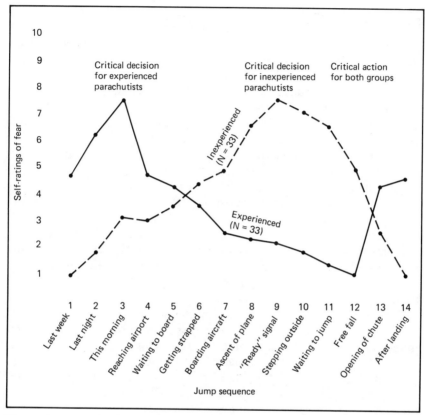

Figure 8.1 Parachutists' self-ratings of fear experienced before, during, and after a jump. Source: Adapted from Epstein & Fonz, 1965.

danger has passed that the experienced jumpers show an increase in fear.

As descriptive terms, "desensitization" and "emotional adaptation" can be applied to the lessening of fear at the airport and in the airplane, when the men are exposed to the series of threat cues that regularly precede the onset of actual danger. But the fact that they show a rise in fear after the danger is over suggests that this change in their fear reaction involves a process of active emotional control or defense, over and beyond any simple extinction or deconditioning that might result from repeated exposures to the conditioned stimuli.

The data shown in Figure 8.1 cannot be regarded as unequivocal evidence of the effects of increased exposure to the danger situation, since the two groups being compared were self-selected. Only a small proportion of novices decided to continue training to the point where they became experienced parachutists; thus this self-selected group might differ in important personality characteristics from the inexperienced men. Nevertheless, the findings are consistent with other evidence that also points to a striking diminution of fear evoked by threat cues as the men progress through the later stages of training. For example, trainers and other observers at sports parachuting centers report that experienced jumpers generally look forward to the jump each day and feel exhilarated, confident, and keyed up for action as the time for each jump approaches. At the beginning of their training these same men had shown the characteristic pattern of increasing fear before their next jump, as well as considerable conflict about wanting to avoid the danger but not wanting to be cowardly.

It seems most probable, therefore, that desensitization and highly discriminatory fear reactions occur among parachutists as a result of repeated exposure to the frightening situation of jumping from a moving airplane—provided, of course, that they continue to survive each jump unscathed. The beginners react strongly to the suspense and uncertainties of the approaching dangerous event. But evidently they gain confidence after a series of successful jumps and become much less emotionally aroused during the waiting period before each scheduled jump. The same type of emotional adaptation or habituation may occur among airplane pilots, scuba divers, professional skiers, mountain guides, and others who face repeated risks while undergoing training for highly dangerous occupations.

EMOTIONAL ADAPTATION IN
COMBAT SOLDIERS

Research during World War II showed that when infantrymen first entered the front lines they usually failed to discriminate between dangerous and nondangerous explosions; they took cover whenever they heard any projectile. They gradually learned to discriminate, eventually taking cover only in response to sounds emitted by projectiles approaching close by (Janis, 1949). Similarly, combat troops learned to discriminate among enemy weapons. For example, they gradually became less afraid of air attacks and more afraid of weapons that had greater potential for inflicting casualties, such as the German 88-millimeter artillery gun.

These wartime observations, like those made of the sports parachutists, indicate that an adaptive process of learning to make discriminations can go on during a period of repeated exposures to a hazardous environment. This process seems to have a dual effect: It decreases the person's fear reactions to exaggerated sources of apparent threat, and it increases his reactions to sources of real danger that he had formerly underestimated. "Green" troops often entered battle with considerable bravado and cockiness, carelessly disregarding the safety precautions they had been taught; their complacency disappeared when they had their "baptism by fire." After becoming seasoned combat men, they made far fewer errors of certain types (Smith, 1949). For example, they were less likely to huddle in groups when the enemy opened fire.

As the men in combat became increasingly responsive to real threats and less fearful of startling sights or sounds that could safely be disregarded, their judgments and actions became more appropriate in the face of danger. Insofar as these acquired discriminations increased the men's chances of survival, they are regarded as adaptive changes in behavior. . . .

EXPERIMENTS ON PREPARATORY COMMUNICATIONS

We have noted that exposure to actual danger can have favorable effects by building up adaptive discriminations and increasing the need for social reassurance. Exposure to warning communications can also initiate an adaptive learning process that enables the person to respond more effectively to subsequent stressful events. Studies of this process are important to understanding the psychology of stress and may lead to valuable practical applications in preventing emotional disturbances. Government agencies and national health organizations, including those in the mental health field, issue a constant stream of warning messages and recommendations to the public via news releases, magazine articles, pamphlets, movies, radio talks, and television programs. These messages in the mass media are "preparatory communications" in that they are intended to prepare people in advance to resist the adverse effects of a variety of stressful events, including illness, accidents, bereavement, economic loss, job dislocation, and divorce. The object of such preparation is to reduce the incidence of preventable emotional disturbance. Similar preparatory messages are often given in a more personal way by men and women in professional roles—attorneys, clergymen, physicians, social workers, teachers, employee counselors, and others—when they help their clients prepare for future adversity.

What makes preparatory communications successful? Studies indicate that a preparatory message can dampen the emotional impact of a subsequent threatening event if it correctly predicts the event, provided that it does not make the potential danger appear to be so overwhelming that nothing can be done to avert or minimize it. In one such study, Janis, Lumsdaine, and Gladstone (1951) investigated the way the impact of a major "bad news" event was modified by preparatory communications given several months in advance. The experiment was started in June 1949, at a time when the United States had a monopoly on atomic weapons. High school students were presented with tape recordings of radio talks that discussed the Soviet Union's ability to produce an atomic bomb in the near future. Three months later, when President Truman unexpectedly announced that Russia had succeeded in producing its first atomic bomb, the same students were given a follow-up questionnaire to assess their emotional reactions and attitude changes.

The findings indicated that the preparatory communication reduced the psychological impact of the bad news event. The students in the control group had not received the advance warning. Following President Truman's announcement, they were much more likely than the forewarned students to believe that Russia would soon have a large supply of A-bombs and that within a few years Russia would launch a nuclear war against the United States. The unwarned students also reported feeling more worried about the possibility that their own city might be destroyed by an atomic bomb than did those who were warned. Thus, the advance warnings tended to prevent pessimism and apprehensiveness in response to the dramatic piece of bad news. These findings indicate that an advance warning of an unfavorable event can have a significant dampening effect even for a relatively nonpersonal type of threatening news involving national security.

The findings from this experiment support the general hypothesis that the intensity of fear evoked by a stressful event can be reduced by prior exposure to a preparatory communication that predicts the event. Further support for this hypothesis comes from a number of laboratory investigations of human reactions to experimentally induced stress. For example, an outstanding series of experiments by Lazarus and his co-workers (1962, 1964, 1966) shows that advance information can significantly reduce the emotional impact of distressing perceptions of bodily damage. In these experiments male college students were shown an anthropological film of a primitive society's puberty rite, during which young boys had to undergo a crude type of circumcision. The stress reactions of the audience as they saw the color film sequence depicting the mutilation of the boys' genital organs were measured by self-ratings of their mood as well as by psychophysiological measures of heart rate and galvanic skin reactions. In one of the experiments Lazarus and Alfert (1964) found that much less fear was aroused when a commentary was given to the students before they saw the distressing scenes. This preparatory communication informed them that the procedure would appear to be very painful but that it was not actually disturbing to the young boys who experienced it in this particular cultural setting.

In such experiments the effectiveness of the forewarnings might involve more than merely changing the subjects' psychological set. The very warning that one will soon be confronted by horrifying sights functions as a mild source of stress, touching off a low or moderate level of fear and motivating the person to seek new forms of reassurance that might reduce fear.

STRESS TOLERANCE IN SURGICAL PATIENTS

A series of studies on surgical patients (Janis, 1958) highlights the crucial importance of developing relevant reassurances for coping with stress. Since major surgery involves pain, a profound threat to bodily integrity, and a variety of frustrations, a great deal can be learned on the surgical wards of a general hospital about the processes of normal adjustment to severe stress.

The investigations were designed to help answer some basic questions pertinent to a general theory of stress tolerance: What is the relationship between the intensity of the patient's fear before surgery and the way he reacts to the pains and discomforts of the postoperative period? Is the popular belief true that the more anxious a person becomes when confronted with the threat of impending danger, the poorer he will adjust to the stress when he encounters it? Is a patient better able to cope with postoperative stress if he has been given realistic information beforehand on what is likely to happen?

With these questions in mind, the author carried out a study on the surgical ward of a large community hospital. As a first step, interviews were given to 23 typical patients before and after they underwent major surgery. Each of the patients was facing a highly dangerous and painful operation, such as removal of a lung or part of the stomach. Hospital records, including the physicians' and nurses' daily notes on each patient's behavior, were used to supplement the intensive interviews.

Three Degrees of Anticipatory Fear

Three general patterns of emotional response were observed:

1. High anticipatory fear. These patients were constantly worried and jittery about suffering acute pain, being mutilated by the surgeon, or dying on the operating table. Openly admitting their *extreme feelings of vulnerability*, they tried to postpone the operation, were unable to sleep without sedation, and continually sought reassurances, even though these gave only momentary relief. After the operation they were *much more likely than others to be anxiety-ridden*. They had stormy emotional outbursts and shrank back in fright when the time came for routine postoperative treatments. Their excessive fears of bodily damage appeared to be based on a chronic sense of personal vulnerability.

2. Moderate anticipatory fear. These patients were occasionally worried and tense about specific features of the impending operation, such as the anesthesia. They asked for and received realistic information about what was going to happen to them from the hospital staff. They were able to be reassured, to engage in distracting activities, and to remain outwardly calm during most, though not every minute, of the day before the operation. They felt *somewhat vulnerable*, but their concerns were focused on realistic threats. After the operation they were *much less likely than others to display any emotional disturbance*. They consistently showed high morale and good cooperation with the hospital staff, even when asked to submit to uncomfortable drainage tubes, injections, and other disagreeable postoperative treatments.

3. Low anticipatory fear. These patients were constantly cheerful and optimistic about the impending operation. They denied feeling worried, slept well, and were able to read, listen to the radio, and socialize without any observable signs of emotional tension. They appeared to have unrealistic expectations of *almost complete invulnerability*. After the operation, however, they became acutely preoccupied with their vulnerability and were *more likely than others to display anger and resentment toward the staff*. Most of them complained bitterly about being mistreated and sometimes became so negativistic that they tried to refuse even routine postoperative treatments.

Anticipatory Fear and Postoperative Adjustment

The main hypotheses suggested by this series of intensive case studies were supported by a second study, a questionnaire survey conducted among more than 150 male college students who had recently undergone surgical operations. Several measures were used as indicators of each patient's postoperative adjustment. The measures included feelings of anger, complaints against the hospital staff, and current emotional disturbance when recalling the operation. Each of these indicators was examined in relation to what the patient had reported about his fear level before surgery. In each instance a curvilinear relation was found, as shown in Figure 8.2. The essential feature of this relation is the location of the peak of the curve somewhere in the middle of the fear continuum, rather than at one end or the other.

This outcome clearly contradicts the popular assumption that placid people—those who are least fearful about an impending ordeal—will prove to be less disturbed than others by subsequent stress. One of the main implications of these findings from the surgical studies is this: Whenever people are exposed to severe stress,

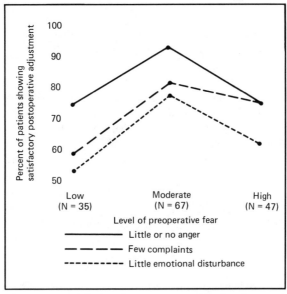

Figure 8.2 Relation between preoperative fear and postoperative adjustment. Source: Adapted from Janis, 1958, 1968

those who had been most calm and most confident about their invulnerability at the outset will tend to become much more upset than those who had been part-time worriers beforehand.

Apparently, a moderate amount of anticipatory fear about realistic threats is necessary for the development of effective inner defenses for coping with subsequent danger and deprivation. The patients who were somewhat fearful before the operation mentally rehearsed various unpleasant occurrences they thought were in store for them. They were motivated to seek and take account of realistic information about the experiences they would be likely to undergo from the time they would awaken from the anesthesia to the end of the period of convalescence. Seldom caught by surprise, these patients felt relatively secure as events proceeded just about as they had expected. Not only were they highly responsive to authoritative reassurances from the hospital staff, but also they could reassure themselves at moments when their fears were strongly aroused. In their postoperative interviews such patients frequently reported instances of self-reassurance; for example, "I knew there might be some bad pains, so when my side started to ache I told myself that this didn't mean anything had gone wrong."

Those who displayed excessively high anxiety before the operation appeared to benefit relatively little from preliminary mental rehearsals of the dangers. In the intensive interviews conducted both before and after the operation they revealed that they felt highly vulnerable to bodily damage and were unable to develop effective inner defenses for coping with the threat. Most of these patients were found to have a history of neurotic disorder, including past episodes of anxiety attacks. Their postoperative emotional reactions can be regarded as a continuation of their long-standing neuroses and not just a response to the external dangers of surgery.

The patients who were relatively free from anticipatory fears before the operation seem to have remained emotionally calm only by denying or minimizing the possibility of danger and suffering. As soon as the inescapable pains and harassments of normal recovery from a major surgical operation began to plague them, they could no longer maintain their expectations of personal invulnerability and became upset.

As an illustrative example, let us consider the reactions of a 21-year-old woman who had earlier undergone an appendectomy. At that time she had been given realistic information by her physician. Before the operation she had been moderately worried and occasionally asked the nurses for something to calm her nerves, but she

showed excellent emotional adjustment throughout her conva-
lescence. About two years later she came to the same hospital for
another abdominal operation, the removal of her gall bladder. In the
preoperative interview with the investigator she reported that her
physician had assured her that "there's really nothing to it; it's a
less serious operation than the previous one." This time she remained
wholly unconcerned about the operation beforehand, apparently
anticipating very little or no suffering. Afterward, experiencing the
usual pains and deprivations following a gall bladder operation, she
became markedly upset, negativistic, and resentful toward the
nursing staff.

   Chronic personality predispositions do not seem to account fully
for this patient's reactions, since she was capable of showing an
entirely different pattern of emotional response, as she had on a
previous occasion. The patient's adjustment to the fear-producing
situation appeared to be influenced mainly by the insufficient and
misleading preparatory communications she was given before the
second operation. Since nothing distressing was supposed to happen,
she assumed that the hospital staff must be to blame for her post-
operative suffering.

   In some persons the lack of preoperative fear may be a manifestation of a type of neurotic predisposition that involves using
extreme defenses of denial and projection of blame in order to ward
off anxiety; probably nothing short of intensive psychotherapy could
change this characteristic personality tendency. Most of the patients
who showed little or no fear, however, seemed to be clinically normal
personalities. Like the patient just described, they never received the
type of realistic information that would induce them to face up to
the distressing implications of the impending surgery. If they are
given clear-cut information by a trustworthy authority, such persons
are capable of modifying their defensive attitude and becoming
appropriately worried about what they now realize is in store for
them. But if they are not given adequate preparatory warnings about
postoperative pain and suffering, they will cling to their expectations
of personal invulnerability as long as possible, until suffering itself
teaches them that they are not invulnerable after all.

The Role of Information

As we have just seen, the patients who did not worry beforehand
appeared to be much less able to cope with the stresses of surgery
than those who had been moderately worried. When the two types

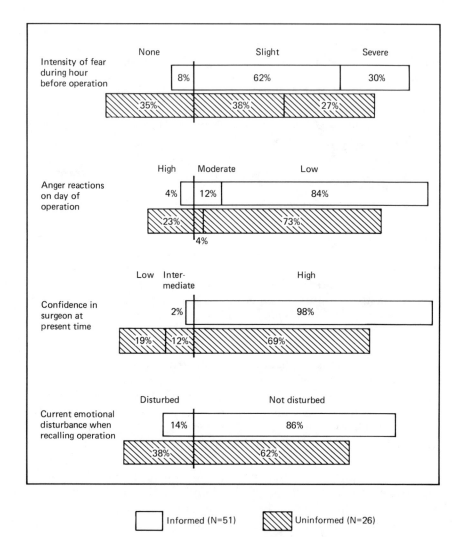

Figure 8.3 Preoperative fear and postoperative adjustment in informed and uniformed surgical patients. Source: Adapted from Janis, 1958, 1968.

of patients were compared on a variety of background factors, the only significant difference turned out to be in the amount of advance information they had obtained. A careful check showed no significant differences as to type of operation, amount of pain, degree of incapacitation, type of anesthesia, or prognosis; nor were there differences between the groups as to age, education, sex, ethnic origin, or the number of prior hospitalizations.

But the two groups did differ on one important factor: the amount of prior information. Patients in the low-fear group had little idea of what to expect, whereas those in the moderate-fear group had been far better informed.

The survey of male surgery cases provided systematic evidence on this point. Illustrative results are shown in Figure 8.3, which compares preoperative fear and postoperative adjustment in the two groups of men who had undergone major surgical operations: 51 men who reported having been informed beforehand about the specific unpleasant experiences in store for them and 26 men who reported having been completely uninformed. The two groups differed in the following ways: (1) the well-informed men were more likely to report that they had felt worried or fearful before the operation; and (2) the well-informed men were less likely to report that they had become angry or emotionally upset during the postoperative period of convalescence.

Since these correlational data are based on retrospective reports, they cannot be accepted as conclusive evidence. Nevertheless, they point in the same direction as the observations made in the intensive case studies, suggesting the following hypothesis: If no authoritative warning communications are given and if other circumstances are such that fear is not aroused beforehand, the normal person will lack the motivation to build up effective inner preparation before the onset of the danger, and he will thus have relatively low tolerance for stress when the crisis is actually at hand.

The "Work of Worrying"

The observations and findings from the surgery research suggested a concept of the "work of worrying," a theoretical construct that emphasizes the potentially positive value of anticipatory fear (Janis, 1958). The "work of worrying" might involve psychological processes similar to the "work of mourning" (Freud, 1917), but there are likely to be some important differences. Freud postulated that the work of mourning begins *after* a blow, such as the death of a loved one, has struck; the work of worrying is assumed to begin *beforehand*, as soon as the individual becomes aware of signs of *impending danger* that might affect him personally.

When the Work of Worrying Is Incomplete

Sometimes an endangered person remains quite unworried and then finds himself unexpectedly confronted with actual danger stimuli.

This is evidently what happens to many surgical patients who are given no explicit warning information that induces them to face up to what is in store for them. They anticipate little or no pain or suffering until the severe stresses of the postoperative period are encountered. Then they are unable to reassure themselves and no longer trust the authorities whose protection they had expected. The patient's failure to worry about the operation in advance seems to set the stage for intense feelings of helplessness as well as resentment toward the members of the staff who, until the moment of crisis, had been counted on to take good care of them, just as good parents would do.

At moments of grave crisis most people are likely to blame the doctors or other authorities for unexpected stress. Many observations of surgical patients and of people exposed to comparable stress situations suggest the following sequence:

Absence of anticipatory fear

↓

Absence of mental rehearsal of the impending danger

↓

Feelings of helplessness when the danger materializes

↓

Increased expectations of vulnerability and disappointment in protective authorities

↓

Intense fear and anger

This sequence can be regarded as the major consequence of *failing to carry out the work of worrying*. Such failures are to be expected whenever a stressful event occurs under any of the following three conditions: (1) if the person is accustomed to suppressing anticipatory fear by means of denial defenses, by overoptimism, and by avoiding warnings that would stimulate the work of worrying; (2) if the stressful event is so sudden that it cannot be prepared for; and (3) if an adequate prior warning is not given, or if strong but false reassurances encourage the person to believe that he is invulnerable.

In order for the work of worrying to be complete, it seems that each source of stress must be anticipated and "worked through" in advance. This necessity is suggested by some outstanding instances of fright and rage observed in surgical patients who had displayed a moderate degree of anticipatory fear.

A young housewife, for example, had been somewhat worried before a lung operation and then, like most others in the moderately

fearful group, showed excellent cooperation and little emotional disturbance throughout the postoperative period—except for one brief crisis she had not expected. She knew in advance about the acute incision pains and other unpleasant aspects of the postoperative recovery treatments, since she had undergone a similar operation once before and had asked her physician many pertinent questions about the impending second operation. But on the first postoperative day a physician entered her room and told her she would have to swallow a drainage tube, which she had never heard about before. She became extremely upset, could not relax sufficiently to cooperate, and finally begged the physician to take the tube away and let her alone. During an interview the following day she reported that she began to have extremely unfavorable thoughts about the physician at the time he made the unexpected demand; she suspected that he was withholding information about the seriousness of her condition, that he was unnecessarily imposing a hideous form of treatment on her, and that he was carrying out the treatment "so badly it was practically killing me." At no other time during the long and painful convalescence following the removal of her lung did she have any such doubts about this physician or any other member of the hospital staff; nor did she at any other time display any form of overt resistance. Evidently this was the one stressful event she had not anticipated and for which she had not, therefore, carried out the work of worrying.

This episode might help to explain why other patients who are caught by surprise display so much fright, anger, and uncooperative behavior. Those calm, seemingly stoic patients who do practically none of the work of worrying beforehand would be likely to encounter the same type of disruptive episode many times over during each day of their convalescence.

Preparatory Communications as a Prerequisite for Constructive Worrying: Some Further Evidence

Other studies on the psychological effects of surgical operations, severe illness, community disasters, and combat dangers provide many bits of evidence that are consistent with the foregoing hypotheses derived from the study of surgical patients (Grinker et al., 1946; Cobb, Clark, McGuire, & Howe, 1954; Cramond & Aberd, 1954; Titchner, Zweling, Gottschalk, Levine, Silver, Cowett, Cohen, & Colbertson, 1957; Janis & Leventhal, 1965). Like the surgery research, these studies suggest that if a normal person is given accurate prior warning of impending pain and discomfort, together with sufficient reassurances so that fear does not mount to a very high level, he will be less likely to develop acute emotional disturbances than a person who is not warned.

We know that there are exceptions, of course, such as neurotic personalities who are hypersensitive to any threat cues. But this does not preclude the possibility that moderately fear-arousing information about impending dangers and deprivations will function as a kind of emotional inoculation, enabling normal persons to increase their tolerance for stress by developing coping mechanisms and effective defenses. This process is called emotional inoculation because it may be analogous to what happens when antibodies are induced by injections of mildly virulent viruses.

If these inferences are correct, we should find that a group of surgical patients given appropriate preparatory communications before their operations will show better adjustment to the stresses of the postoperative period than an equivalent group of patients given no special preparatory communications other than the information ordinarily available to any hospitalized patient.

This prediction was tested and confirmed in a carefully controlled field experiment with 97 adult surgical patients at the Massachusetts General Hospital (Egbert, Battit, Welch, & Bartlett, 1964). The patients, hospitalized for elective abdominal operations, were assigned at random to the experimental and control groups. The two groups were equated on the basis of age, sex, type of operation, and so forth. On the night before his operation each patient was visited by the anesthetist, who gave him routine information about the operation—its time and duration, the nature of the anesthesia, and the fact that he would awaken in the recovery room. The patients in the control group were told nothing more. Those in the experimental group were given four additional types of information intended to help them carry out the work of worrying and to provide some useful coping devices: (1) a description of postoperative pain—where they would feel it, how intense it would be, how long it was likely to last; (2) explicit reassurance that postoperative pain is a normal consequence of an abdominal operation; (3) advice to relax their abdominal muscles in order to reduce the pain, along with special instructions about how to shift from one side to the other without tensing muscles in the sensitive area; and (4) assurance that they would be given pain-killing medication if they could not otherwise achieve a tolerable level of comfort. The information contained in the preparatory communication was repeated to the patients in the experimental group by the anesthetist when he visited them following the operation. Neither the surgeons nor the ward nurses were told about this experiment, to make sure that the experimental (informed) and the control (uninformed) patients would receive equivalent treatment in all other respects.

What difference did the special information make? During the 5 days just after surgery, patients in the experimental group required only half as much sedation as did patients in the control group. Comparisons of the total amounts of morphine administered to the two groups of patients during the postoperative period are shown by the curves in Figure 8.4. On the day of the operation (day zero in the figure) both groups required about the same amount of narcotics, but on each of the next 5 postoperative days the experimental group required significantly less than the control group.

The investigators tried to rule out the possibility that the well-informed patients might be suffering in silence in order to "please the doctor." They arranged to have the interviews conducted on the first and second postoperative days by an anethetist whom the patients had never seen before. This independent observer was completely unaware of the type of treatment any of the patients had

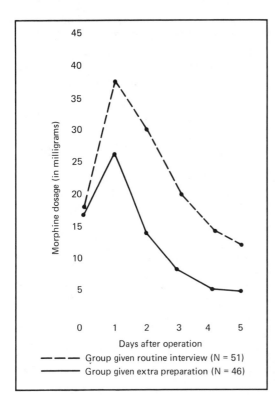

Figure 8.4 Postoperative narcotic treatment for two groups of surgical patients— those given a special preparatory communication and those given a routine interview. Source: Adapted from Egbert, Battit, Welch, & Bartlett, 1964.

received, and his "blind" ratings indicated that the patients in the experimental group were in better emotional and physical condition than the controls. Further evidence of the more rapid improvement of the well-informed patients is provided by data on the duration of hospitalization. Completely unaware of the experiment, the surgeons sent the well-informed patients home an average of 2.7 days earlier than the patients who had not been given the special preparatory communication. In line with the earlier correlational findings shown in Figure 8.3 the investigators also noted that the uninformed controls made many complaints to the staff, such as "Why didn't you tell me it was going to be like this?" Such complaints were rare in the experimental group.

Thus, the experiment provides some systematic evidence concerning the positive value of advance information about postoperative stress [including reassurances and authoritative recommendations about how to cope with it.] In this experiment the preoperative information was reiterated during the first few postoperative days, and this repetition may have contributed to the effectiveness of the preparatory communication. Conceivably, the postoperative reassurances alone might have been responsible for the outcome. There are other possible interpretations that will have to be checked in subsequent studies. It should be noted, however, that the results of this study show essentially the same positive outcome as ... similar controlled experiments on the effects of preparatory communications ... given to children and adults ... before surgery [see Chapter 13]. The studies point to one general conclusion: A person will be better able to tolerate suffering and deprivation if he [or she] worries about it beforehand rather than remaining free from anticipatory fear by maintaining expectations of personal invulnerability. This generalization, if confirmed by research in other stress situations, might turn out to hold true for many nonphysical setbacks and losses such as career failures, marital discord, and bereavement.

REFERENCES

Cobb, B. C., Clark, R. L., Jr., McGuire, C., & Howe, C. D. Patient-responsible delay of treatment of cancer: A social psychological study. *Cancer*, 1954, 7, 920–26.

Cramond, W., & Aberd, D. Psychological aspects of uterine disfunction. *Lancet*, 1954, 2, 1241–45.

Egbert, L., Battit, G., Welch, C., & Bartlett, M. Reduction of postoperative pain by encouragement and instruction of patients. *New England Journal of Medicine*, 1964, 270, 825–27.

Epstein, S., & Fenz, W. D. Steepness of approach and avoidance gradients in humans as a function of experience: Theory and experiment. *Journal of Experimental Psychology*, 1965, *70*, 1–12.

Freud, S. (1917) Mourning and melancholia. *Standard edition*, Vol. 14. London: Hogarth Press, 1957.

Grinker, R. R., Willerman, B., Bradley, A., & Fastovsky, A. A study of psychological predisposition to the development of operational fatigue, 1 and 2. *American Journal of Orthopsychiatry*, 1946, *16*, 191–214.

Janis, I. L. Problems related to the control of fear in combat. In S. Stouffer, A. A. Lumsdaine, R. Williams, M. B. Smith, I. L. Janis, S. A. Star, & L. Cottrell, Jr., *The American soldier.* Vol. 2. *Combat and its aftermath.* Princeton, N. J.: Princeton University Press, 1949. 192–214.

Janis, I. L. *Psychological stress.* New York: Wiley, 1958.

Janis, I. L. When fear is healthy. *Psychology Today*, 1968, *1*, 46–49, 60–61.

Janis, I. L., & Leventhal, H. Psychological aspects of physical illness and hospital care. In B. Wolman (Ed.), *Handbook of clinical psychology.* New York: McGraw-Hill, 1965.

Janis, I. L., Lumsdaine, A. A., & Gladstone, A. I. Effects of preparatory communications on reactions to a subsequent news event. *Public Opinion Quarterly*, 1951, *15*, 487–518.

Lazarus, R. S. *Psychological stress and the coping process.* New York: McGraw-Hill, 1966.

Lazarus, R. S., & Alfert, E. The short-circuiting of threat by experimentally altering cognitive appraisal. *Journal of Abnormal and Social Psychology*, 1964, *69*, 195–205.

Lazarus, R. S., Speisman, J. C., Mordkoff, A. M., & Davison, L. A. A laboratory study of psychological stress produced by a motion picture film. *Psychological Monographs*, 1962, *76*, 1–35.

Smith, M. B. Combat motivations among ground troops. In S. A. Stouffer, A. A. Lumsdaine, R. Williams, M. B. Smith, I. L. Janis, S. A. Star, & L. Cottrell, Jr., *The American soldier*, Vol. 2. *Combat and its aftermath.* Princeton, N.J.: Princeton University Press, 1949. Pp. 105–91.

Titchner, J., Zweling, I., Gottschalk, L., Levine, M., Silver, H., Cowett. A., Cohen, S., & Colbertson, W. Consequences of surgical illness and treatment: Interaction of emotions, personality and surgical illness, and treatment, convalescence. *American Medical Association Archives of Neurology and Psychiatry*, 1957, *77*, 623–634.

9

Coping with Decisional Conflict: An Analysis of How Stress Affects Decision-Making Suggests Interventions to Improve the Process (1976)

"How could I have been so stupid?" President John F. Kennedy asked after realizing how badly he had miscalculated when he approved the Bay of Pigs invasion. Every private citizen asks the same question each time he finds himself embroiled in a personal Bay of Pigs. Why do people so often fail to look into the available alternatives with care even when vital consequences are at stake? Under what conditions are they most likely to make a sound choice that they can live with? Under what conditions are they likely to do such a poor job of appraising the consequences that they head straight for a fiasco?

Recently psychologists have begun to obtain some answers to these questions by investigating the effects of conflict and stress on the quality of a decison-maker's search for and appraisal of alternative courses of action. People know from experience that making a vital decision is worrisome and can cause anxiety reactions, such as agitation, quick temper, sleeplessness, loss of appetite, and other psychosomatic symptoms. Studies of physiological concomitants of decisional conflict have found that there are marked changes in heart rate, finger-pulse amplitude, and galvanic skin response when a per-

Janis, I. L., & Mann, L. Coping with decisional conflict: An analysis of how stress affects decision-making suggests interventions to improve the process. *American Scientist*, 1976, *64*, 657–666. This paper is based on the authors' book, *Decision making: A psychological analysis of conflict, choice and commitment.* Free Press, 1977. Reprinted by permission.

son is required to make a difficult decision (Gerard 1967; Mann, Janis, and Chaplin 1969; Jones and Johnson 1973).

Because the arousal of stress and its implications for the process of decision-making have been neglected by most behavioral scientists, one of the major purposes of our recent work has been to fill this gap by describing the conditions under which psychological stress imposes limitations on the processes of decision-making. Our research has also focused on hypotheses that attempt to explain how and why stress can have functional or adaptive value. This article presents a brief summary of the analysis of decisional conflict that we have developed and tested for over a decade, based on propositions derived from the psychology of stress. We also describe several experiments that bear on derivations from our conflict theory and discuss some promising interventions to improve the quality of decision-making that the theory suggests.

DYNAMICS OF STRESS

Psychological stress arising from decisional conflict stems from at least two sources. First, the decision-maker is concerned about the material and social losses he might suffer from whichever course of action he chooses—including the costs of failing to live up to prior commitments. Second, he recognizes that his reputation and self-esteem as a competent decision-maker are at stake. The more severe the anticipated losses, the greater the stress.

We start with the assumption that the stress itself is frequently a major cause of errors in decision-making. This assumption does not deny the influence of other common causes, such as information overload and the limitations of human information-processing, group pressures, blinding prejudice, ignorance, organizational constraints, and bureaucratic politics (see Janis 1972, 1974; Simon 1976). We maintain, however, that a major reason for many ill-conceived and poorly implemented decisions has to do with the motivational consequences of decisional conflict, particularly attempts to ward off the stresses generated by agonizingly difficult choices.

Linked with the initial assumption is a set of postulates that describe five basic patterns of *coping* with a realistic challenge, each of which is associated with a specific set of antecedent conditions and a characteristic level of stress. These patterns were derived from an analysis of the research literature on how people react to emergency warnings and fear-arousing messages that urge protective action. The five coping patterns are:

1. *Unconflicted adherence*. The decision-maker complacently

decides to continue whatever he has been doing, ignoring information about the risk of losses.

2. *Unconflicted change* to a new course of action. The decision-maker uncritically adopts whichever new course of action is most salient or most strongly recommended to him.

3. *Defensive avoidance.* The decision-maker evades the conflict by procrastinating, shifting responsibility to someone else, or constructing wishful rationalizations and remaining selectively inattentive to corrective information.

4. *Hypervigilance.* The decision-maker searches frantically for a way out of the dilemma and impulsively seizes upon a hastily contrived solution that seems to promise immediate relief, overlooking the full range of consequences of his choice because of emotional excitement, repetitive thinking, and cognitive constriction (manifested by reduction in immediate memory span and simplistic ideas). In its most extreme form, hypervigilance is referred to as "panic."

5. *Vigilance.* The decision-maker searches painstakingly for relevant information, assimilates it in an unbiased manner, and appraises alternatives carefully before making a choice.

While the first two patterns are occasionally adaptive in saving time, effort, and emotional wear and tear, especially for routine or minor decisions, they often lead to defective decision-making if the person must make a vital choice. Similarly, defensive avoidance and hypervigilance may occasionally be adaptive but they generally reduce one's chances of averting serious losses. Consequently, we regard all four as defective patterns of decision-making. The fifth pattern, vigilance, although occasionally maladaptive if danger is imminent and a split-second response is required, generally leads to decisions of the best quality.

The coping patterns are determined by the presence or absence of three conditions: awareness of serious risks for whichever alternative is chosen (i.e. arousal of conflict), hope of finding a better alternative, and belief that there is adequate time to search and deliberate before a decision is required. Figure 9.1 shows the linkages between these conditions, the level of stress, and the coping pattern. The intensity of psychological stress is related to the coping pattern: extremely low stress and extremely intense stress are likely to give rise to defective patterns, while intermediate levels are more likely to be associated with vigilant information-processing. We assume, then, a curvilinear, non-monotonic relationship between magnitude of stress and quality of decision-making, like the relationship that has been described for emotional arousal and responsiveness to persuasive communications (Janis 1967; McGuire 1969).

It seems likely that the psychological processes that come into

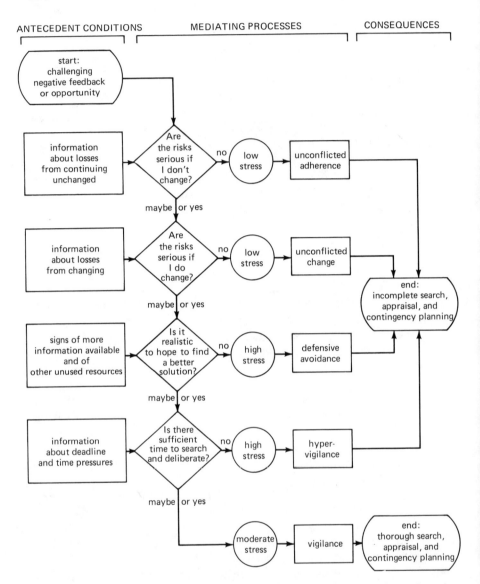

Figure 9.1 The conflict-theory model of decision-making postulates that the way we cope with resolving a difficult choice is determined by the presence or absence of 3 conditions: awareness of the risks involved, hope of finding a better solution, and the time available in which to make the decision. Source: Adapted from Janis and Mann, 1977.

play in emergency and health-oriented decisions are activated by the stress generated by any consequential decision that affects the decision-maker's welfare or that of his family or any organization on whose behalf he is functioning as a policy-maker. We assume that the same five patterns of dealing with the challenge are in the repertoire of every decision-maker, that the use of one pattern rather than another is determined by the same mediating psychological conditions, and that the five patterns lead to somewhat different behavioral consequences, which are summarized in Table 9.1. The columns of the table represent the major criteria that can be used to judge whether a decision made by a person or a group is of high quality with regard to the problem-solving procedures that lead up to the act of commitment. These criteria were extracted from the extensive literature on effective decision-making (Janis and Mann 1977). Although systematic data are not yet available on this point, it seems plausible to assume that "high quality" decisions—in the sense of satisfying these procedural criteria—have a better chance than others of attaining the decision-maker's objectives and of being adhered to in the long run.

What is unique about the model is the specification of conditions relating to conflict, hope, and time pressure that mediate distinctive coping patterns. We do not claim that the five patterns occur *only* as a result of the specified conditions. A habitual procrastinator, for example, may almost invariably approach any decision, large or small, in a defensive manner; a flexible person may display vigilance in response to most threats but become hypervigilant each time he reencounters a situation in which he had once been traumatized. Our claim is that the patterns are linked dependably with the conditions we have specified—a claim that has testable implications about environmental circumstances that generate vigilance and about deliberate interventions that could counteract the beliefs and perceptions responsible for defective coping patterns.

EXPERIMENTAL EVIDENCE

From the conflict model a number of predictions can be made concerning some of the crucial conditions that determine whether a decision-maker's information search will be cursory or thorough, whether his deliberations will be biased or unbiased, and whether his adherence to the decision will be short-lived or persistent. The model postulates, for example, that if the decision-maker is aware that there are serious risks for whatever courses of action are available, and if he

Table 9.1 Predecisional behavior characteristics of the five basic patterns of decision-making (from Janis and Mann, in press)

Pattern of Coping with Challenge	Thorough Canvassing of Alternatives	Thorough Canvassing of Objectives	Careful Evaluation of Consequences of (1) Current Policy	(2) New Policies	Thorough Search for Information	Unbiased Assimilation of New Information	Careful Reevaluation of Consequences	Thorough Planning for Implementation and Contingencies
Unconflicted adherence	-	-	-	-	-	+	-	-
Unconflicted change	-	-	+	-	-	+	-	-
Defensive avoidance	-	-	-	-	-	-	-	-
Hypervigilance	-	-	±	±	±	±	-	-
Vigilance	+	+	+	+	+	+	+	+

Note: + = the decision-maker meets the criterion to the best of his ability

        - = the decision-maker fails to meet the criterion

        ± = the decision-maker's performance fluctuates, sometimes meeting the criterion to the best of his ability and sometimes not

        All evaluative terms such as *thorough* and *unbiased* are to be understood as intrapersonal comparative assessments, relative to the person's performances under the most favorable conditions that enable him to display his cognitive capabilities to the best of his ability.

loses hope of finding a more satisfactory solution, he will attempt to escape the conflict by defensive avoidance.

An experiment to test this hypothesis was carried out with female students at the University of Melbourne, Australia (Mann, Janis, and Chaplin 1969). The women were told that the experiment dealt with the effect of unpleasant physiological stimulation on ability to carry out intellectual tasks. To create the conditions for conflict, subjects were given a choice between noxious taste or noise and were told that each could produce temporary side effects such as nausea, dizziness, headaches, and other disagreeable symptoms. To maintain hope of obtaining additional information that could lead to a better solution, the experimenter told one group of subjects that some estimates about the percentage of people suffering side effects from the different stimulations would be provided later on. In contrast, a second group was told that nothing was definitely known about the percentage of people suffering side effects from the two alternatives. Before and again after these statements the experimenter measured *bolstering* by obtaining ratings of the alternatives.

Bolstering, a prime mechanism of defensive avoidance, consists of magnifying the attractiveness of one of the alternatives and devaluing the other. It is measured by the amount of "spreading" of the ratings of the alternatives from the first to the final predecisional rating, computed according to the formula $(C_2 - N_2) - (C_1 - N_1)$, where C_1 and C_2 are the initial and final ratings of the alternative chosen, and N_1 and N_2 are the initial and final ratings of the alternative not chosen.

As predicted by our conflict theory, when subjects were led to believe that no additional information could be expected, they tended to bolster the alternatives they had originally preferred, evidenced by a spread in the attractiveness of the two alternatives. But when subjects expected more information, there was virtually no tendency to bolster—a finding that is also consistent with the conflict model, which specifies that vigilance will be the dominant coping pattern under these circumstances. This experiment not only bears on our theoretical assumptions about the conditions under which defensive avoidance rather than vigilance will be the dominant pattern but also put to the test a different theoretical position held by Festinger (1964) and his coworkers, which predicts that bolstering, which is a manifestation of dissonance reduction, will never occur before the decision-maker announces his choice to others. The results indicate that bolstering does occur before commitment if the conditions that foster defensive avoidance are present.

Another testable proposition that follows from the conflict-theory model is that people will display vigilant attention when they believe that (1) serious risks are associated with the key alternatives, (2) a satisfactory solution can be found, and (3) there is sufficient time in which to find it. An implication is that if these three conditions are met, decision-makers will be open-minded to both supportive and opposing messages, even if they are already committed to a choice. This implication can be formulated as a "vigilance-despite-commitment" hypothesis. It asserts that vigilance will be the dominant coping pattern after a person has committed himself to a decision if he is exposed to realistic warnings of serious risks entailed by the course of action he has chosen, provided that he believes there is still hope and time for finding an improved way of implementing the decision.

Evidence consistent with this hypothesis has been provided by Janis and Rausch (1970) in a field study of draft resisters at Yale University in the spring of 1968, carried out at a time of growing civil disobedience throughout the United States among students who were opposed to being drafted to fight in Vietnam. . . . Among those who had signed the pledge, there was a relatively high level of interest in both supportive and nonsupportive information, a pattern indicative of vigilance. This finding, consistent with conflict theory, calls into question the well-known selective-exposure hypothesis, which maintains that after making a decision people are motivated primarily to try to reduce cognitive inconsistency, or dissonance, by seeking information that supports their choice and avoiding discrepant, nonsupportive material.

Among the three groups of nonsigners, Janis and Rausch also found information preferences generally consistent with the conflict model and inconsistent with the selective-exposure hypothesis. For example, the unchallenged men, who were firm in their decision not to sign, showed somewhat less interest in either the pro- or anti-pledge articles than the other groups, with no tendency to avoid pro-pledge information. . . .

A major postulate of the conflict model is that each of the five coping patterns is associated with a characteristic mode of information-processing that governs the type and amount of information the decision-maker will prefer. Consistent with the conclusions of many recent investigators who dispute the universality of a selective-exposure tendency, the conflict model suggests that it is futile to look for any single type of information preference that will be dominant in a wide variety of circumstances. Rather, the model points to a number of markedly different tendencies that become dominant under the specific conditions identified with the coping patterns. Thus we expect that unconflicted adherence and unconflicted change will be associated with relatively low interest in pro and con information, with little selective bias. We expect selective exposure to information when defensive avoidance is the prevailing coping pattern under circumstances in which the decision-maker can neither procrastinate nor shift responsibility to someone else. Further, we expect very high, indiscriminate interest in both relevant and irrelevant, supportive and nonsupportive information, when hypervigilance is the dominant pattern. Open-minded and discriminating search for information is to be expected only when the vigilance pattern prevails.

Because so little research on the question of information preferences has been conducted within the framework of the conflict model, little evidence is at hand for testing the exact conditions under which the dominant tendency will be selective exposure motivated by defensive avoidance rather than open-minded vigilance. The Janis and Rausch field study marks an initial step in this direction, but the evidence is correlational and therefore open to other interpretations. Obviously, there are other motivations, such as a tendency to prefer reading unfamiliar ideas rather than familiar ones or a desire to be regarded as a fair and judicious person, that might enter into the decision to expose oneself to messages that run counter to one's own stand. These and related tendencies have been repeatedly mentioned in the literature on selective exposure; they could also be operating among the college students in the Janis and Rausch study and might limit the generality of the findings to college-educated persons who have acquired similar dispositions. To test our assumptions about vigilance definitely a different type of study will have to be carried out, in which subjects are exposed to experimental conditions affecting level of conflict, beliefs about the prospect of finding a satisfactory solution, and perceptions of deadlines.

Although the theory has not yet been adequately tested, a review by Janis and Mann (1977) of the social-psychological studies bearing on openness to nonsupportive information indicates that the findings generally are consistent with the conflict-theory analysis of vigilance. For the present, we conclude that the theory has heuristic value, in that it calls attention to some neglected research problems that should be systematically explored if the field is to advance beyond its current fragmented state. We believe that the conflict model provides a coherent theoretical framework for organizing the interacting variables—such as certainty, curiosity, and expected utility—that affect preferences for being exposed to supportive or nonsupportive information.

THE CONTINUITY PRINCIPLE

According to conflict theory the factors that affect the decision-maker's thinking, including the degree of bias in his search for and evaluation of new information, operate before as well as after a commitment has been made. The two research studies just discussed bear on two major inferences that disagree with the claims of an alternative theoretical position, which maintains that decision-makers are objective before making a decision but become biased as soon as they commit themselves to a choice and tend to remain so until they encounter undeniably disconfirming evidence. The research we have cited suggests that (1) when the conditions that foster defensive avoidance are present, decision-makers will distort evaluations of alternatives *before* (as well as after) they commit themselves to a choice (Mann, Janis, and Chaplin 1969) and (2) when the conditions that favor vigilance are present, decision-makers will be open-minded in exposing themselves to information *after* (as well as before) they make a choice (Janis and Rausch 1970). (For detailed reviews and critical appraisals of other studies bearing on these two propositions, including a few that purport to be disconfirmatory, see Janis and Mann 1977.)

A further implication of the principle of continuity between pre- and postdecisional processes is that residues of conflicts unresolved prior to commitment will continue to exert an effect after commitment. An example may be found in the phenomenon of postdecisional regret, which poses a problem of great interest to social-psychological theorists. According to conflict theory, many of the fluctuations in attractiveness of alternatives that occur after commitment are a sign that the person is coping with residual conflict, rather than evidence of a general tendency toward spontaneous regret after making a decision.

Walster (1964), in a well-known field experiment, reported spontaneous regret among army draftees, each of whom was required to make a vital decision about the job he would be assigned for his two years of military service. The draftees were given a choice between two unattractive job alternatives. Dissonance theorists interpreted fluctuations in attractiveness of the alternatives following the decision as evidence of a brief period of spontaneous regret essential for subsequent dissonance reduction. We offer a different interpretation for the phenomenon. In Walster's study all the conditions were present that make for hypervigilance: the recruits had to make a difficult choice with serious risks attendant on both alternatives; many may have had hope of finding a better solution if they had had a few days to obtain information from others at their military base, but the experimenter allowed them only a few minutes to scrutinize the alternatives before making a choice. Accordingly we find it plausible to interpret Walster's findings as evidence of a hypervigilant reaction, manifested in the form of vacillation that persisted for an hour or so after the premature deadline for the decision was imposed.

This example illustrates how the conflict model can provide alternative explanations for findings that appear puzzling or inconsistent. We also see the model as pointing to testable hypotheses about the conditions under which a person's motivation to reduce conflict will prevail over other social motives, such as the desire to make attributions that justify one's actions (Bem 1972), to reduce inconsistency between cognitive elements (Festinger 1957, 1964), and to reassert freedom of choice (which Brehm, 1966, and Wicklund, 1974, refer to as *reactance*). An example of work in this category is the field experiment by Mann and Dashiell (1975) on the reactions of young men who participated in the 1969 draft lottery. According to conflict theory, the men who drew low numbers in the lottery should have become less attracted toward plans for the following year (such as graduate school or travel) that entailed the high risk of being drafted and accordingly were associated with intense stress. Reactance theory, on the other hand, predicts that when important career decisions are at stake, the alternatives that are no longer available (in this case, because of a marked increase in the threat of being drafted) should become more attractive. Mann and Dashiell found that while there was some evidence of reactance motivation immediately after the draft lottery, the motivation to reduce conflict by derogating the threatened alternatives, as predicted by conflict theory, was more strongly manifested when ratings were obtained ten days later.

INTERVENTIONS TO IMPROVE DECISON-MAKING

One of the values of the conflict model is that it suggests a number of ways counselors could help their clients make more vigilant decisions. For example, a counselor might prevent hypervigilance by correcting gross underestimates of the time remaining for search and deliberation before a momentous decision is required. Confirmatory evidence for such prescriptive hypotheses, while not definitive, would add support to the theory, whereas failure to confirm them would sharply bring into question its heuristic value.

The defective information search and faulty information-processing caused by defensive avoidance have been observed in a variety of dilemmas, including health, marital, and career decisions (Janis and Mann 1977), and we are led to expect that it will be the most difficult pattern to prevent. Advisers may be able to counteract unconflicted adherence, unconflicted change, and hypervigilance by raising questions, presenting corrective information about the risks and costs involved, and giving realistic reassurances about deadlines. But corrective information and explicit reassurances are likely to fail as an antidote to defensive avoidance because the decision-maker's motivation to ward off distressing conflict makes him highly resistant to the influence of factual information. The combination of conflict and pessimism about finding an adequate solution leads to the all-too-human tendency to seek escape via wishful thinking.

Defensive avoidance may take any of three distinct forms: procrastination, based on the wishful belief that nothing will be lost by putting off the decision indefinitely; shifting responsibility, or "buck-passing," based on the wishful belief that nothing will be lost by foisting the decision onto someone else; and bolstering, based on wishful distortions of the gains and losses to be expected from adopting the least objectionable course of action. The special conditions that foster the first two forms are governed by cues as to whether the decision can be postponed at no great cost (e.g. absence of a deadline) and whether someone else is willing and able to take responsibility. When neither of these low-effort types of avoidance is available, bolstering, the classic mode of defensive avoidance, becomes the dominant coping pattern. Bolstering includes distorting, rationalizing, and denying in such a way as to play up the merits of the chosen alternative.

We have developed some new procedures to reduce defensiveness, all of which are based on the assumption that when defensive avoidance in any of its three forms is the dominant pattern, the person will actively resist new information about risks in an effort to avoid reactivating the psychological stress aroused by the conflict. Reed and Janis (1974) developed an "awareness-of-rationalizations" technique for use in antismoking clinics that helps to undermine some of the main rationalizations used to bolster the decision to continue smoking. The technique, which is designed to make the heavy smoker more responsive to challenging information that he or she typically discounts, was tested in a field experiment at the Yale Smokers' Clinic on a sample of 74 men and women who wanted to cut down on cigarette consumption. Half the subjects were randomly assigned to the experimental group that was given the awareness-of-rationalizations procedure, while the other half received a control treatment, which consisted only of films and a lecture.

The counselor's introduction to the awareness-of-rationalizations procedure stressed the importance of "honest exploration and frank acknowledgment of basic, deep-down thoughts and feelings" about giving up smoking. The interviewer then presented the subject with a list of eight statements (referred to as "excuses") and asked him if he was aware of any personal tendencies to use one of the excuses. The list consisted of typical rationalizations made by heavy smokers (e.g. "It hasn't really been proved that cigarette smoking is a cause of lung cancer"; "If I stop smoking I will gain too much weight"). After that the subject was given a recorded lecture that refuted the eight rationalizations, followed by two dramatic antismoking films, and then reactions were measured. The same lecture and films were presented to the control group. Reed and Janis found that subjects who had received the awareness-of-rationalizations treatment expressed greater feelings of susceptibility to lung cancer and emphysema, a stronger belief in the harmfulness of smoking, and a more complete endorsement of the antismoking films.

Follow-up interviews 2–3 months later revealed that, so far as the reported amount of smoking was concerned, the treatment had a significant effect when given by one psychologist but not by the other. Hence the technique cannot be regarded as an adequate cure for smoking. But the procedure of inducing a decision-maker to acknowledge and explore his own tendencies to rationalize appears to have considerable promise for reducing resistance to realistic warning messages. It has much in common with two other successful cognitive confrontation techniques used to undermine defensive attitudes that bolster social prejudices—Katz, Sarnoff, and McClintock's (1956) insight technique and Rokeach's (1971) awareness of inconsistency between values and actions.

Another type of intervention for overcoming defensive avoidance is a psychodramatic technique known as "emotional role-playing" (Janis and Mann 1965; Mann and Janis 1968). In our initial laboratory experiments, we asked heavy smokers to play the role of a lung-cancer patient who receives bad news from a physician. We soon found that this disquieting psychodramatic experience could be so realistic that heavy smokers would, for the first time, acknowledge their personal vulnerability to the threat of lung disease. The typical cognitive defense, "It can't happen to me," can be undermined by this technique. Sufficient research has been done on emotional role-playing in antismoking clinics to show that it is capable of producing long-term changes in attitudes of personal vulnerability and in cigarette consumption among heavy smokers (Janis and Mann 1977). Additional studies suggest that the technique may prove effective for other types of decisions as well—for example, inducing heavy drinkers to stop drinking (Toomey 1972) and evoking student support for changes in university policy to meet the needs of disabled students (Clore and McMillan 1970). Modifications of the technique are now being explored as interventions for a variety of other types of decisions, including policy decisions by executives.

The level of emotion aroused by role-playing may be a crucial determinant of its effectiveness. Sufficient anxiety must be generated to break through the defensive facade and motivate fresh concern about the decision to continue the habit; too much stress, however, could trigger defensive avoidance or hypervigilant panic (see Janis 1971, pp. 138–44).

FOSTERING VIGILANCE

Several new intervention procedures have been developed that attempt to bring about the conditions necessary for the vigilant coping pattern. The "balance-sheet" procedure is a predecisional exercise that requires a decision-maker to confront and answer questions about potential risks and gains he had not previously contemplated. Without a systematic procedure, even the most alert and well-motivated person may overlook vital aspects of the alternatives, remaining unaware of some of the losses that will ensue from the preferred course and maintaining false expectations about potential gains.

In an earlier analysis of decision-making processes (Janis 1959), a balance sheet of incentives was proposed to take account of both the cognitive and the motivational aspects of planning for future action. It was intended to be broadly applicable to all important decisions—both professional and personal. The balance sheet serves as a descriptive schema and as a source of prescriptive hypotheses to supplement the conflict model of coping patterns. We find it especially valuable for analyzing how thoroughly a decision-maker explores the alternatives open to him and appraises the consequences to be expected (Janis and Mann 1977). Some of the main assumptions of the balance-sheet schema are the same as those of various additive gain-loss models suggested by many other behavioral scientists, who assume that a person will not decide to embark on a new course of action or to continue an old one unless he expects the gains to exceed the losses. The expected consequences for each alternative can be classified into the four main categories of the balance sheet: utilitarian gains or losses for self, utilitarian gains or losses for others, self-approval or disapproval, and approval or disapproval from others.

One of the main hypotheses that has grown out of our analysis of the balance sheets of persons making stressful decisions is that *the more errors of omission and commission in the decision-maker's balance sheet at the time he commits himself to a new course of action, the greater will be his vulnerability to negative feedback when he subsequently implements the decision* (Janis 1959, 1971; Janis and Mann 1977). We refer to this as the "defective balance-sheet" hypothesis. Errors of omission include overlooking the losses that will ensue from the chosen course; errors of commission include false expectations about improbable gains that are overoptimistically expected.

A balance-sheet procedure designed primarily to prevent errors of omission was developed in a series of pilot studies by Janis (1968) and was pretested with Yale College seniors several months before graduation, when they were trying to decide what they would do the following year. At the beginning of each interview, the respondent was given a series of questions that asked him to describe all the alternatives he was considering and to specify the pros and cons for each. Then the interviewer showed the subject a balance-sheet grid with empty cells, explained the meaning of each category, and helped him fill in the entries for the alternatives he had rated as most preferable. The subject was then asked to examine each cell in the balance sheet again, this time trying to think of considerations he had not yet mentioned. To focus on things that may have been overlooked, the subject was given a sheet listing the considerations that might be involved in a career choice of the type he was making (see Table 9.2). The majority of time spent on this cognitive exercise was usually devoted to categories that had started off with few or no entries, most often those pertaining to approval or disapproval from the self.

Trial runs were made with 36 Yale College seniors, half of whom were given the balance-sheet procedure, while the other half were given a control interview that spent the same amount of time (about one hour) discussing the decision, using standard interview questions. Each of the 18 subjects given the balance sheet responded by talking

Table 9.2 Considerations that might affect career choice used in the balance-sheet procedure with college seniors facing a decision about what to do after graduation

---

Utilitarian gains and losses for self

   income
   how difficult the work is
   how interesting the work is
   freedom to select work tasks
   chances of advancement
   security
   time available for personal interests
   other (e.g. special restrictions or opportunities with respect to social life, effect of the
      career or job demands on marriage, type of people one will come in contact with)

Utilitarian gains and losses for others

   income for family
   status for family
   time available for family
   kind of environment for family (e.g. stimulating, dull, safe, unsafe)
   being in a position to help an organization or group
   other (e.g. fringe benefits for family)

Self-approval or disapproval

   self-esteem from contributions to society or to good causes
   extent to which work tasks are ethically justifiable
   extent to which work will involve compromising oneself
   creativity or originality of work
   extent to which job will involve a way of life that meets one's moral or ethical standards
   opportunity to fulfill long-range life goals
   other (e.g. extent to which work is "more than just a job")

Approval or disapproval from others (includes being criticized or being excluded from a group as well as being praised or obtaining prestige, admiration, and respect)

   parents
   college friends
   wife (or husband)
   colleagues
   community-at-large
   other (e.g. social, political, or religious groups)

---

about risks and drawbacks not previously mentioned during the standard part of the interview. Hence the procedure seems to be a feasible way of stimulating people to become aware of major gaps, particularly those pertaining to unfavorable consequences of the preferred courses of action. The increased awareness can affect the decision-maker's choice: more than half the 18 subjects who were given the balance-sheet procedure reported at the end of the interview that they regarded a different alternative as most preferable; only one of the 18 subjects given the control interview did so. Obviously these results cannot be taken as definitive evidence, since the verbal reports might merely reflect differences in wanting to please the interviewer rather than genuine effects of the procedure. Nevertheless, the observations suggest that the procedure can function as a goad to vigilance.

This pilot work was followed up by Mann (1972), who conducted a similar study with 50 high school seniors who were deciding which college to attend. The balance-sheet procedure, which was administered three months before a decision was required, again proved effective. On follow-up measures taken approximately six weeks after the students had notified the colleges of their decisions, the 30 students who had been given the procedure expressed less postdecisional regret, were more secure in their choice, and were more open to potentially challenging information about the consequences of their decision than were the 20 students in the control group. . . .

Further evidence of the effectiveness of the balance-sheet procedure comes from a field experiment by Hoyt and Janis (1975) with 40 women who had signed up for an early-morning exercise class. Twenty women, assigned on a random basis to the *relevant* balance-sheet condition, were induced to consider carefully all the advantages and disadvantages of regular participation in the class. Twenty others, randomly assigned to the *irrelevant* balance-sheet condition, were asked to consider all the pros and cons involved in another health-oriented decision—abstaining from cigarette smoking. Records of class attendance for a 7-week period were used as unobtrusive behavioral measures of the effects of these treatments. As predicted by the "defective balance-sheet" hypothesis, the women given the relevant balance sheet attended significantly more classes than those given the irrelevant balance-sheet procedure, whose rate of attendance did not differ from that of a no-treatment (baseline) control group (see Figure 9.2).

Another technique that offers promise of stimulating vigilance is called outcome psychodrama. The client is asked to participate in a scenario that requires him to project himself into the future and to improvise a vivid retrospective account of what happened as a consequence of choosing one or another alternative. The procedure is repeated as many times as necessary to explore the potential risks and consequences of the alternatives under consideration.

Outcome psychodrama was developed by Janis in a series of pilot studies. It was first used with clients having marital difficulties who

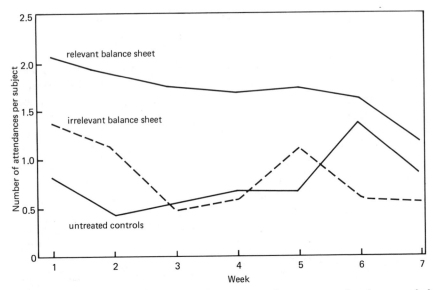

Figure 9.2 Records of weekly attendance at a voluntary exercise class revealed that a relevant balance-sheet procedure helped to stabilize the decision to participate regularly. Relevant balance sheet, N = 20; irrelevant balance sheet, N = 20; untreated controls, N = 10. Source: Hoyt and Janis © 1975 APA; reprinted by permission.

came to a family-service clinic for aid in deciding whether or not to seek divorce. Each went through two psychodramatic enactments to explore the gains and losses that might be sustained from the two main alternatives, obtaining the divorce and reconstituting the marriage. In every case the clients showed signs of having become more vigilant, especially by confronting important new considerations they had not mentioned in earlier interviews.

A similar psychodramatic procedure was tried out in career counseling with 15 college seniors. Each student enacted two scenarios, dealing with an imagined crisis one year after selecting his most preferred career choice and his second choice. Among 12 of the 15 students, new considerations emerged during the psychodrama that affected their evaluation of the alternatives. Four students were so impressed by the undesirable consequences which surfaced during the improvised performance that they reversed their preferences. No controlled field experiments on the effectiveness of outcome psychodrama have been completed as yet (one is currently being conducted by La Flamme and Janis), but from the pilot studies we think the technique will prove useful as a supplement to the balance-sheet procedure for stimulating vigilance. . . .

Various other studies . . . support the generalization that when preparatory information induces a decision-maker to become vigilant concerning potential risks before they materialize, he or she will develop more effective reassurances and contingency plans, which will enable the person to display higher stress tolerance if a post-decisional crisis actually occurs. [See Chapter 13.] This conclusion is consistent with—and therefore adds some weight to—the assumption of conflict theory that a decision -maker is much more likely to display adaptive behavior when making a difficult decision if his or her dominant coping pattern is vigilance rather than defensive avoidance or hypervigilance. When the vigilance pattern is dominant, the decision-maker engages in careful search and appraisal before implementing a new course of action and thereafter remains relatively unshaken by setbacks that challenge his or her decision.

REFERENCES

Bem, D. J. 1972. Self-perception theory. In *Advances in Experimental Social Psychology,* ed. L. Berkowitz. Academic Press.

Brehm, J. W. 1966. *A Theory of Psychological Reactance.* Academic Press.

Clore, G. L., and K. L. McMillan. Role playing, attitude change, and attraction toward a disabled other. Unpublished paper, Univ. of Illinois, 1970. Cited in *The Psychology of Personality,* J. S. Wiggins et al., Addison-Wesley, 1971.

Epstein, S., and S. Clarke. 1970. Heart rate and skin conductance during experimentally induced anxiety: Effects of anticipated intensity of noxious stimulation and experience. *J. Exp. Psych.* 84:105–12.

Festinger, L. 1957. *A Theory of Cognitive Dissonance.* Row Peterson.

——, ed. 1964. *Conflict, Decision and Dissonance.* Stanford Univ. Press.

Gerard, H. B. 1967. Choice difficulty, dissonance, and the decision sequence. *J. Personality* 35:91–108.

Hoyt, M. F., and I. L. Janis. 1975. Increasing adherence to a stressful decision via a motivational balance-sheet procedure: A field experiment. *J. Personality and Soc. Psych.* 31:833–39.

Janis, J. L. 1959. Motivational factors in the resolution of decisional conflicts. In *Nebraska Symposium on Motivation,* vol. 7, ed. M. R. Jones. Univ. of Nebraska Press.

——. 1967. Effects of fear arousal on attitude change: Recent developments in theory and experimental research. In *Advances in Experimental Social Psychology,* vol. 3, ed. L. Berkowitz. Academic Press.

——. Pilot studies on new procedures for improving the quality of decision-making. Mimeo. research report. Yale Studies in Attitude and Decisions, 1968.

——. 1972. *Victims of Groupthink.* Houghton Mifflin.

——. 1974. Vigilance and decision-making in personal crises. In *Coping and Adaptation,* ed. D. A. Hamburg and C. V. Coelho. Academic Press.

——, and L. Mann. 1965. Effectiveness of emotional role-playing in modifying smoking habits and attitudes. *J. Exp. Res. in Personality* 1:84–90.

——, and L. Mann. 1977. *Decision Making: A Psychological Analysis of Conflict, Choice and Commitment.* Free Press.

——, and C. N. Rausch. 1970. Selective interest in communications that could arouse decisional conflict: A field study of participants in the draft-resistance movement. *J. Personality and Soc. Psych.* 14:46–54.

Jones, E. E., and C. A. Johnson. 1973. Delay of consequences and the riskiness of decisions. *J. Personality* 42:613–37.

Katz, D., I. Sarnoff, and C. G. McClintock. 1956. Ego-defense and attitude change. *Human Relations* 9:27–46.

Mann, L. 1972. Use of a "balance-sheet" procedure to improve the quality of personal decision-making: A field experiment with college applicants. *J. Vocational Beh.* 2:291–300.

——, and T. Dashiell. 1975. Reactions to the draft lottery: A test of conflict theory. *Human Relations* 29:155–73.

——, and I. L. Janis. 1968. A follow-up study on the long-term effects of emotional role playing. *J. Personality and Soc. Psych.* 8:339–42.

——, I. L. Janis, and R. Chaplin. 1969. The effects of anticipation of forthcoming information on predecisional processes. *J. Personality and Soc. Psych.* 11:10–16.

McGuire, W. J. 1969. The nature of attitudes and attitude change. In *The Handbook of Social Psychology,* vol. 3, ed. G. Lindzey and E. Aronson. Addison-Wesley.

Reed, H. D., and I. L. Janis. 1974. Effects of a new type of psychological treatment on smokers' resistance to warnings about health hazards. *J. Consulting and Clin. Psych.* 42:748.

Rokeach, M. 1971. Long-range experimental modification of values, attitudes and behavior. *Am. Psychologist* 26:453–59.

Simon, H. A. 1976. *Administrative Behavior: A Study of Decision-making Processes in Administrative Organization,* 3rd ed. Free Press.

Toomey, M. 1972. Conflict theory approach to decision-making applied to alcoholics. *J. Personality and Soc. Psych.* 24:199–206.

Walster, E. 1964. The temporal sequence of post-decision processes. In *Conflict, Decision, and Dissonance,* ed. L. Festinger. Stanford Univ. Press.

Wicklund, R. A. 1974. *Freedom and Reactance.* Lawrence Erlbaum Associates.

10

The Influence of Television on Personal Decision-Making (1980)

POTENTIAL POWER OF TELEVISION

A recent survey of social scientists who are active in research on the behavioral effects of television has identified a number of problem areas that are regarded as warranting high priority for the next decade (Comstock, 1975). The topic of this paper cuts across two of the highest priority areas—the influence of television on socialization of young persons and behavioral effects of the "picture of the world" provided by entertainment programs.

The high priority assigned to these areas is directly or indirectly based on the assumption that in a variety of subtle ways television might prove to have considerable power in shaping the actions of large numbers of people. This assumption seems to be very much alive despite the deadening findings reported by social scientists indicating that television and other mass media have slight, if any, observable effects on the public's attitudes and behavior. As William McGuire (1969) puts it, the outcome of two decades of mass media research "has been quite embarrassing for proponents of the mass media, since there is little evidence of attitude change, much less change in gross behavior such as buying or voting [p. 227]." But there are many diehards around, not only among those responsible for spending billions of dollars each year on television advertising but also among social scientists who maintain that television is a major source of social influence in our society.

Janis, I. L. The influence of television on personal decision-making. In S. B. Withey & R. P. Abeles (Eds.), *Television and social behavior: Beyond violence and children.* Hillsdale, N. J.: Erlbaum, 1980. Pp. 161–189. Reprinted by permission.

Here are a few samples of impressive assertions about the potential power of television by responsible social scientists:

George Comstock (1975), who has spent several years preparing comprehensive reviews and analyses of the extensive literature on the effects of television, speaks of the "vicarious socialization" that television provides—conveying values, norms, and taboos to maturing individuals in a way that could affect how they function in their society. He goes on to say that television has challenged the functions of parents, teachers, peers, and various social institutions that previously were the exclusive sources of socializing communications.

George Gerbner (1972), too, emphasizes the persuasive power of television when he argues that the recurrent themes of popular television dramas exert a subtle cumulative effect on viewers' beliefs and anxieties about the urban environment. He presents evidence from audience surveys indicating that the amount of exposure to television is positively correlated with grossly exaggerated expectations about the likelihood of being involved in violence—exceptions that could affect a variety of personal and political decisions, such as whether or not to move away from the center of the city and whether or not to increase appropriations for law enforcement agencies.

John Platt (1975) emphasizes the politicizing aspects of the transformations brought about by television, the instant spread of new information needed for public participation in new policy decisions, and the general education of the public: . . .

Comstock, Gerbner, and Platt and a number of other social scientists believe, contrary to all the opposing generalizations in social science monographs and textbooks, that the mass media—and television in particular—can exert a marked influence on many different types of decisions made by large numbers of viewers, not just the consumer decisions in which TV advertisers are interested.

At this point, I cannot resist the temptation of invoking a moral equivalent of Pascal's divine wager for the salvation of social science research on television effects. If the demurring monographs and textbooks are completely right, such research will be a waste of time and money. But even if the few commentators just cited are overestimating so grossly that they are only one-tenth right about the power of television to influence the viewing population throughout the world, social scientists had better try to locate samples of the tens of millions of people who might be affected, and learn whatever they can about when, how, and why.

Key Questions

The central problem on which I propose to focus pertains to the influence of television on the courses of action selected by viewers when they are confronted with major choices concerning career, marriage, life style, health, and the welfare of their families. Among which people, in what ways, and under what conditions does television influence vital personal decisions made by viewers? When and how do the words and vivid images conveyed by television become linked up in the minds of viewers as consequences of their own action, even though the producers of the television show may have had no intention of trying to influence the audience in that particular way? In discussing these questions I shall make use of conceptual schemas that have grown out of recent research, including my own research in recent years on social influence in relation to decision-making (Janis, 1972, 1975, 1977; Janis & Mann, 1976, 1977).

These questions are worth investigating, it seems to me, even if the visual medium of television does not prove to be more effective than newspapers and other mass media that rely mainly on the printed word. Television seems to differ from the press not just in the size of its daily audience throughout the world but also in the limited number of themes it presents in the relatively few programs available to regular viewers. It is important to find out exactly what those themes are and what effects they have on the behavior of viewers. Of course within one or two decades many of the findings might become obsolete, except as past history, if the monopolistic character of television programming is greatly reduced as a result of a huge increase in the variety of diverse programs made accessible by cable television, cassettes, and the proliferation of new channels catering to the special interests of different types of people. Even so, we can hope to learn something of lasting importance about the ways mass communications affect the personal choices people make and influence the procedures they use to arrive at their decisions.

AVAILABILITY OF IMAGES AND PERSONAL SCRIPTS

Let me begin with a very simple example of the potential power of visual images on television to influence a minor decision. I have selected this obvious example because it can serve to illustrate some of the key theoretical concepts that might be brought to bear in the analysis of many more complex examples involving more important personal decisions. In New Haven, Connecticut, on the evening of January 28, 1977, a supper meeting of a parent–teachers' association, whose activities were always enthusiastically supported by the members, was poorly attended as a result of forecasts of a bad storm. Throughout the hour before the potluck supper was scheduled to start, many members phoned the organizers to say that although they were all ready to drive to the meeting and had already prepared a big dish of food as their contribution, they wanted to postpone the affair because a blizzard was predicted for that evening. Many spoke about having seen television newcasts of the blizzard that had hit Buffalo, New York, where traffic was brought to a complete stand-still and some people were trapped in cars completely buried by snow drifts. They said they didn't want be caught in anything like that. Actually, at the time of these phone calls, the temperature was 44°F and the weather clear (and remained so for many hours there-after). The organizers decided to hold the meeting despite the dire forecast. But most of the parents and teachers who had phoned to say they were worried after seeing the televised newcast about the blizzard did not show up. Many of those who came had heard about the blizzard from the radio or newspapers.

Perhaps those who rely on television to get the news are more susceptible than those who use the other media. Or perhaps the same weather forecast transmitted by radio or newspaper could not have been as effective in influencing people to decide to stay home when they felt under such a strong social obligation to attend the supper meeting. From the way the absentees spoke about it on the phone that evening and at the school the next day it seems likely that the vivid images of the blizzard they had seen on television played a crucial role in mediating their decision.

Apparently the television newscasts had made the image of a disastrous blizzard *available,* in the sense that Tversky and Kahneman (1974) use that term. These two authors have given a detailed account of various illusions, some notorious and others not yet well known, which make for errors in estimating the probability that given events will occur. Some of their empirical investigations indicate that the risks of a particular course of action are likely to be grossly overesti-mated if decision-makers have *vivid mental images of the possible unfavorable outcomes,* so that it is easy for them to imagine an ensu-ing disaster. Perhaps much of the power of television to influence the decisions of large numbers of people, whether for good or for ill, resides in its capacity to increase the availability of images of specific outcomes, desirable ones as well as undesirable. The greater availabil-ity of an image of any positive or negative outcome increases the probability of that particular image becoming dominant over images of other outcomes when people are trying to decide what to do. This can play a crucial role in determining which course of action they will choose.

In the brief example just given, the image of a blizzard, presented in an impersonal way on a television news program seems to have greatly augmented the influence of the purely verbal forecast that the storm was approaching the local area. A number of viewers evidently took away a personalized message to the effect that "If I go to our parent–teacher association meeting tonight, even though the weather is fine right now, I shall encounter a very dangerous snowstorm when I try to drive home, like the one I just saw." This cognition, which represents a combination of a decision with a visual image of an ensuing outcome, is a simple example of what Shank and Abelson (1975) refer to as a "script." They use the *script* to designate any specific cognitive schema or frame that represents a *"coherent sequence of events expected by the individual, involving him either as a participant or as an observer* (Abelson, 1976, [p. 33])." These psychologists propose to use scripts as a basic unit of psychological analysis in the study of language, memory, attitudes, and decision-making. They distinguish between two main types of scripts. One type, called "situational scripts," pertains to stereotyped sequences of actions in well-known situations, such as what one has to do to get a room in a hotel. A second type of cognitive structure, which is more important for decision making, is what Shank and Abelson call "planning scripts." These scripts specify the choices that one can make when confronted with novel situations or personal problems. We rely on planning scripts, according to their terminology, whenever we tell ourselves what we can or ought to do in order to accomplish a goal. From the standpoint of research on television effects, I propose that we should try to learn more about the *personal* scripts—those situational and planning scripts involving individuals as participants or social actors—that they acquire from vicarious observations of events depicted on the television screen.

Do Fictitious Scenarios Become the Viewers' Personal Scripts?

The personal script just exemplified was acquired from a television newscast and involved a very limited sphere of action pertaining to an immediate source of potential danger. But the images conveyed by entertainment programs and films shown on television can also induce personal scripts in viewers, some of which may unintentionally affect their personal policies that are carried out time and again for many years, perhaps even for the rest of their lives. Let us consider next an example of an implicit script conveyed by a typical entertainment program. The opening of "Queen of the Gypsies," a Kojak episode about bank robberies that was shown on the CBS network during the winter of 1977, depicts a seemingly foolish, bumblingly incompetent young woman who, in a very pleasant way, asks a bank teller to help her out by answering her naive questions, while the bank customers in line behind her grow more and more impatient. The audience soon learns, however, that her naiveté is merely a false front that enables her to con the teller into giving her change for a fake $50 bill. And before the program is over it becomes apparent that the young woman is, in fact, an extraordinarily sophisticated con artist who can use her naive front so skillfully as to con even the great Kojak himself. An unintended message, it seems to me, could be conveyed by this fictitious episode: "Be suspicious of any seemingly helpless female who asks a lot of questions; she could be putting on an act to con you." Perhaps most viewers were too distracted by the exciting events in the drama or too absorbed in the specifics of the story to pick up any such message. But suppose that among the millions of viewers watching the program the minority who got the message included thousands of intelligent people in the business world who must deal with customers' naive questions. This little component in the television writers' scenario could conceivably reduce what little gracious behavior exists in the business world by building up personal scripts in those viewers that influence the way they respond to naive people who ask for help.

One of the problems for television research is to ascertain when and among whom such messages are internalized as personal scripts and thereafter acted upon. Even simple explicit messages may be missed, especially by children, because of distracting cues, lack of opportunity for mental replaying and reflecting, and the rapid shifts of focus that characterize commercial television. As a result of these and other characteristics, television programs may often succeed in keeping the viewers' attention fixed on the screen at the expense of failing to transmit anything more than vague or garbled messages (Singer, 1976). Nevertheless a small percentage of children and a larger percentage of adults may pick up some of the unintended implicit messages that are repeated hour after hour and day after day in entertainment fare (Himmelweit, 1977). A study of school children by Dominick (1974) indicates that their viewing of crime shows on television was positively correlated not only with the belief that criminals usually get caught (which is an ideological theme intentionally introduced by the scenario writers) but also with specific knowledge about an arrested suspect's civil rights (which may be an *unintended* message that could be beneficial for some viewers, especially for anyone encountering police misconduct).

Other unintended messages picked up from those same programs may be socially detrimental because they go counter to democratic values. On the basis of an analysis of television crime shows from 1974 to 1976, Arons and Katsch (1977) conclude that Columbo, Kojak, and other television detectives regularly violate the legal rights of crime suspects, which may subtly convey the message to children and adults that there is nothing wrong with such conduct on the part of the police in their own communities.

Effects of Misleading Stereotypes of Occupational Roles

Of prime importance, from the standpoint of the potential role of television in the socialization of children and youth in our society, are the effects of explicit or implicit messages conveyed by television contents that induce personal scripts pertaining to vital decisions. Consider, for example, the complaints made by representatives of large scientific associations and technological organizations that many bright young people are not choosing careers in science or engineering because scientists and engineers are so often depicted in television stories as evil, power-hungry, and socially irresponsible. To what extent are such complaints based on factually accurate assumptions? Will a content analysis of popular entertainment programs show an imbalance in the direction of unwarranted negative portrayals of scientists and engineers? If so, do the stereotyped portrayals affect the beliefs and attitudes of the young people who see the programs? Do those beliefs and attitudes in turn affect their occupational choices?

Similar questions need to be answered by systematic content analysis, opinion surveys, and audience-response analysis of the portrayals in everyday television fare of each major type of occupation. . . .

One possible approach would be to compare (a) the images that people are given of the usual positive and negative consequences to be expected if they were to pursue a given professional career or go into a given line of nonprofessional work with (b) the knowledgeable reports obtained from men and women who are actively engaged in that type of career. The questions to be answered would be whether or not the typical television characterization (if there is a fairly consistent one) influences the expectations of a sizable percentage of young viewers and differs from the central tendency of the reports obtained from experienced participants. For this purpose it might be worthwhile to use the "balance sheet" of incentives described by Janis and Mann (1977, pp. 135 *ff.*) as a schema to analyze the considerations that people consciously or unconsciously are taking into account when they decide to adopt a new course of action or to stick with the one previously chosen. In this schema the expected consequences for each alternative course of action are classified into four main categories.

1. Utilitarian gains or losses for self.
2. Utilitarian gains or losses for significant others.
3. Self-approval or disapproval.
4. Approval or disapproval from significant others.

. . . . The entries in the four categories of the balance sheet obtained from content analysis of television characterizations could be compared with the most frequent entries obtained from interviews or questionnaires given to representative samples of (a) viewers who are asked to state their expectations about the pros and cons for major occupational choices that they might face in the future and (b) persons currently occupying each major occupational role who are asked to report on the positive and negative incentives for sticking with their occupational choice. (The same comparative method could be adopted for comparing television with other media and for studying correct and incorrect conceptions about other types of decision in addition to career choices.)

Obtaining objective data on the degree of verisimilitude in television characterizations of occupational roles—and identifying the most distorted stereotypes—should be regarded as only the first step in the inquiry. What we next need to know is the extent to which the accurate or inaccurate portrayals influence the personal scripts and the level of aspiration of young people when the time comes for them to choose their own career. Similarly, we need to find out the effects of television portrayals on personal scripts that enter into the subsequent career-related decisions of adult life, such as shifts in occupational role resulting from mid-career crises.

Other Types of Personal Scripts to Be Investigated

At present we know very little about personal scripts acquired from or reinforced by television portrayals on currently popular programs like "Mork and Mindy," "Laverne and Shirley," and "Mary Hartman, Mary Hartman." Dramas, situational comedies, and other entertainment fare often portray vital aspects of adult life that might sooner or later affect some of the viewers' decisions to be married, to become pregnant, to obtain a divorce, to raise a child as a single parent, to move to or from an urban area, or to make a drastic change in life style.

Similarly, we remain quite ignorant about the ultimate impact of the repeated portrayals of health problems, not only in television soap operas, but also on talk shows and in commercials, which could have profound effects on viewers' personal scripts that enter into their health-related decisions. The increased availability of images of physical suffering and of successful and unsuccessful medical treatments undoubtedly influences the actions of many people when they become ill, sometimes when it is a matter of life or death. A study of adolescent boys by Milavsky, Pekowsky, and Stipp (1975) indicates that exposure to television commercials plugging the use of over-the-counter drugs is positively correlated with the use of such drugs but is negatively correlated with the use of illicit drugs. These correlational findings need to be pursued further by other types of research to determine the causal sequences. Does viewing the television commercials exert a causal influence on the decisions of young people to take one type of drug and to avoid the other? Or are the young people who use illicit drugs too busy elsewhere to view television programs and their accompanying commercials? Of special importance are questions concerning long-range effects on drug consumption: Does viewing the commercials or other television presentations bearing on drug-taking have any observable influence on drug consumption in later adult life? If so, when, why, and among whom? Multistage studies are also needed to determine the extent to which positive or negative portrayals of smokers, overeaters, and alcoholics on television entertainment programs and in commercials affect personal scripts that are pertinent to consumption decisions made by youthful and adult viewers.

Similar data are needed to learn about the personal scripts acquired in childhood. A review of 21 studies on the effects of television advertising on young children's attitudes and behavior by Adler (1977) refers to a number of studies showing that children under 8 years of age have great difficulty distinguishing commercials from programs. This may be one of the main reasons why they believe the information and misinformation in advertisements to be true. There is some evidence, for example, indicating that children who are exposed to across-the-counter drug advertising are more likely than others to believe that the advertised medicines are widely needed and effective and to be receptive to their use. Other findings, according to Adler's review, show that as children grow older they can discriminate commercials from other fare and they say that they dislike them more and more. Nevertheless, the older children show little or no decrease in wanting and requesting the advertised products. The demand created by television commercials among older as well as younger children might have some corrosive effects on family life.

Survey research indicates that a substantial proportion of parents complain that their children ask them to buy the things they see advertised on the screen and become disappointed or angry when the parents do not comply.

On the positive side of the ledger, a recent development in America is the deliberate attempt by government health agencies, medical organizations, and various public interest groups to use the power of television to convey messages to adult viewers that could improve the physical health and emotional well-being of the nation. Maccoby and Breitrose (cited in Comstock & Lindsey, 1975), for example, have devised a media campaign to reduce coronary heart disease, sponsored by the National Heart and Lung Institute. The campaign includes television spot announcements, together with radio and newspaper announcements, direct mailings, and instruction classes for volunteers who want to reduce their heart disease risk by improving their diet, increasing exercise, reducing weight, and cutting down on smoking. Assessments of the effectiveness of the campaign, conducted by Maccoby, Breitrose, and others in the Stanford Heart Disease Prevention Program, may provide some useful leads as to which types of persons respond positively to which types of persuasive messages. For this type of campaign it is possible to obtain behavioral measures that are dependable indicators of viewers' decisions to volunteer for classes on personal health-related instruction and to adhere to the public health recommendations. Similar measures could be used to investigate the implicit messages about desirable health practices conveyed by soap operas and other entertainment fare, which could be much more effective for some people than campaigns that are perceived by viewers as deliberate persuasion.

CUMULATIVE EFFECTS OF EXPOSURE TO RECURRENT THEMES

Whether or not spot television announcements alone or in combination with other media prove to be effective in inducing people to take preventative action to avoid heart disease or any other type of illness, the television medium probably exerts enormous influence on health-related decisions of large numbers of viewers. Some of the talk shows, documentary videotapes, and films presented on the television screen deliberately attempt to teach the audience personal scripts about specific ways to cope with medical emergencies, chronic illness, and a variety of other problems involving physical or mental health. For example, during the week of January 24, 1977, a daily talk show on NBC titled "Not for Women Only" concentrated entirely on the topic of breast cancer, featuring physicians who presented scientific information and knowledgeable women who described what it is like to be a breast cancer patient. On the mornings of January 26 and 27, the entire program was devoted to conversations with three patients—Rose Kushner and Betty Rollins, each of whom had written a book based on her personal experiences, and Debre Hamburger, a 25-year-old student who had recently undergone a mastectomy. These three women emphasized a number of themes that could have a direct effect on the decision-making of members of the audience who might have cancer symptoms. One theme emphasized by all three patients was that even when a trusted physician tells you that you must undergo drastic surgery to save your life, you should take an active role as a skeptical decisionmaker—you should try to get a second opinion from an independent cancer specialist as to whether or not surgery is essential, and, if so, how extensive it should be; then, if you decide to undergo the recommended operation, you should consult a plastic surgeon in advance, if possible, and arrange to have him on hand during the operation so that he can influence the life-saving surgeon to take account of the need to plan for satisfactory cosmetic repair.

Perhaps even more important from the standpoint of transmitting personal scripts to the 1 out of every 14 women in the United States who will be afflicted with breast cancer was the repeated emphasis by all three patients on the theme that you can still lead a normal, productive, and self-fulfilling life, including a satisfactory sex life, despite being mutilated by the loss of one of your breasts. A subsidiary theme, which is applicable to any male or female who undergoes any kind of body mutilation, was that there can be some advantages even though one would never choose this means for achieving one's goals if given a free choice—for example, the operation is likely to evoke an immediate increase in tender affection from one's spouse or lover; ultimately, after coming to terms with the continuing threats, the personal disaster can lead one to become a more mature, self-reliant person with a more profound sense of the values one wants to pursue during the remaining days of one's life. This theme was conveyed not just by what was being said but also by the visual images of the three impressive-looking, socially competent women, each of whom was talking frankly, in a self-possessed manner, about how her mastectomy experience had affected her and about her own current assets and liabilities.

Inadvertently, the latter theme made its appearance again in an entertainment program that was viewed by over 70 million people on the evening of each of the two days that the women had discussed their mastectomies on the morning talk show. On those evenings, two installments appeared of "Roots," the serial dramatization of the ABC network of the best-selling saga about an Afro-American family, which had a larger audience than any comparable entertainment program ever had before. These two episodes of the serial dealt with the experiences of Kunta Kinte, a Mandinka warrior who in the early 18th century had been captured by slave traders outside his native village in Gambia and brought to Virginia on a slave ship. In line with one of the explicit themes of "Roots," we see Kunta asserting his manliness and his indomitable striving for freedom by attempting to escape to the north. Two sadistic slave catchers punish him by chopping off his foot with an axe. At this point in the drama, a subsidiary implicit theme makes its appearance. Kunta appears to be in a state of utter despair as he lies deathly ill from an infection in his mutilated foot, and we hear him mutter that he will never walk again. But an attractive slave woman who gives him tender care is clearly not at all repelled by his feeble, mutilated state. With her encouragement, he resolves not only to walk again but also to run and presumably to do other manly things as well.

The next episode shows Kunta functioning effectively despite his permanent mutilation, once again a strong, competent, proud man who has married his loving nurse and has impregnated her. Many of the viewers who had tuned in on the morning talk show about mastectomies would be likely to recognize that here again was essentially the same theme, encouraging anyone who undergoes body mutilation to strive to overcome the handicaps and demoralization. Some of those who had not viewed the morning talk show may well have gotten the same message. But for the ones who had watched and listened to the two morning programs, the reappearance of the theme in the entertainment program on the same two evenings may well have had an interactive or cumulative effect, establishing a more generalized personal script, with more broadly applicable categories: "If you (or anyone else in your family, male or female) are mutilated by a horrible injury or illness"—so runs the more generalized script— "you can still be a competent, well-loved person, living a full life."

Focusing On Recurrent Explicit and Implicit Themes

The foregoing example of a recurrent theme has been given in considerable detail because it calls attention to neglected aspects of television research. Most of the existing research bearing on personal scripts acquired from television is on the effects of single-shot exposures to one particular television program or even just one little snip-pet from one episode. Such research may have value for investigating certain limited hypotheses but can tell us nothing about sensitizing and cumulative effects on the acquisition of personal scripts that arise from recurrences of the same or similar themes on a variety of different television programs—soap operas, situation comedies, news-casts, and commercials, as well as intentionally educational programs. We need to go beyond assessing merely the overall frequency of each theme that could create or reinforce personal scripts bearing on vital personal decisions. We need to learn about the *recurrent* themes that have the most potent effects on the audience. Which are the messages that are constantly being reinforced by multiple presenta-tions and which are the ones that are being contradicted and counter-acted? In order to answer these questions, content assessments should take account of whatever is known about audience appercep-tion in order to include the latent as well as the obvious manifest themes—Kunta's implicit modeling of emotional recovery from mutilation, as well as his explicit modeling of black manliness.

The type of research proposed here need not be deterred by the realization that we cannot hope to obtain dependable answers to sociohistorical questions regarding the extent to which the themes in daily television fare are initiating social change by introducing new ideas into our culture or by making people more aware of their latent fears and aspirations as against merely reinforcing the dominant folk-lore that almost everyone would learn anyhow from other socializing agencies. In any case, we need to know which are the explicit and implicit themes that are repeatedly being presented to the mass audi-ence and to what extent each of those is being registered by the viewers and entering into their personal scripts.

Differential Effects of Explicit Versus Implicit Themes

For certain types of messages, explicit presentations might evoke so much psychological resistance that implicit presentations are more effective. Many mutilated men might reject an explicit statement of the theme about obtaining tender affection as a compensatory gain from mutilation but nevertheless incorporate the theme into a con-structive personal script from seeing the implicit presentation in the mutilation episode of "Roots." It is conceivable that everyone builds up much more potent personal scripts when the themes are acquired as *tacit* knowledge. The themes may be more readily internalized from a variety of implicit presentations than from an equal number of exposures to explicit presentations that can be easily identified as deliberate efforts to influence one's personal beliefs or attitudes. These are some of the more basic research questions that need to be worked on in order to improve our understanding of the role of television as a socializing agency in our society.

Expanding the Scope of Content Analyses

Obviously, one of the first steps in pursuing some of the research questions just discussed is to make use of existing content analysis data on themes that might influence the personal scripts of at least a sizable minority, if not the majority, of viewers. Some new coding schemes may have to be developed to capture themes bearing on all the various types of vital personal decisions that should be examined. Comstock (1975) points out that the socially contructive content of television is likely to continue to be investigated by many research workers because, among other reasons, a coding scheme for content analysis of such themes has already been developed. The same consideration might make it worthwhile to invest research resources into developing specific coding schemes pertaining to depictions of the positive and negative consequences of alternative courses of action for each major type of personal decision. Ultimately, if subsequent research shows that these new coding schemes are of some value for predicting the personal scripts acquired by television viewers, they might be incorporated into a set of comprehensive cultural indicators of the type being developed by George Gerbner and Larry Gross (1976), which are intended "to present annual, cumulative, and comparative indicators of dominant cultural configurations, common conceptions, and trends relevant to issues of social health and public policy" (Comstock, 1975, p. 64).

ACQUISITION OF PERSONAL SCRIPTS

In order to investigate the acquisition of new personal scripts, some of the sophisticated methods developed for basic research on learning, memory, and high-order cognitive processes might be applied (see the section on Cognitive Psychology in Janis, 1977). These methods may be useful for research on questions about when, how, and why content themes presented on television are transformed by viewers into personal scripts, with and without distortion. Similar research questions need to be answered concerning the storage of newly acquired scripts in long-term memory and their retrieval on appropriate and inappropriate occasions when a vital personal decision has to be made.

Earlier I suggested that misleading themes on television that could have adverse effects on the making of career decisions might be detected by a two-step comparative method: First, by examining the results of a content analysis of television protrayals of the favorable and unfavorable features of various types of jobs in relation to comparisons between children who are heavy and light viewers with regard to beliefs about those features in order to see if the content themes are being assimilated by young people; and second, by comparing the assimilated beliefs with the ratings of persons who really know what the favorable and unfavorable features are because they are actually working in those jobs, in order to see if those beliefs are accurate or inaccurate. Essentially the same comparative method could be used to identify other misleading content themes presented on television that could have adverse effects on the marriages, health, or life style of many viewers—misleading in the sense that children, youth, or adults are being led to build up erroneous personal scripts involving false expectations about the consequences of the courses of action they will sooner or later be contemplating, which make for choices that are unduly costly, regrettable, and regretted.

It is especially important to find out how children respond to content themes that could build up or modify personal scripts. . . . On the one hand, children usually do not give undivided, continuous attention to television but engage in active play or do their homework while half-watching the screen (Bechtel, Achelpohl, & Akers, 1972; Lyle & Hoffman, 1972). Furthermore they do not understand some of the important cues to adult intentions and miss nuances in human relationships (Singer, 1976). Consequently they may learn only the most pervasive, uncomplicated, and attention-capturing messages, sometimes with considerable miscomprehension because of their failure to take account of the context. But, on the other hand, young children are sometimes highly attentive to the television screen and when curious they are likely to notice all sorts of little details ignored by adults. Children may be extremely vulnerable to those fictitious representations of the social world that repeatedly give the same messages about the police or any other group in entertainment programs and commercials. Correlational evidence from a study by Robert S. Frank (cited by Comstock and Linsey, 1975, p. 62) suggests that the more they watch television, the more likely they are to regard lying and deceitful practices as acceptable behavior, provided that it is for a good cause. This correlational finding, of course, does not tell us whether television plays a causal role because other factors, such as the presence or absence of parental lying and deceit, might account for the observed relationship. Nevertheless, it suggests yet another type of potentially adverse effect that we probably should worry about. Fairly high priority should be given to new research on television effects designed to tell us something about the extent to which the ideological components of the Watergate coverup mentality are currently being transmitted to and acquired by children.

Exactly what kind of personal *moral* scripts are being acquired by adults as well as children and youth who watch popular television programs? Numerous commentators cry out against the oversimplified, self-serving, antisocial, or corrupt moral content of prime time programs. Others say that prime time programs are not directly antisocial or corrupt, but exert a pernicious moral influence by promoting stereotypes, ideological beliefs, and myths that encourage classifying all persons and social groups into simplistic moral categories (heroes or villians, good guys or bad guys) that are antithetical to democratic values. A few claim that television is doing a fine job of encouraging belief in law, democratic institutions, and "good" moral values. Columnist Benjamin Stein, for example, writing in the *Wall Street Journal* (April 1975), takes the position that it is not at all a bad thing that "television sells its values as well as its soaps and detergents." He argues that shows under attack for being pointlessly violent can be defended on the grounds that they offer counterbalancing moral content. The moral theme that regularly runs through these programs, he says, "is that the bad, evil people who lead criminal, antisocial lives, are punished. Thus it pays to be a good, moral person." He adds that most adventure shows portray the people who are on the side of the law as superior and more worthy of imitation than the criminals. Stein concludes that insofar as television is selling these powerfully important moral messages, along with faith in our government's institutions, it "must be one of the primary stabilizing forces in America today." It follows that we should prize "Kojak," "The Rookies," and "Police Story" as national treasures.

Is there any empirical validity to Stein's ultraconservative position? Or to the opposing position? And for which programs? What we really need to find out is which of the explicit and implied moral themes in television programs are being internalized. If preliminary studies indicate that television scenarios sometimes are acquired as moral scripts that enter into the making of personal decisions by viewers, the next step should be to conduct full-scale studies to determine under what conditions this effect does and does not occur and who are the viewers most likely to be influenced. It certainly will not be an easy task to find the answers. But maybe with some ingenuity, along with intensive effort, social scientists can find ways of obtaining relevant data, especially for school children.

Counteracting the Influence of Television

The vulnerability of the very young to social modeling by the heroes and heroines in television drama is suggested by many survey results. Greenberg and Reeves (1976), for example, found that there was a marked tendency for school children to regard portrayals in television dramas as real. This attribution of reality was positively related to the amount of television viewing but was inversely related to age. Earlier I mentioned parallel findings on children's belief in the truthfulness of television commercials: Older children were found to be much less likely than younger ones to believe that commercials are truthful and display the "best" products (Ward, Wackman, Faber, & Lesser, 1974). All these findings about children's beliefs in the reality of television dramas and commercials suggest that other interacting factors offset or reduce the influence of television as a child grows older. We need to learn exactly what the counteracting factors are that decrease the influence of television on personal scripts and how they operate.

A closely related problem involves the moderating effects of socializing agents who say and do things that correct or modify the ideas children pick up from television. We can expect ongoing research to tell us something about the moderating influence of parents who watch television with their children and make comments about the prosocial and antisocial contents (Chaffee, McLeod, & Atkin, 1971; Comstock, 1975; Hicks, 1968). This topic at present is exciting considerable interest among developmental psychologists, but most of their research seems restricted to obvious pro- and antisocial themes. It could be extended to a variety of other pervasive content themes, such as those pertaining to ways of avoiding common health hazards, to determine how the moderating influence of adults can correct misconceptions or reinforce correct concepts that children might acquire from television. This brings us to a general operational research question, which could lead to advances in theoretical as well as practical knowledge. *What can parents or teachers do to prevent children from acquiring or retaining erroneous personal scripts that could have an adverse influence on their vital decisions, including the ones they make currently or later in life?*

New Objectives for Educational Television

Operational research is obviously needed to develop television programs that effectively induce accurate personal scripts about means-outcome relationships. This type of research could also be oriented toward developing and diffusing new programs for educational television. Research workers in this area could take advantage of findings from other fields of research and also make use of unusual television events as opportunities to obtain some useful leads, if not solid evidence. Here is a relatively simple example of what I have in mind: A fourth-grade class in an innercity school (99% black) was given a special "live" program in which black members of many different professions came to their classroom and told them what their professional work was like, how they prepared for it, how much money they made, and how they felt about what they were doing. The results of questionnaires given to the children suggested that they had changed markedly in their knowledge about the professions represented and had shifted their aspirations upward. If such changes are retained for many years, they could presumably affect the personal planning scripts that will be activated when the time comes for these young people to make career choices. Even more important might be the increase in realistic *hope* of finding a satisfactory career, which could promote a more vigilant pattern of decision-making rather than defensive proscrastinating or wishful thinking (see the final section of this chapter). One obvious research problem would be to see if a similar program prepared for television had any such effects, and, if so, if it attracted a large enough audience, when shown on local educational television programs, to make it worthwhile to prepare and distribute.

Here is a more complicated example: During March and April 1977, Ingmar Bergman's "Scenes From a Marriage," on New York's WNET (Channel 13), was accompanied by a live supplementary program during which viewers could speak via telephone with professional counselors on marriage and family problems. Imaginative research workers might be able to pose a number of practical questions that could be answered by small-scale studies concerning the impact of this combination of a provocative television drama with telephone counseling and other innovative ways of using television to promote effective decision-making. The findings might be useful not just for subsequent showing of one particular program but also for a broad range of productions that depict one or another aspect of life dilemmas involving ubiquitous personal problems. Of course, the most valuable projects might well be those in which research workers collaborate with writers, producers, and others in the television industry to develop and test new educational programs designed to build up accurate means–outcome scripts in the viewers. New programs developed to help children acquire the skills and information necessary for effective personal decision-making might prove to be especially valuable when parents watch them at the same time and discuss them with their children immediately afterward to make sure that the main points are neither missed nor misunderstood (Singer & Singer, 1977). This type of operational research might go a long way toward enabling the industry as well as the public to realize the full potential of the TV medium.

EFFECTS OF CONTENT THEMES BEARING ON DECISION-MAKING PROCEDURES

Up to this point I have been discussing research on the potential effects of television themes pertaining to means–consequence relationships—themes that could induce or reinforce personal scripts in the form of an if–then proposition: "When I have to make such and such a choice, if I select X as the best course of action, then one of the outcomes I should expect to experience is Y (with a high, moderate, or low degree of certainty)." Such scripts determine the dominant entries in the people's decisional balance sheets when they are trying to make up their minds what to do in response to a given threat or opportunity that requires a decision. But television also conveys information and presents social models of effective versus ineffective *procedures* for arriving at a satisfactory decision. Here I am referring to an entirely different type of content theme that can induce or reinforce an entirely different type of personal script pertaining to such questions as, "Where can I go for relevant information about the alternatives that are open to me and about their consequences?" "Who should I trust as an expert?" "What can I do to handle pressures from other people to make my decision before I have sufficient information about the consequences to make a sensible choice?" These and a variety of other *procedural* scripts can affect the degree to which people will explore the full range of alternatives open to them and assess the probable consequences of the alternatives that need to be taken into account in order to achieve their most important goals. If their procedures of information search and appraisal are defective, people are likely to encounter unexpected outcomes that cause unnecessary suffering and that make them regret the decision.

An example of a procedural theme explicitly conveyed by a television program has already been discussed: The three cancer patients on the "Not for Women Only" program urged the audience not to be overwhelmed by the authority of any physician who recommends surgery but to regard him as a fallible expert, respecting his judgment yet delaying action until a second expert opinion is obtained. This advice and the social modeling by the three self-confident women who offered it could lead viewers to change the procedures they use in arriving at a variety of health-related decisions. Many men and women regularly deal with the appearance of incapacitating symptoms and other serious health problems by consulting their regular physician and immediately accepting whatever recommendation is given, they follow a very simple procedural rule: "Tell a qualified expert about your troubles and do whatever the expert says." For such people the message on the talk show could have a profound effect on the subsequent handling of their own health problems and those of others in their families as a result of having acquired a new procedural script.

We know very little about the extent to which television exerts this type of influence on viewers' decision-making behavior. As far as I know, we do not even have any pertinent content analysis data on the extent to which television entertainment programs and commercials present models of impulsive versus deliberative decision-making or the extent to which they portray the favorable consequences of using sound decision-making procedures when people are confronted with the necessity to make a fundamental decision concerning their marriaage, career, health, or physical survival. And yet the portrayal of people making just such decisions is the stuff that television drama is made of.

I have just used a phrase—"sound decision-making procedures"—that could be faulted as a value-laden term that has no place in an objective analysis of how and why people behave as they do. It is true that we have no dependable way of assessing objectively how "good" or "successful" a decision has turned out to be. Nevertheless, we can formulate propositions specifying the conditions that have favorable or unfavorable effects on a person's decision-making activity by focusing on the *quality of the procedures* used by the decision-maker in selecting a course of action.

Criteria for Assessing the Quality of Decision Making

Suppose we want to find out if a group of viewers of a given television program show an increase or decrease, relative to an equated group of nonviewers, in the quality of their personal decisions. Or suppose we want to determine whether or not heavy versus light viewers show any differences in the quality of their personal decisions. Let us assume that we could obtain fairly valid observations of the steps each person in the equated groups has taken in arriving at recent personal decisions concerning career, health, or other vital issues. When it comes to analyzing these observations in terms of the quality of decision-making procedures, what criteria could we use?

From a review of the extensive literature on effective decision-making, Janis and Mann (1977, p. 11) have extracted seven major criteria that can be used to determine whether or not the decision-making procedures used by a person or group are of high quality. They point out that although systematic data are not yet available on this point, it seems plausible to assume that those decisions that are of high quality, in the sense of satisfying these ideal procedural criteria, have a better chance than others of attaining the decision-maker's objectives and of being adhered to in the long run. . . .

Vigilant Versus Nonvigilant Ways of Arriving at Decisions

Coming back to priorities for research on the effects of television, we should give a high rating to the task of determining when, in what ways, and to what extent the words and images conveyed by television foster or impede a vigilant information-processing orientation. Do certain television programs and advertisements present models that promote impulsive or defensive patterns of decision-making that result in failure to meet most or all of the seven criteria? Which types of television content promote vigilant information-processing?

Aside from direct effects of modeling and explicit persuasion, messages conveyed by television, like those presented in other mass media, can indirectly influence the way a person deals with personal crises requring vital personal decisions. The types of message that might exert an indirect influence are specified in an analysis by Janis and Mann (1976, 1977) of the crucial conditions that make for vigilant as against nonvigilant patterns of decision-making. . . .

As indicated in Fig. 9.1, there are three main conditions that determine whether vigilance of one of the other coping patterns will be dominant: (1) awareness of serious risks for whichever alternative is chosen (i.e., arousal of conflict), (2) hope or optimism about finding a better alternative, and (3) belief that there is adequate time in which to search and deliberate before a decision is required. Each of these three mediating conditions can be induced or changed not only by communications from the experts and advisers the person talks with but also by the words and images presented on television or in other mass media. Consider for example the messages that are likely to be extracted from television family dramas about marital discord by those viewers who are themselves contemplating breaking up their marriage. Some of the portrayals in the drama can make the viewers much more keenly aware of the risks both of trying to preserve a hopeless marriage and of breaking up one's home. The events depicted in the drama can also influence viewers to become more optimistic or pessimistic about finding a good solution for their own marital problems and can also influence beliefs pertaining to time pressures—for example, the heroine's actions might convey the message that an imminent deadline set by lawyers for working out the final details of a divorce agreement can be postponed with little cost if one really wants more time to think it over before making a final decision. Insofar as television content can build up personal scripts pertaining to these psychological conditions, it can influence the likelihood that viewers will adopt a vigilant rather than a defective coping pattern in dealing with vital decisions. If subsequent research shows that such scripts are acquired from television presentations by a sizable proportion of viewers, the next step will be to find out when and among whom.

Research on the effects of television on decisional coping patterns could also move in the direction of developing and testing out new types of television programs and new ways of using the medium to help people avoid defective decision-making procedures that lead to failure and regret. Suppose that there were a marked increase in audience viewing of diversified programs on a large number of new channels, including some devoted to public service programs. Or suppose that television cassettes for home screens became popular and readily accessible in public libraries or in low-fee lending libraries in drugstores. Would it be utopian to expect that once the monopoly of current commercial programming has ended, television could take on a new role in meeting educational needs of the mass audience? Television might prove to be effective, more so than any other medium, in transmitting decision-making skills to the tens of millions of persons of all ages who never did and probably never will learn all the essential skills they need from their families, acquaintances, or classroom teachers.

When we look over what little is already known from social science research in general on how people make decisions, one thing is certain: There is plenty of room for improvement in the information-seeking and appraisal activities of most people in our society when they face the necessity of making fundamental decisions that affect their future welfare. Many of the miseries of unanticipated consequences and postdecisional regret among people who make ill-considered personal decisions might be preventable. Although hardly recognized at present as a social problem, those widespread miseries warrant a considerable increase in attention from organizations that sponsor social science investigations and from leading experts who help set the priorities and spark the research. One of the main questions that has been in the back of my mind during the writing of this chapter is this: Whether or not television is part of the problem, couldn't research on media effects make it part of the solution?

REFERENCES

Abelson, R. P. Script processing in attitude formation and decision-making. In J. S. Carroll & J. W. Payne (Eds.), *Cognition and social behavior.* Hillsdale, N.J.: Lawrence Erlbaum Associates, 1976.

Adler, R. P. *Research on the effects of television advertising on children:* Washington, D.C.: U.S. Government Printing Office, 1977.

Arons, S., & Katsch, E. How TV cops flout the law. *Saturday Review,* 1977, *4,* 10–14.

Bechtel, R. B., Achelpohl, C., & Akers, R. Correlates between observed behavior and questionnaire responses on television viewing. In E. A. Rubinstein, G. A. Comstock, & J. P. Murray (Eds.), *Television and social behavior. Vol. 4. Television in day-to-day life: Patterns of use.* Washington, D.C.: U.S. Government Printing Office, 1972.

Chafee, S. H., McLeod, J. M., & Atkin, C. K. Parental influences on adolescent media use. *American Behavioral Scientist,* 1971, *14,* 323–340.

Comstock, G. *Effects of television on children: What is the evidence?* Paper presented at the 1975 Telecommunications Policy Research Conference at Airlie House, Airlie, Virginia, April 1975.

Comstock, G., & Lindsey, G. (Eds.). *Television and human behavior: The research horizon, future and present* (Vol. 2). Santa Monica: The Rand Corporation, 1975.

DeFleur, M. L. Occupational roles as portrayed on television. *Public Quarterly,* 1964, *28,* 57–74.

DeFleur, M.L., & DeFleur, L. B. The relative contribution of television as a learning source for children's occupation knowledge. *American Sociological Review,* 1967, *32,* 777–789.

Dominick, J. R. Children's viewing of crime shows and attitudes on law enforcement. *Journalism Quarterly,* 1974, *51,* 5–12.

Frank, R. S. Home-school differences in political learning: Television's impact on school children's perception of national needs. Cited in G. Comstock & G. Linsey (Eds.), *Television and human behavior: The research horizon, future and present* (Vol. 2). Santa Monica, Calif.: The Rand Corporation, 1975.

Gerbner, G. Violence in television drama: Trends and symbolic functions. In G. A. Comstock & E. A. Rubinstein (Eds.), *Television and social behavior. Vol. 1. Media content and control.* Washington, D.C.: U.S. Government Printing Office, 1972.

Gerbner, G., & Gross, L. Living with television: The violence profile. *Journal of Communications,* 1976, *26,* 173–199.

Greenberg, B.S., & Reeves, B. Children and the perceived reality of television. *Journal of Social Issues,* 1976, *32,* 86–97.

Hicks, D. J. Effects of co-observers sanctions and adult presence on imitative aggression. *Child Development,* 1968, *38,* 303–309.

Himmelweit, H. T. Yesterday's and tomorrow's television research on children. In. D. Lerner & L. Nelson (Eds.), University of Hawaii Press, 1977.

Himmelweit, H. T., Oppenheim, A. N., & Vince, P. *Television and the child.* London: Oxford University Press, 1958.

Janis, I. L. *Victims of groupthink,* Boston: Houghton Mifflin, 1972.

Janis, I. L. Effectiveness of social support for stressful decisions. In M. Deutsch & H. A. Hornstein (Eds.), *Applying social psychology: Implications for research, practice, and training.* Hillsdale, N.J.: Lawrence Erlbaum Associates, 1975.

Janis, I. L. *Current trends in psychology: Readings from American Scientist.* Palo Alto: Kaufmann, 1977.

Janis, I. L., & Mann, L. Coping with decisional conflict. *American Scientist,* 1976, *64,* 657–667.

Janis, I. L., & Mann, L. *Decision making: A psychological analysis of conflict, choice, and commitment.* New York: Free Press, 1977.

Leifer, A. D., & Lesser, G. S. *The development of career awareness in young children.* NIE Papers in Education and Work: Number 1. Washington, D.C.: National Institute of Education, 1976.

Lesser, G. S. *Children and television: Lessons from Sesame Street.* New York: Random House, 1974.

Lyle, J., & Hoffman, H. R. Explorations in patterns of television viewing by preschool age children. In E. A. Rubinstein, G. A. Comstock, & J. P. Murray (Eds.), *Television and social behavior. Vol. 4, Television in day-to-day life: Patterns of use.* Washington, D.C.: U.S. Government Printing Office, 1972.

McGuire, W. J. The nature of attitudes and attitude change. In G. Lindzey & E. Aronson (Eds.), *The handbook of social psychology* (Vol. 3). Reading, Mass.: Addison-Wesley, 1969.

Milavsky, J. R., Pekowsky, B., & Stipp, H. Television exposure and proprietary and illicit drug use. *Public Opinion Quarterly,* 1975, *39,* 457–481.

Platt, J. Information networks for human transformation. In M. Kochen (Ed.), *Information for action.* New York: Academic Press, 1975.

Seggar, J. F. & Wheeler, P. World at work on TV: Ethnic and sex representation in TV drama. *Journal of Broadcasting,* 1973, *17,* 201–214.

Shank, R. C., & Abelson, R. P. *Scripts, plans, and knowledge.* Prepared for presentation at the 4th International Joint Conference on Artificial Intelligence, U.S.S.R.: Tbilisi, Mat, 1975.

Singer, J. *Television-viewing and reading in the light of current research on cognition and information-processing.* Paper presented at the annual meeting of the Magazine Publishers' Association of America, October, 1976.

Singer, D. G., & Singer, J. L. *Partners in play: A step-by-step guide to imaginative play in children.* New York: Harper, 1977.

Tversky, A., & Kahneman, D. Judgment under uncertainty. *Science,* 1974, *185,* 1124–1131.

Ward, S., Wackman, D. B., Faber, R., & Lesser, G. *Effects of television advertising on consumer socialization.* Cambridge, Mass.: Marketing Science Institute, 1974.

11

Psychological and Sociological Ambivalence: An Analysis of Nonadherence to Courses of Action Prescribed by Health-Care Professionals (1980)

This paper discusses the theoretical concepts and findings that have emerged from a research project on which I have been working for the past 10 years. The research program is designed to test hypotheses concerning the conditions under which a professional counselor will and will not have a positive influence on clients' adherence to a recommended course of action. Most of the studies are field experiments conducted in health-care settings. The recommendations typically involve short-term losses in order to attain long-term gains, such as giving up smoking, dieting, or undergoing a surgical operation. The objective of the research is to increase our understanding of when, how, and why the social influence of professionals on clients achieve their goals. Specifically, the studies are intended to enable us to explain and predict when a professional counselor will succeed or fail to help clients to adhere to a recommended course of action that both agree would be in the client's best interests.

My theoretical analysis for developing testable hypotheses took as its point of departure the concept of *reference power* as a major determinant of a person's social influence. This concept owes much

Janis, I. L. Psychological and sociological ambivalence: An analysis of nonadherence to courses of action prescribed by health-care professionals. In T. F. Gieryn (Ed.), *Science and social structure: A Festschrift for Robert K. Merton.* Transactions of the New York Academy of Sciences, Series 11, Vol. 39. New York, 1980. The research reported in this paper was supported by research grants from the National Institute of Mental Health and National Science Foundation. Reprinted by permission.

to the work of Robert Merton (1957) on reference groups and reference individuals.

When Merton's book on *Sociological Ambivalence* was published in 1976, I discovered that another of his key concepts was applicable to my research on adherence and nonadherence. Most of my previous work dealt with psychological ambivalence. It focused on how variations in the counselor's behavior affected the clients' emotions, expectations, attitudes, and actions. But I soon realized that I was encountering sources of ambivalence that are "built into the structure of social statuses and roles," which Merton (1976, p. 5) designates as *sociological* ambivalence.

When people are ambivalent, as Merton notes, they are "pulled in psychologically opposed directions," as when a person feels both love and hate for someone or is inclined both to accept and reject another's demands (1976, p. 6). Latent ambivalence occurs, to some degree, in all our human contacts. When ambivalence becomes sufficiently intense to be manifest in our dealings with a particular person, our relationship with that person tends to become seriously impaired, if not terminated altogether.

Merton (1976, pp. 19-31 and pp. 65-72) gives a vivid account of sentiments unintentionally evoked by physicians who, in keeping with the requirements of their professional role, are more detached, more demanding, and more frustrating than their patients are willing to tolerate. He calls attention to various dysfunctional consequences that result from health-care professionals living up to their roles. These include patients' suspicion that they are being exploited financially, failures to see a physician when serious medical problems occur, hostile attitudes toward the entire profession, and disproportionate tendencies to initiate unwarranted malpractice suits. Incompatible role expectations also have corruptive influences on some of the troubled practitioners themselves who try to avoid generating ambivalence by "departing from what they know to be the most appropriate kind of medical care" (1976, p. 72). Another dysfunctional consequence would be patients' nonadherence to prescriptions and health practices recommended by health-care practitioners.

I am now prompted to reconceptualize my theoretical analysis of practitioner-client relationships in terms of the linkage between the two types of ambivalence, taking account of Merton's plausible assumption that "sociological ambivalence is one major source of psychological ambivalence" (1976, p. 7). The final section of this paper represents a first attempt at a reformulation in terms of a double focus on sociological and psychological ambivalence, as recommended by Merton. The need for linking the two sources of ambivalence will become more apparent after I discuss the main phenomena of nonadherence.

THE PROBLEM OF NONADHERENCE

Numerous studies indicate that patients often disregard physicians' recommendations for dealing with serious health problems. In a study of 47 men and women treated at an out-patient clinic in Liverpool, England, more than half of the medical instructions given by the physicians could not be recalled accurately by the patients immediately after they left the consulting room (Ley and Spelman, 1965). Investigations of American women with acutely ill children suffering from rheumatic fever, streptococcal pharyngitis, or otitis media found that from 34 to 82 percent were seriously endangering the health of their children by not giving them the proper doses of penicillin that had been explicitly prescribed by their physicians (Bergman and Werner, 1963; Chamey *et al.*, 1967; Feinstein, *et al.*, 1959). A study of 154 new adult patients in the general medical clinic of a large teaching hospital found that 37 percent failed to comply substantially with physicians' recommendations and only 14 percent complied fully (Davis, 1971). Reviews of the large number of studies on patients' failure to comply with physicians' recommendations report wide variation in different circumstances, with noncompliance rates ranging from 15 to 93 percent (Davis, 1966; Sacket and Haynes, 1977).

Medical practitioners sometimes express dissatisfaction with their professional life, despite the high prestige and deference accorded them, because a sizeable percentage of their patients fail to follow the regimens they prescribe (see Kasl, 1975). Many physicians avoid the disappointments of nonadherence by not treating patients with certain types of disorder, like hypertension, which require unpleasant medication as well as restrictions on smoking, drinking, and eating (see Maddox, Anderson, and Bogdonoff, 1966; Stamler, Schoenberger, Lindberg, *et al.*, 1969).

Problems of nonadherence have also been well documented in studies of many clinics that offer professional help to heavy smokers and to overweight men and women. In the United States this is a burgeoning industry, quite profitable to private entrepreneurs. Each year hundreds of thousands of new consumers and recidivists pay for their services. But most of their successes appear to be short-lived. A high percentage of those who come to the clinics do cut down on cigarette smoking or lose weight for a few weeks, but most of them fail to adhere to the prescribed regimen after supportive contact terminates (see Atthowe, 1973; Sackett and Haynes, 1977; Shewchuck, 1976). In a review of the literature on the effectiveness of programs for heavy smokers, Hunt and Matarazzo (1973) found that, just as with heroin addicts and heavy drinkers, many people begin to abstain in response to whatever professional treatment they receive, but a very high percentage relapse within a month or two after starting the program.

Why do many people break off before completing the prescribed regimen or backslide after having changed their behavior temporarily? Why do other people successfully adhere to recommended treatments? Some of the pertinent factors have been tentatively identified. One obvious factor in backsliding is intensity of suffering or deprivation, which may be especially hard to take over a long period of time. But social and psychological factors also affect a person's tolerance for pain, frustration, and resisting temptations. Many studies have found that nonadherence is linked with difficulties in patients' relationships with health-care professionals. Disappointment of patients with their physicians has been found to lead to their not keeping subsequent appointments or breaking off the treatment entirely (Davis 1967; Vincent, 1971; Zola, 1973). These disappointment reactions are partly attributable to the physicians' behavior. Physicians often fail to find out the patients' reasons for wanting to be examined and fail to explain the purpose of the treatments they prescribe. These two kinds of deficiency have been singled out as specific sources of patients' failure to act in accordance with medical recommendations.

In a review of the extensive literature on adherence to recommended medical regimens among outpatients, Kasl (1975) concludes that a crucial source of difficulty resides in the conflicting expectations of the health-care professional and the patient, which involve divergent role expectations. In other words, studies of the psychology of adherence point to precisely those factors related to social structure that Merton (1976) emphasizes in his analysis of sociological ambivalence among medical patients. It is not yet possible, however, to determine the relative importance of social structural factors as compared with psychological factors, such as predispositions of the patients making for strong resistance to authoritative demands and idiosyncratic deficiencies of health-care professionals making for insensitive or humiliating treatment of patients.

OBSERVATIONS ON THE SOCIAL POWER OF
HEALTH-CARE PROFESSIONALS

Observations on surgical wards and in hospital clinics (Janis, 1958 and 1975; Janis and Leventhal, 1965) have made me keenly aware that the quality of the affiliative bond between patients and health-care professionals is a crucial factor in sustained adherence. Time and again, I have noted that patients will adhere to the rigorous demands of a medical regimen only so long as they have a warm personal attachment to a particular physician, nurse, physical therapist, or other member of the staff. In observing patients suffering from neurological damage to the spinal cord and various other back injuries, for example, I have noticed some of them rapidly becoming hopeless, demoralized invalids. Others, suffering from just as severe disorders, actively struggle against such demoralization. They work day in and day out to carry out all the prescribed procedures and exercises, whether the medical staff is around or not. Sometimes their physicians express amazement over the large number of seemingly lost functions they have been able to restore. What seems to loom large in these successful cases is their warm affectionate relationship with a member of the medical staff, a relationship that bolsters their self-confidence during the most stressful periods of convalescence.

I have also observed similar, though less intensive relationships with the health counselor among the most successful clients who come to anti-smoking clinics and weight-reduction clinics. The clients who perceive the health-care professional not just as a likeable person but also as benevolent, admirable and accepting are most likely to adhere to the recommended "cold turkey" program of smoking cessation or to the low-calorie diet (Janis, 1982).

The concept of "referent power" is useful for explicating this facilitating type of affiliative bond between the client or patient and the health-care professional. In the form derived from social psychological analyses of the social power of change agents (French and Raven, 1959; Tedeschi and Lindskold, 1976), the concept refers to the power acquired by professionals when their "acceptance" of clients functions as a major incentive for clients' adherence to prescribed courses of action.

"Referent power" was initially used in a more restrictive sense to describe individuals who fulfill a "comparison reference function," i.e., those used by others as a "frame of reference" for evaluating themselves. With this function in mind, French and Raven (1959) contrasted referent power with other bases of social influence, which are effective in inducing acquiescence but in the absence of surveillance are less likely to create sustained change—coercive power, reward power, and expert power. More recently, social psychologists have extended the concept of "referent power" to apply to influential persons who are regarded as significant others and who have a "normative reference function" (Marwell and Schmitt, 1967; Tedeschi and Lindskold, 1976). Tedeschi and Lindskold observe that normative referent power is a relatively independent dimension of influential persons characterized by high perceived attractiveness and high perceived sociability. Their signs of approval or disapproval function as powerful incentives to induce others to adopt and to internalize their values, attitudes, and standards. This conception of referent power can be derived from the early theoretical analysis of reference groups by Merton and Rossi (1950) and Merton's subsequent elaborations of the social power of reference groups and reference individuals who set and maintain standards for others (Merton, 1957).

When health-care professionals acquire some degree of referent power, they are taken as a "normative frame of reference" with regard to a fairly broad range of health-related attitudes and behavior. If referent power increases to a high level, the professionals' normative influence may extend well beyond this sphere to encompass other aspects of life style.

Physicians and other practitioners, of course, display marked individual differences in the degree to which they rely on the various sources of social power. Years ago, many family physicians apparently developed their referent power to such a high degree that their patients would strive to get well partly because they did not want to disappoint their lovable "old doc." This component is often missing in present-day treatment by specialists (see Merton and Gieryn, 1978). Many physicians and other practitioners appear to have little power as reference persons. They rely, in effect, on coercive, reward, legitimate, and expert power, but neglect the potential increase in their ability to influence patients that could come from acquiring referent power as well. These are the practitioners who appear to be most haunted by the spector of nonadherence—of having all their diligence and all their diagnostic and treatment skills come to nothing simply because their patients do not adhere to their recommendations. In contrast, professionals with referent power as well as the other kinds of social power meet with less psychological resistance. Their recommendations are more likely to be internalized and conscientiously adhered to long after the consulting sessions have come to an end. Some of my observations, which will be described shortly, suggest that even when health-care professionals are fully using the other four sources of power, their effectiveness as change agents would increase if they were to adopt one or another means for acquiring social power as reference persons (Janis, 1982).

What are the means available to a professional for building up social power as a reference person? The psychological literature on the effects of *positive social reinforcement,* which appears to be a necessary condition for the development of strong affiliative ties, suggests part of the answer (see Bersheid and Walster, 1969). Three widely used types of social reinforcement are part of the folk wisdom of our time for anyone who wants to win friends and influence people: expressing agreement, giving contingent praise, and displaying benevolent interest. A fourth type, much less popular despite the best efforts of Carl Rogers and his followers to make it so, involves giving noncontingent acceptance to bolster the other person's self-esteem. Dittes (1959) has provided experimental evidence indicating that a person's attraction to others in a group rapidly increases when he or she is given accepting comments that raise self-esteem. Similar results were found in a study of pairs of students working together as partners (Jones, Knurek, and Regan, 1973).

Considerable skill, as well as empathy and interpersonal sensitivity, is needed to avoid the pitfalls of using noncontingent acceptance as a means for building up one's referent power. For example, a professional's acceptance statements can have a boomerang effect on his patients if he lays it on so thick that he is presumed to be either habitually insincere or attempting to be ingratiating with hidden manipulative intent (see Jones, 1964). Another type of boomerang effect is illustrated by a little episode (hitherto unpublished) in the life of Nicholas Murray Butler, reported to me by a physician who was an intern at the time Butler was President of Columbia University. Merton (1957, page 381), incidentally, in a discussion of individual differences in the number and complexity of statuses, singled out Nicholas Murray Butler as an extreme example of someone with "enumerable though seemingly endless statuses occupied at the same time." The following episode occurred at a time when Butler was temporarily occupying the unwelcomed additional status of a patient in Columbia University's Presbyterian Hospital. Late one night Butler got up from bed and walked agitatedly down the corridor in his hospital garb, carrying a urine container attached to an indwelling catheter. Noticing his discomfort, the nurse notified the resident physician on night duty, a man who was very keen on expressing a warm, accepting interest in patients. The resident approached Butler with a broad smile and said in his best bedside manner, "What's the trouble, pop, can't you pee?" Coolly looking the physician in the eye, "pop" asked, "Doctor, what is your name?" After being told, he responded, "And my name, doctor, is Nicholas Murray Butler."

CRISES IN THE RELATIONSHIP BETWEEN PROFESSIONALS AND THEIR CLIENTS

In an effort to learn something more about the way professionals build up their referent power—or fail to do so—in their interactions with clients, I extended the scope of my observations to a variety of professional settings where people come for help. I functioned as a professional counselor in various kinds of clinics where clients seek help with marital problems, choosing or changing their careers, giving up smoking, going on a diet, or undergoing disagreeable medical treatments recommended by a physician (Janis, 1975). I met with each client once or twice a week for several weeks, usually from 3 to 12 sessions. In the case of the dieting clinics, the objective of counseling was to help clients carry out a difficult course of action in the face of temptations to backslide; in other clinics, the objective was to help clients arrive at a decision concerning marriage or career by encouraging them to go through the necessary steps of exploring alternatives, seeking pertinent information, and making unbiased appraisals.

After comparing successful and unsuccessful cases in an impressionistic way, I tried to evaluate the plausibility of my inferences from these clinical observations in the light of the clinical and social psychological literature on helping relationships. The main hypotheses that emerge appear to be consistent with Merton's (1957) account of the norm-setting functions of reference groups and reference individuals. They are also consistent with findings from systematic studies indicating that social support from a significant person or group can have positive effects under two main conditions: (1) the relationship is characterized by a high degree of *cohesiveness*, which is determined by the participants' anticipations of socio-emotional gains (such as friendship and esteem) as well as utilitarian gains (such as improved health or better career opportunities) resulting from the relationship with the significant person or group; and (2) the relationship involves exposure to *norm-setting* communications, which convey the behavioral standards that the significant person or group expects one to live up to (Cartwright and Zander, 1968; Hare, 1976; Shaw, 1971).

The hypotheses pertain to three critical phases that typically arise in helping relationships. These hypotheses specify several new variables in addition to the more familiar ones pertaining to social power and positive social reinforcements that I have just discussed— variables often overlooked by many professional practitioners but which can nevertheless affect the extent to which a client or patient will be favorably influenced. The key variables are listed in Table 11.1, organized according to the three critical phases. Most of the variables have already been subjected to experimental investigation, conducted mainly in smoking-cessation clinics and weight-reduction clinics (Janis, 1982). I shall summarize the evidence from those studies after giving a short theoretical account of the critical phases.

My observations suggest that three critical phases, arising from three major sources of ambivalence, regularly appear in helping relationships. When these crises are surmounted, people are most likely to benefit from the attempts of a professional to help them arrive at or adhere to difficult decisions.

In the first phase, the practitioner dissipates the patient's wariness and acquires motivating power as a significant "reference person." Fears of being exploited, of being dominated, and of being rejected by the stranger (who is supposed to be a professional helper) constitute initial bases for ambivalence. If the practitioner encourages patients to disclose personal feelings, troubles, or weaknesses and responds to the self-disclosures with statements of noncontingent acceptance, the patients tend to develop an attitude of trust and to rely upon the practitioner for enhancing their self-esteem. The patient's image of the practitioner becomes that of a warm, understanding protective figure who can be counted on to accept personal weaknesses and defects. Normative referent power is also increased if practitioners provide fresh insights or explicit encouragement, regardless of how "awful" the patients characterize themselves.

In the second phase, practitioners begin to use their motivating power. However, the relationship built up during the first phase is impaired as the practitioner begins to function as a norm-sending communicator by encouraging or urging the patient to carry out a necessary but stressful course of action. This is a second major source of ambivalence. If the practitioner makes no such demands, either explicitly or implicitly, the relationship will continue in a warm, friendly way but will be ineffectual. The crisis that arises when practitioners recommend a new course of action are more likely to be surmounted if they make it clear that their demands are very limited in scope and that occasional failures to live up to those demands following a sincere attempt to do so will not change their basic attitude of acceptance toward the patients. It may also be helpful for practitioners to attribute the norms that are being endorsed to a respected secondary group and to negotiate an agreement with the patient so that they become committed to those norms.

Norm-sending practitioners are most likely to retain motivating power when they use a selective pattern of social reinforcement. This pattern consists of criticizing patients' counternorm assertions in a nonthreatening way while expressing positive regard the rest of the time, including when the patients admit to personal shortcomings that are irrelevant to the task at hand. By expressing noncontingent acceptance most of the time and restricting contingent acceptance to the agreed-upon task, practitioners can lead patients to develop an authentic image of them as a quasi-dependable source of self-esteem enhancement; this, in turn, facilitates the practitioners' effectiveness.

A modified expectation of partly contingent acceptance from practitioners allows clients to look forward to receiving genuine acceptance and approval much of the time. The clients sometimes think acceptance will be forthcoming practically all the time, almost as much as when acceptance is in fact wholly unconditional—provided only that they make a sincere effort to follow the relatively few recommended rules which pertain to a limited sphere of personal behavior. The image of a quasi-dependable enhancer differs significantly from that of the garden variety of undependable enhancer who offers acceptance only conditionally. The latter type of helper leads clients to expect little or no approval except when they clearly earn it by conforming to many rules laid down by the helper to govern many spheres of personal behavior, much like the rules imposed by strict parents who demand conformity with their entire code of moral behavior and etiquette. Clients know that signs of acceptance from demanding authority figures are few and far between. An image of the helper as supplying a nurturant diet of variable but basic acceptance, rather than either the meagre bones of conditional acceptance or the rich but undigestible fare of unconditional acceptance, is assumed to be optimal for functioning effectively as a constructive motivator.

In the third critical phase, the influence of the supportive norm-sending practitioner is threatened by the patient's disappointment and resentment centered on the termination of direct contact. As the sessions with the practitioner come to an end, the patient may interpret the termination of contact as a sign of rejection or indifference and fail to internalize the norms advocated by the practitioner. The client's disappointment may become so extreme as to lead to deliberate violations of the counselor's norms. Once a relationship with a helper has been established, aggrievement about termination of contact is a major source of psychological ambivalence. Patients whose chronic diabetes has been stabilized, for example, may stop following the prescribed medical regimen within a few months after they no longer have appointments to see the physician. Adverse reactions to separation may be reduced if the practitioner gives assurances of continuing positive regard and arranges for gradual rather than abrupt termination of contact. In order to prevent backsliding and other adverse effects when contact is terminated, the patient must internalize the practitioner's norms. Little is known about the determinants of this process, but it seems plausible that internalization might be facilitated by communications and training procedures that build up appropriate self attributions and a sense of personal responsibility.

The art of effective health care may require dealing with each of the three critical phases in ways designed to minimize adverse reactions. Perhaps relatively few practitioners have the interpersonal skills that enable them to treat most of their clients with consumate artistry in all three phases. Nevertheless, practitioners having modest amounts of skill in dealing with people in trouble may be able to improve their effectiveness by taking account of the prescriptive hypotheses suggested by this analysis.

The foregoing account of three critical phases assumes that a helper's chances of being effective increase if the client develops a differentiated attitude of reliance on, respect for, and emotional attachment to the professional practitioner or other helper. This is a much more complex attitude than simple "liking" for a stranger as measured by standard scales of interpersonal attraction in current social psychological research (see Berscheid & Walster, 1978; Byrne, 1971). One would expect that after patients have started to reveal personal weaknesses, noncontingent acceptance by the practitioner will result in improving their self regard. This, in turn, will make for strong motivation to continue the relationship, with high reliance on the helper as a respected model. From this point the helper becomes a significant reference person for the client and has the potentiality of using his or her social power to influence the client's actions. This power may compare with that of cohesive normative reference groups. It can be used to encourage the client to become committed to a difficult course of action and to overcome temptations to backslide. The important point is that professional counselors acquire far more social power as normative reference persons and will be regarded with far more affection and deference when clients see them as dependable sources for enhancing self esteem, rather than as conditional acceptors, who are at best undependable enhancers.

A vivid illustration of a client's response to a professional counselor who has become a powerfully motivating norm-setter can be cited from the innovative work of Neal Miller and Barry Dworkin on biofeedback training. These investigators were pioneers in developing an instrumental conditioning technique with verbal rewards to help hypertension patients gain control over their blood pressure. A young woman who wrote down her impressions of an arduous 10-week training period, during which she temporarily succeeded in lowering her diastolic pressure from a dangerously high average of 97 to a satisfactory average of about 80, had this to say about her trainer:

> I always depend very heavily on Barry Dworkin's encouragement and on his personality. I think he could be an Olympics coach. He not only seems aware of my general condition but he is never satisfied with less than my best, and I cannot fool him. I feel we are friends and allies—it's really as though *we* were lowering my pressure. (Jonas, 1972.)

When the patient regards the health-care professional as an Olympics coach, she conveys the idea that in some sense she thinks of the coach as treating her like an Olympics star. Not everyone who engages in professional work can expect to function like a successful Olympics coach with all clients. But perhaps a better understanding of the crucial ingredients of an effective helping relationship will lead to improved means for building the type of relationship that is most effective. The key theoretical concepts introduced in the analysis of the three critical phases, including those pertaining to the image of the helper as a quasi-dependable source of self-esteem enhancement, provide a general framework that might account for what happens in a variety of other dyadic relationships—between a student and a teacher, a novice and a guru, a pair of work colleagues, friends, lovers, or marital partners—and also in relationships between group members and their leaders.

RESEARCH ON THE EFFECTS OF BUILDING REFERENT POWER

Only a few of the independent variables listed in Table 11.1 have been sufficiently investigated to provide replicated findings. Much of

Table 11.1 Critical Phases and Twelve Key Variables That Determine the Degree of Referent Power of Professional Practitioners as Change Agents (From Janis, 1982)

Phase 1: Building up referent power	1. Encouraging clients to make self-disclosures *versus* not doing so
	2. Giving positive feedback (acceptance and understanding) *versus* giving neutral or negative feedback in response to self-disclosure
	3. Using self-disclosures to give insight and cognitive restructuring *versus* giving little insight or cognitive restructuring
Phase 2: Using referent power	4. Making directive statements or endorsing specific recommendations regarding actions the client should carry out *versus* abstaining from any directive statements or endorsements
	5. Eliciting commitment to the recommended course of action *versus* not eliciting commitment
	6. Attributing the norms being endorsed to a respected secondary group *versus* not doing so
	7. Giving selective positive feedback *versus* giving noncontingent acceptance or predominantly neutral or negative feedback[a]
	8. Giving communications and training procedures that build up a sense of personal responsibility *versus* giving no such communications or training
Phase 3: Retaining referent power after contact ends and promoting internalization	9. Giving reassurances that the counselor will continue to maintain an attitude of positive regard *versus* giving no such reassurances
	10. Making arrangements for phone calls, exchange of letters, or other forms of communication that foster hope for future contact, real or symbolic, at the time of terminating face-to-face meetings *versus* making no such arrangements
	11. Giving reminders that continue to foster a sense of personal responsibility *versus* giving no such reminders
	12. Building up the client's self-confidence about succeeding without the aid of the counselor *versus* not doing so

[a]By selective feedback is meant a combination of (a) negative feedback in response to any of the client's comments about being reluctant, unwilling or failing to act in accordance with the recommendations and (b) positive feedback in response to all other comments whether relevant to the decision or not.

the pertinent research carried out in our research program at Yale University deals with the variables in phase 1, the acquisition of referent power (Janis, 1982). We have also completed a few studies and have others under way that bear on the variables affecting the other two phases . . .[A number of paragraphs that summarize the evidence are omitted because the same material is covered more fully in Chapter 12.]

The various research studies . . . [which are reviewed in Chapter 12], including controlled field experiments and qualitative analyses of individual case studies, converge on the following conclusion: When a practitioner gives consistently positive feedback, referent power is fostered by eliciting a *moderate* degree of self-disclosure (rather than a very high or low degree) which results in *enhancement of the clients' self esteem* and makes for *increased adherence* to the practitioner's recommendations. There is also evidence in some of the studies indicating that in short-term health counseling, authority figures who remain detached and demanding can also be effective even though they do not enhance self esteem, provided that they are seen by the clients as benign protectors. . . .

Additional evidence from controlled field experiments by Rodin and her colleagues conducted with weight-reduction groups supports the hypothesis that using the clients' self-disclosures to assess and to modify their causal attributions can lead to cognitive reappraisals that facilitate adherence to medical recommendations (Rodin, 1978).

Studies of physician-patient relationships by other investigators provide additional evidence that is consistent with hypotheses about the variables specified in the three phases. [Brownell, Heckerman and Westlake, 1976; Francis, et al., 1969; Freeman, 1971] . . . .

Although pieces of evidence from a variety of systematic investigations support some of the hypotheses derived from the analysis of the three critical stages, the theoretical assumptions concerning the positive effects of self-esteem enhancement have not yet been fully tested. Nevertheless, the main hypotheses appear to be promising in light of existing studies on professional-client relationships.

LINKAGES OF PSYCHOLOGICAL WITH SOCIOLOGICAL AMBIVALENCE

Upon reading Merton's recent book (1976), I realized that in my studies of psychological sources of ambivalence among the clients of health-care professionals I had taken it for granted that the interactions were at least partly governed by role prescriptions. The structural features of the social relations were taken as "facts of historical circumstance," as Merton puts it (p. 4). As I read his analysis of the factors in the structure of social roles that affect the probability of ambivalence arising from the interaction of professionals with their clients, I noticed that some of those factors are similar to the variables listed in my psychological analysis of critical phases. For example, in Merton's account the professional has the authority (a) to induce intimate disclosures of private information, which can have an adverse affect on the client's self esteem (phase 1 in Table 11.1), (b) to prescribe regimens that impose frustrations (see phase 2), and (c) to terminate contact even though the client may want to continue (see phase 3).

In light of Merton's analysis, I am now inclined to view my work as focussing on the psychological ambivalence induced in clients by the behavior of practitioners when they act within the acceptable boundaries of the professional role. The term "boundaries" takes into account the more or less broad range of acceptable ways for practitioners to deal with their clients, including acceptable variations in manners, as well as in the degree to which they use the social power (expert, legitimate, reward and coercive) with which their role is endowed. The resident physician who intercepted Nicholas Murray Butler in the hospital corridor, addressed him as "pop," and asked about his "peeing" was not violating any of the norms governing his professional role. But the role prescriptions gave him options for expressing his interest in an elderly patient on his ward in other acceptable ways that would have had a rather different psychological effect on the patient. . . .

Paul Lazarsfeld (1975, p. 57), commenting on the original sociological ambivalence paper by Merton and his co-author, Elinor Barber, says that it offers a "brilliant program for an empirical study: Why do patients feel uneasy about their physicians?" I would like to add that another research program is also suggested by the same paper—one requiring a combined focus to answer a question about even more profound social consequences: Why do so many patients fail to do what their physicians or other health-care professionals recommend? By using an approach that looks at both the sociological and the psychological sources of ambivalence and their linkages it should be possible to arrive at more complete understanding of the antecedent conditions that give rise to nonadherence.

What kind of hypotheses would link the two types of ambivalence? To sketch out a few examples that might provide some evocative ideas, I shall reformulate the three critical stages specified by the analysis of psychological ambivalence (summarized in Table 11.1) in terms that take account of sociological ambivalence.

From their first contact with clients, physicians and other health-care professionals, by virtue of their social status, have considerable potential for social influence. They wield considerable legitimate and expert power and in some circumstances reward and coercive power as well. There is also, of course, some degree of latent ambivalence right from the outset. When they need the help of a professional, people are wary about the possibility of being exploited or humili-ated, sometimes because of prior unhappy experiences with similar professionals, more often because they have heard cautionary tales from friends or relatives. Merton (1976) points out that disgruntled clients give selective or exaggerated accounts to others of the most dramatic failures which "serve to spread ambivalent attitudes and to provide a context for hearers when next they have dealings with professionals" (p. 30–31). But clients' suspicions are counteracted to some extent by the credentials of professionals, especially by signs that they are affiliated with a prestigious hospital. In any case, the negative components of clients' attitudes toward the professional are likely to be less strong than the positive components. The negative components of the clients' initially ambivalent attitude, which ad-versely affect their willingness to adhere to the professional's recom-mendations, can be expected to increase or decrease depending largely on how the professional behaves in face-to-face sessions.

Professional role prescriptions place numerous constraints on the behavior of health-care practitioners, which prevent them from build-ing up the positive components because the constraints interfere with the acquisition of normative referent power. Consider, for example, the contrasting types of interaction that would be expected to occur when a pair of overweight women agree to use the "buddy system" to help each other stick to a 1200-calorie diet given them by a hos-pital's dietetics clinic, as compared with when the same two clients have individual sessions with a professional counselor. Partners lack the credentials that give professionals a headstart in expert and legiti-mate power, but usually without realizing it find it relatively easy to meet the essential conditions for acquiring normative referent power (see phase 1 in Table 11.1). They can plunge into self-disclosing con-versations, revealing their current hopes, frustrations, concerns, and personal weaknesses, such as their inability to resist temptations to overeat. Typically they respond to each others' disclosures with signs of acceptance, highlighting their similarities and mutual empathy. But equal partners are likely to do a poor job as norm-senders (see phase 2 of Table 11.1). They usually avoid giving selective social reinforcements that are contingent on adherence and are inclined to share the guilt for deviations from the prescribed diet (Janis, 1982). Later on, when the time comes for thinking about termination of the partnership, the partners find it relatively easy to make arrangements that foster hope for future contact and to provide reassurances that they will continue to have positive regard for each other (see phase 3 of Table 11.1). Thus, in terms of the analysis summarized in Table 11.1, each partner will acquire and retain motivating power as a normative reference person, but will fail to use that social power to foster adherence to the diet.

The situation would be entirely different if, instead of forming a partnership, each of the clients had individual sessions with a physician, nurse, or professional health counselor in a weight-reduction clinic that advocates the same 1200-calorie diet. In the professional setting, the client's self-disclosures most likely would be restricted to the business at hand (such as information about eating habits) and the practitioner's response to the disclosures would tend to be neutral and detached, with occasional negative comments indicating disapproval when the client reveals an inability to resist temptations to overeat. (Professional role prescriptions regarding the expression of compassion generally pertain only when patients are in a dire state of physical suffering). Furthermore, tending strictly to business, the professional would be unlikely to take the time to give explanations that might provide insights or cognitive restructuring in response to the client's self-disclosures. To the extent that these features characterize the behavior of professionals, they will fail to build up motivating power as normative reference persons in phase 1. The professionals' social power might actually decrease as a result of their detached impersonal stance and critical comments that lower the self esteem of the clients.

When it comes to norm-sending (phase 2), however, professionals can be counted on to say their piece loud and clear. In accordance with professional role prescriptions, they use whatever social power they have to the fullest extent, laying down the law about the regimen to be followed, giving "doctor's orders." They are also likely to elicit commitment, to give selective social reinforcement (approval for good behavior, disapproval for deviations from the regimen), and to attribute their recommendations to prestigious secondary groups, such as medical research scientists. They are not likely to do anything, however, to build up self-control attributions and a sense of personal responsibility in their clients that would foster adherence to the recommendations in the absence of continued surveillance. Nor are they likely to handle termination of contact (phase 3) in a way that promotes internalization of the recommended course of action.

Insofar as the professional behavior of physicians and other health-care practitioners is characterized by these features, the intensity of psychological ambivalence in their clients can be expected to increase with each contact. Still, when they are feeling miserable and worried about their health, clients have some degree of emotional dependency on the professionals as authority figures to whom they turn for help.

In short, a strictly business-like, no-nonsense style of treatment, which is fostered by professional role prescriptions, can be expected to evoke fears of being humiliated and rejected (phase 1), resentments about being ordered to undergo frustrations (phase 2), and aggrievement about being abandoned after the professional has unilaterally decided that no more appointments are necessary (phase 3). If these reactions occur with a high intensity, the outcome is dysfunctional for attaining the objectives of health-care professionals and of the clients, because the latter will either not come back to complete the series of treatments or will fail to comply with the prescribed regimen.

The objectives of both parties are more likely to be met if the practitioners use in certain ways the *leeway* open to them with regard to how and when the professional role prescriptions are to be lived up to. The intensity of ambivalence induced in clients would be expected to decrease, rather than increase, when a health-care professional's behavior is consistent with the variables (listed in Table 11.1) that are assumed to increase normative referent power. For example, where the medical problem requires little self-disclosure—to set a broken bone, for example—a physician might nevertheless spend an extra few minutes finding out about the patient's worries, since these could be relevant to the regimen that will be prescribed. Even more important, the physician can respond to the patient's disclosures, complaints, and anxious questions in an accepting way, using what the patient says to clear up misunderstandings about the medical problems, which might enable the patient to cope better with suffering and disability. When telling the patient about the recommended course of treatment and the regimen the patient should follow, the physician might avoid reducing acquired normative referent power by making it clear that the demands are as limited in scope as possible and by encouraging the patient to take responsibility as a well-informed decision-maker.

Physicians usually do not think of their patients as decision makers. In America, Europe, and other western countries, the patient role is starting to change somewhat, in part as a result of malpractice suits and new requirements of informed consent (see Merton and Gieryn, 1978). Traditionally, however, the patient role has been defined as a passive one. I suspect that a survey would show that most physicians still expect their patients to do whatever they tell them to do without complaint or questioning. But, in fact, patients are active decision-makers. First, they must decide whether to seek medical treatment and from whom. Then they must decide whether to accept the treatment the doctor recommends. After that, they must make a series of decisions, sometimes every day, about the extent to which they are going to follow the rules laid down for them in the recommended medical regimen.

Without violating any professional role prescriptions, physicians can encourage their patients to function as active decision-makers, giving them a sense of freedom of choice among alternative treatments and alternative regimens (see Janis and Rodin, 1979). This requires giving clarifying communications, inviting and answering questions, and perhaps also introducing some brief training procedures that are specifically designed to build up self-control and a sense of personal responsibility for carrying out the recommended course of action (see variable 8 in Table 11.1). Physicians who do so are less likely to evoke negative reactions. Fostering a sense of perceived control also counteracts debilitating feelings of helplessness, enabling patients to cope more effectively with whatever stress may arise as a consequence of their medical treatments (see Bowers, 1968; Seligman, 1975). Studies of breast cancer patients, for example, have shown that patients do better, as measured by rate of recovery from surgery, when they have a two-stage surgical procedure, as compared with those who undergo a one-stage procedure (Taylor and Levin, in press). The two-stage biopsy allows time for orderly planning and evaluation prior to surgery or therapy and usually includes active participation of the patient in the decision to resort to surgery.

In a field study, Langer and Rodin (1976) assessed the effects of an intervention designed to encourage elderly nursing-home residents to make a greater number of choices and to feel more in control of day-to-day events. Patients given responsibility for making their own decisions showed significant improvement in alertness and fewer deficits of the sort that are commonly regarded as symptoms of senility. From a physician's blind evaluations of the patients' medical records, it was found that during the 6-month period following the intervention, the "responsible" patients showed a significantly greater improvement in health than the comparable patients in the control group. The most striking follow-up data were obtained in death-rate differences between the treatment groups assessed 18 months after the original intervention: 15 percent in the intervention group in contrast to 30 percent in the control group died (Rodin and Langer, 1977). These findings are in line with Ferrare's (1962) original correlational observation that aged people who were re-located in a new nursing home of their own choice lived longer than those who were sent there without being given any choice.

There are both theoretical and empirical grounds for expecting that practitioners who foster a sense of personal responsibility among their patients, while expressing a basic attitude of positive regard (within the accepted boundaries of their professional role), are likely to induce more sustained adherence. This expectation pertains to preventive measures, such as breast self-examination among women in the age group most vulnerable to breast cancer, as well as to con-valescent regimens, such as taking medications and restricting activi-ties among men and women recovering from heart attacks.

Giving patients some degree of control over termination of treat-ments might also alleviate certain sources of ambivalence. If patients feel ready to terminate the treatment and suspect that it is being unduly prolonged, they may become less resistant if the practitioner takes the trouble to brief them about the alternatives and their con-sequences before asking them to make a decision about continuing. Or, if patients feel that the practitioner is terminating the treatment too soon, a similar type of briefing might alleviate feelings of ag-grievement about being abandoned at a time when help is felt to be still needed. This type of briefing, by embodying the variables listed under phase 3 in Table 11.1, could foster internalization of the prac-titioner's recommendations after termination of contact. By relin-quishing the prerogative to exercise full control over termination of treatment, which is one of the sources of sociological ambivalence, the health-care professional can diminish the likelihood of inducing psychological ambivalence in patients without going beyond the boundaries of acceptable role behavior.

In order to meet the essential conditions for becoming effective change agents, practitioners have to overcome their own inner resis-tances when dealing with patients most in need of social incentives. For many professionals it goes against the grain to give options and to make lots of favorable comments conveying positive regard to patients who do little more than complain about their troubles and appear to be unwilling or unable to mobilize themselves to do what they obviously ought to do. Health-care practitioners, like almost all other middle- and upper-class people, can be expected to have a sense of social equity that makes them reluctant to violate the norms asserting that social rewards should be given only to those who have earned them or who are likely to reciprocate (see Walster, Walster and Berscheid, 1978). There are other major deterrents as well—the emotional strain of being genuinely empathic toward suffering people, the additional effort needed to acquire and to use the interpersonal skills of an effective change agent, and, most salient of all, the added time required, for which there is apparently no room at all in professional schedules that are already overfilled. Nevertheless, there is reason to expect that more and more practitioners, as they become aware of the demoralizing statistics on nonadherence, will become *quality* oriented, which means that they will have to renounce quantity ambitions, and expend extra effort in accordance with the primary goal of improving the health of each of their patients as far as possible.

In the foregoing sketch of the linkages between sociological and psychological ambivalence, I have tried to indicate that nonadherence and other adverse outcomes need not be regarded as inescapable consequences of the structure of professional roles. Practitioners have sufficient leeway to act in ways that meet the essential conditions for acquiring a high degree of referent power as change agents. As evidence concerning those conditions accumulates, it should be possible to develop the comprehensive type of psycho-social theory to which Merton has encouraged behavioral scientists to aspire. It should then not be too difficult to work out and test prescriptive hypotheses that have socially beneficial applications for helping people in trouble. With increased understanding of both sources of ambivalence, behavioral scientists at long last could have sufficient expert power to supply valid prescriptions for increasing the effectiveness of all those who have legitimate power to prescribe.

REFERENCES

Atthowe, J. 1973. Behavior innovation and persistence. *Am. Psychol.* **28**: 34–41.

Bergman, A. B. & R. J. Werner. 1963. Failure of children to receive penicillin by mouth. *N. Engl. J. Med.* **268**: 1334–38.

Berscheid, E. & E. H. Walster. 1978. *Interpersonal attraction.* Addison-Wesley. Reading, Mass.

Bowers, K. G. Pain, anxiety, and perceived control. *J. Consult. Clin. Psychol.* **32**: 596–602.

Brownell, K. D., C. L. Heckerman & R. J. Weslake. December 1976. Therapist and group contact as variables in the behavioral treatment of obesity. Paper presented at the annual meeting of the Association for the Advancement of Behavior Therapy, New York, N.Y.

Byrne, D. 1971. *The attraction paradigm.* Academic Press, New York.

Cartwright, D. & A. Zander. (Eds.). 1968. *Group dynamics: Research and theory.* (3rd. ed.). Harper and Row, New York.

Chamey, E., R. Bynum and D. Eldredge. 1967. How well do patients take oral penicillin? A collaborative study in private practice. *Pediatrics.* **40**: 188–195.

Davis, M. S. 1966. Variations in patients' compliance with doctors' orders: Analysis of congruence between survey responses and results of empirical investigations. *J. Med. Educ.* **41**: 1037–1048.

Davis, M. S. 1967. Discharge from hospital against medical advice: A study of reciprocity in the doctor-patient relationship. *Soc. Sci. Med.* **1**: 336.

Davis, M. S. 1971. Variations in patients' compliance with doctors' orders: Medical practice and doctor-patient interaction. *Psychiatry Med.* **2**: 31–54.

Dittes, J. E. 1959. Attractiveness of group as function of self-esteem and acceptance by group. *J. Abnorm. & Soc. Psychol.* **59**: 77–82.

Elling, R., R. Whittemore & M. Green. 1960. Patient participation in a pediatric program. *J. Health Hum. Behav.* **1**: 183–191.

Feinstein, A. R., H. F. Wood, J. A. Epstein, A. Taranta, R. Simpson & E. Tursky. 1959. A controlled study of three methods of prophylaxis against streptococcal infection in a population of rheumatic children. *N. Engl. J. Med.* **260**: 697.

Ferrare, N. A. 1962. Institutionalization and attitude change in an aged population. Unpublished doctoral dissertation, Western Reserve University, Cleveland, Ohio.

Francis, V., B. M. Korsch & M. J. Morris. 1969. Gaps in doctor-patient communications: Patients' responses to medical advice. *N. Engl. J. Med.* **280**: 535.

Freeman, G. 1971. Gaps in doctor-patient communication: Doctor-patient interaction analysis. *Pediatr. Res.* **5**: 298–311.

French, J. R. & B. Raven. 1959. The bases of social power. *In: Studies in Social Power.* D. Cartwright, Ed.:150–167. University of Michigan, Ann Arbor.

Hare, A. P. 1976. *Handbook of small group research.* Second edition. Free Press, New York.

Hunt, W. A. & J. D. Matarazzo. 1973. Three years later: recent developments in the experimental modification of smoking behavior. *J. Abnorm. Psychol.* **81**: 107–114.

Janis, I. L. 1958. *Psychological stress: Psychoanalytic and behavioral studies of surgical patients.* John Wiley & Sons, New York.

Janis, I. L. 1975. Effectiveness of social support for stressful decisions. *In: Applying social psychology: Implications for research, practice, and training.* M. Deutsch and H. Hornstein, Eds. Lawrence Erlbaum Associates, Hilldale, N.J.

Janis, I. L. 1976. Preventing dehumanization. *In: Humanizing Health Care.* J. Howard & A. Strauss, Eds. Wiley & Sons, New York.

Janis, I. L. (Ed.). 1982. *Counseling on personal decisions: Theory and research on short-term helping relationships.* Yale University Press, New Haven, Conn.

Janis, I. L. & H. Leventhal. 1965. Psychological aspects of physical illness and hospital care. *In: Handbook of Clinical Psychology.* B. Wolman, Ed. McGraw-Hill, New York.

Janis, I. L. & J. Rodin. 1979. Attribution, control and decision-making: Social psychology in health care. *In: Health psychology.* G. C. Stone, F. Cohen and N. E. Adler, Eds. Jossey-Bass, San Francisco.

Jonas, G. 1972. Profile: Visceral learning I. *New Yorker Magazine.*

Jones, E. E. 1964. *Ingratiation: A social psychological analysis.* Appleton-Century-Crofts, New York.

Jones, S. C., D. A. Knurek & D. T. Regan, 1973. Variables affecting reactions to social acceptance and rejection. *J. Soc. Psychol.* **90**: 264–284.

Kasl, S. V. 1975. Issues in patient adherence to health care regimens. *J. Hu. Stress.* **1**: 5–17.

Korsch, B. M., E. K. Gozzi & V. Francis. 1968. Gaps in doctor-patient communication: Doctor-patient interaction and patient satisfaction. *Pediatrics.* **42**: 855–871.

Langer, E. J., I. L. Janis & J. A. Wolfer. 1975. Reduction of psychological stress in surgical patients. *J. Exp. Soc. Psychol.* **11**: 155–165.

Langer, E. J. & J. Rodin. 1976. The effects of choice and enhanced personal responsibility for the aged: A field experiment in an institutional setting. *J. Pers. Soc. Psychol.* **34**: 191–198.

Lazarsfeld, P. F. 1975. Working with Merton. *In: The Idea of Social Structure: Papers in Honor of Robert K. Merton.* L. A. Coser, Ed. Harcourt, Brace, Jovanovich, New York.

Ley, P. & M. S. Spelman. 1965. Communications in an out-patient setting. *Br. Jr. Soc. Clin. Psychol.* **4**: 114–116.

Maddox, G. L., C. G. Anderson & M. D. Bogdonoff. 1966. Overweight as a problem of medical management in a public out-patient clinic. *Am. J. Med. Sci.* **252**: 394.

Marwell, G., & D. R. Schmitt. 1967. Dimensions of compliance-gaining behavior: An empirical analysis. *Sociometry.* **30**: 350–364.

Merton, R. K. 1957 and 1968. *Social theory and social structure.* Free Press, New York.

Merton, R. K. 1976. *Sociological ambivalence and other essays.* Free Press, New York.

Merton, R. K. & T. F. Gieryn. 1978. Institutionalized altruism: The case of the professions. *In: Sociocultural change since 1950.* T. L. Smith & M. S. Das, Eds. Vikas, New Delhi.

Merton, R. K. & A. K. Rossi. 1950. Contributions to the theory of reference group behavior. *In: Continuities in Social Research.* R. K. Merton and P. F. Lazarsfeld, Eds. Free Press, New York.

Rodin, J. September, 1978. Cognitive-behavioral strategies for the control of obesity. Paper presented at Conference on Cognitive-behavior Therapy: Applications and issues. Los Angeles, Calif.

Rodin, J. & E. Langer. 1977. Long-term effects of a control-relevant intervention with the institutionalized aged. *J. Personal. Soc. Psychol.* **35**: 897–902.

Sackett, D. L. & R. B. Haynes. 1977. *Compliance with therapeutic regimens.* Johns Hopkins Press, Baltimore, Md.

Shaw, M. E. 1971. *Group Dynamics.* McGraw-Hill, New York.

Seligman, M. E. P. 1975. *Helplessness.* Freeman, San Francisco, Calif.

Shewchuk, L. A. 1976. Special report: Smoking cessation programs of the American Health Foundation. *Prev. Med.* **5**: 454–474.

Stamler, J., J. A. Schoenberger & H. A. Lindberg. 1969. Detection of susceptibility to coronary disease. *Bull. N.Y. Acad. Med.* **45**: 1306.

Taylor, S. & S. Levin. The psychological impact of breast cancer: Theory and practice. *In: Psychological Aspects of Breast Cancer.* A. Enelow, Ed. Oxford University Press, London. (In press.)

Tedeschi, J. T. & S. Lindskold. 1976. *Social Psychology: Interdependence, interaction, and influence.* John Wiley & Sons, New York.

Vincent, P. 1971. Factors influencing patient non-compliance: A theoretical approach. *Nurs. Res.* **20**: 509.

Walster, E., G. W. Walster & E. Berscheid. 1978. *Equity: Theory and research.* Allyn and Bacon, Boston, Mass.

Zola, I. K. 1973. Pathways to the doctor—from person to patient. *Soc. Sci. Med.* **7**: 677.

12

Effective Interventions in Decision Counseling: Implications of the Findings from 23 Field Experiments (1982)

INTRODUCTION

The research summarized in this chapter represents an attempt to move ahead on the task of testing the theoretical ideas concerning the referent power of change agents (Chapter 11) by obtaining systematic evidence in field experiments conducted in counseling clinics. In most of the studies, we gave priority to selecting for our research sites those short-term counseling situations that allow us to make use of clear-cut criteria of the effectiveness of a helper's interventions—such as a dieting clinic, where weight loss can be objectively measured, and a career counseling clinic, where behavioral measures of the degree to which the clients carry out the recommended information-seeking activities can be obtained unobtrusively.

The ultimate purpose of the research is to try to increase our understanding of how and why the influence of one person operates in a constructive way to help another person achieve his or her own goals. More specifically, the studies are intended to enable us to ex-

Janis, I. L. Effective interventions in decision counseling: Implications of the findings from 23 field experiments. In I. L. Janis (Ed.), *Counseling on personal decisions: Theory and research on short-term helping relationships*. New Haven, Conn.: Yale University Press, 1982. This paper discusses the main findings from the field experiments conducted in the author's program of research at Yale University. Some of the studies that are summarized were done in collaboration with Professor Donald Quinlan and others with various graduate students. The introduction is extracted from my opening chapter in the same book. The author wishes to thank the National Institute of Mental Health and the National Science Foundation for supporting this program of research. Reprinted by permission.

plain and predict when only one or a few sessions with a counselor will succeed in helping a client to arrive at and adhere to a recommended course of action that appears to both participants to be in the client's own best interests, with a minimum of postdecisional backsliding and regret. The findings may prove to have practical applications for improving the effectiveness of all sorts of face-to-face counseling in a variety of community settings—wherever psychologists, social workers, lawyers, physicians, nurses, professional counselors or paraprofessional interviewers talk with people and give them advice about their personal decisions in an effort to help them achieve long-term goals of improving their competence, health, or welfare.

By means of naturalistic field experiments, we investigated hypotheses concerning the mediating processes that may account for the main effects and interactions of *two basic types of interventions*: (1) *relationship-building interventions*, such as inducing self-disclosure and responding with explicit acceptance, which influence the client's attitude toward the counselor and motivation to follow the counselor's recommendations (see Chapter 11); and (2) *decisional-process interventions*, such as inducing the client to make contingency plans for anticipated postdecisional setbacks, which can introduce qualitative changes in the way the person arrives at, implements, and sustains his or her personal decision (see Chapter 9).

The field settings in which we conducted our experiments included clinics offering two different kinds of short-term counseling. One type, often practiced in health clinics for people who want to quit smoking or to lose weight, involves giving supportive guidance for executing and sticking with a difficult decision. (See Bandura and Simon, 1977; Cormier and Cormier, 1979; Krumboltz, 1966.) The client already knows what he or she would like to do but seeks help in carrying out the intended course of action. In one or two sessions, the counselor offers direct suggestions, sometimes in an authoritarian manner (e.g., "You should follow carefully every day all the rules of this 1200 calorie diet") and sometimes not (e.g., "You may find it helpful to spend about 10 minutes every day in meditation about your reasons for dieting"). Usually in this type of supportive counseling the counselor also offers information and persuasive arguments to reinforce the decision that the client has already tentatively arrived at before coming to the first session (e.g., by presenting medical facts about the potentially harmful effects of remaining overweight).

The other type is a relatively new form of decision counseling, which involves the joint work of the counselor and the client in diagnosing and improving the latter's decision-making efforts (see Broadhurst, 1976; Janis and Mann, 1977). The counselor attempts to help the person resolve realistic conflicts that arise when he or she is facing a difficult choice, such as whether to be married or divorced, to switch to a different career, or to undergo elective surgery. This type of decision counseling is usually nondirective with respect to substantive issues involved in the decision: The counselor abstains from giving advice about which course of action the clients should choose and even avoids suggesting in any way that he or she regards certain choices as good or bad. Instead, the decision counselor tries to help clients make the fullest possible use of their own resources for arriving at the best possible decision in terms of their own value systems. Much of the counselor's work consists of making clients aware of the decision-making procedures they are using and of alternative procedures that they are not using. The counselor may be somewhat directive, however, in suggesting where to go for pertinent information, how to take account of knowledge about alternative courses of action, how to find out if deadlines need to be taken at face value or can be negotiated, which risks might require preparing contingency plans, and the like.

Among counselors in many different types of settings there appears to be a trend away from the traditional "tell-them-what-they-should-do" approach toward the type of decision counseling just described. (See Cormier and Cormier, 1979; Egan, 1975; Greenwald, 1973.)

In this chapter I shall review the entire set of findings from the 23 field experiments carried out in my research program at Yale University for the purpose of trying to answer fundamental theoretical and practical questions about short-term counseling. The most important questions pertain to when, how, and why short-term counseling is effective. Whenever possible the answers will be presented in the form of empirical generalizations that appear to be warranted by the evidence now at hand.

In addition to pointing out the practical implications for improving the effectiveness of short-term counseling, my discussion of the fundamental questions will include evaluations of the main theoretical assumptions about helping relationships that I and my colleagues had started with (presented in Chapter 11). Those assumptions, which originally were based solely on clinical observations, have been put to the test in many of our field experiments, so that it is now possible to modify and reformulate them on a firmer empirical basis. . . .

IS SHORT-TERM COUNSELING EFFECTIVE?

The first question that has to be answered before we consider any explanatory hypotheses is a simple empirical one: Does short-term counseling of the type we investigated actually work? Although our studies were designed to be analytic experiments rather than descriptive evaluation research, many of the findings nevertheless can be used to answer this initial empirical question.

By and large, the field experiments show that short-term counseling is effective at least for a sizeable minority of the clients, and sometimes, when special procedures are used, for the majority. A fairly high percentage of the clients in our studies show short-term benefits from the two or three counseling sessions that each client typically was given. For a smaller, but nevertheless substantial percentage, some of the short-term counseling procedures we investigated proved to have highly significant long-term effects as well, extending over a period of many months and, in one instance, many years. It must be recognized that most of the evidence is from studies in anti-smoking and weight-reduction clinics whose clients voluntarily come for help because they are motivated to change their behavior.

The very first field experiment reported in the present series (Janis and Hoffman, 1970, 1982) provides clear-cut evidence of the effectiveness of short-term counseling in helping people to get started on cutting down on cigarette smoking. After five weekly meetings with the counselor, all the various treatments groups (irrespective of whether or not the counselor arranged for the clients to form partnerships) showed a marked decrease in number of cigarettes smoked. The majority of the clients showed a marked reduction in smoking over the 5 week period. Control data from other studies in the same smoking clinic, using clients who had been kept on a waiting list for 5 or more weeks, indicate that in the absence of the short-term contact with the counselor no change at all is to be expected over that time interval. The evidence consistently indicates that clients can be helped to start cutting down on cigarette smoking if they meet for a few sessions with a counselor in an anti-smoking clinic.

When we look at the long-term effects in the same study, we see that the outcome depends on whether or not the counselor had used the supplementary procedure of assigning his clients to partnerships, with instructions to phone each other every day for five weeks. The clients who had been given this supplementary procedure during the period when they came for weekly sessions with the counselor showed a highly significant sustained effect after 1 year and also after 10 years. The control clients, who were not given the supplementary partnership treatment, showed no substantial decrease in smoking after 1 year or after 10 years. Later on I shall discuss the factors that are most likely to account for the success of the partnerships. For the present, it suffices to conclude from this field experiment that counselors in anti-smoking clinics who use educational films and other communications about the unhealthy consequences of smoking, together with interviews and discussions that encourage the clients to commit themselves to stop smoking, can help them succeed in getting started on a difficult new regimen of reducing cigarette consumption. But counselors apparently need to introduce special procedures during the few counseling sessions they conduct, such as setting up client partnerships, in order to increase their client's long-term success.

In a comprehensive review of the relevant research on the effectiveness of anti-smoking clinics, Hunt and Bespalec (1974) reported that counseling is generally effective in helping people cut down on cigarette consumption for several weeks but the majority relapse within a few months. Nevertheless, according to these authors a substantial minority show long-term success in abstaining, particularly among those smokers who receive counseling treatments that provide educational information and social support. The findings from the Janis and Hoffman (1970, 1982) study are consistent with those conclusions.

Essentially the same conclusions can be applied to successful dieting, as was shown by the first of the two experiments conducted in a weight-reduction clinic by Nowell and Janis (1982). Again, the short-term counseling sessions were effective in helping clients in all treatments conditions to get started on a rigorous low-calorie diet (when assessed 3 weeks after the first session). By using the special device of setting up partnerships, the counselors were able to help their clients attain longer term success in losing weight (when assessed after a period of 2 1/4 months). A second experiment reported by Nowell and Janis, however, indicates that under certain conditions—which seem to involve promising the clients too much—the effectiveness of short-term counseling is not increased by setting up partnerships (see pp. 236–238).

Subsequent studies in the Yale Weight Reduction Clinic show that even when counselors limit their contacts to only two or three sessions with each client and do not set up any client partnerships, they are generally effective in accomplishing the stated purpose of the counseling clinic, which is to get the clients started on a low-calorie diet. In one study after another we find significant decreases in weight, on the average, for each short-term counseling treatment when assessed after about 1 or 2 months. And again the evidence from the clinic's waiting lists show over and over again that when the clients receive no counseling treatment the average amount of weight loss over either a 1- or a 2-month period is zero. Some counseling treatments, of course, were found to be much more effective than others, but even the least effective treatments generally resulted in a significant average amount of weight loss over a period of about 2 months.

Similar results on the effectiveness of short-term counseling come from our research project's studies in other settings. In these studies the counselors' recommendations deal with different types of clients making a variety of different kinds of decisions: students deciding to donate blood during a Red Cross campaign (Mulligan, 1982), public school teachers deciding to adopt a new method of teaching arithmetic (Smith, 1982), young and middle-aged women deciding to attend an early morning exercise class (Hoyt & Janis, 1975), and hospitalized men and women being prepared to undergo elective surgery (Langer, Janis, & Wolfer, 1975). In each of these settings, one or two sessions with a supportive counselor was found to make a significant difference in the degree of adherence to the decision when assessed from 1 to 7 weeks later.

It must be emphasized that the favorable effects of counseling that we have observed in the 23 field experiments pertain primarily to *short-term adherence* to the counselors' recommendations. When long-term adherence is assessed at 9 months or 1 year after the counseling contact has ended, we find mixed results. Some counseling treatments have detectable long-term effects and some do not. Other investigators who have studied the effectiveness of both short-term and long-term contact with physicians or health counselors have reported essentially the same mixed results, usually with the majority of clients showing backsliding about 1 or 2 months after having started to adhere to the physicians' or counselors' recommendations. (See the reviews of the literature by Hunt & Matarazzo [1973], Marston [1970], and Stone [1979]).

This brings us to a central practical issue of present-day counseling research: How can the long-term effectiveness of counselors be increased? A good psychological theory of helping relationships should be able to provide promising answers to that question by pointing to key factors that determine the extent to which counselors will have a positive influence on their clients long after all contact has terminated. . . .

DOES POSITIVE FEEDBACK RESULT IN MORE ADHERENCE TO THE COUNSELOR'S RECOMMENDATIONS?

Our studies of self-disclosure and positive feedback were designed to test basic theoretical assumptions, which also help to answer a fundamental practical question that confronts all counselors: What is the most effective way to conduct the initial session? This is an extremely important issue especially in short-term counseling when the initial session comprises most, if not all, of the counseling that is provided.

The theoretical model with which we started (see Chapter 11) assumes that a counselor's motivating power can be built up if he or she does certain things in order to take on the role of a quasi-dependable source of self-esteem enhancement for each client. According to this model, at the beginning of a supportive relationship there are two main variables that determine the motivating power of the counselor, both of which involve specific kinds of verbal behavior on the part of the counselor in his or her interactions with the clients: first, encouraging or eliciting some degree of *self-disclosure* and second, responding to self-disclosures with *positive feedback* in the form of acceptance statements. We shall review first the evidence on the effects of positive feedback, which is much less complicated than the evidence on the effects of eliciting different amounts of self-disclosure.

The field experiment by Dowds, Janis, and Conolley (1982) and the replication of it by Conolley, Janis, and Dowds (1982) show the same outcome. Both of these experiments conducted in the Yale Weight-Reduction Clinic clearly indicate that consistently positive feedback from the counselor has favorable effects when given during an interview that induces a moderate amount of self-disclosure. In both experiments, consistently positive feedback was compared with consistently neutral feedback and with predominantly positive feedback marred by a single instance of very mild negative feedback. Of the three forms of feedback treatment, it was the consistently positive that was found to result in the most favorable attitudes toward the counselor and also in the greatest adherence to the counselor's recommendations, as manifested by weight loss 2 months later. (Unexpected findings from these experiments indicating that under certain conditions neutral feedback can also be highly effective will be discussed later in this chapter.)

The findings on the favorable effects of consistently positive feedback have also been replicated in an unpublished doctoral dissertation by Chang (1977), designed under the supervision of Edward Conolley. In a weight-reduction clinic at the University of Southern California, modeled after the one at Yale, Chang compared consistently positive feedback with an ambiguous type of neutral feedback (no response at all from the counselor except for impassive or skeptical facial expressions). He found significantly more weight loss after a period of about three weeks among the clients who had been given positive feedback during their initial interview, irrespective of whether the interview questions induced only positive or only negative disclosures about the self.

Further evidence that consistently positive feedback fosters adherence to the counselor's recommendations comes from another study in the Yale Weight-Reduction Clinic by Greene (1977), which introduced a variation in physical proximity that had not been investigated in the earlier studies. Greene found that when the seating arrangement for the interview placed the client at a normal distance of about 2 feet from the counselor, positive verbal feedback had the expected favorable effect, as shown by significantly greater weight loss 5 weeks after the interview. But when the seating arrangement placed clients at a relatively far distance from the counselor (5 feet away), which they apparently interpreted as a nonverbal sign of withdrawal or detachment, the favorable effect of positive verbal feedback was lost. These results point to the same conclusion suggested by subsidiary findings from the other experiments in the Yale clinic: In order for positive feedback to be effective, the counselor must use it *consistently* throughout the interview, abstaining from saying or doing anything that could be construed by the clients as withdrawing from them or criticizing them.

Additional confirmatory results, which also indicate limiting conditions, were obtained in a pair of field experiments by Mulligan (1982), conducted during a Red Cross campaign to elicit blood donations from college students. Mulligan found that consistently positive feedback from the interviewer, as compared with neutral feedback, increased the amount of adherence to the interviewer's recommendation to donate blood to the Red Cross. This was the outcome when the interview elicited self-disclosures that were not directly relevant to the current decisional conflict. But the opposite outcome was obtained when the interview included the additional issue of whether or not to donate blood, which gave the clients the opportunity to express their reluctance to do so. These findings imply that although positive feedback may generally be more effective than neutral feedback in response to a person's self-disclosures, it can be less effective if it reinforces the "wrong" decision from the recommender's stand-

point. Even though counselors deliberately attempt to avoid reinforcing "bad intentions," they may inadvertently do so by expressing
understanding and empathy during interviews in which clients talk
about not wanting to carry out a recommended healthful or socially
desirable course of action.

In all the studies just cited, positive feedback took the form of
making acceptance statements in response to whatever the clients disclosed about themselves. For example, if a woman who comes for
help in the weight-reduction clinic comments favorably about herself
as being a prudent and conscientious person, the counselor would
respond with a reinforcing comment such as, "it's clear that you do
have a lot going for you." If the client says something unfavorable
about herself by reporting an incident to illustrate her lack of self-
control, the counselor would respond with an empathic comment
that conveys understanding and continued acceptance, such as, "it's
quite understandable that you would feel self-critical at such times
and would want to change." Additional ways of presenting positive
feedback can be used when clients are being monitored after they
have started carrying out a difficult task like dieting. The counselor
can make favorable comments about the progress that the clients are
making and express his or her belief that they have whatever it takes
to succeed at the task. This form of self-esteem enhancement was
used in a field experiment by Smith (1982) in the setting of a weekend workshop for primary school teachers in which they were being
instructed in a difficult new method for teaching arithmetic. On a
random basis, half the teachers in the workshop were privately given
this form of positive feedback by a counselor, focusing on their professional capabilities, during the period when they were attempting
to learn and to practice the new procedures. Unobtrusive observations
made 2 weeks later revealed that those teachers were using the recommended new procedures in their own classrooms to a much greater
extent than were the teachers in the control group, who had received
the same instruction and the same amount of practice but without
the self-esteem enhancement feedback from the counselor.

Riskind (1982) investigated a different type of self-esteem
enhancement in the weight-reduction clinic but found that it did *not*
have the intended effect of increasing adherence to the counselor's
recommendations. He used a "positive-disclosure" interview about
the clients' assets, capabilities, aspirations, and past achievements,
some of which involved activities having nothing to do with dieting.
In response to the positive self-disclosures the counselor made explicitly positive comments. One form of self-esteem enhancement
treatment consisted of pointing out personal strengths and resources

that were applicable to dieting successfully. Another consisted of emphasizing the clients' assets that would help them to be generally successful in life despite any lack of immediate success in dieting. On a random basis, one group of clients was given the first form of treatment, a second group was given the second form, a third group was given both, and a fourth group was given neither.

Riskind's results indicate that both forms of self-esteem enhancement made clients feel much better about themselves (as indicated by their responses on a posttreatment questionnaire), but both failed to have the intended effect on adherence to the low-calorie diet. Contrary to expectations, clients given the self-esteem enhancement treatments showed less weight loss after 8 weeks than those not given either treatment.

Riskind's self-esteem enhancement treatments may have failed to help the clients adhere to the diet for two reasons: In some clients the unearned praise from the counselor may create doubts about the counselor's sincerity; in other clients it may foster complacency, which would reduce their motivation to diet rigorously.

A modified version of the same type of self-esteem enhancement procedure was used with some degree of success in a field experiment by Quinlan, Janis, and Bales (1982). This time the "positive-disclosure" interview was confined to questions relevant to the overweight problem and the counselors' comments encouraged the clients' expectations of success at dieting without using "hard sell" statements about the clients' hitherto unrecognized assets. And this time the "positive-disclosure" interview proved to be effective both in increasing self-confidence about carrying out the tasks of dieting (as indicated by immediate posttreatment questionnaire responses) and in increasing adherence to the diet (as indicated by subsequent weight loss 2 months later) provided that the interview was followed during the first month by weekly telephone calls from the counselor. In the absence of such telephone calls, however, the "positive-disclosure" interview was relatively ineffective. These findings lead us to surmise that among many of the clients given the self-confidence enhancement interview there were still some residual doubts about the counselor's sincerity, which did not clear up until the counselor demonstrated genuine interest by making the phone calls.

Whether or not this explanation accounts for the negative findings on adherence in Riskind's (1982) study, the crucial point is that in six of the seven pertinent studies consistently positive feedback from the counselor (compared with inconsistently positive and/or neutral feedback) had the effect of significantly increasing adherence to the counselor's recommendations. The tentative conclusion that seems warranted from the series of studies is an affirmative answer to the key question of this section, but with some provisos added: When short-term counseling sessions induce a moderate degree of self-disclosure, the degree to which the clients subsequently adhere to the counselor's recommendations will be increased if the counselor responds to the self-disclosures during the sessions by giving positive feedback, provided that it is given consistently and within the obvious limits of plausibility and credibility.

WHEN CLIENTS ARE GIVEN CONSISTENTLY POSITIVE FEEDBACK, DOES INDUCING SELF-DISCLOSURE INCREASE THE COUNSELOR'S EFFECTIVENESS?

Sociolinguists point out that no matter how trivial the topic of conversation may be, every verbal interchange entails at least a slight degree of self-disclosure (see Labov & Fanshel, 1977). But, of course, the amount of self-disclosure by clients that occurs during an initial counseling interview can vary tremendously, depending largely on the questions asked by the interviewer. (The correlation between type of question being asked and amount of self-disclosure elicited is expected to be high when the interviewer is a respected professional counselor, but it would be lower when the interviewer is seen as someone interested only in collecting information in a public opinion poll or, worse yet, a nosey stranger prying into the interviewees' personal life for illegitimate or exploitative purposes.)

In a number of our studies, we have investigated the effects of different levels of self-disclosure by varying the content of the counselor's questions, while holding constant the personality of the counselor, the length of the interview, the recommendations being made, and everything else we could think of that might affect the outcome. In these studies, systematic content analysis of the clients' answers to the counselor's questions consistently indicate very large and significant differences in the amount of self-disclosure and degree of intimacy of the disclosures actually induced by interviews designed to elicit a moderate versus a low level of disclosure and also between those designed to elicit a high versus a moderate level. According to the interviewer's notes, the self-disclosures elicited from the clients generally were given in a spontaneous manner with tone of voice and facial expressions conveying feelings congruent with the intimate information being revealed.

From my own observations of a wide range of different levels of self-disclosure elicited in interviews by professional counselors in many different clinical settings, I rate the routine intake interviews conducted in our weight-reduction clinic as eliciting a relatively "low" level of self-disclosure. Those routine interviews are limited to questions about food preferences, eating habits, and related events of daily life. At the opposite extreme are "high" disclosure interviews, which contain intimate questions about current or past joys and sorrows, body image, sex life, guilt feelings about misbehavior, secret longings, and other such personal information that is sometimes elicited by probing clinicians but is likely to be withheld from most, if not all, members of one's family and close friends. Intermediate between "high" and "low" is the "moderate" type of self-disclosure interview, which includes questions about personal strengths and weaknesses, sources of worry, aspirations, and the like, all of which are likely to be discussed openly with good friends and sympathetic relatives but seldom with strangers, unless they are being consulted as professional counselors.

The theoretical analysis of helping relationships in terms of self-esteem enhancement (Chapter 11) asserts that there are two main conditions which, in combination, build up the motivational power of the counselor. One condition involves eliciting self-disclosure and the other giving positive feedback. Although the theoretical analysis is vague about the upper limit of self-disclosure that might be optimal, it implies the following general hypothesis: Counselors will be more effective in inducing adherence to their recommendations if they first elicit a moderate degree—rather than a very low degree—of self-disclosure in the initial session with each of their clients, provided that they give positive feedback in the form of acceptance responses and display no signs of indifference, rejection, or hostility.

Several experiments in our research project were designed to investigate this self-disclosure hypotheses. The first such experiment, which was conducted in the Yale Weight-Reduction Clinic by Colten and Janis (1982), can be interpreted as tending to confirm the hypothesis. Under conditions where the counselor consistently gave positive feedback in response to whatever the clients said, those who were given only a low disclosure interview showed less adherence to the counselor's recommendations (including less weight loss) than those who were given a moderate disclosure interview combined with a balance-sheet procedure. The latter procedure elicited additional self-disclosures concerning the favorable and unfavorable consequences they would expect to personally experience if they adopted one or another of the alternative courses of action they were considering for dealing with their overweight problem.

Two more experiments conducted in the Yale Weight-Reduction Clinic by Quinlan, Janis, and Bales (1982) yield partially confirmatory evidence in support of the self-disclosure hypothesis, together with some indications of limiting conditions. One of their experiments showed that there was a significantly favorable effect on subsequent adherence when the counselors elicited a moderate degree as against a low degree of self-disclosure from the clients. This outcome (more weight loss after 8 weeks resulting from the moderate disclosure interview) was found, however, only under certain conditions that were also present in the Colten and Janis (1982) study: namely, when (1) a standard type of intake interview was given containing questions about both positive and negative aspects of the self and (2) no contact occurred between the counselor and the clients during the interval between the initial session and the first follow-up interview. When those conditions were changed (by giving interviews that elicited only positive self-disclosures or by having weekly telephone conversations during the 4 weeks following the initial session), the outcome was not the same. In short, the effects of moderate versus low self-disclosure interact in a complex way with type of disclosure and with amount of contact. The most successful of all the conditions investigated in the two experiments (with regard to weight loss after 8 weeks) was one in which *moderate* (rather than low) disclosure was elicited in an interview that was confined to *positive disclosures only* (similar to what is typically done in vocational-counseling interviews) and was followed by weekly telephone conversations for 4 weeks after the first moderate disclosure interview.

The complicated interaction effects seem to detract somewhat from the findings that are confirmatory. (We can only guess about why the standard low disclosure interview was more effective than the standard moderate disclosure interview when the counselor had weekly telephone interviews with the clients during the 4 weeks after the initial session.) Some suggestive evidence from self-reports, however, appears to be consistent with the theoretical assumptions from which the "self-disclosure" hypothesis was derived. In this pair of experiments, there are indications that (a) eliciting self-disclosures about personal shortcomings had a favorable effect with regard to subsequent weight loss when it mobilized a self-confrontation in the clients that generated shame and guilt about continuing to be overweight and (b) eliciting self-disclosures about personal assets had a favorable effect insofar as it built up the clients' self-confidence about achieving future success in changing their undesirable behavior. This combination is consistent with the theoretically-derived expectation (from the assumptions presented in Chapter 11) that as a result of being perceived as an enhancer of the client's self-esteem, a counselor's referent power will increase if he or she consistently gives acceptance and encouragement while conducting a moderate (rather than low) self-disclosure interview.

A more direct test of the crucial combination of variables is provided by Mulligan's research (1982), which was conducted with male college students in the setting of a Red Cross blood donation campaign. Mulligan confirmed the positive effects on compliance of eliciting a moderate degree of self-disclosure as compared with eliciting a low degree of disclosure. He assessed compliance with the interviewer's recommendation by a behavioral measure: the students' signing of pledge cards to donate blood, which was found to be highly correlated with actually making the donation of blood. As I mentioned earlier, Mulligan also found that positive feedback resulted in more compliance than neutral feedback, provided that the clients were not given the opportunity to discuss their disinclinations to donate blood by being asked to talk about their current decisional conflict. The most effective set of conditions, then, was just what was expected on the basis of the theoretical analysis of supportive helping relationships (Chapter 11): when the interviewer (1) gave a *moderate self-disclosure* (rather than low disclosure) interview and (2) gave consistently *positive feedback* (rather than neutral feedback) in response to the disclosures, but (3) *avoided expressing acceptance of the client's reluctance to comply* (by not asking any questions about willingness to comply).

The confirmatory results from Mulligan's research helps to preclude the possibility that the theoretical analysis of the first critical phase in the development of motivating power on the part of a counselor or interviewer, with its emphasis on moderate self-disclosure and positive feedback, holds only for people who are especially defective in self-control. All the other supporting evidence, except for Smith's (1982) study of the effects of positive feedback on women teachers who were seeking help in improving their teaching skills, comes from studies of women who could be regarded as chronically lacking in self-control because they could not control their overeating without external help. Mulligan's findings indicate that inducing a moderate level of self-disclosure and giving positive feedback have essentially the same positive effects on healthy young males (who are not seeking help of any kind) as those we have repeatedly observed among female clients in the weight-reduction clinics.

The available evidence from our studies does not support the notion that the more disclosure the better. Two weight-reduction studies—one by Quinlan and Janis (1982) and the other by Riskind and Janis (1982)—show that eliciting a relatively high level of self-disclosure, as defined at the outset of this section, results in less behavioral adherence to the counselor's recommendations than eliciting a moderate level of disclosure. The high self-disclosure interviews used in these studies elicited a great deal of confidential material about the client's weaknesses and shortcomings that seldom, if ever, is disclosed even to intimate friends. They are similar to the probing intake interviews used by some depth psychologists who treat people seeking help to control their eating, smoking, or drinking habits. The findings suggest that, in the absence of additional sessions devoted to psychotherapeutic treatments, such intake interviews are likely to be far less effective in helping the clients change their behavior than those that elicit only a moderate amount of personal information.

Since one set of experiments shows that moderate disclosure is more effective than low disclosure and another set shows that high disclosure is less effective than moderate disclosure, the obvious inference is that the relationship between amount of induced disclosure and adherence to the counselor's recommendations is nonlinear. The curve for adherence as a function of self-disclosure would be expected to take the form of an inverted U-shaped function, just as has been found for other types of independent variables that have both facilitating and inhibiting effects (see Janis, 1967; McGuire, 1969). This implication of the findings will have to be tested systematically in parametric studies that vary the amount of self-disclosure within each experiment from very low through intermediate levels to very high. As a first approximation to such an experiment, Mulligan's (1982) research provides pertinent data on four different levels of self-disclosure, ranging from very low to relatively high: For those subjects who were given positive feedback by the interviewer, the predicted inverted U-shaped curve emerges if we plot the compliance measure (signing a Red Cross pledge card to donate blood) against amount of self-disclosure induced by the interviewer.[1] In agreement with the prior experiments on effects of self-disclosure, Mulligan's data show that the moderate disclosure interview was more effective than either the low disclosure or the relatively high disclosure interviews.

What accounts for the relatively detrimental effects of high disclosure? Fairly consistent answers to this question are implied by the

---

[1] In order to perceive the inverted U-shape function shown by Mulligan's (1982) data, it is necessary to order the different levels of self-disclosure in the two concurrent experiments from highest to lowest. The results for those given positive feedback by the interviewer are as follows:

process data obtained from the various experiments on self-disclosure, and also from the more sensitive indicators obtained from the small sample study by Janis and Quinlan (1982). In the latter study each client in the weight-reduction clinic was given an intensive process interview immediately after the initial high-disclosure or moderate-disclosure interview. Two main types of detrimental effects were observed. First, numerous signs indicate that participating in a high self-disclosure interview makes the clients somewhat demoralized, despite all the positive comments and acceptance statements made by the counselor. After having revealed all sorts of personal weakness, some clients feel dissatisfied with themselves, as well as with the counseling session, and their self-confidence is shaken. When this occurs, the clients feel less certain than ever that they can succeed in carrying out difficult tasks, like adhering to a low-calorie diet. An initial counseling session that elicits high disclosure from the clients apparently runs the risk of lowering rather than enhancing self-esteem, even when the counselor gives consistently positive feedback.

The second type of detrimental effect, suggested by more indirect and subtle indicators, is a relative increase in conflict about entering into a dependent relationship with the counselor. Many of the clients given a high-disclosure interview express vague uneasiness and dissatisfaction about the counseling session. When an effort is made to

Level of self disclosure	Percentage complying by signing pledge cards to donate blood to the Red Cross
1. *Relatively high:* The moderate disclosure interview combined with questions about the current decisional conflict about donating blood (from Experiment 2)	60%
2. *Moderate:* All questions restricted to past decisional conflicts on important personal issues, such as career choice (from Experiment 1)	90%
3. *Fairly low:* The very low disclosure interview with additional low disclosure questions to make the interview the same length as the relatively high-disclosure interview (from Experiment 2)	60%
4. *Very low:* All questions restricted to recent minor decisions such as which movie to go to (from Experiment 1)	20%

The results for the subjects who were given neutral feedback, however, do not yield an inverted U-shaped curve; the percentages corresponding to the ones just given for position feedback are as follows: (1) 90%, (2) 50%, (3) 30%, (4) 50%. With neutral feedback the relatively high disclosure interview is more effective than any other level of disclosure. The divergences between the neutral feedback and the positive feedback data are somewhat surprising because in this face-to-face interview situation neutral feedback was essentially a form of mild positive feedback. Although the interviewer said little except "Um hum," pin down what is bothering them, some clients admit being concerned about having lost the respect of the counselor or about the threat of somehow being hurt as a result of becoming too trusting, too affectionate, or too dependent upon the counselor. A few explicitly express a sense of vulnerability from having revealed too much. Other clients seem to manifest over-involvement in the emerging dependent relationship by indicating that they really want the counselor to give them more time and more directive advice, not just about the problem at hand (such as being overweight), but also about other problems that were discussed in the high disclosure interview (such as marital difficulties).

The clients given a moderate or low self-disclosure interview seem less likely to regard the counselor as someone who could become an affectionate parental figure or a savior who will solve their problems by telling them exactly what to do. At the end of the initial session they appear to accept with more emotional equanimity a businesslike relationship with the counselor and do not feel deprived because of the limited amount of help offered them. They regard the counselor as friendly, genuinely helpful, and doing a good job; they seem less likely to be hoping to bask in the warmth of intimacy with an affectionate, indulgent parent figure.

---

he smiled, nodded, and looked interested in what the subject was saying, thus giving paralinguistic responses that undoubtedly conveyed interest in and acceptance of whatever the subject was saying. One explanation for the divergence suggested by Mulligan (1982) is that inadvertently the interviewer's positive verbal feedback tended to reinforce the wrong responses when the relatively high disclosure interview was given because some subjects expressed anxiety and reluctance about complying with the request to donate blood. An alternative explanation, suggested by process interviews and questionnaire data from later studies in other settings, is that relatively high disclosure made the subjects so aware of their personal weaknesses and shortcomings that they could no longer accept the counselor's positive feedback as credible, which would incline them to believe that the interviewer was insincere and perhaps would try to manipulate their behavior after giving them a lot of compliments. Whether one or the other or both detrimental processes are operating in this type of interview situation will remain an open question until replications are carried out in which pertinent process data are obtained.

The possibility that inducing a relatively high degree of self-disclosure might result in negative attitudes toward the interviewer was investigated in Mulligan's study and in the other experiments on the effects of self-disclosure. In all of these studies, questionnaire data were obtained immediately after the disclosure interview on attitudes toward the interviewer. The findings consistently indicate that when positive feedback is given throughout the interview, inducing relatively high disclosure does *not* result in less favorable attitudes towards the interviewer than inducing moderate or low levels of disclosure. But these attitudes, as assessed by post-interview questionnaires, are not predictive of compliance with the interviewer's recommendations. The absence of the expected relationship could be due to the low validity of the attitude measures. Clients tend to give conventionally polite answers when printed questionnaires are given right after an interview. There is some evidence that the clients' answers on the printed questionnaires do not correspond to the attitudes they express during an intensive supplemenatary interview in which they are encouraged to speak freely and at length about how they felt during the self-disclosure interview (Janis and Quinlan, 1982).

HOW CAN THE POTENTIALLY UNFAVORABLE
EFFECTS OF HIGH-DISCLOSURE INTERVIEWS
BE MITIGATED?

Although there is clear-cut evidence from a number of our studies showing that high self-disclosure interviews run the risk of being less effective in inducing clients to adhere to the counselor's recommendations than moderate disclosure interviews, many counselors can be expected to continue to ask personal questions that elicit high disclosure in their intake interviews. Even if they become familiar with the evidence and believe it to be correct, there are two main reasons why they are likely to do so. First, a counselor may be convinced that he or she cannot properly evaluate a client's problem and work out an appropriate counseling strategy without learning about how the problem is related to other important aspects of the person's life, which requires obtaining a great deal of personal information during the intake interview. Counselors who are aware of the potential drawbacks of eliciting intimate disclosures may feel that it is still worthwhile to obtain the intimate material they regard as essential for adequate diagnosis, relying on their clinical skills to counteract whatever drawbacks may become apparent. Second, many clients who come to a counselor for help are in a perturbed state, all prepared to talk about what is bothering them. They want to reveal their most pressing difficulties. If the counselor were to try to discourage men and women who are primed to tell their personal story, especially the ones who believe that they should "let it all hang out," those clients would be disappointed and perhaps become less responsive than if they were permitted to unburden themselves despite the drawbacks. (In our studies we regularly encounter a small minority of clients who spontaneously start revealing all sorts of intimate information that is not asked for during low or moderate self-disclosure interviews.)

For these two reasons, despite whatever evidence accumulates on the detrimental effects, I expect that at least for a minority of clients, if not for the majority, intake interviews that elicit high self-disclosure are here to stay. Accordingly, it is worthwhile to continue research on the subsidiary problem of determining the conditions under which people can tolerate a relatively high degree of self-disclosure. Such research could increase our understanding of the psychology of intimacy and point to practical ways of preventing or counteracting potentially unfavorable consequences.

A few leads have emerged from the research carried out in the Yale Weight-Reduction Clinic and in other settings. One hypothesis suggested by intensive process interviews is that the decrease in self-confidence and other unfavorable effects resulting from an initial high self-disclosure interview might be counteracted if a retrospective interview were conducted immediately afterward. A retrospective interview is one in which the counselor asks the clients to discuss their reactions to the earlier high-disclosure interview, allowing them to ventilate whatever misgivings and self-derogatory feelings might have been generated. This type of supplementary interview would, of course, require positive feedback from the counselor to reassure each client that he or she is not despised or thought to be a hopeless case. A crucial component for counteracting the demoralizing effects of high disclosure would be clear-cut signs that the counselor continues to regard the client as worthy of respect and to have high hopes of success on the task at hand, despite all the personal weaknesses and past failures revealed by the client in the intake session.

No systematic study has been done as yet on the effects of a supplementary retrospective interview following high disclosure. But we do have some evidence that a role-playing procedure conveying signs of positive regard on the part of the counselor following a high-disclosure interview can have the expected counteracting effect. Riskind and Janis (1982) tried out in the weight-reduction clinic a new procedure designed to build up expectations of social approval by inducing clients to participate in a psychodrama. The scenario focused on the approval they could expect to receive from the counselor if they succeeded in adhering to the recommended diet. When this social approval training was given after a high self-disclosure interview, the counselor's effectiveness was found to increase. In the absence of social approval training, the clients given a high-disclosure interview were relatively unsuccessful in losing weight as compared with those given a moderate disclosure interview. The findings clearly show that the adverse effects of inducing high disclosure can be markedly reduced by the approval training, as manifested by amount of weight loss 5 weeks later.

Those findings, together with the self-report data indicating changes in level of self-esteem, can be plausibly interpreted in the following way: Clients who were not given the social approval training felt that they had created an unfavorable impression on the counselor as a result of all the derogatory information they had revealed about themselves during the high self-disclosure interview. They had little hope, therefore, of changing the counselor's basically negative attitude toward them even if they were to do all the things recommended. In contrast, when clients were given the approval training after the interview, their hopes in this regard were restored, so that they left the session in essentially the same "steamed up" state as those who had received the moderate self-disclosure interview without approval training. Consequently, during the weeks following the interview, the expected approval of the counselor may have functioned as an incentive for adhering to the diet only among those high self-disclosure clients who had received the approval training. The important point is that the evidence from the Riskind and Janis (1982) study supports the assumption that the potentially adverse effects of eliciting a high degree of self-disclosure can be overcome by using special procedures to restore the motivating power of the counselor.

WHAT ELSE CAN COUNSELORS DO TO INCREASE THEIR EFFECTIVENESS?

Aside from the research on self-disclosure and positive feedback, many [of our] studies present evidence bearing on new procedures that practitioners who engage in short-term counseling might add to might add to their standard procedures in order to increase their following eight supplementary procedures look promising in light of the evidence now available:

Setting Up Partnerships:

The most impressive evidence pertains to the effectiveness of treating clients in pairs, with instructions to function as partners during the intervals between counseling sessions. First of all, there is the Janis and Hoffman (1970) study, which found that clients in an anti-smoking clinic who were assigned to high-contact partnerships were more successful in cutting down on cigarette smoking than those who were assigned to low-contact partnerships or to the control group. The high-contact partnerships were created by the counselor by meeting with the partners once a week and instructing them to phone each other every day for 5 weeks. Long-term follow-up interviews conducted 1 year and 10 years after the clinic treatment was terminated revealed that the clients who had been assigned to the high-contact partnerships were continuing over a very long period of time to be significantly more successful than the others in abstaining from cigarette smoking. These findings suggest that any counselor dealing with clients who want to change unhealthy habits like smoking may find it to be highly efficient to meet with 2 clients at a time, and perhaps even to meet with small groups of perhaps 4 to 8 clients, by assigning pairs to the same type of partnership set up in the Janis and Hoffman study. Obviously, however, the question of whether a counselor typically can save time and still be just as effective if he or she conducts sessions with two or four sets of partners simultaneously would have to be answered empirically by subsequent conceptual replication studies.

Additional evidence from the Janis and Hoffman study suggests that the prime conditions specified in Chapter 11 for the development of effective helping relationships were met by the high-contact partnerships. The partners disclosed a fair amount of personal information to each other, as well as to the counselor, bearing mostly on temptations that made it difficult to cut down on smoking, withdrawal symptoms, and related problems. The partners' disclosures to each other generally were accompanied by mutual acceptance. Hence the conditions for the first phase of acquiring motivational power were met. At each of the weekly meetings, the counselor explicitly conveyed the expected norm by encouraging the partners to make genuine efforts to stop smoking. An analysis of tape recordings of the partners' conversations showed that they repeated this anti-smoking norm to each other. In their spontaneous conversations that were recorded during the clinic sessions, the clients in successful partnerships were much more likely than the other clients to praise each other for success in cutting down, to criticize each other for backsliding, and to be skeptical about excuses for not showing any improvement. Hence the conditions were met for the second phase, which involve using the motivating power acquired during the first phase. The importance of the norm-sending requirement in the second phase was further indicated by evidence from a supplementary study: When the same counselor in the same anti-smoking clinic set up high-contact partnerships without his meeting with the clients to endorse the anti-smoking norm, the partnerships were not at all effective in helping to reduce the amount of cigarette smoking.

With regard to the third phase, the partners who had been meeting with the counselor could look forward to maintaining contact with each other when the time came to terminate the meetings of the three-person groups. This could reduce the disruptive effects of separation from the counselor. Evidence from follow-up interviews indicate that the partners did, in fact, remain in contact with each other for a month or so, on the average, after the final meeting with counselor.

Because contact between the partners dropped off during the subsequent months, the extraordinarily high degree of success of the partnerships in reducing their cigarette smoking, found 1 year and 10 years after the termination of the counseling sessions, cannot be attributed to the partners continuing to give each other direct social support. It appears most likely that the success of the high-contact partnerships is attributable to the increase in motivational power of the three-person clinic group headed by the counselor as group leader, which augmented the degree to which the clients internalized the norms set by the leader.

Confirmatory results from the study by Nowell and Janis (1982) on the effectiveness of high-contact partnerships in a dieting clinic can be interpreted in essentially the same way:

Phase 1: The partners made personal disclosures to each other as well as to the counselor and they received positive feedback in the form of acceptance responses.

Phase 2: At each meeting of the three-person group in the clinic the counselor repeatedly conveyed the norm (to stay on the prescribed low-calorie diet in order to lose weight).

Phase 3: The partners responded to the loss of contact with the counselor by deciding to remain in contact with each other after the last session at the clinic; in follow-up interviews they reported having continued to maintain contact for an average of 3 weeks. Although many of the partners were no longer in contact with each other 6 weeks later, they were still markedly more successful in avoiding overeating, as manifested by their weight loss, than the clients in the two groups that had not been asked by the counselor to form high-contact partnerships.

The success of the partnerships apparently depends upon how the counselor handles the partnership arrangements. We have seen, for example, that no advantages are to be expected when the counselor fails to function as a norm sender. If the other essential conditions for the three critical phases are not met, according to my theoretical analysis (Chapter 11), the partnerships cannot be expected to be successful.

Another condition for a successful outcome, indicated by a serendipitous finding in the Nowell and Janis study (1982), is that the counselor does *not* tell the partners that they are very similar and well-matched on attitudes and background. Contrary to what might be expected from prior research on perceived similarity (e.g., Byrne & Griffitt, 1969), giving clients such information apparently generates overoptimistic expectations that lead to disappointment. This adverse effect is avoided if the partners are told that an attempt was made to match them but that there are some divergences.

Undoubtedly, additional conditions essential for effective partnerships will be discovered in subsequent research. From the evidence now at hand, however, it does not seem premature to conclude that setting up high-contact partnerships can be an effective adjunct to counseling in anti-smoking and weight-reduction clinics—and perhaps in a variety of other clinical settings as well—provided that the counselor takes account of the essential requirements specified in the analysis of the three critical phases in effective helping relationships.

Aside from setting up partnerships, what other things could a counselor do to increase his or her effectiveness in helping people carry out difficult decisions? In answer to this question, I shall summarize several additional procedures which appear to be promising types of intervention for counteracting defensive avoidance and promoting vigilant decision making in some clients, although probably not in all who come for decision counseling.

The "Awareness-of-Rationalizations" Technique:

This procedure requires the client to examine typical "excuses" used by heavy smokers and to state which ones he or she uses. It has been found to be effective in increasing smokers' acceptance of warning messages (endorsed by the counselor), such as American Cancer Society films about the harmful effects of cigarette smoking (Reed and Janis, 1974). Comparable procedures might prove to be useful for other types of personal decisions.

Emotional Role-Playing:

Even more effective with heavy smokers is a psychodramatic procedure in which the client plays the role of a lung cancer victim at the time of receiving the bad news from a physician. Following the psychodrama, the client is likely to show a marked increase in feelings of personal vulnerability to the threat of lung disease and also a sharp decrease in cigarette consumption, an effect that has been found to persist more than a year after the role-playing session (see Janis and Mann, 1977, pp. 350–354).

Stress Inoculation for Postdecisional Setbacks:

This procedure consists of giving clients (a) detailed information about the unfavorable consequences of the new course of action they have decided to carry out, and (b) positive information that fosters self-reassurances and effective coping mechanisms. Evidence of the value of stress inoculation for fostering adherence to stressful courses of action comes from controlled field experiments of surgical patients, medical patients undergoing painful medical treatments, employees who have decided to take a new job, and elderly persons being relocated to a nursing home or hospital (see Chapter 13). But preparatory information about unfavorable consequences of a chosen course of action such as undergoing surgery, may sometimes fail to increase stress tolerance (see Langer, Janis and Wolfer, 1975). The task for the next stage of research will be to test explanatory hypotheses concerning the effective components of stress inoculation for different types of persons and circumstances, which will help to identify the conditions under which stress inoculation is effective.

The Balance-Sheet Procedure:

This type of intervention was originally developed to aid college students and high school students to focus on neglected consequences of the career or training alternatives available to them (see pp. 160–165 in Chapter 9). . . . When the balance-sheet procedure is successful in increasing the clients' subsequent adherence to a difficult course of action, the effective mediating variables may prove to be increased vigilance, self-disclosure, stress inoculation, and/or self-persuasion.

Encouraging a Short-Term Perspective for the Recommended Action:

In order to increase the clients' sense of mastery, and self-confidence about succeeding on a difficult course of action, a decision counselor can structure the task in terms of short-term accomplishments and focus on features of the long-term task that can easily be mastered (see Riskind 1982). For example, clients in a weight-reduction clinic could be encouraged to think about living up to the diet for the next 24 hours, which practically everyone can do. They could be told that approaching the task step by step, just one day at a time, can be the key to ultimate success if they do so repeatedly. In a controlled field experiment, Riskind found that overweight clients who were encouraged to adopt this short-term perspective expressed a greater sense of personal control and showed more compliance with the counselor's recommendation to send in weekly reports than those who were encouraged to adopt a longer time perspective. But the results were somewhat complicated with regard to adherence to the diet itself, as measured by weight loss 2 months later. The day-by-day perspective was found to be more effective than the long-term perspective in increasing weight loss only for those clients who initially expressed a relatively high level of self-esteem. In order to be used effectively to promote adherence, therefore, this time-perspective intervention may require the counselor to assess each client's level of self-esteem in the initial session so as to withhold it from those with relatively low self-esteem.

Outcome Psychodrama:

The purpose of this procedure is to induce clients to explore more fully the consequences of the leading alternatives (see Janis and LaFlamme, 1982). Clients are asked to act out a scenario that involves projecting themselves into the future in order to explore a potential outcome as though it has actually occurred, such as, "the decision has worked out badly." They are required to use their imaginations in order to improvise what specifically could happen, which may enable them to become more aware of expectations and attitudes not previously verbalized even to themselves.

In Janis' pilot studies, outcome psychodrama was used in marital counseling and career counseling. Clients on the verge of committing themselves to a new course of action appeared to benefit from it. For such clients, all of whom were in the later stages of decision making, the procedure seemed to be a promising means for helping them gain access to preconscious worries and other previously unverbalized feelings about alternative courses of action. But negative results were obtained from a field experiment by LaFlamme and Janis in a career decision clinic for men and women who wanted to change their jobs or careers, almost all of whom were in the early stages of decision making. These clients did not seem to benefit from the procedure. Worse yet, it appeared to have an adverse effect on some of them, lowering their self-confidence about finding a good solution and decreasing vigilant information seeking. Consequently, the procedure cannot be recommended for routine use in decision counseling. It might prove to be of value, however, for selected clients in the later stages of decision making, provided that their self-confidence is not shaky and the counselor is prepared to be responsive to any signs of demoralizing effects when the scenarios involve exploring undesirable outcomes.

A Cognitive Reappraisal Procedure for Coping with Postdecisional Stress:

This procedure, which was investigated in a field experiment by Langer, Janis, and Wolfer (1975), was designed to counteract the detrimental effects of defensive avoidance and to promote vigilance after a person has already become committed to a difficult course of action. The experiment assessed the effectiveness of the procedure when introduced by a professional counselor during brief counseling sessions with patients who had recently decided to undergo a major operation (see Chapter 13, pp. 261–264). . . .

The findings consistently show that the procedure had a markedly favorable effect on stress tolerance. The same kind of cognitive-reappraisal intervention involving positive self talk has been applied and evaluated in clinics for helping people manage anxiety, anger, and pain (see Meichenbaum and Turk, 1976). Similar interventions probably can be developed to prevent defensive avoidance tendencies and to foster an effective vigilant coping pattern among clients facing any kind of postdecisional stress, including setbacks entailed by marital and career decisions as well as health decisions.

HOW WELL DOES THE THEORETICAL MODEL OF THE COUNSELOR'S MOTIVATING POWER (PRESENTED IN CHAPTER 11) STAND UP WHEN EVALUATED IN LIGHT OF THE AVAILABLE EVIDENCE?

By and large, the model based on observations of effective versus ineffective long-term counseling and psychotherapy appears to stand up fairly well for short-term counseling. That is to say, the findings from the field experiments on short-term counseling reported in Janis (1982) provide a great deal of confirmatory evidence that the variables specified by the theoretical analysis [listed in Table 11.1 on page 205] do have significant effects in the predicted direction on the clients' adherence to counselors' recommendations. Nevertheless, some changes are needed in the theoretical formulations in order to take account of additional unpredicted findings.

THE FIRST PHASE

Most of the studies in our series of research investigations deal with the variables in the first critical phase of the counselor-client relationship, which pertain to the conditions under which counselors build up their motivating or referent power (see Table 11.1). Three conditions are stipulated:

1. Encouraging clients to engage in a moderate level of self-disclosure vs. not doing so.
2. Giving positive feedback (acceptance and understanding) vs. giving neutral or negative feedback in response to self-disclosures.
3. Using self-disclosures to give insight and cognitive restructuring vs. giving little insight or cognitive restructuring.

Unlike the first two, the third one is not an essential condition but nevertheless is expected to augment somewhat the motivating power of a counselor. The positive findings for the cognitive restructuring procedure described by Langer, Janis, and Wolfer (1975) can be interpreted as supporting this expectation.

The first two conditions, which are assumed to be essential for building up the counselors' motivating power, are embodied in the following basic proposition . . . : Counselors will be most successful in inducing their clients to live up to specific recommendations, such as adhering to a low-calorie diet, if they start off by encouraging a moderate level of *self-disclosure* and respond to the client's disclosures by giving *positive feedback* in the form of explicit acceptance responses. Earlier in this chapter we have seen that most of the pertinent findings bearing on the effects of self-disclosure and of positive feedback are consistent with this proposition. Additional findings, however, were unexpected and indicate that the basic proposition needs to be modified by inserting some important provisos.

One proviso (which is suggested by Mulligan's [1982] study, summarized on p. 230) is that the counselor must *avoid ambiguity* when expressing understanding and empathy in response to clients' disclosures about not wanting to carry out the course of action recommended by the counselor. Ambiguity can inadvertently reinforce the "wrong" decision. The counselor can avoid this error by making favorable comments about the client's honesty (for admitting reluctance to do what is recommended) and then explicitly labeling the client's resistance to the recommended course of action as a problem to be overcome in order for the client to achieve his or her goals.

A second major proviso is that the positive feedback from the counselor must be given *consistently,* with no deviating comments and no nonverbal cues that could be construed by clients as indicating criticism, insincerity, rejection, or exploitative intent. In the summary of the research dealing with the effects of positive versus neutral feedback presented earlier in this chapter, I pointed out that in six out of a series of seven pertinent field experiments, the investigators found that consistently positive feedback from the counselor resulted in a significant increase in subsequent adherence to the counselor's recommendations, just as predicted by the theoretical model. But from three of the confirmatory studies carried out in the weight-reduction clinic we obtained the following surprising, additional results, which were not predicted:

(1) The study reported by Dowds, Janis, and Conolley (1982) showed that positive feedback from the counselor throughout a moderate disclosure interview resulted in more subsequent adherence to dietary recommendations (as manifested by weight loss) only if the counselor also gave a positive evaluation to each client's performance when he imposed a minor task (a motivation test). If the counselor told the client that she did not perform as well as expected on the minor task, neutral feedback from the counselor throughout the interview resulted in more subsequent adherence than did positive feedback.

(2) The study reported by Connolley, Janis, and Dowds (1982) showed that positive feedback throughout a moderate disclosure interview resulted in more subsequent adherence to dietary recommendations (as manifested by weight loss) only if the minor task (a motivation test) imposed by the counselor was relatively easy. If the minor task was very difficult (making the clients feel that they failed), neutral feedback throughout the interview resulted in more subsequent adherence than did positive feedback.

(3) The study reported in Greene (1977) showed that positive feedback throughout a moderate disclosure interview in a face-to-face session resulted in more subsequent adherence to the dietary recommendations (as manifested by weight loss) only if the counselor seated himself at a normal distance from the client (about 2 feet away). If the counselor seated himself at a relatively remote distance (about 5 feet away), neutral feedback throughout the interview resulted in more subsequent adherence than did positive feedback.

To these unpredicted findings, we must add that the study by Riskind (1982) not only failed to obtain the expected increase in adherence but obtained a decrease in adherence (as manifested by amount of weight loss) when the counselor gave a supplementary interview in which he responded with consistently positive feedback to whatever answers the clients gave to a series of questions that were designed to elicit self-disclosures only about the clients' personal assets and past successes. The counselor's acceptance of these positive self-disclosures may have induced in some clients a sense of complacency or self-satisfaction which could lower the overweight clients' motivation to make the effort to adhere to the recommended dietary restrictions. Also, since the counselor gave unearned praise, sometimes accompanied by favorable comments about personal strengths that the clients had not mentioned, some clients may have been skeptical about the counselor's sincerity.

All of these unexpected findings, from four different investigations of weight loss, indicate that under certain conditions we can expect that counselors will *not* increase their effectiveness if they respond with positive feedback during an interview that elicits a moderate level of self-disclosure. Counselors can be expected to fail if they give a great deal of unearned praise or if they are somewhat inconsistent about giving positive feedback in response to the self-disclosures elicited from their clients. The inconsistency may take the form of making just one slight criticism of a client's behavior, demanding the client to carry out a difficult task that is not directly pertinent to the problem for which the client is seeking help, or presenting nonverbal cues that can be construed as signs of detachment or withdrawal, as when the counselor sits at a relatively remote distance from the client. It must be emphasized that in all three studies each one of these disturbing events was presented in such a mild form that the investigators had not expected it to have any adverse effect at all. Nevertheless, each proved to have a profoundly disturbing and long-lasting effect which was revealed by significantly less weight loss at the time of the follow-up interview 5 to 8 weeks later. The findings suggest that if counselors for any reason find it necessary to expose clients to a disturbing event, such as giving clients an unfavorable rating on a test, they will be better off (from the standpoint of motivating the clients to adhere to their recommendations) if they give neutral feedback, rather than positive accepting feedback, throughout the entire intake interview.

Most surprising is the evidence that the disturbing events, as I have been calling them, actually had a favorable effect on clients who were given neutral feedback. The study by Dowds, Janis, and Conolley (1982) showed that the amount of adherence of the clients who received neutral feedback, when assessed by weight loss eight weeks later, proved to be significantly higher if they had been given an unfavorable rather than favorable rating on the extraneous motivation test. The studies by Conolley, Janis, and Dowds (1982) (in which the disturbing event consisted of a high demand made during the motivation test) and by Greene (1977) (in which the disturbing event consisted of a remote seating arrangement) showed the same trend, again implying that among clients who are given neutral feedback, subsequent adherence might be increased by inserting one or another of these disturbing events into the intake interview.

The paradoxical findings just reviewed suggest that building up an image of the counselor as a firm, demanding authority figure by withholding positive feedback throughout the entire initial session, and by occasionally expressing mild disapproval or withdrawal, can sometimes have considerable motivating power. Nevertheless, in each of the three experiments, when counselors gave neutral feedback along with one or another disturbing event (unfavorable rating, high demand, or remote seating), they were not as successful in inducing subsequent adherence as when they gave consistently positive feedback (with no disturbing event). The difference is statistically significant, however, in only one of the studies (Conolley, Janis, and Dowds, 1982). If this trend continues to show up and proves to be statistically significant in subsequent conceptual replications of these field experiments with clients who meet with a counselor individually or in groups, it will carry the implication that when counselors are seen by their clients as nurturant supportive helpers they tend to be more successful in inducing adherence than when they are seen as businesslike authority figures who are critical, withdrawn, or excessively demanding.

By a nurturant supportive helper I mean a person who is seen by the clients as someone who can be counted on to enhance their self-esteem, provided only that they make a conscientious effort to do what he or she recommends. The evidence I have reviewed indicates that counselors can build up this kind of image and thereby elicit increased adherence if, as specified in Phase 1 of the theoretical model for acquiring referent power, they induce a moderate degree of self-disclosure and give positive feedback, with due regard to the provisos inferred from the unpredicted findings. But the evidence bearing on the provisos suggests that in the first stage when counselors are starting to build up their motivating power in this way, that power is rather fragile. Clients evidently are extremely sensitive to cues that might show that the counselor has a low opinion of them or will be too hard to please. Any little comment or gesture by the counselor could unintentionally be misconstrued as a sign of rejection and greatly reduce the counselor's motivating power. Clinical observations from longer-term counseling, however, suggest that if the counselor continues to express positive regard most of the time during subsequent sessions, clients can tolerate quite well an occasional criticism of their behavior and an occasional stringent demand that might have had an adverse effect if presented during the first session. That is to say, the motivating power of the counselor might be expected to increase and to become much more robust if the counselor continues to meet the conditions for Phase 1 during the second, third, and fourth sessions. The fragility we noted in our studies might, therefore, prove to be characteristic only of *short-term counseling that is limited to just one initial session* before the client is expected to adhere to a diet or to carry out some other recommended course of action, as in ten of the eleven studies that investigated the variables in Phase 1.

. . . The main conclusion from the available evidence on frequency of contact was that the number of sessions *per se* is less important as a determinant of adherence than what the counselor does during each session. That conclusion does not preclude the plausible suggestion that if the counselor continues to do the appropriate things specified for Phase 1 to build up his or her motivating power, each additional session will strengthen the positive effect, contribute to building up a more robust relationship, and lead to more adherence.

THE SECOND PHASE

For Phase 2 of the theoretical model (Table 11.1), the various studies in our series provide only fragmentary evidence, which bears on three of the following five variables:

4. Making directive statements or endorsing specific recommendations regarding actions the client should carry out vs. abstaining from any directive statements or endorsements.
5. Eliciting commitment to the recommended course of action vs. not eliciting commitment.
6. Attributing the norms being endorsed to a respected secondary group vs. not doing so.
7. Giving selective positive feedback after making recommendations vs. giving non-contingent acceptance or predominantly neutral or negative feedback.
8. Giving communications and training procedures that build up self-control attributions and a sense of personal responsibility vs. giving no such communications or training.

For variable #4, which involves making directive statements or endorsements, indirect evidence comes from the first study in which adherence to recommendations (assessed by reported number of cigarettes smoked per day) was found to increase when clients in a smoking clinic were assigned to partnerships (Janis and Hoffman, 1970). The partners not only phoned each other every day to disclose mutual problems but also met once a week with a *norm-sending* counselor for five weeks. A supplementary study of 20 smokers (reported by Janis and Hoffman, 1970) showed that in the absence of any contact with a directive counselor at the clinic (except for an initial phone call in which partners were assigned), the partnerships had a brief effect of decreasing cigarette consumption during the first month, but after that backsliding occurred in all cases. In contrast, when the same type of partners attended five weekly meetings with a directive counselor who explicitly endorsed the anti-smoking recommendations, they showed a marked and sustained reduction in cigarette consumption that was still observable 10 years later.

Similar findings concerning the need for contact with a directive leader were obtained in an earlier study by Miller and Janis (1973). This study showed that student partnerships without any exposure to norm-sending communications had the opposite effect from what was intended. Instead of providing mutual support that would improve the students' morale and adjustment to college life, the partnerships had an adverse effect.

After obtaining this indirect evidence from two studies, I surmised that clients who come to a clinic for help with their smoking, overeating, or any other such problem of self-control would not be likely to benefit from whatever treatments they were given if the counselors were to abstain from making any recommendations. Consequently, it seemed to me to be unethical to assign any such clients to the control treatment condition required to carry out an experiment designed to test variable #4 in Phase 2 of the theoretical analysis.

No systematic research has been carried out as yet on two of the other variables listed under Phase 2: attributing the norms being endorsed to a respected secondary group, and giving selective positive feedback after the recommendations are presented. These variables are represented in the experiments conducted in clinical settings, such as the weight-reduction clinic, in that we arrange for the counselors to endorse recommendations that are truthfully attributed to appropriate medical authorities and to give contingent positive feedback after presenting the recommendations, so as to avoid reinforcing the clients' reluctance to comply. The only study in which a systematic variation was introduced was the one by Quinlan and Janis (1982), in which the effects of noncontingent versus contingent feedback throughout the initial interview was systematically compared. The findings on weight loss and other behavioral measures of adherence showed that it was equally effective to give either contingent or noncontingent feedback throughout the initial interview. But this outcome might hold only in certain types of clinical settings, such as weight-reduction clinics, in which clients seldom express any intentions that go counter to the counselor's recommendations. In other settings, contingent reinforcement throughout the initial interview might prove to be more effective, as is suggested by Mulligan's study, (1982) discussed earlier in this chapter, in which the counselors' noncontingent positive feedback appears to have inadvertently reinforced the subjects' reluctance to comply with the recommendation to donate blood to the Red Cross.

The other two subsidiary variables listed in Phase 2 could be investigated to some extent without posing ethical issues concerning responsibility to offer genuine help to clients in clinical settings. Such research does not necessarily require assigning clients to control conditions that are expected to have unfavorable effects that might undermine the effectiveness of whatever else the counselor might do in an effort to help the clients. Prior research on one of the variables (commitment) suggests that it can have positive effects on adherence to difficult decisions, but the limiting conditions remain to be determined. (See the review of the research literature in Janis & Mann, 1977, pages 279–308, and in Kiesler, 1971). In several pilot studies in our weight-reduction clinic, my colleagues and I have compared the standard commitment procedure used in all such studies with an additional procedure intended to make commitment even more salient. The standard procedure involves asking clients at the end of the session if they are willing to try conscientiously to stick to the recommended low-calorie diet; the additional procedure involves asking clients to sign contracts asserting that they will avoid eating their favorite fattening foods and will conscientiously stay on the diet for as long as it takes to reach their target weight.

In these pilot studies we have found no evidence of any effect of the additional commitment on adherence (as measured by weight loss). These unpromising findings may be attributable to the use of the standard commitment procedure as the control condition, which may be so potent that it is already at the ceiling so far as commitment effects are concerned. We have been reluctant to take the next step in pursuing commitment effects in our weight-reduction clinic, which would be to compare the standard commitment procedure with a control condition in which no commitment at all is elicited. Again, the reason is that ethical standards require that we do not use a control condition which prior research indicates could run the risk of undermining the effectiveness of the counseling sessions, which would deprive the clients of genuine help. In future research some way might be found to investigate commitment effects in field experiments without violating ethical standards, perhaps by carrying out the research in a setting like that used by Mulligan (1982) (in which clients were encouraged to contribute blood to the Red Cross drive) where the interviewers do not recruit subjects by offering a genuine clinical service but can nevertheless make legitimate recommendations.

The remaining variable specified for Phase 2—building up attributions of self-control and personal responsibility—was systematically investigated in the study reported by Riskind and Janis (1982), which included a special procedure intended to promote long-term adherence by training clients to give themselves self-approval for successful adherence to dieting rules. Each client was asked to engage in two psychodramatic enactments in order to "look into the future." One of the role-playing scenarios stipulated failure to follow the diet and the other stipulated success. While acting out each scenario in turn, the client was required to say out loud what she would think of herself, particularly her thoughts and feelings concerning self-pride. Unexpectedly, the results came out in the opposite direction from what was predicted for clients who were given a standard type of intake interview that induced a moderate degree of self-disclosure. Those clients also expressed less confidence about their ability to diet successfully and more self-derogation than clients who were not given the self-approval training. Evidently the attempt to get the clients to focus on their own personal responsibility and to anticipate self-approval for successful dieting had a boomerang effect.

Perhaps enacting the failure scenario (which was always done first) had such a demoralizing effect that it could not be counteracted by enacting the success scenario. In any case, the unfavorable outcome from the psychodramatic self-approval procedure has made us very wary about trying out any similar procedure because of the danger that it may do the clients more harm than good. Nevertheless, my colleagues and I are now trying out other approaches that we think may prove to be more effective for building up self-control attributions and a sense of personal responsibility in a way that will facilitate long-term adherence.

What little evidence is available bearing on the facilitating conditions listed for phase 2 seems to be consistent with the theoretical model (except perhaps for the last variable, since the one attempt to represent it in a field experiment yielded the opposite outcome from what was predicted). But the variables for phase 2 remain largely uninvestigated, partly because of ethical considerations.

THE THIRD PHASE

Ethical constraints again loom large when it comes to investigating the first of the following four variables specified for handling Phase 3 (in Table 11.1), but not for the last three:

9. Giving reassurances that the counselor will continue to maintain an attitude of positive regard vs. giving no such reassurances.
10. Making arrangements for phone calls, exchange of letters, or other forms of communication that foster hope for future contact, real or symbolic, at the time of terminating face-to-face meetings vs. making no such arrangements.
11. Giving reminders that continue to foster self-control attributions and a sense of personal responsibility vs. giving no such reminders.
12. Building the client's self-confidence about succeeding without the aid of the counselor vs. not doing so.

In all our studies carried out in clinical service settings, before saying goodbye the counselors always convey reassurance that they will continue to maintain a positive attitude toward each client, often by explicitly expressing their confidence that the client has what it takes to achieve and retain self-control over the problem behavior if he or she makes a genuine effort. Taking account of extensive clinical observations of clients' spontaneous fear of being rejected in response to the termination crisis, we have not tested the hypothesis that withholding this type of reassurance will have a demoralizing effect on many clients.

There is no reason to expect, however, that if such reassurances are given, demoralization or any other such adverse effect will result from withholding the other three conditions specified for promoting a satisfactory outcome to the termination crisis. Accordingly, there appears to be no basis for ethical objections to investigating those ameliorative variables.

Arrangements for future contact were systematically varied in the experimental research reported by Quinlan, Janis, and Bales (1982), in which half of the clients had weekly telephone calls from the counselor after the initial session, while the other half had no contact at all until the brief follow-up session 1 month later. The latter (low-contact) condition corresponds to the standard amount of contact arranged in all other studies in the Yale Weight-Reduction Clinic. The arrangement to have the additional telephone contact had complicated effects on adherence, including both favorable and unfavorable outcomes, depending upon whether the clients had been induced to disclose positive or negative personal information and whether the level of self-disclosure was low or moderate. It is noteworthy, however, that under certain conditions (moderate level of disclosure in an interview that elicited only positive personal information) arranging for the additional telephone contact was found to result in much more weight loss than any other condition in this experiment or in any other of our experiments on dieting (a mean weight loss of 10 pounds after 8 weeks). Consequently it appears worthwhile to continue investigating this enigmatic variable to find out how and why it results in such a marked increase in success under certain limited conditions and why it reduces success under other conditions.

Variable 11 in Phase 3, which involves reminders that encourage self-reliance, is very similar to variable 8 in Phase 2. Both variables were investigated in combination in the study reported by Riskind and Janis (1982) on weight reduction, which yielded results indicating that the attempts at building up reliance on self-approval rather than on approval from others failed to increase adherence (as measured by subsequent weight loss) and appeared to have reduced the clients' self confidence at the end of the initial interview.

We cannot be at all optimistic about the kind of self-approval training used in that field experiment, without making major changes. Nevertheless, we need not be pessimistic about finding some way to foster self-reliance that will increase rather than decrease self-confidence. One possibility, for example, would be to drastically modify the Riskind and Janis procedure by focusing only on expected successful outcomes in the future, leaving out possible failures.

A new approach to transforming other-directed to self-directed approval motivation is suggested by clinical observations in the Yale Weight-Reduction Clinic, particularly from process interviews such as the ones used in the study reported by Janis and Quinlan (1982). These observations fit in with an hypothesis suggested by Riskind and Janis (1982) which asserts that transitory dependency on the counselor helps the client get started on a stressful course of action but continued adherence requires that the client develop self-attributions of personal responsibility, with a corresponding decline in dependency upon the counselor. Our clinical observations seem to be in agreement with those of Davison and Valins (1969) who conclude from their research in a completely different setting that behavior change is more likely to be maintained when clients attribute the cause of the change to themselves rather than to an outside agent. A direct implication of this conclusion is that people who seek help in self-regulation will be more likely to adhere in the long run to a new course of action, such as dieting, if the counselor stresses the client's own role in whatever behavior change occurs (see S. Brehm, 1976, p. 168).

I have noticed that some of our most successful clients go through a progression of steps in which other-directed approval motivation seems to be transformed into self-directed approval motivation, much as was proposed by Riskind and Janis (1982). First, they start off feeling that with the counselor's help they will be able to stick to the diet. The second step comes during the first week or so of dieting, when they begin to feel like "I can do it on my own most of the time, as long as you are still available to give me some support and encouragement." The third step comes after they start losing some weight when they see that, in fact, they have basically been doing it on their own for a while. They feel, "at first I needed your help, but now I can do it on my own with a little support from someone else besides you." Finally, the last step comes when they realize that they are able to control their eating. Then they feel "I can do it entirely on my own and I have already shown that I can do it." I have the impression that the final attitude of self-reliance is predominant among those clients who are most successful at resisting temptations to backslide.

I suspect that this sequence of steps, moving from dependency to self-reliance, could be facilitated in many clients if counselors give their clients step-by-step guidance in self-talk about personal responsibility. In the initial session the counselors might make a frank statement about the problem of dependency and set up the ultimate goal of self-reliance, after describing the successive steps. Then, at the appropriate times, they could encourage the clients to try to move on to the next step. For example, in a telephone conversation with a client who reports having lost weight for 2 successive weeks, a counselor might remind the client of the third step in the sequence and raise the question as to which one of the clients' friends or relatives might be most suited to function as an additional helper. Later on, after the client has demonstrated weight loss in a follow-up interview, the counselor could encourage self-talk that embodies the final attitude of self-reliance, as specified by variable 12 in Phase 3. This type of procedure is currently being tried out in a pilot study, to see if it looks sufficiently promising to warrant systematic testing in a field experiment.

HOW FAR HAVE WE GONE IN ATTAINING OUR PRIMARY GOAL—TO HELP TRANSFORM THE ART OF COUNSELING INTO A SCIENCE?

A little way, in my judgment, but not very far. Earlier I pointed out that in our research on short-term counseling my colleagues and I were attempting to move ahead on the two-fold task of formulating testable theoretical ideas and of obtaining systematic evidence bearing on them. The theoretical model based on observations of successful versus unsuccessful long-term counseling has proved to be useful in guiding the choice of variables for most of the studies of short-term counseling discussed in this chapter. The key variables pertaining to the first phase of forming an effective counselor-client relationship, as we have just seen, have stood up quite well in replicated field experiments as determinants of adherence to counselors' recommendations. The variables specified for Phases 2 and 3, however, must be regarded as an unfinished agenda on which research work is still in progress. For some of those variables, fragmentary findings have been obtained, and they appear to be sufficiently promising to warrant further systematic investigation. From unexpected findings in the research completed so far, we have obtained a few fresh leads, particularly bearing on the crucial mediating role of building up the clients' self-confidence about improving their self-control, which also appear well worth pursuing. But all these small advances carry us only a short distance and we cannot console ourselves with the overoptimistic view that they have brought us to the verge of a big breakthrough.

Those of us carrying out research on helping relationships, like psychologists working on many other problems of human behavior, evidently must resign ourselves to snail-like progress. As we systematically test the most promising hypotheses, using the best available research methods, we would like to achieve some quantum jumps in the science of counseling. But can we realistically expect much more than a slow accumulation of piecemeal evidence that may tell us a little something that is dependable about when, how, and why counselors can succeed in helping clients achieve their goals? If not, we need to function like a good counselor to ourselves, to build up our own hope and self-confidence about being successful in the long run.

REFERENCES

Bandura, A., & Simon, K. The role of proximal intentions in self-regulation of refractory behavior. *Cognitive Therapy and Research*, 1977, *1*, 177–193.

Brehm, S. *The application of social psychology to clinical practice*. New York: Halsted Press (Wiley), 1976.

Broadhurst, A. Applications of the psychology of decisions. In M. P. Feldman and A. Broadhurst (Eds.), *Theoretical and experimental bases of the behavior therapies*. London: Wiley, 1976.

Byrne, D., & Griffitt, W. Similarity and awareness of similarity of personality characteristics as determinants of attraction. *Journal of Experimental Research in Personality*, 1969, *3*, 179–186.

Chang, P. *The effects of quality of self-disclosure on reactions to interviewer feedback*. Unpublished doctoral dissertation, University of Southern California, 1977.

Colten, M. E., & Janis, I. L. Effects of moderate self-disclosure and the balance-sheet procedure. In I. L. Janis (Ed.), *Counseling on personal decisions: Theory and research on short-term helping relationships*. New Haven, Conn.: Yale University Press, 1982.

Conolley, E., Janis, I. L., & Dowds, M. M., Jr. Effects of variations in the type of feedback given by the counselor. In I. L. Janis (Ed.), *Counseling on personal decisions: Theory and research on short-term helping relationships*. New Haven, Conn.: Yale University Press, 1982.

Cormier, W. H., & Cormier, L. S. *Interviewing strategies for helpers: A guide to assessment, treatment and evaluation*. Monterey, Calif.: Brooks/Cole, 1979.

Davison, G. C. and Valins, S. Maintenance of self-attributed and drug attributed behavior change. *Journal of Personality and Social Psychology*, 1969, *11*, 25–33.

Dowds, M. M., Jr., Janis, I. L., & Conolley, E. Effects of acceptance by the counselor. In I. L. Janis (Ed.), *Counseling on personal decisions: Theory and research on short-term helping relationships*. New Haven, Conn.: Yale University Press, 1982.

Egan, G. *The skilled helper: A model for systematic helping and interpersonal relating*. Monetary, Calif.: Brooks/Cole, 1975.

Greene, L. R. Effects of field dependence on affective reactions and compliance in dyadic interactions. *Journal of Personality and Social Psychology*, 1976, *34*, 569–577.

Greene, L. R. Effects of verbal evaluative feedback and interpersonal distance on behavioral compliance. *Journal of Counseling Psychology*, 1977, *24*, 10–14.

Greenwald, H. *Decision therapy*. New York: Wyden, 1973.

Hoyt, M. and Janis, I. L. Increasing adherence to a stressful decision via a motivational balance sheet procedure: A field experiment. *Journal of Personality and Social Psychology*, 1975, *31*, 833–839.

Hunt, W. A., & Bespalec, D. A. An evaluation of current methods of modifying smoking behavior. *Journal of Clinical Psychology*, 1974, *30*, 431–438.

Hunt, W. A., & Matarazzo, J. D. Three years later: Recent developments in the experimental modification of smoking behavior. *Journal of Abnormal Psychology*, 1973, *81*, 107–114.

Janis, I. L. Effects of fear-arousal on attitude change. In L. Berkowitz (Ed.), *Advances in experimental social psychology* (Vol. 3). New York: Academic Press, 1967.

Janis, I. L. (Ed.), *Counseling on personal decisions: Theory and research on short-term helping relationships*. New Haven, Conn.: Yale University Press, 1982.

Janis, I. L., & Hoffman, D. Facilitating effects of daily contact between partners who make a decision to cut down on smoking. *Journal of Personality and Social Psychology*, 1970, *17*, 25–35. (Reprinted with additional evidence from a 10-year follow up study in I. L. Janis (Ed.), *Counseling on personal decisions: Theory and research on short-term helping relationships*. New Haven, Conn.: Yale University Press, 1982.

Janis, I. L., & LaFlamme, D. Effects of outcome psychodrama as a supplementary technique in marital and career counseling. In I. L. Janis (Ed.), *Counseling on personal decisions: Theory and research on short-term helping relationships*. New Haven, Conn.: Yale University Press, 1982.

Janis, I. L., & Mann, L. *Decision making: A psychological analysis of conflict, choice, and commitment*. New York: Free Press, 1977.

Janis, I. L., & Quinlan, D. M. What disclosing means to the client: Comparative case studies. In I. L. Janis (Ed.), *Counseling on personal decisions: Theory and research on short-term helping relationships*. New Haven, Conn.: Yale University Press, 1982.

Kiesler, C. A. (Ed.). *The psychology of commitment*. New York: Academic Press, 1971.

Krumboltz, J. D. (Ed.). *Revolution in counseling*. Boston: Houghton Mifflin, 1966.

Labov, W., & Fanshel, D. *Therapeutic discourse*. New York: Academic Press, 1977.

Langer, E. J., Janis, I., & Wolfer, J. Reduction of psychological stress in surgical patients. *Journal of Experimental Social Psychology*, 1975, *1*, 155–166.

Marston, M. V. Compliance with medical regimens: A review of the literature. *Nursing Research*, 1970, *19*, 312–323.

McGuire, W. J. The nature of attitudes and attitude change. In G. Lindzey and E. Aronson (Eds.), *The handbook of social psychology* (Vol. 3, 2nd ed.). Reading, Mass.: Addison-Wesley, 1969.

Meichenbaum, D. H., & Turk, D. C. The cognitive-behavioral management of anxiety, anger, and pain. In P. O. Davidson (Ed.), *The behavioral management of anxiety, depression and pain*. New York: Brunner/Mazel, 1976.

Miller, J. C., & Janis, I. L. Dyadic interaction and adaptation to the stresses of college life. *Journal of Consulting Psychology*, 1973, *3*, 258–264.

Mulligan, W. L. Effects of self-disclosure and interviewer feedback: A field experiment during a Red Cross blood donation campaign. In I. L. Janis (Ed.), *Counseling on personal decisions: Theory and research on short-term helping relationships*. New Haven, Conn.: Yale University Press, 1982.

Nowell, C., & Janis, I. L. Effective and ineffective partnerships in a weight-reduction clinic. In I. L. Janis (Ed.), *Counseling on personal decisions: Theory and research on short-term helping relationships*. New Haven, Conn.: Yale University Press, 1982.

Quinlan, D. M., & Janis, I. L. Unfavorable effects of high levels of self-disclosure. In I. L. Janis (Ed.), *Counseling on personal decisions: Theory and research on short-term helping relationships*. New Haven, Conn.: Yale University Press, 1982.

Quinlan, D. M., Janis, I. L., & Bales, V. Effects of moderate self-disclosure and amount of contact with the counselor. In I. L. Janis (Ed.), *Counseling on personal decisions: Theory and research on short-term helping relationships*. New Haven, Conn.: Yale University Press, 1982.

Reed, H. B., & Janis, I. L. Effects of a new type of psychological treatment on smokers' resistance to warnings about health hazards. *Journal of Consulting and Clinical Psychology*, 1974, *42*, 748.

Riskind, J. H. The clients' sense of personal mastery: Effects of time perspective and self-esteem. In I. L. Janis (Ed.), *Counseling on personal decisions: Theory and research on short-term helping relationships.* New Haven, Conn.: Yale University Press, 1982.

Riskind, J. H., & Janis, I. L. Effects of high self-disclosure and approval training procedures. In I. L. Janis (Ed.), *Counseling on personal decisions: Theory and research on short-term helping relationships.* New Haven, Conn.: Yale University Press, 1982.

Smith, A. D. Effects of self-esteem enhancement on teachers' acceptance of innovation in a classroom setting. In I. L. Janis (Ed.), *Counseling on personal decisions: Theory and research on short-term helping relationships.* New Haven, Conn.: Yale University Press, 1982.

Stone, G. C. Patient compliance and the role of the expert. *Journal of Social Issues,* 1979, *35,* 34–59.

13

Stress Inoculation in Health Care: Theory and Research (1982)

Stress inoculation involves giving people realistic warnings, recommendations, and reassurances to prepare them to cope with impending dangers or losses. At present stress inoculation procedures range in intensiveness from a single 10-minute preparatory communication to an elaborate training program with graded exposure to danger stimuli accompanied by guided practice in coping skills, which might require 15 or more hours of training. Any preparatory communication is said to function as stress inoculation if it enables a person to increase his or her tolerance for subsequent threatening events, as manifested by behavior that is relatively efficient and stable rather than disorganized by anxiety or inappropriate as a result of denial of real dangers. Preparatory communications and related training procedures can be administered before or shortly after a person makes a commitment to carry out a stressful decision, such as undergoing surgery or a painful series of medical treatments. When successful, the process is called stress inoculation because it may be analogous to what happens when people are inoculated to produce antibodies that will prevent a disease.

OBSERVATIONS DURING WORLD WAR II

The notion that people could be prepared for stress was very much in the air during World War II. I was rather forcibly introduced to

Janis, I. L. Stress inoculation in health care: Theory and research. In D. Meichenbaum and M. Jaremko (Eds.), *Stress prevention and management: A cognitive-behavioral approach.* New York: Plenum, 1982. Preparation of this paper was supported in part by Grant No. 1R01 MH32995-01 from the National Institute of Mental Health. The author wishes to thank Marjorie Janis, Leah Lapidus, Donald Meichenbaum, and Dennis Turk for valuable criticisms and suggestions for revising earlier drafts. Reprinted by permission.

that notion shortly after I was drafted into the Army in the fall of 1943. Like millions of other American soldiers who received basic military training at that time, I was put through what was called a "battle inoculation" course. It included not only films, pamphlets, and illustrated lectures about the realities of combat dangers but also gradual exposure to actual battle stimuli under reasonably safe conditions. The most impressive feature of the battle inoculation course was that each of us had to crawl about eighty yards under live machine-gun fire in a simulated combat setting that was all too realistic.

Later on, as a member of an Army research team of social psychologists under the leadership of Samuel Stouffer and Carl Hovland, I had the opportunity to collect and analyze pertinent morale survey data and clinical observations bearing on stress tolerance. In an analysis of fear in combat in *The American Soldier: Combat and its Aftermath* [Chapter 2], I discussed the battle inoculation course. Although its effectiveness had not been systematically investigated during the war, I noted that correlational data from morale surveys indirectly supported the conclusion that "having the experience of escaping from danger by taking successful protective action and having practice in discriminating among [battle] sound cues can be critical factors in the reduction of fears of enemy weapons in combat" (1949, p. 241). In a more speculative vein, I also suggested other ways in which exposure to stress stimuli during basic military training might facilitate coping with the stresses of combat: Battle inoculation training could "increase motivation [of the soldier] to acquire combat skills" and to "develop some personal techniques for coping with his emotional reactions—such as focusing his attention upon the details of his own combat mission as a form of distraction, frequently asserting to himself that he can take it, or some other . . . verbalization which reduces anxiety" (1949, p. 224).

Battle inoculation training was given only after trainees had received ample training opportunities to build up a repertoire of combat skills. I pointed out that this type of preparation for combat could help to reduce the disruptive effects of fear in two ways:"(1) the general level of anxiety in combat would tend to be reduced in so far as the men derived from their training a high degree of self-confidence about their ability to take care of themselves and to handle almost any contingency that might threaten them with sudden danger; and (2) the intensity of fear reactions in specific danger situations would tend to be reduced once the man began to carry out a plan of action in a skilled manner." (1949, pp. 222-223).

In a recent critical review of the evidence bearing on fear in combat, Rachman (1978, p. 64) concludes that with minor exceptions the available correlational data support these propositions, which are consistent with Bandura's (1977) recent emphasis on the positive behavioral changes resulting from an improved sense of self-efficacy. . . .

A few years after the end of World War II, I reviewed the studies bearing on fear reactions of civilians exposed to air war [see Chapters 3 and 4]. Here again I encountered indications that realistic warnings and gradual exposure to stress stimuli might have positive effects as "psychological preparation for withstanding the emotional impact of increasingly severe air attacks" (Janis, 1951, p. 155). I was especially impressed by Matte's (1943) observations of Londoners standing for long periods of time silently and solemnly contemplating the bombing damage. These observations, together with his clinical interviews, led him to infer that the Londoners were "working-through" the current air raid experience in a way that prepared them psychologically for subsequent ones. He surmised that their gradual realization of the possibility of being injured or killed minimized the potentially traumatic effects of a sudden confrontation with air raid dangers and at the same time heightened their self-confidence about being able to take it. Rachman's (1978) review of the evidence from wartime research emphasizes the unexpectedly high level of stress tolerance displayed by heavily bombed people in England, Germany, and Japan, during World War II. He points out that "some of the strongest evidence pointing to the tendency of fears to habituate with repeated [non-traumatic] exposures to the fear-provoking situation, comes from these [World War II] observations of people exposed to air raids." (Rachman, 1978, p. 39).

The value of psychological preparation was also implied by impressionistic observations of how people reacted to social stresses during World War II. Romalis (1942), for example, reported clinical observations suggesting that the American women who became most upset when their husbands or sons were drafted into the Army tended to be those who had denied the threat of being separated. These women, according to Romalis, were psychologically unprepared because they had maintained overoptimistic beliefs that their husbands or sons would somehow be exempt from the draft. When the threat of being separated actually materialized, they reacted with much more surprise, resentment, and anxiety than those women who had developed realistic expectations.

RESEARCH ON SURGERY

While studying stress reactions in a series of case studies of surgical patients during the early 1950s, I observed numerous indications that preparatory information could affect stress tolerance [see Chapter 8]. My first series of case studies on the surgical wards led me to surmise that the earlier observations on psychological preparation of people exposed to military combat and air war disasters might have broad applicability to all sorts of personal disasters, including surgery and painful medical treatments. I was able to check on this idea by obtaining survey data from seventy-seven young men who had recently undergone a major surgical operation (Janis, 1958, pp. 352-394). The results indicated that those surgical patients who received information beforehand about what to expect were less likely than those given little information to overreact to setbacks during the postoperative period. Although no dependable conclusions about the causal sequence could be drawn from those correlational results, they led to subsequent experiments on the effects of giving patients various kinds of preparatory information intended to increase their tolerance for the stresses of surgery.

Supporting evidence for the effectiveness of anticipatory preparation for stress—information about what to expect combined with various coping suggestions—has come from a variety of controlled field experiments with adult surgical patients (e.g., DeLong, 1971; Egbert, Battit, Welch, and Bartlett, 1964; Johnson, 1966; Johnson, et al., 1977; Schmidt, 1966; Schmitt and Wooldridge, 1973; Vernon and Bigelow, 1974). Similar positive results on the value of giving psychological preparation have also been reported in studies of childbirth (e.g., Breen, 1975; Dick-Read, 1959; Lemaze, 1958; Levy and McGee, 1975) and noxious medical procedures (e.g., Johnson and Leventhal, 1974).

The research with surgical patients indicates that preparatory information can inoculate people to withstand the disruptive emotional and physical impact of the severe stresses of surgery. Like people traumatized by an overwhelming wartime disaster, those who are not inoculated experience acute feelings of helplessness and react with symptoms of acute fright, aggrievement, rage, or depression. In this respect, the natural tendency of ill people to deny impending threats during the preoperative period is likely to be pathogenic.

A number of interrelated cognitive and motivational processes that may mediate the effects of stress inoculation are suggested by case studies of how hospitalized men and women react to severe postdecisional setbacks after having decided to accept their physician's recommendation to have an operation (Janis, 1958, pp. 352-394; 1971, pp. 95-102). Most of the case studies deal with surgical patients who for one reason or another were not psychologically prepared. These patients were so overwhelmed by the usual pains, discomforts, and deprivations of the postoperative convalescense period that they manifestly regretted their decision and on some occasions actually refused to permit the hospital staff to administer routine postoperative treatments. Before the disturbing setbacks occurred, these patients typically received relatively little preparatory information and retained an unrealistic conception of how nicely everything was going to work out, which functioned as a blanket immunity type of reassurance, enabling them for a time to set their worries aside. They sincerely believed that they would not have bad pains or undergo any other disagreeable experiences. But then, when they unexpectedly experienced incision pains and suffered from all sorts of other unpleasant deprivations that are characteristic of post-operative convalescence, their blanket immunity type of reassurance was undermined. They thought something had gone horribly wrong. They could neither reassure themselves nor accept truthful reas-surances from physicians and nurses.

Taking account of the surgery findings and the earlier research from World War II, I suggested that it should be possible to prevent traumatic reactions and to help people cope more effectively with any type of anticipated stress by giving them beforehand some form of "emotional inoculation", as I then called it (Janis, 1951, pp. 220–221 and 1958, p. 353 ff.). (Subsequently, Donald Meichenbaum [1977] called it "stress inoculation", which I now think is a better term). For people who initially ignore or deny the danger, the inocu-lation procedure, as I have described it (1971, pp. 196–197), includes three counseling procedures: (1) giving "realistic information in a way that challenges the person's blanket immunity reassurances so as to make him aware of his vulnerability" and to motivate him "to plan preparatory actions for dealing with the subsequent crisis"; (2) counteracting "feelings of helplessness, hopelessness, and de-moralization" by calling attention to reassuring facts about personal and social coping resources that enable the person "to feel reasonably confident about surviving and ultimately recovering from the im-pending ordeal"; and (3) encouraging "the person to work out his own ways of reassuring himself and his own plans for protecting himself." The third procedure is important because in a crisis many people become passive and overly dependent on family, friends, and authority figures, such as physicians; they need to build up cognitive defenses involving some degree of self reliance instead of relying exclusively on others to protect them from suffering and loss. The first two counseling procedures require careful dosage of both dis-tressing and calming information about what is likely to happen in order to strike "a balance between arousal of anticipatory fear or grief on the one hand and authoritative reassurance on the other." (1971, p. 196). For persons whose initial level of fear is high, however, only the second and third procedures would be used.

In my theoretical analysis of the psychological effects of preparatory information, I introduced the concept of "the work of worrying" to refer to the process of mentally rehearsing anticipated losses and developing reassuring cognitions that can at least partially alleviate fear or other intense emotions when a crisis is subsequently encountered (1958, pp. 374–378). The "work of worrying" is assumed to be stimulated by preparatory information concerning any impending threat to one's physical, material, social, or moral well-being. For example, it may play a crucial role among men and women exposed to the physical and social stresses of tornadoes, floods, and other natural disasters. Wolfenstein (1957) reports having the impression from her review of disaster studies that the people who seemed to cope best and to recover most quickly were those who received unambiguous warnings beforehand and who decided to take precautionary action on the assumption that they personally could be affected. She suggests that among people who deny that any protective measures are necessary up to the last moment, "the lack of emotional preparation, the sudden shattering of the fantasy of complete immunity, the sense of compunction for failing to respond to warnings contribute to the disruptive effect of an extreme event" (1957, p. 29).

RESEARCH ON OTHER POSTDECISIONAL CRISES

Essentially the same adaptive cognitive and emotional changes that were discerned following stress inoculation in surgical patients have been noted in many case studies and in a few field experiments that focus on people who have encountered setbacks and losses when carrying out other decisions, including typical problems arising after choosing a career, taking legal action to obtain a divorce, and making policy decisions on behalf of an organization (Janis and Mann, 1977). Stress inoculation is also pertinent to the problem of backsliding recidivism, which plagues those health-care practitioners who try to help their clients to improve their eating habits, stop smoking, cut down on alcohol consumption, or change their behavior in other ways that will promote physical or mental health [see Chapter 11]. Similarly, preparatory communications given prior to relocation of elderly patients to a new nursing home or to a hospital have been found to be effective in reducing protests and debilitation (Schulz and Hanusa, 1978).

Recently stress inoculation has begun to be used in schools to help prevent teen-aged children from becoming cigarette smokers. A controlled field experiment with seventh graders showed that significantly fewer teen-agers became smokers by the end of the school year if they were exposed to an experimental program of stress inoculation designed to counteract the overt and subtle social pressures, such as dares from friends, that frequently induce smoking (McAlister, Perry, and Maccoby, 1979). The stress inoculation procedures, which were given after the students committed themselves to the decision to be non-smokers, included role-playing skits to represent the various social inducements to smoke, specific suggestions about how to handle difficult situations when confronted with peer group pressures, and rehearsals of appropriate cognitive responses of commitment to resist the pressures.

All of the various studies just cited on postdecisional crises support the same general conclusion that emerged from the earlier surgery studies, namely that many people will display higher stress tolerance in response to losses and setbacks when they attempt to carry out a chosen course of action if they have been given realistic warnings in advance about what to expect together with cogent reassurances that promote confidence about attaining a basically satisfactory outcome despite those losses and setbacks.

CLINICAL USES IN TREATING EMOTIONAL AND PHYSICAL DISORDERS

During the past decade stress inoculation has been extensively used by clinical practitioners who have developed what they call a "cognitive-behavioral modification" form of therapy (see Goldfried, Decenteco, and Weinberg, 1974; Meichenbaum, 1977; Meichenbaum and Turk, 1976 and in press; Meichenbaum and Jaremko, 1982). In the earlier work I have just reviewed, stress inoculation was introduced to *prevent* the damaging psychological consequences of subsequent exposures to stress, such as demoralization, phobias, and psychosomatic disorders. In contrast, this new trend in clinical psychology uses stress inoculation to *alleviate* or *cure* the stress-related disorders from which patients are already suffering.

The procedures described by Donald Meichenbaum and his associates for clients suffering from phobic anxiety, such as excessive fear of needles used in injections and blood tests, include three main steps. The first step is to give preparatory information about the stressful situations that evoke the anxiety symptoms. Just as in the surgery cases, the client is told about (a) the negative features of the situations that arouse anxiety, including the possibility of high physiological arousal and feelings of being emotionally overwhelmed, and (b) the positive features that are reassuring and that can lead to the development of more effective ways of managing the situation. A major goal of this initial educational phase, which is usually conducted by means of questions in a Socratic-type of dialogue, is to help the clients reconceptualize their anxiety symptoms so that what they say to themselves when they are confronted with the phobic situation will no longer be self-defeating but will be conducive to effective action. Another somewhat related goal is to enable the client to grasp a more differentiated view of anxiety as comprising both cognitive appraisals of threat and physiological arousal. This differentiation sets the stage for the next phase.

The second phase is intended to help the client develop a new set of coping techniques that modify distressing cognitions and physiological arousal. The client is not only encouraged to make use of coping skills already in his or her repertoire but is also given training in new "direct-action" skills, such as relaxation exercises that can be used to reduce emotional arousal in anxiety-provoking situations. A major goal of this phase is to prepare the client to react in a constructive way to early warning signs, before the full onset of the anxiety symptoms. In addition to direct-action skills, cognitive coping skills are also discussed in collaborative interchanges designed to help the client work out his or her own coping strategies. The counselor gives suggestive examples of positive self-talk that might promote effective coping, such as "I can handle this situation by taking one step at a time." Some of the recommended self-talk is also likely to enhance the client's sense of self-efficacy after each successful trial— for example, "I can do it, it really worked; I can control my fear by controlling my ideas."

The third phase involves applying the new coping skills to a graded series of imaginary and real stress situations. The procedures used in this phase are based on the pioneering work of Seymour Epstein (1967), who emphasized the importance of "self-pacing" and exposure to small doses of threat in the acquisition of coping skills for mastery of stress among men engaging in dangerous activities such as parachuting and combat flying. In the graduated practice phase of stress inoculation, the patient is given role playing exercises and also a series of homework assignments involving real-life exposures that become increasingly demanding.

Favorable results from using this type of stress inoculation have been reported in clinical studies of clients suffering from a variety of emotional symptoms, including persistent phobias (Meichenbaum, 1977); test anxiety (Goldfried, Linehan, and Smith, 1978; Meichenbaum, 1972); social anxiety and shyness (Glass, Gottman, and Shmurack, 1976; Zimbardo, 1970); speech anxiety (Fremauw and Zitter, 1978; Meichenbaum, Gilmore, and Fedoravicious, 1971); depression (Taylor and Marshall, 1977); and outbursts of anger (Novaco, 1975). Essentially the same procedures have also been used successfully with patients suffering from certain kinds of physical ailments, most notably those involving sporadic or chronic pain (Turk, 1977; Turk and Genest, 1979). From the clinical research that has been done so far, it appears that a package treatment combining the various kinds of intervention that enter into this type of stress inoculation can sometimes be effective with some patients, but it is not yet known which interventions are essential and which are not (see Meichenbaum and Turk, in press). Nor do we know very much at present about the conditions under which giving preparatory information or administering any of the other component interventions is likely to succeed or fail.

WHEN PREPARATORY INFORMATION FAILS

Here and there in the prior research on stress inoculation one can discern a few rudimentary indications of the conditions under which preparatory information is ineffective or even detrimental. From the very outset of my research on surgery it was apparent that although preparatory information is advantageous for many patients it definitely is not for some of them (Janis, 1958, pp. 370–374). In numerous instances of failure the main source of difficulty seems to be that the message is too meagre to influence the patients. Very brief preparatory messages that take only a few minutes to convey information about impending threats are usually too weak to change a patient's expectations or to stimulate the development of effective self-assurances and therefore have no effect at all. At the opposite extreme, some patients receive very strong preparatory communications from their physicians and friends, which unintentionally stimulate anxiety and feelings of helplessness that decrease rather than increase stress tolerance. Like an overdose of antigens, an overenthusiastic inoculation attempt can produce the very condition it is intended to prevent.

Other sources of detrimental effects have to do with the nature of the stress to which the person is subsequently exposed. For example, I have observed that at least a small minority of surgical patients become extremely upset when told in advance that they are going to be given certain intrusive treatments such as enemas, catheterization, or injections (Janis, 1958, p. 387). These patients apparently imagine each of these routine treatments as being much worse than it really is. When the time comes to have it, they become so emotionally aroused that they are unresponsive to the physicians' or nurses' reassurances and resist to such an extent that the treatment is either botched or cannot be carried out at all. Some practitioners report that they obtain better cooperation if they give no preparatory information about a disturbing procedure of short duration, such as an enema, until they administer it, at which time they give the patient reassurances along with instructions about what to do. (See Janis, 1958, p. 394).

In the instances I have just been discussing the stress episode itself is relatively mild because the patients do not undergo acute pain or prolonged discomfort and an authority figure is present to reassure them that they are doing fine. Perhaps stress inoculation is most applicable for those episodes of stress that are painful or of long duration and that are likely to occur at times when no one will be around to give reassurances.

More recent research with surgical patients has shown that, as expected, preparatory information is not uniformly effective. (For a review of inconsistent effects of preparatory information given to surgical patients see Cohen and Lazarus, 1979). In a number of studies that found no significant effects on psychological or physical recovery only brief messages were given to the patients describing what the stressful experiences would be like in the operating room and during convalescence. For example, a field experiment by Langer, Janis, and Wolfer (1975) found that a brief message containing standard preparatory information that presented accurate forecasts about what would happen to each patient was ineffective, whereas a special form of psychological preparation that presented detailed instructions about a cognitive coping device . . . proved to be highly effective in helping patients to tolerate postoperative stress [see pages 273–274].

Johnson, Rice, Fuller, and Endress (1977) found that preparatory information about what to expect was ineffective for patients having one type of operation (herniorraphy) but highly effective for those having another type (cholecystectomy). These findings may be in line with the earlier observations suggesting that the success of inoculation attempts will vary depending upon the nature of the stress.

Psychological preparation for childbirth, which for several decades has been extensively applied to hundreds of thousands of women, has often been investigated (e.g., Chertok, 1959; Doering and Entwhistle, 1975; Huttel, Mitchell, Fischer, and Meyer, 1972; Tanzer, 1968; Velvoysky, Platonov, Ploticher, and Shugon, 1970). In general, most of the studies of pregnant women, like those of surgical patients, document the value of giving preparatory information and coping suggestions. But occasional failures have also been reported (e.g., Davenport-Slack and Boylan, 1974; Javert and Hardy, 1951). Some women experience severe pains during childbirth despite being given one or another form of psychological preparation. Essentially the same can be said about psychological preparation for other types of pain. Turk and Genest (1979) have reviewed over two dozen systematic evaluation studies of psychological treatments designed to help people suffering from persistent backaches, recurrent headaches, or other chronic pains. Most of the treatments include giving preparatory information about recurrent distressing events that might precipitate or exacerbate the patient's pains together with suggestions about how to cope more effectively with the stresses. A major conclusion that emerges from all these studies, according to Turk and Genest, is that when the psychological treatments include preparatory information about expected stresses and suggestions about how to cope with the stresses, they are generally effective in helping to alleviate chronic pains, but not with all patients in all situations.

Turk and Genest suggest a number of important factors that may influence the outcome of stress inoculation for patients suffering from chronic pain—the degree of threat perceived by the patient, the perceived effectiveness of the information, the mode or channel used to present the preparatory message, and individual differences in coping style and self-confidence. They point out, however, that these factors await systematic investigation, as do the various ingredients of the treatments that have been found to be effective.

In summary: Many findings, both old and new, from studies of psychological preparation for surgery, childbirth, and the stresses associated with chronic pain show that stress inoculation often works but sometimes does not. Obviously the time has come to move on to a more sophisticated phase of research, to investigate systematically the conditions under which stress inoculation is effective. In this new phase of research, which has just recently begun, the investigators' primary purpose is no longer merely to evaluate the overall effectiveness of stress-inoculation procedures, to find out if one or another compound treatment program is successful in building up tolerance for one or another type of stress. Rather, the purpose is to find out which are the *effective components* of the stress inoculation treatments that have already been found to be at least partially successful in past research and to determine the conditions under which each component has a positive effect on stress tolerance. This new phase of analytic research on components includes investigating several factors simultaneously in an analysis of variance design so that interaction effects can be determined, which help to specify in what circumstances and for which types of persons certain of the components of stress inoculation are effective. In my opinion this is where stress inoculation research should have started to go a long time ago and fortunately is now actually going.

From prior studies, we have already obtained important clues about what could prove to be the crucial components. The variables that appear to be leading candidates are discussed in the sections that follow.

PREDICTABILITY

According to a number of laboratory investigations, a person's degree of behavioral control is increased by reducing uncertainty about the nature and timing of threatening events (Averill, 1973; Ball and Vogler, 1971; Pervin, 1963; Seligman, 1975; Weiss, 1970). Several experiments indicate that people are less likely to display strong emotional reactions or extreme changes in attitude when confronted with an unpleasant event if they were previously exposed to a preparatory communication that accurately predicted the disagreeable experience (Epstein and Clark, 1970; Janis, Lumsdaine, and Gladstone, 1951; Lazarus and Alfert, 1964; Staub and Kellett, 1972). These experiments show that advance warnings and accurate predictions can have an emotional dampening effect on the impact of subsequent confrontations with the predicted adverse events. Predictability may therefore be a crucial component in increasing stress tolerance. This hypothesis implies that when a person is given realistic preparatory information about the unpleasant consequences of a decision, he or she will be more likely to adhere to the chosen course of action despite setbacks and losses.

Although the hypothesis has not been systematically investigated in relation to postdecisional behavior, it appears to be plausible in light of a field experiment by Johnson, Morrissey, and Leventhal (1973) on psychological preparation of patients who had agreed to undergo a distressful gastrointestinal endoscopic examination that requires swallowing a stomach tube. In this study one of the preparatory communications was devoted mainly to predicting the perceptual aspects of the unpleasant procedures—what the patient could expect to feel, see, hear, and taste. Photographs of the examining room and the apparatus were also presented. Effectiveness was assessed by the amount of medication required to sedate the patients when the distressing endoscopic procedure was given, which is presumed to be an indicator of stress tolerance. The preparatory communication that predicted the unpleasant perceptual experiences proved to be highly effective, significantly more so than a control communication that described the procedures without giving any perceptual information. The effectiveness of the preparatory communication with the perceptual information cannot, however, be ascribed unequivocally to the increased predictability of the unpleasant events because here and there it also contained reassuring information about the skill of the health-care practitioners and various explanations, which may have involved another variable (discussed in the next section).

If future research verifies the hypothesis that predictability is a crucial variable which is capable of increasing stress tolerance, a subsidiary variable to be considered will be the *vividness* of the perceptual information that is presented, which might make images of expected stressful events more *available*, in the sense that Tversky and Kahneman (1973, 1974) use that term. Psychodramatic role playing, films, and other vividness-enchancing techniques might increase the effectiveness of stress inoculation procedures by increasing the availability of images of the predicted stressful events.

ENHANCING COPING SKILLS BY ENCOURAGING CONTINGENCY PLANS

Another component of standard stress inoculation procedures consists of information about means for dealing with the anticipated stressful event, which provides people with more adequate coping skills. If this component is essential, we would expect to find that people will show more adherence to an adaptive course of action, such as following well-established health rules, if they are given preparatory communications containing specific recommendations for coping with whatever adverse consequences of the decision are most likely to occur. In most of the examples of stress inoculation used in the prior research that has already been cited, two different types of coping recommendations are included. One type pertains to *plans for action* that will prevent or reduce objective damage that might ensue if the anticipated stressful events occur. The second type involves *cognitive coping devices*, including attention-diversion tactics, mentally relaxing imagery, and replacing self-defeating thoughts with reassuring and optimistic self-talk, all of which can prevent or reduce excessive anxiety reactions.

A good example of the first type is to be found in the highly successful stress inoculation procedure for surgical patients used by Egbert, Battit, Welch, and Bartlett (1964), which included giving instruction regarding physical relaxation, positions of the body, and deep breathing exercises that can help to keep postoperative pains to a minimum. Such instruction can be conceptualized as providing a set of contingency plans for dealing with setbacks, suffering, and other sources of postdecisional regret for a course of action that entails short-term losses in order to obtain long-term gains. For example, surgical patients in the study by Egbert and his associates were encouraged to develop the following contingency plan: "If I start to feel severe incision pains, I will use the relaxation and breathing exercises to cut down on the amount of suffering".

Other investigators also report evidence of the effectiveness of stress inoculation procedures that include instruction about behavioral coping techniques for medical or surgical patients (Fuller, Endress and Johnson, 1977; Johnson, 1977; Lindeman, 1972; Lindeman and Van Aernam, 1971; Schmitt and Wooldridge, 1973; Wolfer and Visintainer, 1975). In all of these studies, the recommendations about coping actions were presented in compound communications, accompanied by other types of information, such as predictions about what stressful events are likely to be experienced. There is no way of knowing, therefore, whether the coping action recommendations were wholly, partially, or not at all responsible for the successful outcome of the stress inoculation. One major study, however, has attempted to tease out the relative effectiveness of the coping recommendations. In their second study of patients who were about to undergo a distressing endoscopic examination, Johnson and Leventhal (1974) compared a preparatory communication that told about the discomforts and other sensations that would most likely be experienced with one that gave specific behavioral coping instructions about how to use rapid breathing to reduce gagging during throat swabbing and what to do to avoid discomforts while the stomach tube was being inserted into the esophagus. These investigators found that each of these preparatory communications was more effective than a standard (control) communication that was limited to describing the endoscopic examination procedures (given to all subjects in the experiment), but the combined effect was significantly greater than either alone. Thus, the combination of predicting the adverse events that would be experienced with recommending coping actions proved to be the maximally effective form of stress inoculation. If this outcome is replicated in subsequent analytic research on the effectiveness of different components of stress inoculation, a major controversial issue might be settled. We should be able to find out whether information about coping strategies is essential and which combinations with other components are most effective for various types of individuals.

ENHANCING COGNITIVE COPING CAPABILITIES

We turn next to research on the second type of coping recommendations—those pertaining to positive self talk and other cognitive changes that might increase stress tolerance without necessarily involving any overt coping actions. A few studies provide evidence that people can be helped by preparatory communications that induce them to reconceptualize in an optimistic way the stresses they will undergo. The coping device developed by Langer, Janis, and Wolfer (1975), which involves encouraging an optimistic reappraisal of anxiety-provoking events, was tested in a field experiment with surgical patients by inserting it in a brief preoperative interview conducted by a psychologist. Each patient was given several examples of the positive consequences of his or her decision to undergo surgery (for example, improvement in health, extra care and attention in the hospital, temporary vacation from outside pressure). Then the patient was invited to think up additional positive examples that pertained to his or her individual case. Finally the patient was given the recommendation to rehearse these compensatory favorable consequences whenever he or she started to feel upset about the unpleasant aspects of the surgical experience. Patients were urged to be as realistic as possible about the compensatory features, so as to emphasize that what was being recommended was not equivalent to trying to deceive oneself. The instructions were designed to promote warranted optimism and awareness of the anticipated gains that outweighed the losses to be expected from the chosen course of action. The findings from the controlled experiment conducted by Langer, Janis, and Wolfer (1975) supported the prediction that cognitive reappraisal would reduce stress both before and after an operation. Patients given the reappraisal intervention obtained lower scores on nurses' blind ratings of preoperative stress and on unobtrusive postoperative measures of the number of times pain-relieving drugs and sedatives were requested and administered.

Additional evidence of the value of encouraging cognitive coping strategies comes from a study by Kendall, Williams, Pechacek, Graham, Shisslak, and Herzoff (1977) on the effectiveness of stress inoculation for patients who had agreed to undergo cardiac catheterization. This is a particularly stressful medical procedure that involves working a catheter up into the heart by inserting it into a vein in the groin. One group of patients was given stress inoculation that included discussion of the stresses to be expected together with suggestions to develop their own cognitive coping strategies, which were encouraged by suggesting various reassurances, modeling cognitive coping strategies, and reinforcing whatever personal cognitive coping responses the patient mentioned. Two other equivalent groups of patients were given different preparatory treatments—an educational communication about the catheterization procedure and an attention placebo intervention. There was also a no-treatment control group. The patients given the stress inoculation procedure that encouraged them to develop their own cognitive coping strategies showed higher stress tolerance during the cardiac catheterization than those in the other three treatment groups, as assessed by self-ratings and by ratings made by observers (physicians and medical technicians).

One cannot expect, of course, that every attempt to encourage positive thinking among patients facing surgery or distressing treatments will succeed in helping their recovery during convalescence. One such attempt with surgical patients by Cohen (1975), using different intervention procedures from those in the preceding studies, failed to have any effect on indicators of psychological and physical recovery.

Although few studies have been done among patients who are not hospitalized, there is some evidence of favorable effects which suggests that encouraging positive self-talk and related cognitive coping strategies might prove to be successful in many different spheres of health care. In a controlled field experiment, a stress inoculation procedure designed to encourage positive self talk was found to be effective in helping patients reduce the frequency, duration, and intensity of muscle-contraction headaches (Holroyd, Andrasik, and Westbrook, 1977).

Cognitive coping procedures may also be effective for increasing adherence to health-related decisions, such as dieting. That this is a likely prospect is suggested by the findings from a doctoral dissertation by Riskind (1982), which was carried out in the Weight-Reduction Clinic under my research program. In this field study, all the clients were given counseling and information about dieting but only one experimental group was given additional instructions to adopt a day-by-day coping perspective rather than a long-term perspective. Riskind found that the coping instructions resulted in a greater sense of personal control and more adherence to the diet (as measured by weight loss) over a period of two months among clients with a relatively high initial level of self esteem. The results are similar to those reported by Bandura and Simon (1977) for obese patients being treated by behavior modification techniques. The patients who were instructed to adopt short-term subgoals on a *daily* basis ate less and lost more weight than the patients who were instructed to adopt a longer-term subgoal in terms of *weekly* accomplishments.

From the few systematic studies just reviewed, it seems reasonable to expect that recommendations about coping strategies may prove to be essential ingredients of successful stress inoculation. The evidence is particularly promising, as we have seen, with regard to increasing the stress tolerance of medical and surgical patients by encouraging them to replace self-defeating thoughts with positive coping cognitions. A similar conclusion is drawn by Girodo (1977) after reviewing the positive and negative outcomes of treating phobic patients with the type of stress inoculation procedures recommended by Meichenbaum (1977). Girodo goes so far as to say that the only successful ingredients of stress inoculation are those that induce the person to reconceptualize the threat into nonthreatening terms and that all other ingredients are of limited value, merely serving temporarily to divert attention away from threat cues. Any such generalization, however, gives undue weight to a limited set of findings and would be premature until we have well-replicated results from a variety of investigations that carefully test the effectiveness of each component of stress inoculation.

SELF-CONFIDENCE, HOPE, AND PERCEIVED CONTROL

Many innovative clinical psychologists who have developed stress inoculation procedures and use them in their practice emphasize that teaching patients new cognitive skills is a necessary but not a sufficient condition for helping them to deal effectively with stressful situations. They say that the patients not only need to acquire adequate coping skills but, in order to use them when needed, must feel some degree of self-confidence about being successful. (See, Cormier and Cormier, 1979; Meichenbaum and Turk, in press; Turk and Genest, 1979). Inducing the patients to believe that a recommended course of action will lead to a desired outcome is only one step in the right direction; they must also be able to maintain a sense of personal efficacy with regard to being able to "take it" and to do whatever is expected of them (see Bandura, 1977). Over and beyond the coping recommendations themselves, reassuring social support may be needed to build up the patients' self-confidence and hope about surviving intact despite whatever ordeals are awaiting them (see Caplan and Killilea, 1976).

For medical and surgical patients, the key messages include two types of statements along the lines that I have just suggested. One type asserts that the medical treatment or surgery they are about to receive will be successful, which makes them feel it is worthwhile to put up with whatever suffering, losses, and coping efforts may be required. The second type asserts that the patient will be able to tolerate the pain and other sources of stress. Among the "coping thoughts" recommended in the stress inoculation procedure used by Meichenbaum and Cameron (1973) for fear-arousing situations and by Turk (1977) for chronic pain are some that are specifically oriented toward building a sense of self-confidence and hope—for example, "You can meet this challenge;" "You have lots of different strategies you can call upon;" "You can handle the situation." Even the standard recommendations concerning positive self talk, such as "Don't worry, just think about what you can do about the pain," tends to create an attitude of self-confidence about dealing effectively with the stresses that are anticipated. Similarly, the positive effects of the cognitive coping technique used with surgical patients by Langer, Janis, and Wolfer (1975) may be at least partly attributable to attitude changes in the direction of increased self-confidence. The patients are encouraged to feel confident about being able to deal effectively with whatever pains, discomforts, and setbacks are subsequently encountered, which may help them to avoid becoming discouraged and to maintain hope about surviving without sustaining unbearable losses.

The crucial role of statements about the efficacy of recommended means for averting or minimizing threats of body damage is repeatedly borne out by social psychological studies of the effects of public health messages that contain fear-arousing warnings (see Chu,

1966; Janis, 1971; Leventhal, 1973; Leventhal, Singer and Jones, 1965; Rogers and Deckner, 1975; Rogers and Thistlethwaite, 1970). A study by Rogers and Mewborn (1976), for example, found that assertions about the efficacy of recommended protective actions had a significant effect on college students' intentions to adopt the practices recommended in three different public health communications dealing with well-known hazards—lung cancer, automobile accident injuries, and venereal disease. The findings from this study and from the other studies just cited are consistent with the hypothesis that when a stress inoculation procedure presents impressive information about the expected efficacy of a recommended protective action, it instills hope in the recipients about emerging without serious damage from the dangers they may encounter, which increases their willingness to adhere to the recommended action.

Obviously, it is difficult to test this hypothesis independently of the hypothesis that information inserted to increase coping skills is a potent ingredient of successful stress inoculation. Nevertheless, as I have already indicated, there are certain types of messages that can induce attitude changes in the direction of increased self-confidence and hope without necessarily changing coping skills, which could be used in field experiments designed to determine whether the postulated attitude changes mediate successful stress inoculation. For example, a patient's self-confidence about surviving the ordeal of a painful medical treatment might be increased by a persuasive communication containing an impressive example of a similar patient who had a successful outcome, which may counteract a defeatist attitude and foster an optimistic outlook without increasing coping skills.

There are theoretical grounds for assuming that communications fostering self-confidence and hope will prove to be effective components of stress inoculation, particularly for preventing backsliding among patients who decide to comply with a troublesome medical regimen. Janis and Mann (1977) describe several basic patterns of coping with realistic threats derived from an analysis of the research literature on how people react to emergency warnings and public health recommendations. [See Chapter 9] . . . .

Observations from prior studies by my colleagues and I in weight-reduction and anti-smoking clinics indicate that clients often start carrying out a health-oriented course of action without having engaged in vigilant search and appraisal of the alternatives open to them (Janis, 1982). The dominant coping pattern in many cases appears to be defensive avoidance—deciding without deliberation to adopt the recommended course of action, which appears at the moment to be the least objectionable alternative, and bolstering it with rationalizations that minimize the difficulties to be expected when carrying it out. Defensive avoidance also appears to be a frequent coping pattern among hospitalized surgical and medical patients (Janis, 1958; and Janis and Rodin, 1979).

In order to prevent defensive avoidance, according to Janis and Mann (1977), preparatory communications are needed to meet [an] . . . essential condition for promoting a vigilant coping pattern: Assuming that the clients are already aware of the problems to be expected, interventions are needed that foster hope of solving these problems. Such interventions may also be essential for maintaining a vigilant problem-solving approach to whatever frustrations, temptations, or setbacks subsequently occur when the decision is being implemented.

On the basis of prior studies in clinics for heavy smokers and overweight people, it appears plausible to assume that backsliding occurs when one or more major setbacks make the clients lose hope about finding an adequate solution (Janis, 1982). If this assumption is correct, we would expect stress inoculation to be most effective in preventing patients from reversing their decisions to follow a medical regimen if the preparatory communications contain information or persuasive messages that foster hope of solving whatever problems may arise from that regimen.

Closely related to patients' attitudes of self-confidence and hope are their beliefs about being able to *control* a stressful situation. Stress inoculation may change a patient's expectations of being in control of a dangerous situation, both with regard to the external threats of being helpless to prevent physical damage and the internal threats of becoming panic-stricken and losing emotional control. The stress inoculation procedures used with surgical and medical patients typically include statements designed to counteract feelings of helplessness and to promote a sense of active control. For example, in the stress inoculation procedures designed by Turk (1978) for patients suffering from chronic pains, the coping thoughts that are explicitly recommended and modeled include "Relax, you're in control" and "When the pain mounts you can switch to a different strategy, you're in control."

There is now a sizeable literature indicating that perceived personal control sometimes plays an important role in coping with stress (Averill, 1973; Ball and Vogler, 1971; Bowers, 1968; Houston, 1972; Janis and Rodin, 1979; Lapidus, 1969; Pranulis, Dabbs, and Johnson, 1975; Kanfer and Seider, 1973; Pervin, 1963; Seligman, 1975; Staub, Tursky and Schwartz, 1971; Weiss, 1970). Some preparatory interventions may make patients feel less helpless by making them more active participants, increasing their personal involvement in the treatment. Pranulis and others (1975), for example, redirect hospitalized patients' attention away from their own emotional reactions as passive recipients of medical treatments to information that makes them feel more in control as active collaborators with the staff. Perhaps many of the preparatory communications used for purposes of stress inoculation have essentially the same effect on the patients' perceived control over distressing environmental events, which could increase their self confidence and hope.

INDUCING COMMITMENT AND PERSONAL RESPONSIBILITY

Another psychological component that may contribute to the positive effects of stress inoculation is the heightening of commitment. As part of the stress-inoculation procedure for a new course of action, such as accepting medical recommendations to undergo surgery, painful treatments, or unpleasant regimens, patients are induced to acknowledge that they are going to have to deal with anticipated losses, which is tantamount to making more elaborated commitment statements to the health-care practitioners. Prior psychological research on commitment indicates that each time a person is induced to announce his or her intentions to an esteemed other, such as a professional counselor, the person is anchored to the decision not just by anticipated social disapproval but also by anticipated self disapproval (Janis and Mann, 1977; Kiesler, 1971; McFall and Hammen, 1971). The stabilizing effect of commitment, according to Kiesler's (1971) research, is enhanced by exposure to a mild challenging attack, such as counterpropaganda that is easy to refute. A stress inoculation procedure for medical treatments or surgery might serve this function by first calling attention to the obstacles and drawbacks to be expected (which is a challenging attack) and then providing impressive suggestions about how those obstacles and drawbacks can be overcome (which may dampen the challenging attack sufficiently to make it mild).

Along with inducing increased commitment, stress inoculation tends to build up a sense of personal responsibility on the part of the patient. After hearing about the unpleasant consequences to be expected from undergoing a prescribed treatment and about ways of coping with the anticipated stresses, the patient realizes all the more keenly that he or she is personally responsible for the decision to undergo the recommended treatment and for doing his or her share to help carry it out as effectively as possible, rather than simply being a passive recipient of whatever it is that the physician decides to do.

Predictions about each source of stress to be expected and accompanying coping suggestions convey to the patient the theme "This is yet another problem you must solve yourself; no one else can do it for you." My recent research in weight-reduction and anti-smoking clinics suggests that such messages may foster long-term adherence to difficult regimens because sticking to it requires that the patients develop attributions of personal responsibility, with a corresponding decline in dependency upon the counselor (Janis, 1982). . . .

My theoretical analysis of supportive helping relationships [Chapter 11] postulates that when people have the intention of changing to a new course of action that requires undergoing short-term deprivation in order to attain long-term objectives, the incentive value of gaining the approval of a professional advisor or counselor can help to get them started. . . .

[Later on, however,] to prevent backsliding and other adverse effects when contact with the helper is terminated, the person must internalize the norms sponsored by the helper by somehow converting *other-directed* approval motivation into *self-directed* approval motivation. Little is known as yet about determinants of this process, but it seems plausible to expect that internalization might be facilitated by communication themes in stress inoculation procedures that enhance commitment by building up a sense of personal responsibility.

COPING PREDISPOSITIONS

For certain types of persons, as I mentioned earlier, stress inoculation has been found to have no effect and occasionally even adverse effects. The Janis and Mann (1977) theoretical model of coping patterns has some implications for personality differences in responsiveness to stress inoculation. Certain people can be expected to be highly resistant to communications that attempt to induce the conditions essential for a coping pattern of vigilant search and appraisal [see Chapter 9]. The difficulty may be that they are unresponsive to authentic information that promotes one or another of the three crucial beliefs (that there are serious risks for whichever alternative course of action is chosen; that it is realistic to be optimistically hopeful about finding a satisfactory solution; and that there is adequate time in which to search and deliberate before a decision is required). Such persons would be expected to show consistently defective coping patterns that often would lead to inadequate planning and overreactions to setbacks. In response to acute postdecisional stress, they would be the ones who are most likely to reverse their decisions about undergoing painful medical treatments.

Elsewhere (Janis, 1982, Chapter 20), I have more fully elaborated these theoretical assumptions and reviewed the research findings on specific personality variables related to responsiveness to stress inoculation. In the discussion that follows I shall highlight the main findings and conclusions.

A number of studies employing Byrne's (1964) repression-sensitization scale and Goldstein's (1959) closely related coper versus avoider test suggest that persons diagnosed as chronic repressors or avoiders tend to minimize, deny, or ignore any warning that presents disturbing information about impending threats. Such persons appear to be predisposed to display the characteristic features of defensive avoidance. Unlike persons who are predisposed to be vigilant, these avoiders would not be expected to respond adaptively to preparatory information that provides realistic forecasts about anticipated stressful experiences along with reassurances. Relevant evidence is to be found in the reports on two field experiments conducted on surgery wards by Andrew (1970) and DeLong (1971). In both studies, patients awaiting surgery were given Goldstein's test in order to assess their preferred mode of coping with stress and then were given preparatory information. The reactions of the following three groups were compared: (1) copers who tended to display vigilance or sensitizing defenses; (2) avoiders, who displayed avoidant or denial defenses; and (3) nonspecific defenders who showed no clear preference. In Andrew's (1970) study, preparatory information describing what the experience of the operation and the postoperative convalescence would be like had an unfavorable effect on the rate of physical recovery of avoiders but a positive effect on nonspecific defenders. Copers recovered well irrespective of whether they were given the preoperative information. In DeLong's (1971) study, avoiders were found to have poorest recovery regardless of whether they were given preparatory information; copers showed the greatest benefit from the preparatory information. The findings from the two studies show some inconsistencies but they agree in indicating that persons who display defensive avoidance tendencies do not respond well to preparatory information.

Correlational evidence from studies of surgical patients by Cohen and Lazarus (1973) and Cohen (1975) appears to contradict the implications of the studies just discussed bearing on vigilance versus defensive avoidance. These investigators report that patients who were rated as "vigilant" before the operation showed poorer recovery from surgery than those rated as "avoidant." This finding seems not only to contradict the earlier surgery findings but also to go against the expectation from the conflict-theory model that people who are vigilant will cope better with unfavorable consequences of their decisions than will those whose dominant coping pattern is defensive avoidance. But there are two important considerations that need to be taken into account. One is that Sime (1976) attempted to replicate Cohen and Lazarus' (1973) finding using the same categories but was unable to do so. When there are disagreements like this, one suspects that either there are unrecognized differences in the ways in which the variables were assessed or the relationship between the two variables is determined by an uninvestigated third variable, such as severity of the patient's illness. A second consideration has to do with the way Cohen and Lazarus define "vigilance." A careful examination of their procedures reveals that they did not differentiate between hypervigilance and vigilance. The investigators state that they classified as vigilant any patient who sought out information about the operation (which hypervigilant people do even more than vigilant ones) or who were sensitized in terms of remembering the information and displaying readiness to discuss their thoughts about the operation. (Again, the hypervigilant people tend to be much more preoccupied with information about threatening consequences than those who are vigilant.) According to the criteria given in Janis and Mann (1977) the one example Cohen and Lazarus give of a so-called vigilant reaction would be classified as "hypervigilant": "I have all the facts, my will is all prepared [in the event of death] . . . you're put out, you could be put out too deep, your heart could quit, you can have shock . . . I go not in lightly." Consequently, the correlation observed by these investigators might be attributable to the relationship between preoperative *hypervigilance* and low tolerance for postoperative stress, which has been observed by other investigators (Auerbach, 1973; Janis, 1958; Leventhal, 1963). Auerbach (1973), for example, found that surgical patients who showed a high state of preoperative anxiety relative to their normal or average level (as assessed by the State-Trait Anxiety Inventory developed by Spielberger, Gorsuch, and Lushene, 1970) obtained poorer scores on a measure of postoperative adjustment than those who showed a relatively moderate level of preoperative anxiety.

In Auerbach's study, the postoperative adjustment of the patients who showed moderate preoperative anxiety was found to be superior to the patients who showed relatively low anxiety as well as those who showed relatively high anxiety before the operation. In disagreement with contradictory findings reported by Cohen and Lazarus (1973) and by several other investigators, Auerbach's data tend to confirm Janis' (1958) earlier finding of a curvilinear relationship between the level of preoperative anxiety and postoperative adjustment. Such data are consistent with the "work of worrying" concept, which assumes that inducing vigilance in surgical patients (manifested by a moderate level of preoperative fear or anxiety) is beneficial for postoperative adjustment (Janis, 1958; Janis and Mann, 1977). But it is essential to take note of the disagreements in the correlational results obtained from many non-intervention studies in the research literature on the relationship between level of preoperative fear or anxiety and postoperative adjustment, which can be affected by a number of extraneous variables that are difficult to control even when they can be recognized (see Cohen and Lazarus, 1979). It would not be worthwhile, it seems to me, for investigators to carry out more such correlational studies because even a dozen or two of them cannot be expected to settle the issue. I think it is realistic, however, to hope for dependable conclusions about the postoperative effects of arousal of vigilance before surgery—and also about the interacting effects of such arousal with personality characteristics—if a few more well-controlled *intervention* studies are carried out in which preparatory information designed to induce vigilance is used as an independent variable and is not confounded with social support or with any other potentially potent variable. . . .

The complex findings from the many studies of personality variables suggest that in order to increase the percentage of patients who benefit from stress inoculation it will be necessary to hand-tailor the preparatory information in a way that takes account of each individual's coping style.

When opportunities for stress inoculation are made available, personality factors may play a role in determining who will choose to take advantage of those opportunities and who will not. A study by Lapidus (1969) of pregnant women indicates that when preparatory information about the stresses of childbirth is offered free of charge, passive-submissive women who are most in need of stress inoculation are unlikely to obtain it if it is left up to them to take the initiative. On various indicators of field dependence-independence, cognitive control, and flexibility, the pregnant women who chose to participate in a program that offered psychological preparation for childbirth differed significantly from those who chose not to participate.

The participants were more field independent and displayed stronger tendencies toward active mastery of stress than the nonparticipants, many of whom showed signs of strong dependency and denial tendencies.

In order to take account of individual differences in coping style and other personality predispositions it may be necessary in each clinic or hospital to set up a number of different preparation programs, rather than just one standard program. The patients would probably have to be screened in advance for their knowledge about the consequences of the treatment they have agreed to undergo as well as for their capacity to assimilate unpleasant information. At present, health-care professionals have to use their best judgment in selecting what they think will be the most effective ingredients of stress inoculation for each particular individual facing a particular type of stress. Until more analytic research is carried out on responsiveness to each of the major components of stress inoculation, the hand-tailoring of preparatory information and coping recommendations will remain more of an art than a science.

CONCLUSION

The main point emphasized throughout this chapter is that sufficient research has already been done on the effectiveness of stress inoculation to warrant moving to a new stage of attempting to identify the factors that are responsible for the positive effects. Analytic experiments are needed that attempt to determine the crucial variables by testing hypotheses based on theoretical concepts about basic processes. These can be carried out as field experiments in clinics and hospitals where large numbers of patients are awaiting distressing medical treatments or surgery. With regard to the problems of internal validity and replicability of the findings, investigators can use standard methodological safeguards, including random assignment of patients to conditions, which have evolved in experimental social psychology and personality research during the past three decades. The major goal should be to pin down as specifically as possible the key variables (and their interactions) that are responsible for the positive effects of stress inoculation on increasing tolerance for adverse events that disrupt adherence to health-promoting regimens.

The key variables that should be given priority, in my opinion, are the ones suggested by theory and prior research, as discussed in the preceding sections—(1) increasing the predictability of stressful events, (2) fostering coping skills and plans for coping actions, (3) stimulating cognitive coping responses such as positive self talk and reconceptualization of threats into nonthreatening terms, (4) encouraging attitudes of self confidence and hope about a successful outcome with related expectations that make for perceived control, and (5) building up commitment and a sense of personal responsibility for adhering to an adaptive course of action.

REFERENCES

Andrew, J. M. Recovery from surgery, with and without preparatory instruction, for three coping styles. *Journal of Personality and Social Psychology,* 1970, *15,* 223–226.

Auerbach, S. M. Trait-state anxiety and adjustment to surgery. *Journal of Consulting and Clinical Psychology,* 1973, *40,* 264–271.

Auerbach, S. M., Kendall, P. C., Cuttler, H. F., & Levitt, R. Anxiety, locus of control, type of preparatory information and adjustment to dental surgery. *Journal of Consulting and Clinical Psychology,* 1976, *44,* 809–818.

Averill, J. R. Personal control over aversive stimuli and its relationship to stress. *Psychological Bulletin,* 1973, *80,* 286–303.

Ball, T. S., & Vogler, R. E. Uncertain pain and the pain of uncertainty. *Perceptual Motor Skills,* 1971, *33,* 1195–1203.

Bandura, A. Self-efficacy: Toward a unified theory of behavioral change. *Psychological Review,* 1977, *89,* 191–215.

Bandura, A., & Simon, K. The role of proximal intentions in self-regulation of refractory behavior. *Cognitive Therapy and Research,* 1977, *1,* 177–193.

Bowers, K. G. Pain, anxiety, and perceived control. *Journal of Consulting and Clinical Psychology,* 1968, *32,* 596–602.

Breen, D. *The birth of a first child: Towards an understanding of feminity.* London: Tavistock, 1975.

Brehm, S. *The application of social psychology to clinical practice.* New York: Wiley (Halsted Press), 1976.

Byrne, D. Repression-sensitization as a dimension of personality. In B. A. Maher (Ed.), *Progress in experimental personality research* (Vol. 1). New York: Academic Press, 1964.

Caplan, G. and Killilea, M. (Eds.), *Support systems and mutual help.* New York: Grune & Stratton, 1976.

Cartwright, D., & Zander, A. (Eds.), *Group dynamics: Research and theory* (3rd ed.). New York: Harper and Row, 1968.

Chertok, L. *Psychosomatic methods in painless childbirth.* New York: Pergamon, 1959.

Chu, C. C. Fear arousal, efficacy, and imminency. *Journal of Personality and Social Psychology,* 1966, *4,* 517–524.

Cohen, F. Psychological preparation, coping, and recovery from surgery. Unpublished doctoral dissertation, University of California, Berkeley, 1975.

Cohen, F., & Lazarus, R. S. Active coping processes, coping disposition, and recovery from surgery. *Psychosomatic Medicine,* 1973, *35,* 375–389.

Cohen, F., & Lazarus, R. S. Coping with the stresses of illness. In G. C. Stone, F. Cohen, & N. E. Adler (Eds.), *Health psychology.* San Francisco: Jossey-Bass, 1979.

Cormier, W. H., & Cormier, L. S. *Interviewing strategies for helpers: A guide to assessment, treatment and evaluation.* California: Brooks/Cole Publishing Co., 1979.

Davenport-Slack, B., & Boylan, C. H. Psychological correlates of childbirth pain. *Psychosomatic Medicine,* 1974, *36,* 215–223.

Davison, G. C., & Valins, S. Maintenance of self-attributed and drug-attributed behavior change. *Journal of Personality and Social Psychology,* 1969, *11,* 25–33.

DeLong, R. D. Individual differences in patterns of anxiety arousal, stress-relevant information, and recovery from surgery. *Dissertation Abstracts International,* 1971, *32*(3), 554.

Dick-Read, G. *Childbirth without fear: The principles and practices of natural childbirth* (2nd ed. rev.). New York: Harper & Row, 1959.

Doering, S. G., & Entwisle, D. R. Preparation during pregnancy and ability to cope with labor and delivery. *American Journal of Orthopsychiatry,* 1975, *45,* 825–837.

Egbert, L., Battit, G., Welch, C., & Bartlett, M. Reduction of post-operative pain by encouragement and instruction. *New England Journal of Medicine,* 1964, *270,* 825–827.

Epstein, S. Toward a unified theory of anxiety. In B. Maher (Ed.), *Progress in experimental personality* (Vol. 4). New York: Academic Press, 1967.

Epstein, S., & Clark, S. Heart rate and skin conductance during experimentally induced anxiety: Effects of anticipated intensity of noxious stimulation and experience. *Journal of Experimental Psychology,* 1970, *84,* 105–112.

Fremauw, W. J. & Zitter, R. E. A comparison of skills training and cognitive restructuring—relaxation for the treatment of speech anxiety. *Behavior Therapy,* 1978, *9,* 248–259.

Fuller, S. S., Endress, M. P., & Johnson, J. E. Control and coping with an aversive health examination. *Paper presented at the annual meeting of the American Psychological Association,* San Francisco, 1977.

Giordo, M. Self-talk: Mechanisms in anxiety and stress management. In C. D. Spielberger and I. G. Sarason (Eds.), *Stress and anxiety* (Vol. 4). New York: John Wiley & Sons, 1977.

Glass, C., Gottman, J., & Shmurack, S. Response acquisition and cognitive self-statements modification approaches to dating skill training. *Journal of Counseling Psychology,* 1976, *23,* 520–526.

Goldfried, M. R., Decenteco, E. T., & Weinberg, L. Systematic rational restructuring as a self-control technique. *Behavior Therapy,* 1974, *5,* 247–254.

Goldfried, M. R., Linehan, M. M., & Smith, J. L. The reduction of test anxiety through rational restructuring. *Journal of Consulting and Clinical Psychology,* 1978, *46,* 32–39.

Goldstein, M. J. The relationship between coping and avoiding behavior and response to fear-arousing propaganda. *Journal of Abnormal and Social Psychology,* 1959, *58,* 247–252.

Hare, A. P. *Handbook of small group research* (2nd ed.). New York: Free Press, 1976.

Holroyd, K. A., Andrasik, F., & Westbrook, T. Cognitive control of tension headache. *Cognitive Therapy and Research,* 1977, *1,* 121–134.

Houston, B. K. Control over stress, locus of control, and response to stress. *Journal of Personality and Social Psychology,* 1972, *21,* 249–255.

Huttel, F. A., Mitchell, I., Fischer, W. M., & Meyer, A. E. A quantitative evaluation of psychoprophylaxis in childbirth. *Journal of Psychosomatic Research,* 1972, *16,* 81.

Janis, I. L. Problems related to the control of fear in combat. In S. A. Stouffer, et al., (Eds.), *The American soldier: Vol. II: Combat and its aftermath.* Princeton, N.J.: Princeton University Press, 1949.

Janis, I. L. *Air war and emotional stress.* New York: McGraw-Hill, 1951.

Janis, I. *Psychological stress.* New York: John Wiley & Sons, 1958.

Janis, I. L. *Stress and frustration.* New York: Harcourt, Brace, Jovanovich, 1971.

Janis, I. L. (Ed.), *Counseling on personal decisions: Theory and research on short-term helping relationships.* New Haven, Conn.: Yale University Press, 1982.

Janis, I. L., Lumsdaine, A. H., & Gladstone, A. I. Effects of preparatory communication on reactions to a subsequent news event. *Public Opinion Quarterly,* 1951, *15,* 488–518.

Janis, I. L., & Mann, L. *Decision making: A psychological analysis of conflict, choice, and commitment.* New York: Free Press, 1977.

Janis, I. L., & Rodin, J. Attribution, control and decision-making: Social psychology in health care. In G. C. Stone, F. Cohen and N. E. Adler (Eds.), *Health psychology.* San Francisco: Josey-Bass, 1979.

Javert, C. T., & Hardy, J. D. Influence of analgesia on pain intensity during labor ("with a note on natural childbirth"). *Anesthesiology,* 1951, *12,* 189–215.

Johnson, J. E. The influence of purposeful nurse-patient interaction on the patients' postoperative course. *A.N.A. Monograph series No. 2.: Exploring medical-surgical nursing practice.* New York: American Nurses' Association, 1966.

Johnson, J. E. Information factors in coping with stressful events. Paper presented at the eleventh annual convention of the Association for the Advancement of Behavioral Therapy, December 11, 1977, Atlanta.

Johnson, J. E., & Leventhal, H. Effects of accurate expectations and behavioral instructions on reactions during a noxious medical examination. *Journal of Personality and Social Psychology,* 1974, *29,* 710–718.

Johnson, J. E., Morrissey, J. F., & Leventhal, H. Psychological preparation for endoscopic examination. *Gastrointestinal Endoscopy,* 1973, *19,* 180–182.

Johnson, J. E., Rice, V. H., Fuller, S. S., & Endress, P. Sensory information, behavioral instruction, and recovery from surgery. *Paper presented at annual meeting of the American Psychological Association,* San Francisco, 1977.

Kanfer, F., & Seider, M. L. Self-control: Factors enhancing tolerance of noxious stimulation. *Journal of Personality and Social Psychology,* 1973, *25,* 381–389.

Kendall, P., Williams, L., Pechacek, T. F., Graham, L. E., Shisslak, C., & Herzoff, N. *The Palo Alto medical psychology project: Cognitive-behavioral patient education interventions in catheterization procedures.* Unpublished manuscript, University of Minnesota, 1977.

Kiesler, C. A. (Ed). *The psychology of commitment.* New York: Academic Press, 1971.

Langer, E., Janis, I., & Wolfer, J. Reduction of psychological stress in surgical patients. *Journal of Experimental Social Psychology,* 1975, *1,* 155–166.

Lapidus, L. B. Cognitive control and reaction to stress: Conditions for mastery in the anticipatory phase. *Proceedings, 77th annual convention, APA (American Psychological Association),* 1969.

Lazarus, R. S., & Alfert, E. The short-circuiting of threat by experimentally altering cognitive appraisal. *Journal of Abnormal and Social Psychology,* 1964, *69,* 195–205.

Lemaze, F. *Painless childbirth: Psychoprophylactic method.* London: Burke, 1958.

Leventhal, H. Patient responses to surgical stress in regular surgery and intensive care units. *Progr. Rep. Div. Hosp. Med. Facilities, U.S. Public Health Service, 1963* (Mimeographed).

Leventhal, H. Changing attitudes and habits to reduce chronic risk factors. *American Journal of Cardiology,* 1973, *31,* 571–580.

Leventhal, H., Singer, R. E., & Jones, S. Effects of fear and specificity of recommendations. *Journal of Personality and Social Psychology,* 1965, *2,* 20–29.

Lindeman, C. A. Nursing intervention with the presurgical patient: The effectiveness and efficiency of group and individual preoperative teaching. *Nursing Research,* 1972, *21,* 196–209.

Lindeman, C. A., & Van Aernam, B. Nursing intervention with the presurgical patient—the effects of structured and unstructured preoperative teaching. *Nursing Research,* 1971, *20,* 319–332.

Levy, J. M., & McGee, R. K. Childbirth as crisis: A test of Janis' theory of communication and stress resolution. *Journal of Personality and Social Psychology,* 1975, *31,* 171–179.

Matte, I. Observations of the English in wartime. *J. Nervous Mental Diseases,* 1943, *97,* 447–463.

McAlister, A. L., Perry, C., & Maccoby, N. Adolescent smoking: Onset and prevention. *Pediatrics,* 1979, *63,* 650–680.

McFall, R. M., & Hammen, L. Motivation, structure, and self-monitoring: Role of nonspecific factors in smoking reduction. *Journal of Consulting and Clinical Psychology,* 1971, *37,* 80–86.

Meichenbaum, D. Cognitive modification of test anxious college students. *Journal of Consulting and Clinical Psychology,* 1972, *39,* 370–380.

Meichenbaum, D. *Cognitive-behavior modification: An integrative approach.* New York: Plenum, 1977.

Meichenbaum, D., & Cameron, R. An examination of cognitive and contingency variables in anxiety relief procedures. Unpublished manuscript, University of Waterloo, Ontario, 1973.

Meichenbaum, D., Gilmore, J. B., & Fedoravicous, A. A group insight vs. group desensitization in treating speech anxiety. *Journal of Consulting and Clinical Psychology*, 1971, *36*, 410–421.

Meichenbaum, D., & Jaremko, M. (Eds.). *Stress prevention and management: A cognitive-behavioral approach.* New York: Plenum, 1982.

Meichenbaum, D. H., & Turk, D. C. The cognitive-behavioral management of anxiety, anger, and pain. In P. O. Davidson (Ed.), *The behavioral management of anxiety, depression and pain.* New York: Brunner/Mazel, 1976.

Meichenbaum, D., & Turk, D. Stress, coping, and disease: A cognitive-behavioral perspective. In R. Neufeld (Ed.), *Relations between psychological stress and psychopathology.* New York: McGraw-Hill, in press.

Meichenbaum, D. H., & Turk, D. Stress inoculation: A preventive approach. In R. W. J. Neufeld (Ed.), *Relations between psychological stress and psychopathology.* New York: McGraw-Hill, in press.

Novaco, R. *Anger control: The development and evaluation of an experimental treatment.* Lexington, Mass.: Heath & Co., 1975.

Pervin, L. A. The need to predict and control under conditions of threat. *Journal of Personality*, 1963, *34*, 570–587.

Pranulis, M., Dabbs, J., & Johnson, J. General anesthesia and the patients' attempts at control. *Social Behavior and Personality*, 1975, *3*, 49–51.

Rachman, S. J. *Fear and courage.* San Francisco: W. H. Freeman & Co., 1978.

Riskind, J. The client's sense of personal control: Effects of time perspective and self-esteem. In I. L. Janis (Ed.), *Counseling on personal decisions: Theory and research on short-term helping relationships.* New Haven, Conn.: Yale University Press, 1982.

Rodin, J. R. Somatopsychics and attribution. *Personality and Social Bulletin*, 1978, *4*, 531–540.

Rogers, R. W., & Deckner, W. C. Effects of fear appeals and physiological arousal upon emotion, attitudes, and cigarette smoking. *Journal of Personality and Social Psychology*, 1975, *32*, 220–230.

Rogers, R. W., & Mewborn, C. R. Fear appeals and attitude change: Effects of threat's noxiousness, probability of occurrence, and the efficacy of coping responses. *Journal of Personality and Social Psychology*, 1976, *34*, 54–61.

Rogers, R. W., & Thistlethwaite, D. L. Effects of fear arousal and reassurance upon attitude change. *Journal of Personality and Social Psychology*, 1970, *15*, 227–233.

Romalis, F. The impact of the war on family life. Part I. Reactions to change and crisis. *The Family*, 1942, *23*, 219–224.

Rotter, J. B. Generalized expectancies for internal versus external control of reinforcement. *Psychological Monographs*, 1966, *80*(1), No. 609.

Schmidt, R. L. An exploratory study of nursing and patient readiness for surgery. Unpublished master's thesis, School of Nursing, Yale University, 1966.

Schmitt, F. E., & Wooldridge, P. J. Psychological preparation of surgical patients. *Nursing Research*, 1973, *22*, 108–116.

Schulz, R., & Hanusa, B. M. Long term effects of control and predictability enhancing interventions: Findings and ethical issues. *Journal of Personality and Social Psychology,* 1978, *36,* 1194–1201.

Seligman, M. *Helplessness.* San Francisco: W. H. Freeman, 1975.

Shaw, M. E. *Group Dynamics.* New York: McGraw-Hill, 1971.

Sime, A. M. Relationship of preoperative fear, type of coping, and information received about surgery to recovery from surgery. *Journal of Personality and Social Psychology,* 1976, *34,* 716–724.

Spielberger, C. D., Gorsuch, R. L., & Lushene, R. E. *Manual for the state-trait anxiety inventory.* Palo Alto, Calif.: Consulting Psychologist Press, 1970.

Staub, E., & Kellett, D. Increasing pain tolerance by information about aversive stimuli. *Journal of Personality and Social Psychology,* 1972, *21,* 198–203.

Staub, E., Tursky, B., & Schwartz, G. E. Self-control and predictability: Their effects on reactions to aversive stimulation. *Journal of Personality and Social Psychology,* 1971, *18,* 157–162.

Tanzer, D. Natural childbirth: Pain or peak experience. *Psychology Today,* 1968, *2,* 17–21.

Taylor, F. G., & Marshall, W. L. Experimental analysis of a cognitive-behavioral therapy for depression. *Cognitive Therapy and Research,* 1977, *1,* 59–72.

Turk, D. C. Cognitive control of pain: A skills-training approach. Unpublished master's thesis, University of Waterloo, 1977.

Turk, D. Cognitive behavioral techniques on the management of pain. In J. P. Foreyt & D. J. Rathgen (Eds.), *Cognitive behavior therapy: Research and application.* New York: Plenum Publishing Co., 1978.

Turk, D. C., & Genest, M. Regulation of pain: The application of cognitive and behavioral techniques for prevention and remediation. In P. Kendall & S. Hollon (Eds.), *Cognitive-behavioral interventions: Theory, research, and practices.* New York: Academic Press, 1979.

Tversky, A., & Kahneman, D. Availability: A heuristic for judging frequency and probability. *Cognitive Psychology,* 1973, *5,* 207–232.

Tversky, A., & Kahneman, D. Judgment under uncertainty: Heuristics and biases. *Science,* 1974, *185,* 1124–1131.

Velvoysky, I., Platonov, K., Ploticher, V., & Shugon, E. *Painless childbirth through psychoprophylaxis.* Moscow: Foreign Languages Publishing House, 1960.

Vernon, D. T. A., & Bigelow, D. A. The effect of information about a potentially stressful situation on responses to stress impact. *Journal of Personality and Social Psychology,* 1974, *29,* 50–59.

Weiss, J. M. Somatic effects of predictable and unpredictable shock. *Psychosomatic Medicine,* 1970, *32,* 397–409.

Wolfenstein, M. *Disaster.* Glencoe: The Free Press, 1957.

Wolfer, J. A., & Visintainer, M. A. Pediatric surgical patients' and parents' stress responses and adjustment as a function of psychologic preparation and stress-point nursing care. *Nursing Research,* 1975, *24,* 244–255.

Zimbardo, P. G. The human choice. In W. Arnold & D. Levine (Eds.), *Nebraska Symposium on Motivation* Vol. 17, 1969. Lincoln: University of Nebraska Press, 1970.

14

Counteracting the Adverse Effects of Concurrence-Seeking in Policy-Planning Groups: Theory and Research Perspectives (1982)

This paper discusses the concurrence-seeking or "groupthink" phenomena described in my writings on *Groupthink* (1972, 1982) and the . . . explanatory hypotheses developed by Janis and Mann (1977) that have direct implications for improving the quality of decision making by policy planning groups. First I shall present a set of analytic and prescriptive hypotheses that specify how changes in the antecedent conditions that foster groupthink increase the probability of effective group work in carrying out the tasks of search and appraisal when the members are engaged in making policy recommendations or decisions. Then I shall describe the type of research needed to test the hypotheses (some of which is now underway). This will include: (1) laboratory experiments to develop new interventions and to test them in a preliminary way; (2) field experiments with ad hoc policy planning groups (e.g., with American graduate students in economics and policy sciences who volunteer to prepare a position paper on proposed means for dealing with the dangers of relying upon atomic fission as a source of energy, to be circulated within the U.S. Department of Energy and other relevant governmental agencies); and (3) field experiments in organizational settings (starting with aides who are relatively low in the organizational hierarchy and then, if the evidence shows that certain interventions are effective, replica-

Janis, I. L. Counteracting the adverse effects of concurrence—seeking in policy-planning groups: Theory and research perspectives. In H. Brandstätter, J. H. Davis, and G. Stocker-Kreichgauer (Eds.), *Group decision making*. New York: Academic Press, 1982. Reprinted by permission.

ting the study by moving up the hierarchy to higher-level policy planners).

. . . One major source of defective decision-making has been described in my analysis of fiascoes resulting from foreign policy decisions made by presidential advisory groups (Janis, 1982). I call attention to a *concurrence-seeking tendency* that occurs among moderately or highly cohesive groups. When this tendency is dominant, the members use their collective cognitive resources to develop rationalizations in line with shared illusions about the invulnerability of their organization or nation and display other symptoms of "groupthink".

A number of historic fiascoes appear to have been products of defective policy-planning on the part of a misguided government leader who obtained social support from his advisors. My analysis of case studies of historic fiascoes suggests that the following groups of policy advisors were dominated by concurrence-seeking (referred to as "groupthink"): 1) Neville Chamberlain's inner circle, whose members supported the policy of appeasement of Hitler during 1937 and 1938, despite repeated warnings and events indicating that it would have adverse consequences; 2) Admiral Kimmel's group of Naval Commanders whose members failed to respond to warnings in the fall of 1941 that Pearl Harbor was in danger of being attacked by Japanese planes; 3) President Truman's advisory group, whose members supported the decision to escalate the war in North Korea despite firm warnings by the Chinese Communist government that United States entry into North Korea would be met with armed resistance from the Chinese; 4) President John F. Kennedy's advisory group, whose members supported the decision to launch the Bay of Pigs invasion of Cuba despite the availability of information indicating that it would be an unsuccessful venture and would damage United States relations with other countries; 5) President Lyndon B. Johnson's "Tuesday luncheon group", whose members supported the decision to escalate the war in Vietnam despite intelligence reports and other information indicating that this course of action would not defeat the Viet Cong or the North Vietnamese and would entail unfavorable political consequences within the United States. In all these "groupthink"-dominated groups, there were strong pressures toward uniformity, which inclined the members to avoid raising controversial issues, questioning weak arguments, or calling a halt to soft-headed thinking. Other social psychologists (Green and Conolley, 1974; Raven, 1974; Wong-McCarthy, 1978) have noted similar symptoms of groupthink in the way Nixon and his inner circle handled the Watergate coverup.

Eight main symptoms of groupthink run through the case studies of historic decision-making fiascoes (Janis, 1982). Each symptom can be identified by a variety of indicators, derived from historical records, observers' accounts of conversations, and participants' memoirs. The eight symptoms of groupthink are:

1. An illusion of invulnerability, shared by most or all of the members, which creates excessive optimism and encourages taking extreme risks;
2. Collective efforts to rationalize in order to discount warnings which might lead the members to reconsider their assumptions before they recommit themselves to their past policy decisions;
3. An unquestioned belief in the group's inherent morality, inclining the members to ignore the ethical or moral consequences of their decisions;
4. Stereotyped views of rivals and enemies as too evil to warrant genuine attempts to negotiate, or as too weak and stupid to counter whatever risky attempts are made to defeat their purposes;
5. Direct pressure on any member who expresses strong arguments against any of the group's stereotypes, illusions, or commitments, making clear that this type of dissent is contrary to what is expected of all loyal members;
6. Self-censorship of deviations from the apparent group consensus, reflecting each member's inclination to minimize to himself the importance of his doubts and counterarguments;
7. A shared illusion of unanimity concerning judgements conforming to the majority view (partly resulting from self-censorship of deviations, augmented by the false assumption that silence means consent);
8. The emergence of self-appointed mindguards—members who protect the group from adverse information that might shatter their shared complacency about the effectiveness and morality of their decisions.

In our book [on *Decision Making* (1977)], Leon Mann and I have elaborated on the theory of concurrence-seeking, or "groupthink," as a defective pattern of decision making that is fostered by certain social conditions affecting most, if not all, members of a group. Our assumption is that the symptoms of groupthink are behavioral consequences of a coping pattern of defensive avoidance, which is mutually supported by the group members.

The schematic analysis in Figure 14.1 (based on Janis and Mann, 1977) shows the major antecedent conditions of concurrence-seeking, which lead to the symptoms of groupthink. The main variables shown in this figure form the basis for the independent and dependent variables that need to be investigated in comparative case studies, field experiments, and other systematic investigations. This analysis leads us to attempt to develop interventions that change the antecedent conditions in such a way that group processes are less likely to produce the symptoms of groupthink, with the result that symptoms of defective decision-making will also be less likely to occur.

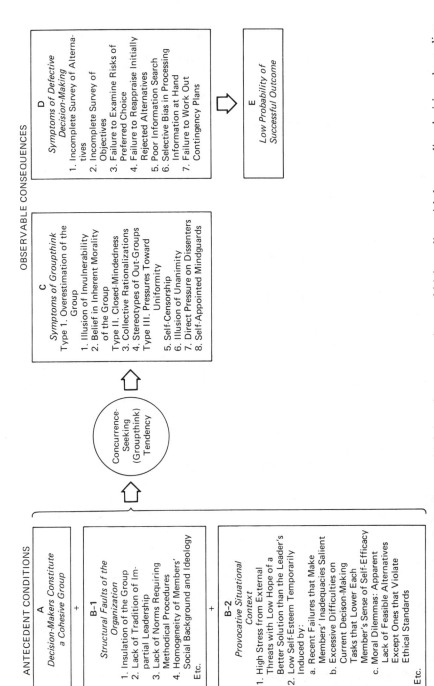

Figure 14.1 Theoretical analysis of groupthink based on comparisons of high-quality with low-quality decisions by policy-making groups. Source: Adapted from Janis, 1982.

One of the factors listed as an antecedent condition in Figure 14.1 is the lack of standard operating procedures involving methodical procedures for search and appraisal. . . .

. . . Interventions designed to counteract the defective decision-making patterns, which may prove to be effective in preventing groupthink, include the balance-sheet procedure and stress inoculation for postdecisional setbacks. (These procedures and the series of research studies that indicate their value for individual decision makers are described in Janis and Mann, 1977, Chapter 14.) The same basic procedures, which could easily be modified for use in group meetings, might prove to be effective in preventing defensive avoidance and promoting vigilance among members of decision-making groups.

Not all cohesive groups suffer from groupthink, though all may display some of its symptoms from time to time (Janis, 1982). A group whose members are highly competent and who have properly defined roles, with traditions and standard operating procedures that facilitate critical inquiry, is probably capable of making better decisions than any individual in the group who works on the problem alone (see Davis, 1969; Steiner, 1966). And yet the advantages of having policy decisions made by groups are often lost because of psychological pressures that arise when the members work closely together, share the same values, and above all, face a crisis situation in which everyone realizes at the outset that whatever action the group decides to take will be fraught with serious risks and that there is little hope for obtaining new information that will point to a satisfactory solution. In these circumstances, the leader and the members of his in-group are subjected to stresses that generate a strong need for affiliation.

As conformity pressures begin to dominate, the striving for unanimity fosters the pattern of defensive avoidance, with characteristic lack of vigilance, unwarranted optimism, "sloganistic" thinking, and reliance on shared rationalizations that bolster the least objectionable alternative. That alternative is often the one favored by the leader or other influential persons in the policy-making group on the basis of initial biases that remain uncorrected despite the availability of impressive evidence showing it to be inferior to other feasible courses of action.

PRESCRIPTIVE HYPOTHESES
TO BE TESTED

In my analysis of the conditions that foster groupthink (Janis, 1982), I suggest ten prescriptive hypotheses.

One general hypothesis, which pertains to the effects of training, is presented in my discussion of the question, "Is a little knowledge of groupthink a dangerous thing?" (pp. 275–276). The training hypothesis is as follows:

Hypothesis 1. Information about the causes and consequences of groupthink will have a beneficial deterring effect.

Impressive information from case studies can augment the members' resolve to curtail group encroachments on their critical thinking and can increase their willingness to try out antidote prescriptions, "provided . . . that they are aware of the costs in time and effort and realize that there are other disadvantages they must also watch out for before they decide to adopt any of them as a standard operating procedure" (p. 275).

Six more prescriptive hypotheses pertain to decision-making procedures that can be carried out within the policy-making group itself and can usually be put into operation if the chairman of the group decides to try them out:

Hypothesis 2. The leader, when assigning a policy-planning mission to a group, should be impartial instead of stating preferences and expectations at the outset.

This practice requires each leader to limit his briefings to unbiased statements about the scope of the problem and the limitations of available resources, without advocating specific proposals he would like to see adopted. This allows the conferees the opportunity to develop an atmosphere of open inquiry and to explore impartially a wide range of policy alternatives.

Hypothesis 3. The leader of a policy-forming group at the outset should assign the role of critical evaluator to each member, encouraging the group to give high priority to airing objections and doubts.

This practice needs to be reinforced by the leader's acceptance of criticism of his own judgements in order to discourage the members from soft-pedaling their disagreements.

Hypothesis 4. At every meeting devoted to evaluating policy alternatives, one or more members should be assigned the role of devil's advocate.

In order to avoid domesticating and neutralizing the devil's advocates, the group leader will have to give each of them an unambiguous assignment to present his arguments as cleverly and convincingly as he can, as a good lawyer would, challenging the testimony of those advocating the majority position.

Hypothesis 5. Throughout the period when the feasibility and effectiveness of policy alternatives are being surveyed, the policy-planning group should from time to time divide into two or more subgroups to meet separately, under different chairmen, then come together to hammer out their differences.

Hypothesis 6. Whenever the policy issue involves relations with a rival organization or out-group, a sizable block of time (perhaps an entire session) should be spent surveying all warning signals from the rivals and constructing alternative scenarios of the rivals' intentions.

Hypothesis 7. After reaching a preliminary consensus about what seems to be the best policy alternative, the policy-planning group should hold a "second chance" meeting at which every member is expected to express as vividly as he can all his residual doubts and to rethink the entire issue before making a definitive choice.

Three additional hypotheses specify procedures that require the participation of other units and persons in the organization outside of the policy-planning group:

Hypothesis 8. One or more outside experts or qualified colleagues within the organization who are not core members of the policy-planning group should be present at each meeting on a staggered basis and should be encouraged to challenge the views of the core members.

Hypothesis 9. Each member of the policy-planning group should discuss periodically the group's deliberations with trusted associates in his own unit of the organization and report back their reactions.

Hypothesis 10. The organization should routinely follow the administrative practice of setting up several independent policy-planning and evaluation groups to work on the same policy question, each carrying out its deliberations under a different chairman.

The last three of the above ten prescriptive hypotheses, in contrast to all the others, cannot be applied unless cooperation is obtained from key persons throughout an organization, with appropriate directives issued by the chief executive or the board of directors.

WHAT TYPE OF RESEARCH CAN BE DONE?

In the preceding sections, I have presented a number of analytic and prescriptive hypotheses concerning the conditions under which the quality of group decisions can be improved by preventing groupthink. The analytic hypotheses are represented in Figure 14.1, which lists the key situational factors that are expected to increase the concurrence-seeking tendencies of the members of a group and thereby decrease vigilant search and appraisal. The ten prescriptive hypotheses are intended to reduce or moderate the influence of one or more of these factors. All of these hypotheses must be validated before they can be applied with any confidence. Each of the proposed remedies may prove to have undesirable side effects and other drawbacks, but these hypotheses appear sufficiently promising to warrant the trouble and expense of being tested as potentially useful means for counteracting groupthink whenever a small number of policy-planners or executives in any organization meet with their chairman or chief executive to work out new policies. Some of the anti-groupthink procedures might also help to counteract initial biases of the members, prevent pluralistic ignorance, and eliminate other sources of error that can occur independently of groupthink.

The next question that arises is: How can the analytic and prescriptive hypotheses be tested? My answer is that the full range of behavioral research methods could be used, including comparative case studies, experiments in social psychological laboratories, and field experiments in natural settings.

In limited ways, comparative case studies can provide evidence pertinent to analytic hypotheses about the causes and consequences of groupthink. One study that illuminates some of the politically relevant consequences of groupthink was completed by Phillip Tetlock (1979) when he was a graduate student at Yale working with me. Tetlock systematically reinvestigated the Bay of Pigs fiasco and the two other historic fiascoes in U.S. foreign policy that were analyzed in the main case studies presented in my book on *Victims of Groupthink* (1972). Tetlock carried out systematic content analyses of the relevant public speeches made by the President of the United States and by the Secretary of State during the period when each of the three policy decisions was being made, which presumably would reflect the quality of their thinking at that time. He compared the content analysis results from the three groupthink decisions with those obtained from comparable public speeches made during the time when two non-groupthink decisions were being made (the Marshall Plan and the Cuban Missile Crisis), both of which I had also analyzed for comparative purposes in *Victims of Groupthink*. Using a measure of cognitive complexity developed by Peter Suedfeld, Tetlock found that when the groupthink decisions were being made, the public speeches obtained significantly lower scores than when the non-groupthink decisions were being made. Tetlock also found that when the groupthink decisions were under discussion there were certain signs of stereotyped thinking in the public speeches. In our future research, we plan to apply the comparative method used in Tetlock's study to other verbal products produced in connection with group meetings, including memoranda, memoirs, minutes, and verbatim transcripts of the sessions.

A somewhat different type of comparative study has been initiated by William Wong-McCarthy, when he was a Yale graduate student working with me. Wong-McCarthy systematically compared two samples of Watergate tapes from two different periods. One sample was from a period when Nixon and his main advisors (Haldemann, Erlichman, and Dean) were keenly aware of the threat of public exposure, felt little hope for finding a better solution than to continue the cover-up policy, and displayed coordinated group action. The other sample was from a period when the in-group disintegrated as more and more devastating revelations implicated one member after another. He found that the transcripts of the meetings held during the period of coordinated action contained significantly more supportive statements, which are symptomatic of groupthink, than those of the meetings held during the period when the participants were no longer a cohesive group. This comparative method, in which each policy-making group is used as its own control, could be extended to obtain objective data on the relationship between various external conditions and blind ratings of the symptoms of groupthink—provided, of course, that the investigators can obtain recordings or detailed minutes of group meeting.

Concurrently with the fully controlled experimental research I shall describe shortly, my co-workers and I are planning to continue conducting quasi-experimental studies based on existing records of historic policy decisions. We hope to obtain the cooperation of other social scientists in developing a cross-organization file that will contain indexed case studies of policy-planning. One purpose is to provide comparative case study material for the *discovery phase* of the research, to suggest plausible hypotheses about the conditions under which high-quality policy-making is facilitated. We expect to pursue the most promising hypotheses in designing the field experiments on the effects of interventions intended to improve the quality of group decisions. A second purpose is to build up a data bank on a large sample of high-quality versus low-quality policy decisions for the *verification phase* of the research. The data bank will provide correlational evidence for testing the hypotheses (derived from a few comparative case studies) with large samples of policy decisions. For example, the conditions shown in the causes-of-groupthink model in Figure 14.1 above, which were inferred from a small number of comparative case studies, might be tested systematically by comparing 25 high-quality decisions with 25 low-quality decisions made by governmental committees. The comparison would focus on degree of group cohesiveness, degree of insulation of the group, . . . and other variables specified by the model. . . .

The comparative methods I have been discussing so far are quasi-experimental and suffer from a number of obvious disadvantages with regard to achieving experimental control over the independent variables under investigation, but have the great advantage of high external validity by dealing with real-life decisions by policy makers. The reverse advantages and disadvantages are to be expected, of course, for laboratory experiments, where relatively high control over the variables can be achieved but at the expense of obtaining findings that may prove to have little validity outside the laboratory. Controlled field experiments in actual organizational settings might prove to be feasible, in which case we can hope to observe cause-and-effect relationships that will have a high degree of external validity. If field experiments as well as laboratory experiments and comparative case studies of historic decisions all point to the same general conclusion when we are testing a hypothesis about the conditions that foster groupthink, we can feel reasonably confident about the generality of the findings.

When I speak of controlled field experiments I have in mind studies in which the investigator (a) introduces an experimental intervention under natural conditions with policy planners facing real decisions and (b) determines the effects of the intervention by comparing groups assigned on a random basis to the experimental and control conditions. No such studies bearing on groupthink have been carried out as yet.

Prior to attempting to carry out field experiments in order to test the interventions specified by the prescriptive hypotheses, I think it is sensible to develop and test them first in laboratory experiments. A few laboratory studies that have already been carried out are indirectly relevant to the causes and consequences of groupthink. Some of the symptoms noted in my studies, for example, are similar to those observed in experiments on group polarization effects (see Davis, 1969). An article by Myers and Lamm (1977) discusses the dozens of laboratory experiments carried out during the 1960s that purported to demonstrate that the average individual was more prone to take risks after participating in a group discussion than when making a decision on his own (e.g., Brown, 1965, 1974; Kogan and Wallach, 1967; Stoner, 1961; Wallach, et al., 1962). They also take account of more recent findings and analyses that call into question the generality of the so-called "risky-shift" tendency (e.g., Cartwright, 1971; Pruitt, 1971). Their analysis of the accumulated evidence, in agreement with Davis (1969) and others, points to a *group polarization tendency* such that the group decision enhances whichever point of view, risky or conservative, that is initially dominant within the group. (See, for example, Lamm and Sauer, 1974; Moscovici and Zavalloni, 1969; Rabbie and Visser, 1972.)

> Some of the literature cited presents experimental demonstrations of groupthink processes which Irving Janis (1972) has proposed to help explain decision fiascoes. . . . For example, his suggestion that group members "show interest in facts and opinions that support their initially preferred policy and take up time in their meetings to discuss them, but they tend to ignore facts and opinions that do not support their initially preferred policy" (p. 10) is confirmed by a recent finding that discussion arguments more decisively favor the dominant alternative than do written arguments. (Myers and Lamm, 1977.)

More direct evidence bearing on the conditions that foster groupthink comes from a few other laboratory experiments. In a simulation experiment of the historical decision by Mexican authorities which led to the Alamo episode, Crow and Noel (1975) found symptoms analogous to those of groupthink. When consensus was induced as an experimental condition, many groups chose a much more aggressive course of action than many individual members initially preferred.

Flowers (1977), in "a laboratory test of some implications of Janis's groupthink hypothesis," divided 40 teams of students into different treatment groups and asked all of them to work on the same hypothetical decision (imagining that they were a group of school administrators deciding what to do about a formerly good teacher who as a result of illness had become incompetent). Group leaders were trained to conduct meetings according to two different leadership styles. One was an *open* style—in line with prescriptive hypotheses about preventing groupthink, the leader avoided stating his own position on the issue until after the others in the group had discussed their own solutions, continually encouraged free discussion of alternatives, and explicitly conveyed the norm of airing all possible viewpoints. The second leadership style was *closed*—the leader stated his own position at the outset, did not encourage free discussion of alternatives, and explicitly conveyed the norm that the most important thing was for the team to agree on its decision. Flowers found that, as predicted, the teams exposed to the open leadership style offered significantly more solutions to the problem and during their discussion cited significantly more facts from the information made available to them before arriving at a consensus than the teams exposed to the closed leadership style.

Another variable investigated in Flowers's laboratory experiment was cohesiveness of the groups, which she manipulated by comparing groups of acquaintances with groups of strangers. Contrary to one of the analytic hypotheses about factors that promote groupthink, the teams made up of acquaintances, who were assumed to be more cohesive, did not differ significantly from the teams made up of strangers on either measure of decision-making activity. Flowers suggests that the failure to find the predicted differences may imply that cohesiveness is not a necessary condition for groupthink, but she also points out that the student groups she studied might differ on many dimensions from the groups described in *Victims of Groupthink*—such as degree of consequentiality of the decision, salience of real rivals or enemies, length of time the group works together, and quality of interaction among the members. Any of these different factors could prove to be an interacting variable that moderates the effects of differences in cohesiveness. Another possibility is that differences in decision making activities at relatively low levels of cohesiveness (strangers versus mere acquaintances) may be too slight to be detected, whereas differences between low and high degrees of cohesiveness (e.g. strangers versus close friends who are somewhat dependent upon each other for self-esteem enhancement) might emerge quite clearly.

The laboratory experiments I have just described illustrate the type of research that can provide some pertinent evidence and that can help investigators to pose more sharply the issues to be pursued in much more costly experiments dealing with real-life decisions by policy-making groups in natural settings. Additional studies are discussed [in a recent paper] by Ivan D. Steiner [1982].

Among the additional variables specified in Figure 14.1 that could be assessed in laboratory studies are the following:

1. *Insulation of the group*. The laboratory environment permits control over communication from outside the group. The flow of information and contact with neutral non-group members can be restricted to produce a high degree of insulation.

2. *Lack of norms requiring methodical procedures.* The tendency of problem-solving groups to avoid planning and discussion of procedural methods has been pointed out by Hackman and Morris (1974). They discuss the assumptions apparently made by many decision-makers in public and private institutions that everyone already knows how to go about the task and that discussion about how to tackle the problem is a waste of time. It is therefore unlikely that methodical procedures will be used unless a group is specifically instructed to employ the balance sheet procedure, which I mentioned earlier, or other methodical procedures.

3. *High stress with low hope*. A number of stressful policy-planning tasks could be compared in order to determine the ones most likely to produce concurrence-seeking. Stress and hope could be varied by modifying the difficulty of the decision and the resources available to work on it.

By testing the prescriptive hypotheses in controlled experiments we can expect to gain some further information about the effects of the antecedent conditions. Insulation of the group, for example, is counteracted by Prescriptive Hypotheses 8 and 9, which involve having outside experts at each meeting, and consultation with "home-base" colleagues. The antecedent condition of lack of methodical procedures for search and appraisal is counteracted by Prescriptive Hypotheses 3, 4, 5, 6, and 7. Also, low hope of finding a better solution than the one stated by the leader (Antecedent Condition 5) is counteracted by Prescriptive Hypothesis 2, which requires that the leader be impartial in stating the problem without expressing a preference for a particular solution. Consequently, the effects of these antecedent conditions can be evaluated as part of the study of the relative effectiveness of the different prescriptive hypotheses.

PERSPECTIVES FOR CONTROLLED
EXPERIMENTS ON GROUPS MAKING
REAL DECISIONS

Increasing criticism of laboratory studies (cf. Argyris, 1968; McGuire, 1973; Meehl, 1967; Rosenthal and Rosnow, 1969) has spurred efforts to develop approaches which avoid some of their short-comings. As I mentioned earlier, laboratory experiments have the advantage of control over the manipulation of independent variables and therefore more certain identification of cause-effect relations than is the case with survey or field studies. However, the many background variables that are held constant by the nature of the experimental setting potentially could affect the extent and direction of the relationships observed between the independent and dependent variables. Often these "interactions" contribute to the failure of observed relationships to hold up in new, untested situations.

A research strategy that may help to solve this problem without going to the enormous expense in time and effort of doing field experiments in large organizations is to carry out small laboratory-like experiments using *ad hoc* groups of qualified policy-planners who agree to cooperate with a research team in exchange for having the opportunity to participate in policy-planning on an issue about which they are deeply concerned. Working with advanced graduate students in administrative sciences and related fields at Yale University, I have developed the prototype for this type of field research: (1) announcements are made to recruit well-qualified candidates for a policy-planning group with the promise that their policy recommendations will be circulated to people who have the power to change the current unsatisfactory policy; (2) volunteers are selected with an eye to representing appropriate expertise and varying viewpoints, comparable to what is done when a government agency sets up a group to recommend policy changes; (3) the working sessions of the planning group are recorded and are unobtrusively observed by one or more members of the research team; and (4) when the group submits its final report on the policy recommendations, the head of the research team carries out his promise by circulating it, via informal university social networks, to key persons in the local, state or federal government who could initiate a change in policy.

As an example, . . . years ago, in collaboration with David Adams, who was a psychology graduate student at that time, I recruited a policy-planning group of administrative scientists, economists and political scientists from among the graduate students at Yale University to prepare a "white paper" for the U.S. Government on proposals for overcoming economic deterrents to ending the war in Vietnam. The members of the group were highly motivated to do a good job and reinforced each other's hopes that the product of their deliberations could have a positive effect on the policy-planning in Washington. When the group submitted its "white paper," I had it duplicated and, with the aid of various federal government advisors on the faculty in the Law School and in the Department of Political Science, circulated it to a number of key government officials. The group's efforts were rewarded by encouraging responses from several officials, including a detailed critique of the group's "white paper" indicating that even though it was not going to bring about an immediate end to the Vietnam war, at least it was being read carefully and taken seriously. The data obtained from the tape recordings of those sessions of the *ad hoc* planning group were used to investigate phases in group development, which turned out to be parallel to those I had reported on the basis of research on self-study groups in management training workshops and mutual aid groups in antismoking clinics and weight-reduction clinics (Janis, 1966). . . .

The approach used in introducing anti-groupthink interventions could be similar to "process counseling", which is oriented toward improving interaction processes within policy-making groups by changing group norms concerning problem-solving strategies "to help group members discover and implement new, more task-effective ways of working together" (Hackman and Morris, 1975). Some suggestive evidence is cited by Hackman and Morris in support of the assumption that task effectiveness and creativity of solutions might be increased by inducing participants to engage in a preliminary discusssion of the strategy of solving the problem before they start to work on it. They point out, however, that while a few pertinent studies show promising results, other studies indicate that interventions designed to improve problem-solving procedures give rise to only temporary improvements with little or no carryover to subsequent problem-solving tasks (Hackman, et al., 1974; Maier, 1963; Shure, et al., 1962; Varela, 1971). The interventions we propose to develop and test differ from these earlier efforts in that we try to counteract certain of the conditions that motivate the participants to rely on group consensus, which interferes with open-minded, vigilant problem-solving.

After evidence from *ad hoc* planning groups is available concerning the effectiveness of an anti-groupthink program, the heads of local and national organizations could be approached. Professional services might be offered free of charge to introduce the program to executive groups in their organization in exchange for the opportunity to obtain additional data on its effectiveness. It would be desirable to try out the program first with executive groups that are relatively low in the organizational hierarchy and then, if evidence shows it to be effective, to move up in the hierarchy to top level groups of policy makers. I have started to discuss this idea with a few high-level executives and they seem to be highly receptive to the proposed research. It seems to me, therefore, that controlled field experiments on preventing groupthink in actual organizational settings will prove to be feasible.

If sufficient progress is made from field experiments with *ad hoc* groups, I see no reason why the necessary arrangements could not be made to test the most promising interventions in a few organizations interested in improving the quality of policy-making procedures. And if I permit myself to be a little grandiose about imagining what might be done in the future, I can envisage the same type of research on prescriptive hypotheses being carried out in many different organizations in different countries, so as to accumulate evidence on the generality of the conclusions in different organizational and national contexts.

REFERENCES

Allison, G. T. *Essence of decision: Explaining the Cuban missile crisis*. Boston: Little, Brown, 1971.

Argyris, C. Some unintended consequences of rigorous research. *Psychological Bulletin*, 1968, 70, 185–197.

Blake, R. R., & Mouton, J. S. *Managing intergroup conflict in industry*. Houston, Texas: Gulf Publishing, 1964.

Brody, R. A. Some systemic effects of nuclear weapons technology: A study through simulation of a multi-nuclear future. *Journal of Conflict Resolution*, 1963, 7, 663–753.

Brown, R. *Social psychology*. New York: Free Press, 1965.

Brown, R. Further comments on the risky shift. *American Psychologist*, 1974, 29, 468–470.

Campbell, D. T., & Stanley, J. C. *Experimental and quasi-experimental designs for research*. Chicago: Rand McNally, 1963.

Cartwright, D. Risk taking by individuals and groups: An assessment of research employing choice dilemmas. *Journal of Personality and Social Psychology*, 1971, 20, 361–378.

Crow, W. J., & Noel, R. C. An experiment in simulated historical decision-making. In M. G. Hermann & T. W. Milburn (Eds.), *A psychological examination of political leaders*. New York: Free Press, 1975.

Davis, J. H. *Group performance*. Menlo Park, Calif.: Addison-Wesley, 1969.

Etzioni, A. *Active society*. New York: Free Press, 1968.

Flowers, M. L. A laboratory test of some implications of Janis's groupthink hypothesis. *Journal of Personality and Social Psychology*, 1977, *35*, 888–896.

Green, D., & Conolley, E. "Groupthink" and Watergate. Paper presented at the annual meetings of the American Psychological Association, 1974.

Guetzkow, H., Alger, C., Brody, R., Noel, R., & Snyder, R. *Simulation in international relations: Developments for research and teaching*. Englewood Cliffs, N. J.: Prentice-Hall, 1963.

Hackman, J. R., & Morris, C. G. Group tasks, group interaction process, and group performance effectiveness: A review and proposed intergration. In L. Berkowitz (Ed.), *Advances in experimental social psychology, Vol. 8*. New York: Academic Press, 1975.)

Hackman, J. R., Weiss, J. A., & Brousseau, K. *Effects of task performance strategies on group performance effectiveness*. Technical Report No. 5, Department of Administrative Sciences, Yale University, 1974.

Hall, J., & Williams, M. A comparison of decision-making performance in established and ad hoc groups. *Journal of Personality and Social Psychology*, 1966, *3*, 214–222.

Hoffman, L. R. Group problem solving. In L. Berkowitz (Ed.), *Advances in experimental social psychology, Vol. 2*. New York: Academic Press, 1965.

Holsti, O. R. *Content analysis for the social sciences and humanities*. Reading, Mass.: Addison-Wesley, 1969.

Hovland, C. I., Janis, I. L., & Kelley, H. H. *Communication and persuasion*. New Haven: Yale University Press, 1953.

Janis, I. L. *Psychological stress*. New York: Wiley & Sons, 1958.

Janis, I. L. Field and experimental studies of phases in the development of cohesive face-to-face groups. *XVIII International Congress of Psychology abstracts of communication: Problems of mental development and social psychology*. Moscow, USSR: International Union of Scientific Psychology, 1966. P. 397.

Janis, I. L. *Stress and frustration*. New York: Harcourt, Brace & Jovanovich, 1971.

Janis, I. L. *Victims of groupthink: A psychological study of foreign-policy decisions and fiascoes*. Boston: Houghton Mifflin, 1972.

Janis, I. L. *Groupthink: Psychological studies of policy decisions and fiascoes*. (Revised and enlarged edition of *Victims of Groupthink*). Boston: Houghton-Mifflin, 1982.

Janis, I. L. Vigilance and decision-making in personal crises. In D. A. Hamburg & C. V. Coelho (Eds.), *Coping and adaptation*. New York: Academic Press, 1974.

Janis, I. L., & Mann, L. *Decision-making: A psychological analysis of conflict, choice and commitment*. New York: Free Press, 1977.

Kogan, N., & Wallach, M. Risk taking as a function of the situation, the person and the group. In G. Mandler, et al., *New Directions in Psychology, Vol. 3*. New York: Holt, Rinehart & Winston, 1967.

Lamm, H., & Sauer, C. Discussion-induced shift toward higher demands in negotiation. *European J. of Soc. Psychology*, 1974, *4*, 85–88.

Maier, N. R. F. Group problem solving. *Psychological Review*, 1967, *74*, 239–249.

McGuire, W. J. The nature of attitudes and attitude change. In G. Lindzey & E. Aronson (Eds.), *The handbook of social psychology, Vol. 3* (2nd ed). Reading, Mass.: Addison-Wesley, 1969.

McGuire, W. J. The yin and yang of progress in social psychology: Seven koan. *Journal of Personality and Social Psychology*, 1973, *26*, 446–456.

Meehl, P. Theory testing in psychology and physics. *Philosophy of Sciences*, 1967, *34*, 103–115.

Moscovici, S., & Zavalloni, M. The group as a polarizer of attitudes. *Journal of Personality and Social Psychology*, 1969, *12*, 125–135.

Myers, D. D., & Lamm, H. The polarizing effect of group discussion. In I. Janis (Ed.), *Current trends in psychology: Readings from American Scientist*. Los Altos, Calif.: Kaufmann, 1977.

Paige, G. D. *The Korean decision*. New York: Free Press, 1968.

Pfeiffer, J. W., & Jones, J. E. *A handbook of structured experiences for human relations training, Vol. 5*. La Jolla, Cal: University Associates, 1975.

Pruitt, D. Conclusions: Toward an understanding of choice shifts in group discussion. *Journal of Personality and Social Psychology*, 1971, *20*, 495–510.

Rabbie, J. M., & Visser, L. Bargaining strength and group polarization in intergroup negotiations. *European J. of Soc. Psychology*, 1972, *2*, 401–416.

Raven, B. H. The Nixon group. *Journal of Social Issues*, 1974, *30*, 297–320.

Raven, B. H., & Rubin, J. Z. *Social psychology: People in groups*. New York: Wiley, 1977.

Rosenthal, R., & Rosnow, R. *Artifact in behavioral research*. New York: Academic Press, 1969.

Shure, G. H., Rogers, M. S., Larsen, I. M., & Tassone, J. Group planning and task effectiveness. *Sociometry*, 1962, *25*, 263–282.

Simon, H. Administrative behavior (2nd ed.). New York: Macmillan, 1957.

Steiner, I. D. Models for inferring relationships between group size and potential group productivity. *Behavioral Science*, 1966, *11*, 273–283.

Steiner, I. Heuristic models of groupthink. In H. Brandstatter, J. H. Davis, and G. Stocker-Kreichgauer (Eds.). Group decision making. N.Y.: Academic Press, 1982.

Stoner, J. A. F. A comparison of individual and group decisions involving risk. M. S. thesis, Mass. Institute of Technology, 1961.

Tetlock, P. E. Identifying victims of groupthink from the public statements of key decision makers. *Journal of Personality and Social Psychology*, 1980.

Varela, J. A. *Psychological solutions to social problems*. New York and London: Academic Press, 1971.

Wallach, M. A., Kogan, N. and Bem, D. J. Group influence on individual risk taking. *Journal of Abnormal and Social Psychology*, 1962, *65*, 75–86.

Wong-McCarthy, W. An analysis of 17 unedited Nixon tapes of presidential conversations. Preliminary draft, 1977.

15

Postscript:
Improving Research Strategies (1982)

In the course of carrying out the various studies on psychological stress, attitude change, and decision making reported in the preceding chapters, I have arrived at a number of suggestions for improving research in these and related areas. In this chapter I shall try to formulate these suggestions as tentative prescriptions, specifying what it is that theory-oriented investigators in personality and social psychology might do to increase the chances that their findings will be valid contributions to knowledge about human behavior.

Some of the main prescriptive ideas, as I indicated in the first chapter, were learned early in my career from Carl Hovland, Kurt Lewin, and others who shaped my research orientation. Later on, those prescriptions were elaborated and several more were acquired on the basis of my own experience. The ones I shall focus on are those that are not often discussed in the research literature, although quite a few investigators might be tacitly following them.

ARRIVING AT WARRANTED
GENERALIZATIONS THAT ARE NOT TRIVIAL

I expect that most behavioral scientists would agree that there are at least two prime goals of basic research in human psychology. One is to obtain evidence that warrants drawing general conclusions about cause-and-effect relationships that will prove to have external as well as internal validity. Another is to arrive at new generalizations that are not substantively trivial but are of considerable theoretical interest in the sense that they increase our understanding of how or why certain conditions lead to certain behaviors that make a difference in people's lives. This is what I had in mind when I said earlier that the most highly prized studies from the standpoint of advancing our knowledge are those that start and end with a theory, but not exactly the same one.

Taking account of these considerations and the special problems encountered in experimental social psychology, I propose to supplement the well-known rules for designing methodologically sound investigations with the following two prescriptive suggestions for productive research in this field. *First,* the specific independent and dependent variables to be investigated should represent plausible instances of antecedent conditions and behavioral consequences that are of theoretical interest; they should potentially have high generality, embracing a wide variety of specific social phenomena. *Second,* even if some or all of the assumptions that enter into the judgments made about the first prescriptive rule were to prove to be false, the findings of the investigation should, in any case, be of inherent interest as social psychological phenomena. That is to say, the empirically observed relationships between the independent and dependent variables should help to specify determinants of at least a limited class of socially important behavior.

In order to illustrate these two formidable sounding rules in a way that will convey their meaning more concretely, I shall briefly summarize the judgments that entered into the planning of the series of field experiments discussed in Chapter 12. Most of these studies investigated the condition under which social support is effective in helping people to adhere to personal decisions that are difficult to carry out because they have stressful consequences. I deliberately set up a diet clinic as one of the main research sites for working on this problem because it appeared to satisfy the criteria specified in the two prescriptive rules.

With regard to the first rule, prior research has established that among the vast majority of people who are not seriously ill, weight loss is to a large extent a function of the amount and kind of food they eat; consequently it provides an objective indicator of adherence to the decision to go on a recommended low-calorie diet. Furthermore, dieting entails a variety of distressing consequences—such as feeling hungry at night, undergoing conflict when exposed to tempting fattening foods, and being socially embarrassed at dinner parties where abstaining is not regarded by fellow guests as appropriate behavior and is sometimes resented by the host or hostess. Consequently weight loss is a plausible indicator of the main dependent variable specified by the hypotheses under investigation, namely, adherence to a personal decision that has stressful consequences. This category includes a variety of other decisions that lead to a similar combination of stressful physiological and social consequences—for example, giving up smoking, cutting down on alcohol or hard drug consumption, and doing daily exercises.

The category might be much broader if we think in terms of any sort of stressful consequences, whether or not they include physiological distress. The more extensive category would include career decisions that require long hours of study and marital decisions that entail sacrifices of former personal freedoms. This broad category might also include policy decisions to conform voluntarily with socially desirable standards, such as those pertaining to pollution control, which require top policymakers in a commercial organization to make sacrifices in the form of a reduction in annual income from profits and most likely being exposed to the disapproval of others in the organization who object.

It seems reasonable to assume that whatever we learn about the conditions that make for adherence to the decision to lose weight has a very good chance of proving to be applicable to decisions most similar to going on a diet, such as quitting smoking. Also there is a fair chance that the conclusions could prove to be applicable to some or all of the career decisions, marital decisions, and policy decisions that are in the more inclusive category as well. In other words, we can expect that whatever conclusions are supported by the evidence from our studies of the determinants of long-term weight loss will be broadly applicable to some other, if not all, decisions that are difficult to stick with.

Now let us consider the second prescriptive rule, which specifies, in effect, that each study should investigate empirical relationships that are inherently important. In order to apply this rule, we must force ourselves to be pessimists temporarily, because we have to worry about what would happen if the main assumptions and expectations stated in the preceding paragraph turn out to be wrong. For example, here is the train of thought that led me to select the diet clinic as an acceptable research site for testing hypotheses about helping relationships: Suppose that by pursuing whatever leads we pick up in our initial studies we discover after a time that adherence to the decision to lose weight among the people we study (who are 15 to 45 pounds overweight) proves to be largely determined by a variable that is relevant only to successful dieting, such as physiological tolerance for hunger between meals. What good will our research be if it does not apply to any kind of decision except the one particular kind we have chosen to investigate? In that unfortunate case, it seems to me, the findings would still be worthwhile because they would tell us something about the conditions under which people succeed or fail to carry out their decision to lose weight, which is an important type of behavior to understand in its own right.

With two prescriptive rules in mind, I deliberately decided to transform my social psychology laboratory in the Yale Department of Psychology, with its one-way vision screen and recording equipment, into a community weight-reduction clinic. All that I and my collaborators had to do from a physical point of view was to add a balance scale to our equipment and to put up a new sign on the door. In the same way, by removing the scale and changing the sign on the door, we sometimes used the laboratory space to set up a decision counseling service for people seeking help on giving up smoking or on choosing a new career. But while these changes could easily be carried out from a strictly physical point of view, they required a great deal of time and effort to meet high standards of clinical service to the community. For the diet clinic we had to line up a medical consultant and a nutritionist, check carefully on the best available counseling techniques for helping overweight people to lose weight, train graduate students to serve in the dual role of field experimenter and clinical counselor, and carry out all the necessary public relations work to recruit large numbers of clients to come to the new clinic.

Although my decision to transform the laboratory into a clinic was largely governed by efforts to maximize external validity, it did not entail any great risk of reducing internal validity. Unlike the situation where research psychologists obtain permission to do research in a clinic run by someone else, this entire operation remains under our own control as investigators, so that we can easily arrange to carry out properly-designed field experiments. Of course there are constraints because of the essential ethical and practical demands of operating a clinical service, but they do not preclude us from trying out new treatment interventions that our theory leads us to believe will be beneficial. Nor do those constraints prevent us from assigning clients on a random basis to different treatment conditions or from using standardized procedures to prevent differential demand characteristics, unconscious experimenter bias, and other sources of artifact that are threats to internal validity. Thus, the standards and procedures that have been developed in experimental social psychology can be applied in field investigations of real-life attitudes and decisions.

BEHAVIORAL MEASURES

Implicit in what I have already said is another prescriptive rule: In order to test hypotheses about the determinants of any socially important type of behavior, investigators should try to find research sites that permit them to obtain behavioral measures rather than having to rely entirely on the verbal reports of the subjects. When objective behavioral measures, such as weight loss or records of attendance at exercise classes, are used to assess adherence to personal decisions, the chances are reduced that the findings will subsequently be shown to be questionable or trivial because of experimental artifacts. The findings are much less likely to be trivialized by differential demand characteristics, the subjects' efforts to present themselves as behaving in a socially desirable way, or other well-known sources of distortion that so frequently plague research based solely on the subjects' verbal responses in a laboratory session. In retrospect, I now realize that my own laboratory experiments that relied on verbal reports, such as those on the effects of induced role playing (Chapter 7), are subject to multiple sources of distortion that make for considerable uncertainties about generalizing the findings to real-life situations.

If the only source of data consists of the subjects' verbal reports, as in most survey research and panel studies dealing with personal decisions concerning smoking, career plans, and sex life, the investigator should at least attempt to devise quasi-behavioral indicators by asking subjects to give precise descriptions of their own current behavior (for example, "How many cigarettes did you smoke yesterday?") Answers to such questions, of course, are subject to demand characteristics and other sources of distortion, but usually less so than questions that ask subjects to express attitudes or intentions (for example, "Do you intend to cut down on smoking?") or that ask for retrospective comparisons (for example, "Do you smoke less nowadays than you did about a year ago?")

Despite all the limitations of verbal measures of attitudes, however, I strongly favor using attitude scales based on questionnaires and content analyses of open-ended interviews as supplementary measures. These verbal data can provide valuable clues to mediating psychological processes that might account for observed relationships between experimental treatments and behavioral (or quasi-behavioral) measures. In many of the field experiments discussed in the preceding chapters, we used verbal reports to investigate mediating processes. Occasionally, the analysis of those data has led to discoveries that pointed to interacting factors, which then became the focus of attention in the next investigation. For example, in a series of studies on the effects of relationship-building interventions on adherence to the decision to go on a diet, we used a variety of verbal reports, some obtained from interviews and some from a verbal self-rating scale for assessing temporary changes in level of self-esteem, from which we learned something about why eliciting self-disclosures under conditions where the counselor gave consistently favorable feedback sometimes had positive effects on weight loss and sometimes had negative effects. (See Chapter 12).

Clues to mediating processes can also be inferred from studies that include personality measures, such as those that assess chronic level of self-esteem, anxiety, repression versus sensitization tendencies, locus of control, and need for approval. Such investigations are particularly valuable when the findings show an interaction effect between a personality measure and a situational variable. For example, the findings from the Janis and Feshbach study (Janis, 1954, 4) of fear-arousing communications showing an interaction effect (between chronic level of anxiety and strength of threat appeal in a persuasive communication) were used to make inferences about the resistances to threat appeals mobilized when there is a high level of residual emotional arousal following exposure to a persuasive warning communication (Janis, 1967). Other examples are to be found in my review of studies showing that when surgical patients are given preparatory information, different types of personalities (as assessed by a repression-sensitization scale or the coper versus avoider test) respond differently. The findings provided the basis for inferring that when a person's dominant coping pattern is defensive avoidance, he or she will tend to deny or ignore any warning that presents disturbing information about impending stress (See Chapter 13).

In my investigations of mediating processes, I have tried to take account of the logic of the *modus operandi* approach as formulated by Michael Scriven (1976). This approach formalizes what many investigators sometimes do intuitively when they examine puzzling clues from their research in essentially the same way that a good detective does. It involves formulating all the alternative causal sequences one can conceive of that might account for the puzzling outcome and then attempting to discern which of them appears to be the most probable cause. This requires careful examination of every shred of evidence that might provide tell-tale signs indicating the step-by-step ways in which each of the alternative causes is most likely to operate.

Even when the results of an experiment are not at all puzzling and show a gratifying confirmation of the theoretically-derived hypothesis that the study was designed to test, I think it still pays to use essentially the same approach to see what can be learned about the intervening details of the causal sequence running from the manipulated experimental variable to the observed behavioral effect. Sometimes one can pick up important clues suggesting limiting conditions—those under which a seemingly confirmed hypothesis does not hold true. Such clues may enable one to specify the interacting variables that need to be investigated in the next study. William McGuire (1980) has pointed out that all plausible-sounding hypotheses in social psychology are likely to be true at least under certain limited conditions and consequently the most useful observations for advancing our knowledge are those that show when a hypothesis does and does not predict accurately. If so, we have to expect that at best the results of our systematic inquiries will be warranted generalizations about interaction effects. But even when any such generalization is substantiated by converging evidence from dozens of studies, it is still a hypothesis that can be expected to hold only under certain conditions that remain to be discovered.

Taking account of the omnipresence of limiting conditions, it is prudent for investigators to abstain from presenting any hypothesis about interaction effects as definitively established merely on the basis of the results from one or even several carefully controlled experiments. The obvious prescriptive rule would be to start off making quite modest claims with regard to the generality of any such hypothesis—even though it is confirmed when tested in a well-designed study—and gradually to become less modest if the hypothesis continues to be confirmed. Confidence in the generality of the observed relationship can legitimately increase if it repeatedly makes its appearance in a variety of different settings when different methods are used for testing it with different types of people who vary widely in social background, education, and personality. Unfortunately, however, conceptual replications in social psychology and personality research usually show that few, if any, main effects or simple interactions turn out to be dependable generalizations. All too often the key variables turn out to enter into quadruple and higher-order interactions (see Cronbach, 1975; McGuire, 1969). Nevertheless, this bleak prospect should not deter us from trying to pin down the interacting variables that produce powerful effects at least some of the time in some circumstances. Such efforts will continue to increase our understanding of the conditions under which many, if not all, instances of psychological trauma, self-defeating attitudes, and defective decision making occur and can be prevented.

The prescriptive rules and suggestions presented in this chapter are intended to supplement the well-known methodological principles that are generally covered in graduate training in psychology. The latter usually emphasize the value of methodological rigor in the laboratory for attaining the highest possible degree of internal validity. Comparatively speaking, the problems of external validity are neglected. Most of my suggested rules are intended to redress this imbalance, to encourage investigators to give due emphasis to reducing threats to external validity, which sometimes require settling for using somewhat less rigorous controls in a field experiment than can be attained in the laboratory.

In a carefully designed experiment, Slovic (1969) found that when gambling decisions had real consequences, subjects were much more cautious about the threat of losses than when the gambling decisions were hypothetical choices. Additional research during the past decade on other types of choices also indicates that there is often a large gap between the way most people think and act when coping with the stresses of real-life decisions and the seemingly lawful phenomena observed in laboratory experiments in which the subjects (over 90 percent of whom are college students) are asked to make hypothetical decisions or to play simple games requiring them to make choices that are supposed to represent analogues of real-life decisions (see Janis and Mann, 1977, 2, pp. 417–419; McGuire, 1973; Smith, 1973). This evidence has led me to surmise that *rigor methodologicus* can be the terminal stage before *rigor mortis*.

In advocating several precepts for advancing social psychology and personality research, I do not mean to imply that all an investigator has to do is to follow a set of rules in order to guarantee that his or her research will be successful. I expect trouble even when investigators follow all the best rules and use what I regard as the best combination of research strategies (selecting hypotheses for their theoretical relevance to issues that pose significant social problems and testing them by controlled experiments in naturalistic field settings). They will still make errors and belatedly discover that certain of their studies have been a waste of time, or worse yet, have produced misleading conclusions. Nature will continue to be ingenious in finding unexpected ways to fool even the most vigilant investigators. The main thing that can be said for following the proposed prescriptive rules is that investigators will reduce their chances of being badly fooled and, when they are, they will be likely to find it out, mercifully, before others do.

Obviously, it takes a lot more than merely following a set of prescribed rules to be a productive research worker in any field. What else is required? A great deal of creative inventiveness together with a tremendous apperceptive mass of tacit knowledge as well as a bit of good luck. Sigmund Koch, 1976, p. 509) puts it this way:

> Once we give up a rule-regulated conception of science . . . we must perceive . . . the intensely creative character of genuine advance . . . and acknowledge that a well conducted experiment is a work of art, often of a very high order. Quite aside from the essentially connoisseurlike assessment determining the choice of a significant "consequence" for test, there is the largely open-ended creative task of arriving at a relevant, sensitively discriminating, and rigorous design, and the still more artistic task of shaping, out of the world-flux, a material context which "truly" realizes the theoretical variables selected for study and their appropriate ensemble of initial conditions.

Following the prescriptive rules cannot guarantee that a conscientious investigator will ever in his entire lifetime perform a creative piece of research that could be regarded as a great work of art. But these rules can, nevertheless, increase the chances that an investigator will in the long run obtain some worthwhile results.

REFERENCES

Cronbach, L. J. Beyond the two disciplines of scientific psychology. *American Psychologist*, 1975, *30*, 116-127.

Koch, S. Language communities, search cells, and the psychological studies. In J. K. Cole (Ed.), *Nebraska symposium on motivation, 1975*. Lincoln, Neb.: University of Nebraska Press, 1976.

McGuire, W. J. The nature of attitudes and attitude change. In G. Lindzey & E. Aronson (Eds.), *The handbook of social psychology* Vol. 3, (2nd ed.). Reading Mass.: Addison-Wesley, 1969.

McGuire, W. The yin and yang of progress in social psychology: Seven koan. *Journal of Personality and Social Psychology*, 1973, *28*, 446-456.

McGuire, W. The development of theory in social psychology. In R. Gilmour & S. Duck (Eds.), *The development of social psychology*. London: Academic Press, 1980.

Scriven, M. Maximizing the power of causal investigations: The modus operandi method. In G. V. Glass (Ed.), *Evaluation studies*. Review Annual Vol. 1. Beverly Hills, Calif.: Sage Publications, 1976.

Slovic, P. Differntial effects of real versus hypothetical payoffs on choices among gamblers. *Journal of Experimental Psychology*, 1969, *80*, 434-437.

Smith, M. B. Criticism of a social science: Review of *The Context of Social Psychology*, J. Israel & H. Tajfel (Eds.), *Science*, 1973, *180*, 610-612.

Biographical Sketch (1982)

Before deciding to become a psychologist, Janis seemed headed toward becoming a school drop-out or a critic of the arts, or both. At the age of 16 he was nearly expelled for playing hookey from Lafayette High School in Buffalo (the city where he was born on May 26, 1918). Instead of attending classes, Janis was spending much of his time at libraries reading art history and music history or looking at art works at the Albright Art Gallery. Janis was not expelled, however, after trying to convince the principal that what he was doing was more germane to his intended career than attending classes. Later Janis learned that the main reason he was not expelled or suspended was because he played cello in the school orchestra and was especially needed for the featured cello part in Mendelssohn's first piano concerto, scheduled for the annual spring concert.

As a high school senior, Janis's main achievement was a long essay he wrote on contemporary art, published in part in the school's literary magazine, the *Lafayette Oracle*. In an uninhibited attempt to be oracular, Janis predicted that three contemporary artists would sooner or later be regarded by the art world as great modern masters—Fernand Leger, who in 1934 was generally rated by art lovers as merely one of many minor cubists; Piet Mondriaan, whose simple rectangular compositions were scorned, except by a small sector of the avant-garde; and Arshile Gorky, whose surrealistic abstractions were then known only to the artist's friends and acquaintances. The young Janis was one of those privileged few (twice he was taken by Gorky on personal guided tours through the Metropolitan Museum). Sometimes he visited Gorky's Union Square studio in the company of his parents, Martin and Etta Janis, who were using the modest profits from their family shoe business to form an excellent collection of 20th-century art. The family had been introduced to Gorky by Janis' art mentor—his uncle, Sidney Janis, who was then emerging as a luminary in the art world.

Janis says that over the years he has often looked back with great consternation at those three speculative predictions in the essay written at age 16. With consternation because in none of his many writings as a research psychologist have his behavioral predictions

This biographical sketch is reprinted with slight modifications from the one published in the *American Psychologist* January 1982, reporting the author's Distinguished Scientific Contribution Award from the American Psychological Association.

based on psychological theory turned out to be so smashingly well confirmed.

At the University of Chicago where Janis received his B.S. in 1939 and then did his first year of graduate work, he had fine instructors in psychology who inspired him to acquire the skills essential for sound research on significant problems—Harold Gulliksen, Ward Halstead, Heinrich Kluver, L. L. Thurstone, and above all, Dael Wolfle, who was his main advisor.

During his undergraduate years, Janis acquired a thorough background in the philosophy of science. He participated in formal and informal seminars with Rudolph Carnap, Morris R. Cohen, Carl Hempel, and Bertrand Russell. All that good instruction might have been quickly forgotten were it not for the frequent gatherings at living-room seminars set up by Janis and his wife with fellow-students Abraham Kaplan (who was to become an illustrious philosopher of science) and his wife Iona Kaplan (who was to become an outstanding child therapist). The Janises and the Kaplans, as life-long friends, have continued their informal floating seminar in Los Angeles, Haifa, and elsewhere.

Two other close friends at the University of Chicago stimulated a deepening of Janis' appreciation of psychological wisdom in literary works—Saul Bellow and Isaac Rosenfeld, both well on their way to distinguished careers as novelists and essayists.

Janis says that "the most important of all personal events in my life occurred in September 1939—my marriage to Marjorie Graham, my best lover, best friend, best critic of my ideas, best editor of all my writings. She is now also the best applier of my recent theory of helping relationships, which she uses in an innovative way to deal with withdrawn or overactive children who have trouble learning in the early grades in inner-city schools."

In 1940, Janis entered the Ph.D. program at Columbia University, where he became intrigued with social psychology in a seminar with Otto Klineberg. He also obtained advanced training in experimental methods, particularly in a seminar conducted by Robert S. Woodworth.

After his first year at Columbia, Janis accepted a government job with Harold D. Lasswell at the Library of Congress, to carry out research analyzing fascist propaganda using systematic content analysis techniques. Drafted into the Army in the fall of 1943, Janis was recruited by Samuel Stouffer and Carl Hovland to be a military research psychologist under their supervision in the War Department. There he obtained considerable experience carrying out surveys and field experiments on factors influencing morale attitudes. After the war these studies were published in *The American Soldier*. Janis was one of the co-authors, along with a number of other leading social psychologists, including Arthur A. Lumsdaine and M. Brewster Smith, with whom he became life-long friends and from whom he learned a great deal.

After the war, Janis returned to Columbia University. He worked with Carney Landis and Joseph Zubin on his dissertation—a well-controlled field experiment on the psychological effects of electro-convulsive treatments on psychotics. He discovered that the clinical lore of that time was not true; the patients did *not* fully recover their memory functioning within a few weeks after the treatments but, instead, were left with persistent subtle amnesias that appeared to be linked with the alleviation of their depressive feelings.

In the fall of 1947, Janis joined the Psychology faculty of Yale University. He says that for him it is as close to being the ideal place to work as he can imagine. He has never been tempted to accept attractive job offers elsewhere, mainly because of the extraordinarily talented people among both the faculty and students, and the social atmosphere of the department, which facilitates constant interchange of ideas and collaborative research.

During his early years at Yale, Janis worked closely with Carl I. Hovland, who headed a famous research project on communication and attitude change until his untimely death in 1962. The psychologists who participated in that project now stand out on the roster of America's leading social psychologists—Robert Abelson, Jack Brehm, A. Robert Cohen, Merrill Carlsmith, William McGuire, Howard Leventhal, Herbert Kelman, Harold Kelley, Milton Rosenberg, Phillip Zimbardo, and others. Hovland, who has been characterized as an "intellectual genius" and "the world's most non-directive leader", held ad hoc meetings where he, Janis and the others could obtain critical feedback and develop new research plans. Leonard Doob and Fred Sheffield also participated, as did occasional visiting luminaries— Donald Campbell, Leon Festinger, Robert Merton, Theodore Newcomb, and Muzafer Sherif. . . .

During the late 1940s and the 1950s Janis' research included pioneering work on the effects of fear-arousing appeals (in collaboration with Seymour Feshbach), individual differences in responsiveness to persuasive communications (in collaboration with Peter Field), and facilitating effects of role-playing on internalization (first in collaboration with Bert King and later, during the early 1960s, with Alan Elms, Barney Gilmore, and Leon Mann).

Janis' studies of psychological stress began with attempts to explain the severe psychological disturbances observed among disaster victims. His major work on *Psychological Stress* (1958, 3) presents systematic data and case study observations on reactions of surgical patients. In that book he introduced new theoretical concepts— "the work of worrying" and "emotional inoculation" (or "stress inoculation"), which help to explain how maladaptive behavior can be prevented by appropriate preparatory communications. These concepts are influenced by Freud, whose writings especially on anxiety and defense he studied intensively during his post-doctoral training at the New York Psychoanalytic Institute.

Late in the 1950s Janis' research gradually changed in the direction of investigating real-life personal decisions, such as giving up smoking or going on a low-calorie diet. He selected these decisions for investigation partly because of his interest in health psychology. One of his major contributions is his book in collaboration with Leon Mann on *Decision Making* (1977, 3), which presents a descriptive theory of how choices are made under stress together with an integrative analysis of pertinent research findings from the behavioral sciences. A few years ago Janis extracted the main practical implications in *A practical guide for making decisions*. This nontechnical book was written in collaboration with Daniel Wheeler, a cognitive psychologist who added useful leads from his thorough knowledge of problem-solving. Their book has the distinction of being one of the rare volumes in which two male collaborators dedicate their work to one woman—"to Cathy". Cathy turns out to be Daniel Wheeler's wife and Janis' older daughter. Dr. Cathy Janis Wheeler is a research worker on the cutting edge of the newly developing field of experimental linguistics.

Janis has also contributed to the study of group dynamics in relation to decision making. His *Victims of Groupthink* (1972, 1), which presents detailed case studies of ill-conceived foreign-policy decisions, delineates a pattern of concurrence-seeking that fosters over-optimism, lack of vigilance, and sloganistic thinking among members of cohesive executive groups. He includes testable hypotheses about the conditions under which the concurrence-seeking tendency will interfere with critical thinking and suggests prescriptive hypotheses for preventing the most deleterious effects. Janis . . . [has just completed] a revised edition (1982,) expanding the theory and presenting a new illuminating case study of the Watergate cover-up, based largely on unedited transcripts of Nixon's tapes.

Janis' work on group decision making began about 15 years ago when he noticed that Arthur M. Schlesinger Jr.'s account of the Bay of Pigs contained hints of group processes leading to shared illusions, similar to those he was observing in anti-smoking and weight-reducing groups. He decided to pursue the groupthink hypothesis after his daughter, Charlotte, prepared a paper at his suggestion on the Bay of Pigs fiasco for a high school course. The material she turned up in her library research led him to take the hypothesis seriously enough to examine additional historic fiascos. Charlotte also prepared detailed editorial critiques of the draft of that book and of his subsequent writings. Now Charlotte Janis Mervin is the mother of Janis' only grandchild, Alexis. She pursues a career as a family nurse practitioner. In the publicity she writes for Physicians for Social Responsibility, she makes use of her father's work, especially on fear appeals, vigilance, and decision making.

Janis' recent research has centered on the social influence of counselors on adherence to stressful decisions. It involves testing hypotheses derived from his theory of self-esteem enhancement induced by a supportive relationship with a nurturant, norm-setting communicator. In collaboration with Donald Quinlan, Leon Mann, and 12 former graduate students at Yale, he has just completed a new monograph. The volume presents the theory and reports 23 controlled field experiments that help to explain when, how, and why people succeed in adhering to difficult decisions, such as going on a diet, as a consequence of verbal interchanges with a counselor.

Janis' national professional activities include participation in NSF and NIMH research panels, membership in the Surgeon General's Scientific Advisory Committee on the Social Effects of Television (1969–1972), and in various committees of APA and the Social Science Research Council. He has served on the editorial board of *American Scientist* and several APA journals; currently he is chair of the editorial board of the *Journal of Conflict Resolution.*

Among Janis' many special honors and awards are a Fulbright Research Award (1957–1958), the Hofheimer Prize of the American Psychiatric Association (1958), the Socio-Psychological Prize of the American Association for the Advancement of Science (1967), Fellow at the Center for Advanced Study in the Behavioral Sciences (1973–74), a Guggenheim Foundation Fellowship (1973–74), election to the American Academy of Arts and Sciences (1974) and election to the Academy of Behavioral Medicine Research (1978). During 1981–82 he is a Fellow-in-Residence at the Netherlands Institute for Advanced Study, located near The Hague.

Janis reports that in making the selection of his papers for inclusion in the present volume, he has one regret: "I couldn't find any reasonable excuse to work in my high school essay containing all those nice predictions about Leger, Mondriaan, and Gorky that came out so much better than most of my subsequent predictions based on what I think are sound psychological theories."

Publications:
A Comprehensive Bibliography

1943

1. Meaning and the study of symbolic behavior. *Psychiatry, 6,* 425–439.
2. With R. Fadner. A coefficient of imbalance for content analysis. *Psychometrika, 8,* 105–119.
3. With F. Frick. The relationship between attitudes toward conclusions and errors in judging logical validity of syllogisms. *Journal of Experimental Psychology, 33,* 73–77.
4. With M. Janowitz & R. Fadner. The reliability of a content analysis technique. *Public Opinion Quarterly, 7,* 292–296.

1945

Psychodynamic aspects of adjustment to army life. *Psychiatry, 8,* 159–176.

1946

With M. G. Janis. A supplementary test based on free associations to Rorschach responses. *Rorschach Research Exchange, 10,* 1–19.

1948

Memory loss following electric convulsive treatments. *Journal of Personality, 17,* 29–32.

1949

1. Problems related to the control of fear in combat. In S. Stouffer (Ed.), *The American Soldier: II. Combat and its aftermath.* Princeton, N.J.: Princeton University Press.
2. Morale attitudes of combat flying personnel in the Air Corps. In S. Stouffer (Ed.), *The American Soldier: II. Combat and its aftermath.* Princeton, N.J.: Princeton University Press.
3. Objective factors related to morale attitudes in the aerial combat situation. In S. Stouffer (Ed.), *The American Soldier: II. Combat and its aftermath.* Princeton, N.J.: Princeton University Press.
4. The problem of validating content analysis. In H. D. Lasswell & N. C. Leites (Eds.), *Language of politics: Studies in quantitative semantics.* New York: George W. Stewart, Inc.
5. With R. Fadner. The coefficient of imbalance. In H. D. Lasswell & N. C. Leites (Eds.), *Language of politics: Studies in quantiative semantics.* New York: George W. Stewart, Inc.

1950

1. Psychological problems of A-bomb defense. *Bull. Atomic Scientists, 6,* 256–262.
2. Psychologic effects of electric convulsive treatments: I. Post-treatment amnesias. *Journal of Nervous and Mental Diseases, 111,* 359–382.
3. Psychologic effects of electric convulsive treatments: II. Changes in word association reactions. *Journal of Nervous and Mental Diseases, 111,* 383–397.
4. Psychologic effects of electric convulsive treatments: III. Changes in affective disturbances. *Journal of Nervous and Mental Diseases, 111,* 469–489.

1951

1. *Air war and emotional stress: Psychological studies of bombing and civilian defense.* New York: McGraw-Hill.
2. With M. Astrachan. The effects of electroconvulsive treatments on memory efficiency. *Journal of Abnormal and Social Psychology, 46,* 501–511.
3. With A. A. Lumsdaine & A. I. Gladstone. Effects of preparatory communications on reactions to a subsequent news event. *Public Opinion Quarterly, 15,* 487–518.

1953

1. With S. Feshbach. Effects of fear-arousing communications. *Journal of Abnormal and Social Psychology, 48,* 78–92.
2. With C. I. Hovland & H. H. Kelley. *Communication and persuasion: Psychological studies of opinion change.* New Haven: Yale University Press.
3. With A. A. Lumsdaine. Resistance to "counterpropaganda" produced by a one-sided versus a two-sided "propaganda" presentation. *Public Opinion Quarterly, 17,* 311–318.

1954

1. Personality correlates of susceptibility to persuasion. *Journal of Personality, 22,* 504–518.
2. Problems of theory in the analysis of stress behavior. *Journal of Social Issues, 10,* 12–25.
3. *Psychological effects of atomic disasters.* Publication No. L54-134, Industrial College of the Armed Forces, Washington, D.C.
4. With S. Feshbach. Personality differences associated with responsiveness to fear-arousing communications. *Journal of Personality, 23,* 154–166.
5. With B. T. King. The influence of role playing on opinion change. *Journal of Abnormal and Social Psychology, 49,* 211–218.
6. With W. Milholland. The influence of threat appeals on selective learning of the content of a persuasive communication. *Journal of Psychology, 37,* 75–80.

1955

1. Anxiety indices related to susceptibility to persuasion. *Journal of Abnormal and Social Psychology, 51,* 663–667.
2. With D. W. Chapman, J. P. Gillin, & J. Spiegel. The problem of panic. Civil Defense Technical Bulletin T. B.-19.2 (Prepared for the Committee on Disaster Studies of the National Research Council and National Academy of Sciences. Washington: U.S. Government Printing Office.

1956

1. With P. Field. A behavioral assessment of persuasibility: Consistency of individual differences. *Sociometry, 19,* 241–259.
2. With B. T. King. Comparison of the effectiveness of improvised versus non-improvised role-playing in producing opinion changes. *Human Relations, 9,* 177–186.
3. With R. Williams & B. Fisher. Educational desegregation as a context for basic social science research. *American Sociological Review,* 577–583.

1957

1. Attitude change and the resolution of motivational conflicts. *Proceedings of the 15th International Congress of Psychology,* Acta Psychologica, Amsterdam: North Holland Publishing Co.
2. Appendix B. Motivational effects of different sequential arrangements of conflicting arguments: A theoretical analysis. In C. I. Hovland (Ed.), *The order of presentation in persuasion.* New Haven: Yale University Press.
3. With R. L. Feierabend. Effects of alternative ways at ordering pro and con arguments in persuasive communications. In C. I. Hovland (Ed.), *The order of presentation in persuasion.* New Haven: Yale University Press.

1958

1. Emotional inoculation: Theory and research on effects of preparatory communications. In W. Muensterberger & S. Axelrad (Eds.), *Psychoanalysis and the social sciences Vol. V.* New York: International Universities Press.
2. The psychoanalytic interview as an observational method. In G. Lindzey (Ed.), *Assessment of human motives.* New York: Holt, Rinehart and Winston.
3. *Psychological stress: Psychoanalytic and behavioral studies of surgical patients.* New York: Wiley & Sons.

1959

1. Decisional conflict: A theoretical analysis. *Journal of Conflict Resolution, 3,* 6–27.
2. Motivational factors in the resolution of decisional conflicts. In. M. R. Jones (Ed.), *Nebraska Symposium on Motivation.* Lincoln: Univ. of Nebraska Press.
3. With C. I. Hovland et al. *Personality and persuasibility.* New Haven: Yale University Press.

4. With D. Katz. The reduction of intergroup hostility: Research problems and hypotheses. *Journal of Conflict Resolution, 3,* 85–100.

1962

1. Psychological effects of warnings. In D. Chapman & G. Baker (Eds.), *Man and society in disaster.* New York: Basic Books.
2. With R. Terwilliger. An experimental study of psychological resistances to fear-arousing communications. *Journal of Abnormal and Social Psychology, 65,* 403–410.

1963

1. Group identification under conditions of external danger. *British Journal of Medical Psychology, 36,* 227–238.
2. Personality as a factor in susceptibility to persuasion. In W. Schramm (Ed.), *The science of human communication.* New York: Basic Books.

1964

With C. Sofer & L. Wishlade. Social and psychological factors in changing food habits. In J. Yudkin & J. McKenzie (Eds.) *Changing food habits.* London: MacGibbon and Kee.

1965

1. Professional roles, norms, and ethics—A social psychological viewpoint. *The Canadian Psychologist, 6a,* 143–154.
2. Psychodynamic aspects of stress tolerance. In S. Klausner (Ed.), *The quest for self control.* Glencoe: Free Press.
3. With J. Dabbs, Jr. Why does eating while reading facilitate opinion change?— An experimental inquiry. *Journal of Experimental Social Psychology, 1,* 133–144.
4. With A. C. Elms. Counter-norm attitudes induced by consonant versus dissonant conditions of role-playing. *Journal of Experimental Research in Personality, 1,* 50–60.
5. With B. Gilmore. The influence of incentive conditions on the success of role playing in modifying attitudes. *Journal of Personality and Social Psychology, 1,* 17–27.
6. With D. Kaye & P. Kirschner. Facilitating effects of "eating-while-reading" on responsiveness to persuasive communications. *Journal of Personality and Social Psychology, 1,* 181–186.
7. With H. Leventhal. Psychological aspects of physical illness and hospital care. In B. Wolman (Ed.), *Handbook of clinical psychology.* New York: McGraw-Hill.
8. With L. Mann. Effectiveness of emotional role-playing in modifying smoking habits and attitudes. *Journal of Experimental Research in Personality, 1,* 84–90.
9. With M. B. Smith. Effects of education and persuasion on national and international images. In H. Kelman (Ed.), *International behavior.* New York: Holt.

1966

Field and experimental studies of phases in the development of cohesive face-to-face groups. In *XVIII International Congress of Psychology Abstracts of Communications: Problems of Mental Development and Social Psychology*. Moscow, U.S.S.R.: International Union of Scientific Psychology.

1967

Effects of fear arousal on attitude change: Recent developments in theory and experimental research. In L. Berkowitz (Ed.), *Advances in experimental social psychology*. Vol. 3. New York: Academic Press.

1968

1. Attitude change via role playing. In R. P. Abelson, E. A. Aronson, W. J. McGuire, T. M. Newcomb, M. J. Rosenberg, & P. H. Tannenbaum (Eds.), *Theories of cognitive consistency: A sourcebook*. Chicago: Rand McNally.
2. Biography of Carl I. Hovland. In *International encyclopedia of the social sciences*. New York: MacMillan & The Free Press.
3. Group identification under conditions of external danger. In D. Cartwright & A. Zander (Eds.) *Group dynamics: Research and theory* (3rd ed.). New York: Harper & Row.
4. (Editor, also co-author with G. Mahl, J. Kagan, & R. Holt). *Personality: Dynamics, development, and assessment*. New York: Harcourt Brace and World.
5. Persuasion. In *International encyclopedia of the social sciences*. New York: MacMillan & The Free Press.
6. Stages in the decision-making process. In R. P. Abelson, E. A. Aronson, W. J. McGuire, T. M. Newcomb, M. J. Rosenberg, & P. H. Tannenbaum (Eds.), *Theories of cognitive consistency: A sourcebook*. Chicago: Rand McNally.
7. When fear is healthy. *Psychology Today, 1*, 46–49, 60–61.
8. With H. Leventhal. Human reactions to stress. In E. Borgatta & W. Lambert (Eds.), *Handbook of personality theory and research*. New York: Rand McNally.
9. With L. Mann. A conflict-theory approach to attitude change and decision making. In A. Greenwald, T. Brock, & T. Ostrom (Eds.), *Psychological foundations of attitudes*. New York: Academic Press.
10. With L. Mann. A follow-up study on the long-term effects of emotional role playing. *Journal of Personality and Social Psychology, 8*, 339–342.

1969

1. Some implications of recent research on the dynamics of fear and stress tolerance. In F. Redlich (Ed.), *Social psychiatry*. New York: The Association for Research in Nervous and Mental Disease.
2. With L. Mann & R. Chaplin. Effects of anticipation of forthcoming infor-

mation on predecisional processes. *Journal of Personality and Social Psychology, 11,* 10–16.

1970

1. With D. Hoffman. Facilitating effects of daily contact between partners who make a decision to cut down on smoking. *Journal of Personality and Social Psychology, 17,* 25–35.
2. With C. N. Rausch. Selective interest in communications that could arouse decisional conflict: A field study of participants in the draft-resistance movement. *Journal of Personality and Social Psychology, 14,* 46–54.

1971

1. Groupthink among policy makers. In N. Sanford & C. Comstock (Eds.), *Sanctions for evil: Sources of destructiveness.* San Francisco: Jossey-Bass.
2. *Stress and frustration.* New York: Harcourt Brace & Jovanovich.

1972

1. *Victims of groupthink: A psychological study of foreign-policy decisions and fiascos.* Boston: Houghton Mifflin.
2. With I. H. Cisin and other members of the Surgeon General's Scientific Advisory Committee on Television and Social Behavior. *Television and growing up.* Washington, D.C.: U.S. Government Printing Office.

1973

1. Groupthink and group dynamics: A social psychological analysis of defective policy decisions. *Policy Studies Journal, 2,* 19–25.
2. With J. C. Miller. Dyadic interaction and adaptation to the stresses of college life. *Journal of Consulting Psychology, 3,* 258–264.

1974

1. Vigilance and decision-making in personal crises. In D. A. Hamburg & C. V. Coelho (Eds.), *Coping and Adaptation.* New York: Academic Press.
2. With H. Reed. Effects of induced awareness of rationalizations on smokers' acceptance of fear-arousing warnings about health hazards. *Journal of Consulting and Clinical Psychology, 42,* 748.

1975

1. Field experiments on the effectiveness of social support for stressful decisions. In M. Deutsch & H. Hornstein (Eds.), *Problems of applying social psychology.* Hillsdale, N.J.: Erlbaum (Wiley & Sons).
2. Groupthink among policy makers. In R. S. Lazarus (Ed.), *Clues to the riddle of man.* Englewood Cliffs, N.J.: Prentice-Hall.
3. What group dynamics can contribute to the study of policy decisions. In S. S. Nagel (Ed.), *Policy studies and the social sciences.* Lexington, Mass.: D. C. Heath & Co.

4. With M. Hoyt. Increasing adherence to a stressful decision via a motivational balance sheet procedure: A field experiment. *Journal of Personality and Social Psychology, 31,* 833–839.
5. With E. J. Langer & J. A. Wolfer. Effects of a cognitive coping device and preparatory information on psychological stress in surgical patients. *Journal of Experimental Social Psychology, 11,* 155–165.

1976

1. Preventing dehumanization. In J. Howard & A. Strauss (Eds.), *Humanizing health care.* New York: Wiley & Sons.
2. With L. Mann. Coping with decisional conflict: An analysis of how stress affects decision-making suggest interventions to improve the process. *American Scientist, 64,* 657–667.

1977

1. (Ed.) *Current trends in psychology: Readings from American Scientist.* Los Alto, CA.: Kaufmann.
2. With L. Mann. *Decision-making: A psychological analysis of conflict, choice and commitment.* New York: Free Press.
3. With L. Mann. Emergency decision making: A theoretical analysis of responses to disaster warnings. *Journal of Human Stress, 3,* 35–48.

1978

With D. Wheeler. Thinking clearly about career choices. *Psychology Today,* 66–122.

1979

1. With J. Rodin. Attribution, control, and decision making: Social psychology and health care. In G. C. Stone, F. Cohen, & N. E. Adler (Eds.), *Health Psychology,* San Francisco: Jossey-Bass.
2. With J. Rodin. The social power of health-care practitioners as agents of change. *Journal of Social Issues, 35,* 60–82.

1980

1. Discussion with Irving Janis, pgs. 97–111. In R. I. Evans, *The making of social psychology: Discussions with creative contributors.* New York: Gardner Press.
2. An analysis of psychological and sociological ambivalence: Nonadherence to courses of action prescribed by health-care professionals. In T. F. Gieryn (Ed.), *Science and social structure: A festschrift for Robert K, Merton.* New York: Transactions of The New York Academy of Sciences, Series II, Vol. 39.
3. The influence of television on personal decision-making. In S. B. Withey and R. P. Abeles (Eds.), *Television and social behavior: Beyond violence and children.* Hillsdale, N.J.: Laurence Erlbaum Associates.

4. Personality differences in decision making under stress. In K. R. Blankstein, P. Pliner, & J. Polivy (Eds.) *Assessment and modification of emotional behavior.* New York: Plenum Publishing Corp.
5. With D. Wheeler. *A practical guide for making decisions.* New York: Free Press.

1982

1. Preventing groupthink in policy-planning groups: Theory and research perspectives. In H. Brandstetter, J. Davis, & C. Stocker-Kreichgauer (Eds.), *Group decision making.* London: Academic Press.
2. Preventing pathogenic denial by means of stress inoculation. In S. Breznitz (Ed.), *Stress and denial.* New York: Plenum.
3. *Groupthink: Psychological studies of policy decisions and fiascoes.* (Revised and enlarged edition of *Victims of Groupthink,* 1972). Boston: Houghton Mifflin.
4. (With Collaborators). *Counseling on personal decisions: Theory and research on short-term helping relationships.* New Haven: Yale University Press.
5. With L. Mann. Conflict theory of decision making and the expectancy-value approach. In N. Feather (Ed.), *Expectations and actions: Expectancy-value models in psychology.* New York: Erlbaum.

In Press

1. Coping patterns among patients with life-threatening diseases. In P. Defares, C. Spielberger, & I. Sarason (Eds.), *Stress and anxiety.* Vol. 9. New York: Wiley (Halsted).
2. Decision-making under stress. In L. Goldberger & S. Breznitz (Eds.), *Handbook of stress.* New York: Free Press.
3. Groupthink. In H. H. Blumberg & P. Hare (Eds.), *Small groups.* London: Wiley and Sons.
4. The patient as decision maker. In D. Gentry (Ed.), *Handbook of behavioral medicine.* New York: Guilford Press.
5. Improving adherence to medical recommendations: Prescriptive hypotheses derived from recent research in social psychology. In A. Baum, J. E. Singer, and S. E. Taylor (Eds.), *Handbook of Medical Psychology.* Vol. 4. New York: Erlbaum.
6. Stress inoculation in health care: Theory and research. In D. Meichenbaum & M. Jaremko (Eds.), *Stress prevention and management: A cognitive-behavioral approach.* New York: Plenum.
7. With P. Defares & P. Grossman. Hypervigilant reactions to threat. In H. Selye (Ed.), *Selye's guide to stress research.* Vol. 3. Van Nostrand, Reinhold.
8. With L. Mann. Interpersonal conflict and decision making. In D. Johnson & D. Tjosvold (Eds.), *Conflicts in organizations.* New York: Irvington Publishers.
9. With J. R. Rodin. The social influence of physicians and other health-care practitioners as agents of change. In H. S. Friedman & M. R. DiMatteo (Eds.), *Interpersonal issues and health care.* New York: Academic Press.

Author Index

Abeles, R. P., 167n, 330
Abelson, R. P., 113n, 171, 189, 191, 321, 328
Aberd, D., 141, 144
Achelpohl, C., 181, 189
Adams, D., 304
Adler, N. E., 215, 286, 287, 330
Adler, R. P., 175, 189
Akers, R., 181, 189
Alfert, E., 133, 145, 270, 288
Alger, C., 307
Allison, G. T., 306
Allport, G. W., 70, 89
Anderson, C. G., 195, 215
Andrasik, F., 274, 287
Andrew, J. M., 281, 285
Argyris, C., 304, 306
Arnold, W., 290
Arons, S., 173, 189
Aronson, E. A., 113n, 166, 190, 256, 308, 317, 328
Astrachan, M., 325
Atthowe, J., 196, 213
Atkin, C. K., 183, 189
Auerbach, S. M., 282, 283, 285
Averill, J. R., 270, 278, 285
Axelrod, S., 90, 326

Baker, G. W., 57n, 91, 327
Bales, V., 226, 229, 251, 256
Ball, T. S., 270, 278, 285
Ballach, J., 77, 89
Bandura, A., 218, 254, 261, 275, 276, 285
Barber, E., 207

Bartlett, M., 142, 143n, 144, 262, 272, 286
Battit, G., 142, 143n, 144, 262, 272, 286
Baum, A., 331
Bechtel, R. B., 181, 189
Bem, D. J., 157, 165, 308
Bergman, A. B., 195, 213
Berkowitz, L., 165, 255, 307, 328
Bernstein, S., 86, 89
Berscheid, E., 199, 203, 213, 216
Bespalec, D. A., 221, 255
Bigelow, D. A., 262, 290
Blake, R. R., 306
Blankstein, K. R., 331
Blumberg, H. H., 331
Bodgonoff, M. D., 195, 215
Borgatta, E., 328
Bowers, K. G., 211, 213, 278, 285
Boylan, C. H., 269, 286
Bradley, A., 145
Brandstätter, H., 291n, 308, 331
Braswell, L. R., 89
Breen, D., 262, 285
Brehm, J. W., 116, 117, 124, 125, 157, 165, 321
Brehm, S., 252, 254, 285
Breitrose, 176
Breznitz, S., 331
Broadhurst, A., 219, 254
Brock, T., 124, 328
Brody, R. A., 306, 307
Brousseau, K., 307
Brown, R., 301, 306
Brownell, K. D., 206, 213
Brues, A. M., 30, 37

Butler, N. M., 199, 200, 207
Bynum, R., 214
Byrne, D., 203, 214, 238, 254, 281, 285

Cameron, R., 276, 288
Campbell, D. T., 306, 321
Carlsmith, J. M., 117, 122, 123, 124, 321
Caplan, G., 276, 285
Carroll, J. S., 189
Cartwright, D., 93n, 200, 214, 285, 301,
    306, 328
Chaffee, S. H., 183, 189
Chamey, E., 195, 214
Chang, P., 224, 254
Chaplin, R., 148, 153, 156, 166, 328
Chapman, D. W., 57n, 72, 90, 91, 326, 327
Chertok, L., 269, 285
Chu, C. C., 276, 285
Cisin, I. H., 329
Clark, R. L., Jr., 141, 144
Clark, S., 270, 286
Clarke, S., 165
Clifford, R. A., 77, 89
Clore, G. L., 160, 165
Cobb, B. C., 141, 144
Coelho, C. V., 166, 307, 329
Cohen, A. R., 116, 117, 124, 125, 321
Cohen, F., 215, 268, 274, 281, 282, 283,
    285, 286, 287, 330
Cohen, S., 141, 145
Colbertson, W., 141, 145
Cole, J. K., 317
Collins, B. E., 123, 124
Colten, M. E., 228, 229, 255
Comstock, C., 329
Comstock, G. A., 167, 168, 176, 180, 181,
    183, 189, 190
Conolley, E., 223, 224, 244, 245, 246, 255,
    292, 307
Cormier, L. S. 218, 219, 255, 276, 286
Cormier, W. H., 218, 219, 255, 276, 286
Coser, L. A., 215
Cottrell, L., Jr., 145
Cowett, A., 141, 145
Cramond, W., 141, 144
Cronbach, L. J., 315, 317
Crow, W. J., 301, 306
Cuttler, H. F., 285

Dabbs, J., 278, 289
Dabbs, J., Jr., 327

Danzig, E. R., 72, 89
Das, M. S., 215
Dashiell, T., 157, 166
Davenport-Slack, B., 269, 286
Davidson, P. O., 256
Davis, J. H., 291n, 295, 301, 306, 308, 331
Davis, M. S., 195, 196, 214
Davison, G. C., 252, 255, 286
Davison, L. A., 145
Decenteco, E. T., 265, 286
Deckner, W. C., 277, 289
Defares, P., 331
De Fleur, L. B., 189
De Fleur, M. L., 189
DeLong, R. D., 262, 281, 286
Deutsch, M., 190, 214, 329
Dick-Read, G., 262, 286
Diggory, J. C., 61, 89
DiMatteo, M. R., 331
Dittes, J. E., 199, 214
Doering, S. C., 269, 286
Dominick, J. R., 172, 189
Dowds, M. M., Jr., 223, 244, 245, 246, 255
Duck, S., 317
Dworkin, B., 204

Egan, G., 219, 255
Egbert, L., 142, 143n, 144, 262, 272, 286
Eldredge, D., 214
Elling, R., 214
Elms, A. C., 115, 117, 118, 119, 120, 123,
    124, 321, 327
Endress, M. P., 272, 286
Endress, P., 268, 287
Entwistle, D. R., 269, 286
Epstein, J. A., 214
Epstein, S., 128, 129n, 145, 165, 266, 270,
    286
Ericsson, K. A., 7, 9
Erikson, E. H., 97, 110
Etzioni, A., 307

Faber, R., 183, 191
Fadner, R., 324
Fanshel, D., 227, 256
Fastovsky, A., 145
Feather, N., 331
Fedoravicous, A., 267, 289
Feierabend, R. L., 326
Feinstein, A. R., 195, 214
Feldman, M. P., 254

Fenichel, O., 101, 105, 110
Fenz, W. D., 128, 129n, 145
Ferrare, N. A., 212, 214
Feshbach, S., 57, 90, 314, 321, 325
Festinger, L., 81, 89, 116, 117, 122, 124, 153, 157, 165, 166, 321
Field, P., 321, 326
Fischer, W. M., 269, 287
Fisher, B., 326
Flowers, M. L., 302, 307
Flugel, J., 95, 101, 111
Foreyt, J. P., 290
Form, W. H., 88, 89
Francis, V., 206, 214, 215
Frank, R. S., 181, 190
Fraser, R., 39, 43, 55, 83, 89
Freeman, G., 206, 214
Fremauw, W. J., 267, 286
French, J. R., 197, 214
Freud, S., 2, 61, 89, 95, 103, 104, 111, 139, 145, 322
Frick, F., 324
Friedman, H. S., 331
Fritz, C. E., 70, 77, 78, 83, 89
Fuller, S. S., 268, 272, 286, 287

Galanter, Lila R., 89
Garner, H., 73, 89
Genest, M., 267, 269, 276, 290
Gentry, D., 331
Gerard, H. B., 148, 165
Gerbner, G., 168, 180, 190
Gieryn, T. F., 193n, 198, 211, 215, 330
Gillespie, R. D., 55
Gillin, J. P., 72, 90, 326
Gilmore, B., 321, 327
Gilmore, J. B., 114, 117, 118, 124, 267, 289
Gilmour, R., 317
Giordo, M., 275, 286
Gladstone, A. I., 132, 145, 270, 287, 325
Glass, A. J., 111
Glass, C., 267, 286
Glass, G. V., 317
Glover, E., 55, 56, 73, 74, 75, 82, 83, 88, 89
Goldberger, L., 331
Goldfried, M. R., 265, 267, 286
Goldstein, M. J., 281, 287
Gorsuch, R. L., 282, 290
Gottman, J., 267, 286

Gottschalk, L., 141, 145
Gozzi, E. K., 215
Graham, L. E., 274, 288
Green, D., 292, 307
Green, J. B., 66, 89
Green, M., 214
Greenberg, B. S., 183, 190
Greene, L. R., 224, 244, 245, 255
Greenwald, A., 124, 328
Greenwald, H., 219, 255
Griffitt, W., 238, 254
Grinker, R. R., 56, 141, 145
Gross, L., 180, 190
Grossman, P., 331
Guetzkow, H., 307

Hackman, J. R., 303, 305, 307
Hagashi, T., 29
Hall, J., 307
Hamburg, D. A., 307, 329
Hammen, L., 279, 288
Hanusa, B. M., 265, 289
Hardy, J. D., 269, 287
Hare, A. P., 200, 214, 287
Hare, P., 331
Harrisson, T., 41, 53, 55, 56
Hartmann, H., 2
Hastings, 21, 22
Haynes, R. B., 195, 196, 216
Heckerman, C. L., 206, 213
Helmreich, R. L., 123, 124
Hermann, M. G., 306
Hersey, J., 29, 37
Herzoff, N., 274, 288
Hicks, D. J., 183, 190
Himmelweit, H. T., 172, 190
Hoffman, D., 220, 221, 236, 237, 247, 255, 329
Hoffman, H. R., 181, 190
Hoffman, L. R., 307
Hollon, S., 290
Holroyd, K. A., 274, 287
Holsti, O. R., 307
Holt, R. R., 127n, 328
Hornstein, H. A., 190, 214, 329
Houston, B. K., 278, 287
Hovland, C. I., 4, 5, 6, 9, 57, 63, 68, 89, 260, 307, 309, 320, 321, 325, 236, 328
Howard, J., 214, 330
Howe, C. D., 141, 144
Hoyt, M. F., 163, 165, 222, 255, 330

Hudson, B. B., 74, 77, 90
Hunt, W. A., 196, 214, 221, 222, 255
Huttel, F. A., 269, 287

Israel, J., 317

Jacobson, E., 2
Jaffe, A. J., 11n
Janis, I. L., 3, 4, 5, 11n, 25n, 39n, 55, 57,
    57n, 61, 67, 69, 72, 73, 74, 75, 77, 79
    81, 82, 83, 84, 87, 88, 89, 90, 93n,
    111, 113, 113n, 114, 115, 117, 118,
    119, 120, 123, 124, 127n, 130, 132,
    133, 135n, 138n, 139, 141, 145, 147n,
    148, 149, 150n, 151, 152n, 153, 154,
    155, 156, 158, 159, 160, 161, 163, 164,
    165, 166, 167n, 169, 173, 187, 190,
    193n, 197, 199, 200, 201, 205n, 206,
    209, 211, 214, 215, 217n, 219, 220,
    221, 222, 223, 226, 228, 229, 230, 231,
    232n, 233, 235, 236, 237, 238, 239,
    240, 241, 242, 243, 244, 245, 246,
    247, 248, 249, 250, 251, 252, 255, 256,
    257, 259n, 261, 262, 263, 264, 267,
    268, 270, 273, 274, 276, 277, 278, 279,
    280, 281, 282, 283, 287, 288, 289, 291,
    291n, 292, 293, 294n, 295, 302, 305,
    307, 308, 314, 316, 319, 320, 321, 322,
    323, 324–331
Janis, M. G., 259n, 320, 324
Janowitz, M., 324
Jansen, M. J., 123, 124
Jaremko, M., 259n, 265, 289, 331
Javert, C. T., 269, 287
Johnson, C. A., 148, 166
Johnson, D., 331
Johnson, J., 278, 289
Johnson, J. E., 262, 268, 271, 272, 286,
    287
Jonas, G., 294, 215
Jones, E. E., 148, 166, 199, 215
Jones, J. E., 308
Jones, M. R., 124, 165, 326
Jones, S., 277, 288
Jones, S. C., 199, 215

Kagan, J., 127n, 328
Kahneman, D., 170, 191, 271, 290
Kanfer, F., 278, 288
Kasl, S. V., 195, 196, 215
Katsch, E., 173, 189

Katz, D., 159, 166, 327
Kaye, D., 327
Kellett, D., 270, 290
Kelley, H. H., 57, 89, 307, 321, 325
Kelman, H. C., 113, 124, 327
Kendall, P. C., 274, 285, 288, 290
Kiesler, C. A., 249, 256, 279, 288
Killian, L. M., 77, 80, 81, 83, 88, 89, 90
Killilea, M., 276, 285
King, B. T., 113, 123, 321, 325, 326
Kirschner, P., 327
Klausmeir, H. J., 115, 125
Klausner, S., 327
Klein, E., 55
Klineberg, O., 3, 320
Knurek, D. A., 199, 215
Koch, S., 316, 317
Kochen, M., 190
Kogan, N., 301, 307, 308
Korsch, B. M., 214, 215
Kris, E., 2, 50, 56
Krumboltz, J. D., 218, 256

Labov, W., 227, 256
La Flamme, D., 164, 241, 256
Lambert, W., 328
Lamm, H., 301, 307, 308
Langdon-Davies, J., 55
Langer, E. J., 211, 212, 215, 222, 240, 241,
    243, 256, 268, 273, 274, 276, 288, 330
Lapidus, L. B., 259n, 278, 283, 288
Larsen, I. M., 308
Lasswell, H. D., 4, 320, 324
Lazarsfeld, P. F., 207, 215
Lazarus, R. S., 132, 133, 145, 268, 270,
    282, 283, 286, 288, 329
Leifer, A. D., 190
Leites, N. C., 324
Lemaze, F., 262, 288
Lerner, D., 190
Leslie, I. M., 39, 43, 55, 83, 89
Lesser, G. S., 183, 190, 191
Leventhal, H., 141, 145, 197, 215, 262,
    271, 272, 277, 282, 287, 288, 321,
    327, 328
Levin, S., 211, 216
Levine, D., 290
Levine, M., 141, 145
Levitt, R., 285
Levy, J. M., 262, 288
Lewin, K., 5, 6, 9, 309

Ley, P., 195, 215
Lifton, R. J., 115, 125
Lindberg, H. A., 195, 216
Lindeman, C. A., 272, 288
Lindemann, E., 87, 90
Lindskold, S., 197, 198, 216
Lindzey, G., 166, 176, 181, 189, 190, 256, 308, 317, 326
Linehan, M. M., 267, 286
Logan, L., 66, 77, 83, 88, 89, 90
Lumsdaine, A. A., 4, 11n, 132, 145, 321, 325
Lumsdaine, A. H., 270, 287
Lumsdaine, M. H., 11n
Lushene, R. E., 282, 290
Lyle, J., 181, 190

Maccoby, N., 176, 265, 288
MacCurdy, J. T., 2, 9,, 41–43, 44, 45, 46, 48, 49, 55, 56, 79, 83, 90
Mackintosh, J. M., 55
Maddox, G. L., 195, 215
Madge, 55
Maher, B. A., 285
Mahl, G., 127n, 328
Maier, N. R. F., 305, 308
Mandler, G., 307
Mann, L. A., 3, 6, 114, 124, 147n, 148, 150n, 151, 152n, 153, 155, 156, 157, 158, 159, 160, 161, 163, 166, 169, 173, 187, 190, 219, 239, 249, 256, 264, 277, 278, 279, 280, 282, 283, 287, 291, 293, 295, 307, 316, 321, 322, 323, 327, 328, 330, 331
Marks, E. S., 70, 77, 78, 83, 89
Marrs, W., 77, 83, 90
Marshall, W. L., 267, 290
Marston, M. V., 222, 256
Marwell, G., 198, 215
Matarazzo, J. D., 196, 214, 222, 255
Matte, I., 55, 261, 288
McAlister, A. L., 265, 288
McClintock, C. G., 159, 166
McFall, R. M., 279, 288
McGee, R. K., 262, 288
McGuire, C., 141, 144
McGuire, W. J., 113n, 120, 121, 123, 124, 125, 149, 166, 167, 190, 231, 256, 304, 308, 315, 316, 317, 321, 328
McKenzie, J., 327
McLeod, J. M., 183, 189

McMillan, K. L., 160, 165
Meehl, P., 304, 308
Meerloo, A. M., 56
Meichenbaum, D. H., 242, 256, 259n, 263, 265, 267, 275, 276, 288, 289, 331
Merton, R. K., 194–195, 196, 198, 199, 200, 206, 207, 208, 211, 213, 215, 321
Mewborn, C. R., 277, 289
Meyer, A. E., 269, 287
Milavsky, J. R., 175, 190
Milburn, T. W., 306
Milholland, W., 325
Miller, J. C., 248, 256, 329
Miller, N., 204
Mitchell, I., 269, 287
Moore, H. E., 83, 84, 85, 90
Mordkoff, A. M., 145
Morris, C. G., 303, 305, 307
Morris, M. J., 214
Morrissey, J. F., 271, 287
Moscovici, S., 301, 308
Mouton, J. S., 306
Muensterberger, W., 90, 326
Mulligan, W. L., 222, 224, 230, 231, 231n, 232n, 243, 249, 256
Murray, J. P., 189, 190
Myers, D. D., 301, 308

Nagai, T., 31, 37, 38
Nagel, S. S., 329
Nelson, B., 110
Nelson, L., 190
Neufeld, R. W. J., 289
Newcomb, T. M., 113n, 321, 328
Nisbett, R. E., 7, 9
Noel, R. C., 301, 306, 307
Nosow, S., 88, 89
Novaco, R., 267, 289
Nowell, C., 221, 238, 256

Oppenheim, A. N., 190
Ostrom, T., 124, 328

Paige, G. D., 308
Payne, J. W., 189
Pechacek, T. F., 274, 288
Pekowsky, B., 175, 190
Perry, C., 265, 288
Pervin, L. A., 270, 278, 289
Pfeiffer, J. W., 308

Phelps, D., 39, 43, 55, 83, 89
Platonov, K., 269, 290
Platt, J., 168, 190
Pliner, P., 331
Ploticher, V., 269, 290
Polivy, J., 331
Postman, L., 70, 89
Powell, J. W., 58–60, 87, 90
Pranulis, M., 278, 279, 289
Pruitt, D., 301, 308

Quinlan, D. M., 217n, 226, 229, 230, 232n,
    233, 248, 251, 252, 256, 323

Rabbie, J. M., 116, 125, 301, 308
Rachman, S. J., 260, 261, 289
Rado, S., 49, 56
Rathgen, D. J., 290
Rausch, C. N., 154, 155, 156, 166, 329
Raven, B. H., 197, 214, 292, 308
Rayner, J. F., 89
Redl, F., 95, 105, 111
Redlich, F., 328
Reed, H., 329
Reed, H. B., 239, 256
Reed, H. D., 158, 159, 166
Reeves, B., 183, 190
Regan, D. T., 199, 215
Rice, V. H., 268, 287
Rickman, J., 56
Riskind, J. H., 225, 226, 230, 235, 236,
    240, 244, 250, 252, 257, 275, 289
Rodin, J. R., 206, 211, 212, 215, 278, 287,
    289, 330, 331
Rogers, C., 199
Rogers, M. S., 308
Rogers, R. W., 277, 289
Rokeach, M., 159, 166
Romalis, F., 261, 289
Rosenberg, M. J., 113n, 117, 123, 125,
    321, 328
Rosentahal, R., 304, 308
Rosnow, R., 304, 308
Rossi, A. K., 198, 215
Rotter, J. B., 289
Rubin, J. Z., 308
Rubinstein, E. A., 189, 190

Sackett, D. L., 195, 196, 216
Sandler, J., 111
Sanford, N., 329

Sarason, I. G., 286, 331
Sarnoff, I., 159, 166
Sauer, C., 301, 307
Schachter, S., 74, 90
Schein, E. H., 115, 125
Schmideberg, M., 39, 50, 54, 55, 56, 88, 90
Schmidt, R. L., 262, 289
Schmitt, D. R., 198, 215
Schmitt, F. E., 262, 272, 289
Schramm, W., 327
Schoenberger, J. A., 195, 216
Schulz, R., 265, 289
Schwartz, G. E., 278, 290
Scriven, M., 314, 317
Seggar, J. F., 191
Seider, M. L., 278, 288
Seligman, M. E. P., 211, 216, 270, 278, 290
Seydewitz, M., 44, 55
Shank, R. C., 171, 191
Shaw, M. E., 200, 216, 290
Shewchuk, L. A., 196, 216
Shisslak, C., 274, 288
Shmurack, S., 267, 286
Shugon, E., 269, 290
Shure, G. H., 305, 308
Siemes, Father, 29, 37
Silver, H., 141, 145
Sime, A. M., 282, 290
Simon, H. A., 7, 9, 148, 166, 308
Simon, K., 218, 254, 275, 285
Simpson, R., 214
Singer, D. G., 185, 191
Singer, J. E., 331
Singer, J. L., 172, 181, 185, 191
Singer, R. E., 277, 288
Slovic, P., 316, 317
Small, S., 86, 89
Smith, A. D., 222, 225, 230, 257
Smith, J. L., 267, 286
Smith, M. B., 4, 55, 131, 145, 316, 317,
    321, 327
Smith, T. L., 215
Snyder, R., 307
Sobel, R., 102, 111
Sofer, C., 327
Speisman, J. C., 145
Spelman, M. S., 195, 215
Spiegel, J. P., 72, 77, 88, 90, 91, 326
Spielberger, C. D., 282, 286, 290, 331
Stamler, J., 195, 216
Stanley, J. C., 115, 125, 306

Star, S. A., 145
Staub, E., 270, 278, 290
Stein, B., 182
Steiner, I. D., 295, 303, 308
Stern, J., 55
Stipp, H., 175, 190
Stocker-Kreichgauer, G., 291n, 308, 331
Stolorow, L. M., 123, 124
Stone, G. C., 215, 222, 257, 286, 287, 330
Stoner, J. A. F., 301, 308
Stouffer, S. A., 4, 11n, 55, 94, 111, 145, 260, 287, 320, 324
Strauss, A., 214, 330
Suedfeld, P., 299
Sullivan, H. S., 74, 91

Tajfel, H., 317
Tannenbaum, P. H., 113n, 328
Tanzer, D., 269, 290
Taranta, A., 214
Tassone, J., 308
Taylor, F. G., 267, 290
Taylor, S., 211, 216, 331
Tedeschi, J. T., 197, 198, 216
Terwilliger, R., 327
Tetlock, P. E., 298–299, 308
Thayer, P. W., 89
Thistlethwaite, D. L., 277, 289
Titchner, J., 141, 145
Titmuss, R. M., 55
Tjosvold, D., 331
Toomey, M., 160, 166
Turk, D. C., 242, 256, 259n, 265, 267, 269, 276, 278, 289, 290
Tursky, B., 278, 290
Tursky, E., 214
Tversky, A., 170, 191, 271, 290

Valins, S., 252, 255, 286
Van Aernam, B., 272, 288
Varela, J. A., 305, 308
Velvoysky, I., 269, 290
Vernon, D. T. A., 262, 290
Vernon, P. E., 53, 55, 56, 82, 91
Vince, P., 190
Vincent, P., 196, 216
Visintainer, M. A., 272, 290
Visser, L., 301, 308
Vogler, R. E., 270, 278, 285

Wackman, D. B., 183, 191
Wallach, M. A., 301, 307, 308
Walster, E. H., 156, 157, 166, 199, 203, 213, 216
Walster, G. W., 213, 216
Ward, S., 183, 191
Weinberg, L., 265, 286
Weiss, J. A., 307
Weiss, J. M., 270, 278, 290
Welch, C., 142, 143n, 144, 262, 272, 286
Werner, R. J., 195, 213
Westbrook, T., 274, 287
Westlake, R. J., 206, 213
Wheeler, D., 322, 330, 331
Wheeler, P., 191
Whittemore, R., 214
Wicklund, R. A., 157, 166
Wiggins, J. S., 165
Wilde, O., 127
Willerman, B., 145
Williams, L., 274, 288
Williams, M., 307
Williams, R. M., Jr., 4, 11n, 55, 145, 326
Wilson, T. D., 7, 9
Wineman, D., 105, 111
Wishlade, L., 327
Withey, S. B., 71, 91, 167n, 330
Wittkower, E. A., 87, 91
Wolfenstein, M., 61, 70, 74, 82, 83, 84, 91, 264, 290
Wolfer, J. A., 215, 222, 240, 241, 243, 256, 268, 272, 273, 274, 276, 288, 290, 330
Wolman, B., 145, 215, 327
Wong-McCarthy, W., 292, 299, 308
Wood, H. F., 214
Woodworth, R. S., 3, 320
Wooldridge, P. J., 262, 272, 289
Wright, 21

Yudkin, J., 327

Zander, A., 93n, 200, 214, 285, 328
Zavalloni, M., 301, 308
Zimbardo, P. G., 123, 125, 267, 290, 321
Zitter, R. E., 267, 286
Zola, I. K., 196, 216
Zweling, I., 141, 145

Subject Index

A-Bomb attacks, results of, 26, 34
Abandonment, fears of, 74, 104
Acceptance, contingent, noncontingent and unconditional, 202
Accidents. *See* Disasters
Acute: anxiety, 27, 39, 94; depression, 27; emotional shock, 33; fear, 27, 39; pain, 268; panic, 68, psychoses, 28
Adaptive: attitudes, 4, 165; emotions, 79–80, 128–131; compromise formations, 80, 84; defenses, 100; discriminations, 131; learning processes, 130;
Adherence: factor of, 194, 231, 244; long-term, 250; unconflicted, 148
Adjustment: human, 25; postdanger, 140; postoperative, 283
Administrative sciences, 304
Adult relationships, 97
Advertising and advertisements, 187; television, 175
Advisory groups, presidential, 292
Age, factor of, 138, 142
Agencies: governmental, 131, 291, 304; health, 176; law enforcement, 168
Aggrandizement, personal, 108
Aggrievement, feelings of, 212, 262
Agitation, factor of, 147
Air attacks, 27; conventional, 25, 28, 35; magnitude of, 40–42
Air crews and officers: in combat, 19–24, 47, 51; motivations of, 22
Air raids: anxiety over, 52–53; shelters for, 37, 48
Air Surgeon, Office of the, 22

Air War and Emotional Stress (Janis), cited, 25–26, 39, 94
Alcoholism and alcoholics, problems of, 175, 195, 231, 264, 311
Alternative courses of action, 147
Ambiguity, hypothesis of, 70, 88, 243
Ambivalence: latent, 194; psychological, 194, 208–210; sociological, 194, 196, 206–212; source of, 201, 207
American Cancer Society, 239
American Psychiatric Association, Military Mobilization Committee of, 43
American Soldier, The: Combat and its Aftermath (Stouffer, ed.), cited, 4, 11, 94, 260
Amplitude, finger-pulse, 147
Anger and rage, feelings of, 135, 242, 262
Antecedent warnings, 75
Anti-group think program, 298, 305
Anti-smoking campaigns and clinics, 160, 197, 220–221, 237, 239, 248, 277, 280, 305, 322
Anti-social attitudes and behavior, 27, 95, 107–108, 182–183
Anticipated: anxieties, 49; danger, 62–63, 72; disaster, 71; fear, 134–137, 140, 144, 264; restriction of activity, 73–74; stress, 263
Anxiety: acute, 27, 39, 94; air-raid, 52–53; anticipatory, 49; chronic, 102; events, 273; levels of, 2, 33, 242, 259–260, 314, 322; neurotic, 61; objective, 28, 61; phobic, 265; preoperative, 282–283 reactions to, 11–12, 272; reduction of,

14, 54; on separation, 96; severe, 29, 136; social, 105, 267; sources, 88; symptoms, 19–24, 40, 47, 51, 266
Apathy: feelings of, 31–33, 36, 53; prolonged, 28
Appeals, effects of, 5, 323
Appetite, loss of, 147
Apprehensiveness: extreme, 58; feelings of, 36, 40, 105; prevention of, 132
Approval: group, 107; motivation, 280
Arkansas, tornadoes in, 77
Arousal: of conflict, 149; emotional, 314; of fear, 5, 276, 314; of hostility, 115; physiological, 266; and reassurance needs, 62; of stress, 148
Atlanta, Georgia, 63
Atomic warfare, 23–26, 33–34
Attitude(s): adaptive, 4, 165; anti-social, 27, 95, 107–108, 182–183; changes, 1, 3–8, 63, 114–115, 124, 309; combat, 18; maladaptive, 4, 165; morale, 4; negative, 235; postdisaster, 26; questionnaires on, 117; research on, 3–6; self-defeating, 315; source of, 4; types of, 180, 198; verbal measures of, 7, 313
Authority figures, factor of, 74, 88, 95–96, 100, 202, 206, 210, 246, 263
Automatic habitual responses, 13
Avoidance: ambiguity, 243; defensive, 149, 155–158, 160, 239, 278, 281, 293, 295, 314; overt behavior, 30
Awareness: of danger, 68; of rationalization technique, 159, 239

Backsliding: factor of, 222, 237, 248, 253, 277–278, 280; postdecisional, 218; recidivism, 264, temptation to, 203
Balance sheet hypothesis, 165, 173, 185; defective, 163, 174; irrelevant and relevant, 163; procedure, 160–163, 228, 240, 295, 303
Battle inoculation features, stimuli for, 12, 14–15, 18, 266
Bay of Pigs fiasco, 322–323
Behavior: adaptive, 4; decision-making, 186, delinquent, 104–106; deviant, 109; disaster, 57; emotional, 40; exploitative, 109; group, 95, 110; human, 254, 309; hypervigilant, 80, 88; maladaptive, 2, 4, 57, 60–61, 66–67, 78, 84, 86; overt, 26–27, 30; panic, 27; patterns of, 101;

personal, 202; postdecisional, 270; social, 6, 96; verbal, 223
Behavioral: control, 270; disturbances, 34; effects, 167, 315; measures, 313–315; quasi indicators, 313; research methods, 298; scientists, 1–2, 8, 148, 161, 213; standards, 200; symptoms, 22
Beliefs: changes in, 63; ideological, 180, 182. See also Attitudes
Bereavement, feelings of, 131, 144
Biofeedback, training in, 204
Biological effects, delayed, 28
Black marketeering, factor of, 109
Blanket reassurances, 63–70, 85–86, 89
Blitztowns, factor of, 41
Blood donations, 230, 249
Bolstering, mechanism of, 153–154
Bombing attacks, 25–26, 29–35, 52–53
Breakdowns, neurotic, 51
Buck passing, habit of, 158
Buffalo, New York, 170
Bureaucracy and politics, 148

Career: changes, 164, 200; counseling, 217, 241; decisions, 181, 241, 311; failures, 144; plans, 313; types of, 169, 173, 184, 186, 219, 240
Casualties, psychiatric, 33–34, 41, 102. See also Disasters
Catastrophes, impact of, 25
Cause and effect relationships, 309
Censure, social, 110
Change and changes: agents of, 3, 217; attitude, 1–8, 63, 114–115, 124, 309; career, 164, 200; research on, 3–6; unconflicted, 149
Chicago, University of, 320
Childbirth: preparation for, 269; stress of, 283
Children, socialization of, 173
Chronic: anxiety, 102; mental disorder, 28, pain, 267, 269; tension, 47; traumatic neuroses, 39
Civil disobedience, examples of, 154
Civilian population, British, 39, German, 44
Clinical: psychoanalysts, 49; psychologists, 265, 275
Coercion, power of, 198
Cohesiveness, degrees of, 200, 299, 302
Columbia University, 3, 320–321
Combat: attitude toward, 18; danger, 12;

duty, 22; experience, 15; fear, 260; groups, 94; skills, 12–13; stress, 11; troops, 19–24, 47, 51; veterans, 18

Commercials, value of, 175, 179, 181, 183, 186

Communications: absence of, 75; educational, 274; emotion arousing, 8; fear arousing, 314; forms of, 203, 211, 251; mass, 57, 169; norm-sending, 248; persuasive, 149, 277, 314, 321; preparatory, 131–132, 141–143, 259, 264, 278; public health, 5; telephone, 88; verbal, 70, 87; warning, 57–58, 62, 131

Community: disasters, 61, 72, 75, 141; leadership, 73; life, 29, 218; resources, 69

Compassion and complacency, feelings of, 209, 244

Complaints: physical, 23; psychosomatic, 21

Compromise formations: adaptive, 80, 84; development of, 63–66, 85, 89

Concurrence-seeking tendencies, 292, 298, 303

Conduct, standards of, 95

Conflict: arousal of, 149; effects of, 147; models of, 155–157, 282; theory of, 114, 117, 120, 153–155, 165, 282

Conformity, group, 101

Conscience and conscious defense mechanizations, 49, 107

Constraints, ethical, 250

Contamination, worries over, 36

Contingency plans, 202, 271–272

Continuity, principle of, 156–157

Control(s): behavioral, 270; cognitive, 283; data, 220; disaster, 69, 73, 88; fear, 12–16; groups, 51, 113, 132, 142, 212, 274; interviews, 161; personal, 240

Conventional: morality, 63; warfare, 25, 28, 35, 47

Conversion hysteria, 33

Coping techniques, need for, 239, 266, 272–273, 284

Counseling: career, 217, 241; decision, 218–219; health, 206; interviews, 227; long-term, 242, 246, 253; marital, 241; session procedures, 3, 132–134, 233–236, 242, 263, 312; short-term, 220–223, 236, 247, 253–254; vocational, 229

Counselor(s), 218–222, 225, 229; and client relationship, 242; health, 222; norms of, 203; professional, 3, 184, 193, 200, 208, 228; sincerity of, 245

Crime shows, suspect entertainment value of, 173

Criticism: acceptance of, 296; factor of, 243–246; of laboratory studies, 304

Cues: danger, 86; environmental, 62; nonverbal, 245; threat, 71

Culture, indicators of, 180

Danger: anticipated, 62–63, 72; awareness of, 68–69; combat, 12; cues, 86; disruptive effects of, 127; exposure to, 47, 62; external, 93; indifference to, 77; physical, 11, 26, 95; potential, 57, 66, 69–70, 139; reactions to, 16; of surgery, 136; wartime situations, 94

Death: fear of, 50; losses through, 78

Decisions, decision-making and decision makers, 1, 6, 114, 147–149, 156, 159, 165, 170, 177, 184, 309, 322; behavior, 186; career, 158, 181, 241, 311; conflict coping, 2; consumer, 168; counseling, 218–219; emergency, 3; fiascoes, 188, 293–295; foreign policy, 292; group, 298; groupthink, 299; health-related, 151, 158, 176, 186; informed, 210; marital, 158, 311; morality, 293; non-groupthink, 299; personal, 7, 168, 180; policy, 295, 311; political, 168; procedural states, 115, 160, 185–187, 218, 241, 296; quality of, 186–188, 291; research on, 6–8; vigilant, 157, 239

Defeatism, feelings of, 4, 35, 45

Defective balance sheet hypothesis, 161, 163, 174

Defenses: adaptive, 100; mechanisms of, 2, 49; psychological, 14, 52

Defensive avoidance, effects of, 3, 149, 153–160, 239, 278, 281, 293, 295, 314

Defensiveness, reduction in, 158

Delinquency, problems of, 104–106

Democracy, values of, 182

Demoralization: factor of, 4, 57, 178, 197, 213, 233, 251, 263, 265; group, 101

Dependency: emotional, 210; phenomenon of, 96; problem of, 253

Depression: acute, 27; classical symptoms

of, 103; feelings of, 2, 22, 31–33, 53, 262, 267, 321; mild, 39; pathological forms of, 102; reaction to, 27, 36, 102–104
Desensitization, feelings of, 129–130
Determinants, factors of, 87–88
Deviant behavior informal code, 107, 109
Devil's advocate, role of, 296
Diets and dieting: and clinics, 217, 238, 310–311; problem of, 193, 195, 200, 208, 225, 231, 240, 243, 249, 252, 275, 280, 322
Disability and disapprovals, 210, 279
Disaster: anticipated, 71; behavior, 57, 131; control, 69, 73, 88; community, 61, 72, 75, 141; flood, 10; nonprecipitant, 78; precipitant, 78; studies, 264; toxicological, 61; victims, 2; wartime, 27, 33, 262
Disclosure interviews: high, 234–236; intimate, 234–235; moderate, 234–235, 244; positive, 225–226
Discovery phase, factor of, 300
Discrimination and job dislocation, 131
Disobedience, civil, 154
Disorder(s): chronic mental, 28; emotional, 265–266; neurotic, 136; physical, 265–266; psychopathological, 33; psychosomatic, 265
Dissonance: effects of, 120, 122; magnitude of, 116; theory, 114, 116, 118, 156
Disturbances: behavioral, 34; emotional, 36, 48, 58, 131; post-disaster, 34
Divine protection, call on, 63
Divorce, effects of, 131, 164, 174, 219, 264
Dizziness, causes of, 21, 153
Docility, excessive, 53
Drugs, illicit, 175
Dysphoria, problem of, 99, 105

Economists and the economy, 131, 291, 304
Education: college educated persons, 155; communications in, 274; factor of, 138, 315; films used in, 221; student morale, 248; and teaching skills; television use in, 184–185
Efficiency, mental, 68, 102
Ego: functions, 64, 123; ideals, 95, 101
Electroconvulsive treatments, 321
Emergency: centers, 48; decisions, 3;

medical, 176; reactions, 71; warnings, 78, 148
Emotional: adaptation, 79, 128–131; arousal, 8, 314; behavior, 40; communications, 8; dependency, 210; disorders, 265–266; disturbances, 30, 36, 48, 58, 131; excitement, 27, 149; inoculation, 2, 142, 263, 322; learning, 86; needs, 97; reactions, 15; recovery, 179; role-playing, 159–160, 239; shock, 28, 33, 39; status, 14; stress, 29, 47; tension, 26, 53, 62, 135; trauma, 27
Empathy: feelings of, 199, 213, 243; mutual, 208
Energy, Department of, 291
Entertainment programs, 167, 171–174, 177, 181, 186
Environment and environmental conditions, 67; influence of, 62; physical and social, 72; stress caused by, 25; urban, 168
Epidemics, problem of, 87
Equity, need for, 212
Errors of omission, factor of, 161, 174
Escape routes and opportunities, 72, 74, 78
Esteem, loss of, 95
Ethical: constraints, 250; standards, 249, 293
Ethnic origins, influence of, 138
Europe, customs in, 210
Examinations, medical, 22
Excitement, emotional, 27, 149
Experience(s): childhood separation, 74; narrow-escape, 26, 28; near-miss, 46–47, 50, 53, 83; remote-miss, 83; stress, 4; wartime, 3, 15
Experimental: evidence, 151–156; linguistics, 322; psychology, 3, 113; research, 251, 299; studies, 300
Experiments: field, 1, 8–9, 206, 217, 220, 223–226, 241–242, 246, 252, 274, 284, 291, 298, 300, 310, 312, 320–321, 323; laboratory, 8, 291; preparatory communications, 131–132
Expert power, 198–199
Explanatory theories, 5
Explicit versus implicit themes, 179–181
Exploitation, intent of, 109, 243

Face-to-face: groups, 93–95, 100; sessions, 208, 244, 251
Failures, career, 144

Factory employees, factor of, 110
False alarms: episodes of, 82, 87; sensitizing effects of, 80–82
Family: problems, 184, 263; service clinic, 164
Fantasies, factor of, 49–50
Fatigue: excessive, 34, 36; neurotic, 33; operational, 22; unremitting, 47
Fear(s): of abandonment, 74, 104; acute, 27, 39; alleviation of, 98; anticipatory, 134–137, 140, 144, 264; appeal effects of, 323; arousal of, 5, 57, 276, 314; in combat, 260; conditioned, 48; of contamination, 36; control of, 12–16; of death, 50; levels of, 11, 71, 85; neurotic, 62; normal, 61; postoperative, 135–137; preoperative, 283; of punishment, 52; reaction to, 12, 18, 36, 40, 45, 48, 52; reduction of, 14, 85; reflective, 61–63; 66, 68; sharing of, 100; stimuli, 13
Feedback: factor of, 314; negative, 161, 223, 243, 247; neutral, 223–226, 230, 232, 243–245, 247; positive, 206, 223–232, 236, 238, 243–244, 246–248; verbal, 224
Fiascoes, decision-making, 188, 293–295, 322–323
Fictitious scenarios, factor of, 171–172
Field: experiments, 1, 8–9, 206, 217, 220, 223–226, 241–242, 246, 252, 274, 277, 284, 291, 298, 300, 310, 312, 320–321, 323; research methods, 6; studies, 6
Films, education, entertainment and training, 221, 239, 271
Financing and funding: federal, 41; personal, 3
Finger-pulse amplitude, 147
Firemen and fire alarms, 76, 83, 88
Fires, incendiary, 41–42
First aid, cases of, 43
Flexibility, physical and mental need for, 283, 22
Floods and flooding, problems of, 70, 76, 88
Folklore, influence of, 70
Food and food supplies, 29–30
Foreign policy, decisions on, 292
Friends, influence of, 263, 267
Frustration, feelings of, 196, 208, 210

Galvanic skin response, factor of, 147

Germany, 27–28, 46, 261; army of, 94; civilians in, 44
Governmental agencies, 131, 291, 304
Great Britain, 27–28, 41, 43–46, 54, 64, 77, 88, 261; army of, 94; civilians in, 39
Group(s): approval, 107; behavior, 95, 110; combat, 94; conformity, 101; consensus, 293; control, 51, 113, 132, 142, 212, 274; decisions, 298; demoralization, 101; face-to-face, 93–95, 100; identification, 93–94, 102, 104; peer, 105; polarization, 301; policy planning, 291, 296–299; pressure, 148; primary, 74, 93, 97, 105; psychology, 97; public interest, 176; self-study, 305; social, 182; solidarity, 93; work, 98, 103, 291
Group Psychology (Freud), cited, 104
Groupthink hypothesis, 3, 293, 299, 301–302; consequences of, 298, 301, 305; counteracting, 298, 305; decisions of, 299; phenomena, 291–292; symptoms of, 292
Guilt: factor of, 94, 105, 119, 229; feelings of, 36, 53, 94, 102, 107, 109, 228; reactions to, 31, 52; sharing of, 105, 110; survivor, 31

Hamburg, Germany, 44
Handicaps, overcoming of, 178
Headaches, causes of, 21, 153
Health: agencies, 176; care, 194, 197–199, 208, 210, 212, 218; concern over, 21, 23; counseling, 206, 222; decisions on, 151, 158, 163, 176, 186; hazards, 3, 61, 169, 183; instructions, 176; mental, 131, 176, 264; organizations, 131; professionals, 194, 197–199, 208, 210, 212; public, 5; social, 180–181, 197–199
Heart rate, causes of, 147
Helplessness, feelings of, 50, 84, 140, 211, 262–263
Hierarchy, organizational, 306
Hiroshima, bombing of, 25–26, 29–32, 35, 37
Hope and hopelessness, feelings of, 32, 225, 263, 275, 278, 303
Hospital(s): facilities, 32, 197–198; need for, 208, 284; teaching, 195
Hostility, arousal of, 115
Housing facilities, restoration of, 32

Human: adjustment, 25; behavior, 254,
   309; reactions, 132; relationships, 181
Humiliation, feelings of, 95
Hurricane damage and warnings, 80-82
Hurricane Florence, scare of, 80, 82
Hyperaggressiveness, tendency to, 22
Hypertension, problem of, 195, 204
Hypervigilance hypothesis, 3, 83, 85, 149,
   151, 155, 157, 282; and behavior, 80,
   88; extreme, 71; maladaptive, 86; and
   panic, 160; reactions to, 66-68, 75
Hypovigilance: extreme, 70-71; reactions
   to, 67
Hysteria, problem of, 59

Identification: group, 93-94, 102, 104;
   post-bereavement, 101; process of, 103
Ideologies and ideals, 101, 180, 182
Illicit drugs, use of, 175
Illness and ill-health, 131; psychosomatic,
   34; severe, 141; threat of, 61, 96
Images: body, 228; mental, 170; visual,
   169
Immorality, factor of, 106, 116
Implicit versus explicit themes, 179-181
Incendiary battle attacks, 28, 41-42
Incentives, social, 212
Information: preparatory, 262, 264, 267-
   270, 281; processing, 2, 149, 154, 187;
   role of, 137; search, 151-152; unambig-
   uous, 69-70
Information-Education Division, Research
   Branch of, 4
Inhibitions, unlearning of, 107
Injury, losses to, 78
Inoculation: battle, 14, 266; emotional, 2,
   142, 263, 322; stress, 2, 239, 259,
   265, 267, 270, 272-275, 321-322
Insights, technique of, 159
Insincerity, feelings of, 243
Instructions, health-related, 176
Internationalization, role playing in, 5
Interpersonal: contacts, 3, 99; sensitivity,
   199; skills, 203
Intervention: decisional process, 218;
   effects of, 1; placebo, 274; relationship
   building, 218; studies, 283
Interviews: intensive, 80, 136; clinical, 58,
   261; control, 161; counseling, 227;
   follow up, 229, 237-238, 245; high disclosure, 234-236; intake, 229-231, 234,

245, 250; moderate disclosure, 234-
   235, 244; morale, 30-33; open-ended,
   313; positive disclosure, 225-226; responses, 45; results of, 6, 34, 94, 143,
   164, 174, 224; routine, 228; self-
   disclosure, 163; standard, 26; telephone,
   229
Intimate disclosures, 234-235
Introjection, process of, 100-101
Investigations, research, 242
Involvement, personal, 43-44, 53
Invulnerability: feelings of, 48-52, 63, 136,
   292; illusion of, 293; personal, 2, 136,
   144
Irrelevant balance-sheet condition, 163
Irresponsibility, problem of, 173
Irritability, feelings of, 22

Japan and the Japanese, 27-28, 46, 73,
   261; morale of, 26
Job dislocations, problem of, 131

Kansas City, floods and fires in, 76-77, 88

Laboratory: experiments, 8, 291; sessions,
   313; studies, 304
Lafayette Oracle, 319
Law enforcement and lawyers, 168, 218
Leaders and leadership; civic, 75; com-
   munity, 73; position styles of, 16, 302
Learning: adaptive process of, 130; emo-
   tional, 86; principles of, 2, 180
Leedy, Oklahoma, 77
Libraries, lending and public, 188
Life styles: changes in, 174; factor of,
   169, 181, 198; and love life, 3
Linguistics, experimental, 322
Liquor episode, poison, 58-61, 87
Liverpool, England, 195
Long-term: adherence, 250; counseling,
   242, 246, 253
Low-threat reactions and warnings, 66, 70

Maladaptive: behavior, 2, 4, 57, 60-61,
   66-67, 78, 84, 86, 165; hypervigilance,
   86
Malnutrition, problem of, 29
Malpractice suits, 194, 211
Man, Morals and Society (Flugel), cited, 95
Marital: counseling, 241; decisions, 158,
   311; differences, 233; problems, 144,
   163, 184, 188, 200

Marriage, state of, 169, 181, 186, 188, 200, 219

Mass: communications, 57, 169; media, 75, 131

Medical: aid, 31, examinations, 22; emergencies, 176; research, 209; treatment, 4, 174. *See also* Health

Meditation, need for, 218–219

Melancholia, features of, 103

Melbourne, University of, 153

Memory, functioning of, 180, 321

Mental: chronic disorders, 28; efficiency, 68, 102; health, 131, 176, 264; images, 170; processes, 22

Methanol poisoning, 59

Miami, Oklahoma, floods in, 77

Military: morale, 4; personnel, 19–24, 36, 47, 51; research, 4; stress, 100; training, 4

Military Mobilization Committee of the American Psychiatric Association, 43

Moderate disclosure interviews, 234–235, 244

Moral: code, 109; scripts, 182; standards, 101

Morale: attitudes, 4; deterioration in, 44; high, 134; interviews, 30, 32–33; Japanese, 26; military, 4; research organizations, 94; student, 248; surveys of, 4, 32, 34, 44, 97; of survivors, 34–35

Morality: conventional, 63; decisions on, 293

Motivation: approval, 280; factor of, 157, 218; norm-setter, 204; power, 201, 209, 223, 228, 230, 236, 238, 242, 246, 280; sources of, 101; test of, 245

Motor dexterity, 22

Mourning: and introjection, 100–101; pathological, 101; work of, 100, 103, 139

Mourning and Melancholia (Freud), cited, 103

Muscular tension, 62

Mutilation, fear of, 179–182

Nagasaki, bombing of, 25–26, 30–32, 35–37

Narcissism: feelings of, 52, 105; reactive, 103

Narrow-escape experiences, 26, 28, 50

National Archives, 26

National health organizations, 131

National Heart and Lung Institute, 176

National Research Council, 72

National Science Foundation (NSF), 323

Nausea, causes of, 21, 153

Naziism and evilness, 4

Near-miss: concepts of, 2, 41–44, 48; experiences, 46–47, 50, 83; reinterpretation of, 82–87

Negativism: feedback on, 161, 223, 243, 247; feelings of, 114, 135, 137, 235

Neuroses: chronic, 39; signs of, 34; traumatic, 28, 36, 39, 83

Neurotic: anxiety, 61; breakdowns, 51; disorders, 136; fatigue reaction, 33; fear, 62; personalities, 142; symptoms, 43

Neutral feedback, 223–226, 230–232, 243–247

New York Psychoanalytic Institute, 2

News services and releases, 75, 131

Newscasts, 171–173, 179

Newspapers, influence of, 170, 176. *See also* Mass media

Nonadherence, specter of, 194–198

Noncontigent acceptance, 202

Nongroupthink decisions, 299

Nonovert role-playing conditions, 117–118

Nonprecipitant disasters, 78

Nonverbal cues, 245

Norm-setting functions, 200–201, 204, 209

Normative reference power, 198, 201, 208

North Sea, floods caused by, 88

NSA scores, 21

Nurses and nursing home residents, 211, 218, 263

Obedience, postponed, 101

Objective anxiety, 28, 61

Occupations: hazardous, 63; role of, 173–175

Oklahoma, University of, 76, 88

"Old Sergeant" syndrome, 102–104

Omission, errors of, 161, 174

Open-ended interviews, 313

Operational fatigue, symptoms of, 22

Operations, surgical, 2, 141, 193

Opportunities, escape, 72–74, 78

Optimism, feelings of, 42; unwarranted, 295

Organizations: health, 131; and hierarchical procedures, 306

Outcome psychodrama, results of, 163, 141-142

Overeating, results of, 238, 248. *See also* Diets and dieting

Overreactions, 67-68, problems of,

Overt: behavior, 26-27, 30; role playing, 116-119

Pain, 196, 242; acute, 268; chronic, 267, 269; unbearable, 12

Panama City, Florida, 80, 82

Panic, 149; acute, 68; behavior, 278; hypervigilant, 160

Paraprofessionals, positions of, 218

Parent Teachers' Association, 169, 171

Parents: figure status of, 233; as surrogates 74, 95

Partnerships: high-contact, 237-238; setting up of, 236-238

Passivity, feelings of, 84

Pathological: depression forms of, 102; mourning, 101

Patients; surgical, 67, 100, 103, 133-134

Peer groups, 105; pressures of, 265

Permissiveness, atmosphere of, 98

Persistent phobias, 34-36, 267

Personal: aggrandizement, 108; behavior, 202; conscience, 107; control, 240; decision-making, 7, 168, 180; finances, 3; involvement, 43-44, 53; invulnerability, 2, 136, 144; losses, 53; responsibility, 203, 209, 211; safety, 50; survival, 26; scripts, 169-172, 175; vulnerability, 82, 160, 239

Personality: characteristics, 16, 130, 309; measures, 314; neurotic, 142; predispositions, 51; research, 284, 315-316; variables, 280, 283

Personnel: occupation troops, 109; military, 19-24, 36, 47, 51, 73, 93, 96-97, 107

Persuasion, tactics of, 149, 277, 314, 321

Pessimism: feelings of, 158, 311; prevention of, 132

Phenomena, ranges of, 291-292

Phobias, 265-266; persistent, 34, 36

Physical: complaints, 23; conditions, 21-22; dangers, 11, 26, 95; disorders, 265-266; environment, 72; therapists, 197

Physicians: patient relationships of, 206-

210; professional role of, 194, 196-199, 211, 218, 222, 263, 267, 280

Physicians for Social Responsibility organization, 323

Pitcher, Oklahoma, 77

Placebos, use of, 274

Plans and planning, concept of, 171, 291, 297-298, 304, 313

Poisons and poisoning episodes, liquor, 58-61, 87; methanol, 59

Polarization tendencies, factor of, 301

Policy: decisions, 295, 311; making, 3, 151, 296, 299; planning, 291, 297-298, 304

Politics and political activities, 148, 168, 304

Positive: disclosure interviews, 225-226; feedbacks, 206, 223-226, 228-232, 236, 238, 243-248; self-talk, 266, 285; social reinforcement, 199

Post-bereavement identification, 101

Post-danger adjustments, 40

Post-decisional: behavior, 270; backsliding, 218; crisis, 264-265; regrets, 156; setbacks, 218, 239, 262, 295; stress, 241, 281

Postdisaster: attitudes, 26; disturbances, 34; periods, 29, 32, 36; reactions, 28-30

Postoperative: adjustments, 135-137; periods, 133, 139, 142; stress, 144, 282

Power: coercive, 198; expert, 198-199; motivating, 201, 209, 223, 228, 230, 236, 238, 242, 246, 280; referent, 193, 197-201, 204-205, 208, 213, 217, 230, 242, 246; social, 197-201, 209; source of, 198

Powerlessness, feelings of, 51

Precipitant disasters, 78

Predictability, factor of, 151-152, 270

Predisaster: periods of, 70, 87; reactions, 65; warnings, 72

Predispositions, influence of, 51

Prejudices: blind, 148; social, 159

Preoperative anxiety, 282-283

Preparatory communications and information, 131-132, 141-143, 259, 264, 267-270, 278, 281

Prescriptive hypothesis, 298-301, 303, 315

Presidential advisory groups, effects of, 292

Pressures: group, 148; peer, 265; psychological, 295

Primary groups, factor of, 74, 93, 97, 105

Problem-solving techniques, 305, 322
Procrastination, problem of, 151, 155, 158
Professional: counselors, 3, 184, 193, 200, 208, 228; health roles, 110, 194–199, 208, 210
Propaganda, Fascist and Nazi, 4
Protective action, need for, 81
Psychiatric: casualties, 33–34, 41, 102; studies, 39
Psychoanalysis and psychoanalysts, 96; clinical, 49; Freudian, 2
Psychodrama: outcome of, 163, 241–242; procedures of, 164, 235, 239, 250; role of, 271
Psychological: ambivalence, 194, 208–210; arousal, 266; defenses, 14, 52; pressures, 295; replacement, 97; social hypothesis, 6, 8, 155–156, 200, 203, 276; stress, 1, 4, 11, 48–49, 61, 94, 100, 148–149, 158, 309; ttauma, 2–3, 8
Psychologists, 147, 171, 218, 254; clinical, 275; developmental, 183; research, 4, 312, social, 6–7, 198, 260, 292
Psychology: experimental, 3, 113; group, 97; social, 3, 5, 113, 284, 309–312, 315–316, 320; of stress, 131; training in, 316; of warnings, 57
Psychoneurotic: manifestations, 43; patients, 96; symptoms, 61; tendencies, 21
Psychopathological disorders, 33
Psycho-social theory, 213
Psychoses, 36; acute, 28; increase in, 39; signs of, 34
Psychosomatic: disorders, 34, 265; complaints, 21; symptoms, 147
Psychotherapy, 3, 98, 137, 231, 242
Psychotics, problem of, 67, 321
Public: health, 5; libraries, 188; interest groups, 176; opinion polls, 227; utilities, 32
Punishment, fear of, 52

Quality of decision-making, 186–188, 291
Quasi-: behavioral indicators, 313; experimental studies, 300; projection mechanisms, 105
Queens, New York, 87
Questionnaires: attitude, 117; post-treatment, 226; surveys, 135; use of, 6, 19, 128, 174, 184, 313

Questions: priming, 117–118; socio-historical, 179

Radiation, sickness from, 29–31, 36, 87
Radio, use and influence of, 170, 176
Rationalizations, making of, 106, 149, 158–159, 239
Reactance theory and reactions, patterns of, 11–15, 28–31, 52, 59, 65–68, 71, 75, 82–87, 97, 157, 263–264, 272
Readiness, actional, 71–74
Realism and real life, 6–7, 259
Reassurance, 263; blanket, 63–70, 85–86, 89; need for, 62, 84, 97–100; social, 131; source of, 74; tendencies, 67–70
Recidivism and recidivists, 195, 264
Recognition and recovery, 31, 179
Recurrent themes, exposure to, 176–178
Red Cross organization, 222, 224, 230–231, 249
Referent power: building of, 204–205; concept of, 193, 197, 200, 213, 217, 230, 242, 246; normative, 198, 201, 208
Reflective fear: functional properties of, 61–63; levels of, 64, 68–69, 73, 78, 85; mild, 66
Regressive thought processes, 68
Regret, postdecisional reflections on, 156
Rejection, feelings of, 243, 246
Relationship building interventions, 218
Relaxation, exercises for, 266
Remorse, feelings of, 105
Remote-misses, hypothesis on, 2, 42, 47–49, 53, 83, 85, 87
Replacement and repression, 97, 314
Research: on attitude changes, 3–6; behavioral, 298; clinical, 267; on decision making, 6–8; experimental, 251, 299; field methods of, 6; investigations, 242; literature, 249; medical, 209; morale, 94; orientation, 309; personality, 284, 315–316; priorities, 187; projects, 6, 188, 228, 230; programs, 193, 207, 219, 304; social, 6, 203; psychological, 4, 6, 203, 312; stress, 1–5; surgical, 261–263, 267; systematic, 248; television, 172; types of, 298–301; workers, 184–316,
Research Branch of the Information-Education Division, 4, 22
Research Institute of the University of Oklahoma, 76, 88

Resentment, feelings of, 114–115, 140
Resources: community, 69; social coping, 263
Responsibility: personal, 203, 209, 211, 250–253, 279–281, 285; sense of, 73, 88; shifting of, 155, 158; social, 323; taking of, 158
Responsiveness and responses, 5; interview, 45; symbolic, 50
Restrictions of activity, anticipated, 73–74
Roles and role-playing: assignment, 88; effects of, 113; emotional, 159–160, 239; in internalization, 5; non-overt, 117–118; overt, 116–119; performance scenarios, 117, 121–122, 250; psychodramatic, 271; task and techniques of, 115, 118–119, 235
Routine interviews and sequences, 13, 228
Rumors, problem of, 70
Rural areas, factor of, 46

Sadism and sadness, traits of, 32, 105
Safety, feelings of, 50
San Angelo, Texas, tornadoes in, 83, 85
Scenarios, role-playing, 250
Science(s): administrative, 304; conception of, 317; philosophy of, 320; policies on, 291; social, 188–189
Scientists: behavioral, 1–2, 8, 148, 161, 213; medical research, 209; political, 304; social, 113, 167–168, 183
Scripts: moral, 182; personal, 169–172, 175; procedural, 185
Security, promises of, 50
Selective-exposure hypothesis, 154
Self-appraisal, 71
Self-approval, 250–252
Self-assurances, 267
Self-censorship, 293
Self-confidence, 197, 229, 233, 240–241, 251–252, 254, 260, 260, 269, 275–278; changes in, 4; degrees of, 14–16; loss of, 102
Self-control, 209, 230, 250, 254; lack of, 225; problem of, 248
Self-defeating policies, 272, 315
Self-derogatory feelings, 235
Self-disclosure hypothesis, levels of, 163, 206, 218, 223–224, 227–232, 243, 314
Self-efficacy, sense of, 261, 266

Self-esteem, feelings of, 98, 148, 201–202, 206, 226, 229, 235, 240, 275, 280, 303, 314; improvement in, 204, 223, 225; loss of, 105; maintenance of, 3; raising of, 199
Self-evaluation, 22
Self-initiated action, 72–73
Self-pacing, importance of, 266
Self-persuasion hypothesis, 114, 120–123, 240
Self-pride, 250
Self-rating, 19; verbal scale, 314
Self-reassurance, 136, 239
Self-regulation, 280
Self-reliance, need for, 177, 252–253, 263
Self-report data, 235
Self-reproaches, forms of, 104
Self-satisfaction, 244
Self-study groups, 305
Self-talk, positive, 266, 285
Sensitivity and sensitization: effects of, 75, 80–82; interpersonal, 79–80, 199, 314
Separation, anxiety and experiences, 74, 96
Setbacks, postdecisional, 218, 239, 262, 295
Sex: factor of, 138, 142, 228, 313; exploitation of, 108
Sharing: of fear, 100; of guilt, 105, 110
Shelters, air raid, 37, 48
Shifting of responsibility, 155, 158
Shock, emotional, 28, 33, 39
Short-term counseling, 220–223, 236, 247, 253–254
Shyness, trait of, 267
Sickness: radiation, 29–31, 36, 87; rate of, 22–23; severe, 141
Sincerity, feelings of, 245
Skills: combat, 12–13; coping, 284; direct-action, 266; interpersonal, 203; teaching, 230
Sleeplessness, causes of, 147
Smoking, problem of, 159, 174–176, 193–196, 200–201, 218–220, 231, 236–237, 247, 264, 311, 313
Soap operas, dubious value of, 175
Social: anxiety, 105, 267: approval training, 235; background, 75, 315; behavior, 6, 96; censure, 110; conditions 242, 293; coping resources, 263; disapproval, 279; environment, 72, 98; equity, 212; groups, 182; health, 180–

181, 197–199; incentives, 212; influence, 3, 167, 193, 208, 217; irresponsibility, 173; life, 29, 95; losses, 148; motives, 157; power, 197–201,209; prejudices, 159; problems, 189; psychologists, 6–7, 198, 260, 292; psychology, 3, 5–8, 113, 155–156, 200, 203, 213, 276, 284, 309–312, 315–316, 320; reassurance, 131; recognition, 31; reinforcement, 199; research, 6, 203; responsibility, 323; role, 88, 207; science, 188–189; scientists, 113, 167–168, 183; status, 208; stresses, 261, 264; structure, 185, 196; support, 221, 276, 283, 292, 310; surveys, 8; training, 68, 235; values, 121; workers, 218
Socialization: of children, 173; vicarious, 168
Society, influence of, 167, 173, 180
Sociohistory, factor of, 179
Sociolinguists, 227
Sociological Ambivalence (Merton), cited, 194
Sociology, ambivalence of, 194, 196, 206–212
Solidarity, group, 93
Southern California, University of, 224
Standard(s): behavioral, 198–200; of conduct, 95; ethical, 249, 293; of interviewing, 26; moral, 101
Standard operating procedures (SOP), 295–296
Starvation, fear of, 29
Status: loss of, 95; social, 208
Stereotyping, misleading, 173–175
Stimuli: battle, 12–15, 18; fear-eliciting, 13
Strategic Bombing Survey, United States (USSBS), 26, 30, 32, 35, 46, 73
Stress: anticipated, 263; arousal, 148; of childbirth, 283; combat, 11; dynamics, 148–151; emotional, 29, 47; environmental, 25; experiences, 4; induced, 132; inoculation, 2, 239, 259, 265, 267, 270–275, 321–322; levels of, 148–149, 303; military, 100; post-decisional, 241, 281; postoperative, 144, 282; psychological, 1, 4, 11, 48–49, 61, 94, 100, 148–149, 158, 309; psychology of, 131; research on, 1–5; situations, 2; social, 261, 264; sources, 133; of surgery, 137, 262; tolerance of, 133, 260

Students, morale of, 248
Studies: disaster, 264; field, 6; intervention, 283; laboratory, 304; psychiatric, 39; quasi-experimental, 300; social, 155
Subjective feelings, 26
Substitutive processes and persons, 97, 103
Super-ego functions, factor of, 95, 104
Superstitions, practice of, 63
Supportive actions, 221, 276, 283, 292, 310
Surgery: danger of, 136; elective, 219, 222; factor of, 4, 61, 94, 96, 174,186, 211, 240, 273, 279, 282; and patients, 67, 100, 103, 133–134; research in, 261–263, 267, stress of, 137, 262
Surrogate parents, 74, 95
Surveys: social, 8; morale, 4, 32, 34, 44, 97; questionnaire, 135
Survival and survivor reactions, 26, 31, 34–35
Suspicions, feelings of, 115, 119
Sylvania Laboratories, 87
Symbolism, responses to, 50, 88
Systems analyses, results of, 2

Taboos, subject of, 168
Teacher associations, 169, 171
Teaching: hospitals, 195; skills, 230
Telephone: contacts, 88, 251, interviews, 229
Television: cable, 169; commercial, 172, 175; dramas, 183; educational, 184–185; influence of, 183–184; potential power of, 167–169, 180; research on, 172; themes on, 181
Temper, exhibition of, 147
Temptation: to backslide, 203; resistance of, 196, 208
Tendencies: concurrence-seeking, 292, 298, 303; polarization of, 301; psychoneurotic, 21; reassurance, 67–70
Tenseness and tensions, 22; chronic, 47, emotional, 26, 53, 62, 135; muscular, 62
Terrorism, uncontrollable, 12
Texas city disaster, 83
Therapy and therapists, 197, 211, 265
Threats, reactions to, 61, 66, 70–71, 96
Tolerance, to stress, 133–134, 260
Tornadoes, damage caused by, 77, 83, 85
Toxicology, factory of, 61
Training: biofeedback, 204; effects of, 296;

military, 4, 12–16; procedures, 203, 211, 259; psychological, 316; self-approval, 250; social, 68, 235
Transference hypothesis, 95–97, 108, 110
Trauma and traumatic activities: emotional, 27; psychological, 2–3, 8; neuroses, 28, 36, 39, 83; reactions to, 263–264
Treatment: medical, 4, 174; psychotherapeutic, 231

Unambiguous information, 69–70
Unanimity, striving for, 295–296
Unconflicted: adherence, 148; change, 149
Underreaction, forms of, 60, 67–68
Understanding, need for, 243
United States: army of, 94; Morale Division and Survey, 25, 55; Strategic Bombing Survey, 26, 30, 32, 35, 46, 73
Unlearning of inhibitions, 107
Unwarranted optimism, 295
Urban: areas, 174; environment, 168; population, 46, 69
Utilities, public, 32

Vacillation, problem of, 157
Values and validity, internal and social, 6, 121
Verbal: attitudes, 7, 313; behavior, 223; communications, 70, 87; feedback, 224; reports, 313; self-rating scale, 314; warnings, 86
Verbalizations, forms of, 15, 260
Veterans, army, 18
Vicarious socialization and verification phase, 168, 300
Victimization: degrees of, 72, 83, 85; disaster, 2; flood, 76
Victims of Groupthink (Janis), cited, 291, 299, 302, 322
Videotapes, documentary, 176
Vietnam War, tragedy of, 154

Vigilance hypothesis, 3, 60–63, 69, 72, 149, 154, 157, 160–163, 239, 305
Viruses and epidemics, 87
Visual images, 169
Vocational counseling, 229
Vomiting, emotional causes of, 21
Vulnerability: feelings of, 64, 70, 134, 140, 183, 233, 263; personal, 82, 160, 239

Wall Street Journal, cited, 182
War Department, 4
Warfare and war weariness, 45; atomic, 23–26, 33–34; conventional, 25, 28, 35, 47
Warning(s), communications, 57–58, 62, 131; emergency, 78, 148; hurricane, 80–82; preliminary, 72–75, 79; psychology of, 57; reaction to, 58–61; realistic, 154, 259; stimuli, 87; unambiguous, 68; verbal, 86
Wartime: catastrophes, 25; danger and disasters, 27, 33, 94, 262; experiences, 3, 15
Weekend workshops, factor of, 225
Weight-reduction and clinics for, 196–197, 201, 220–225, 228–231, 234, 239–240, 249, 251–252, 277, 280, 305, 312–313, 322
"Wolf-wolf" fable, 80
Work groups, 98, 103, 291
Work of mourning, concept of, 100, 103, 139
Work of worrying hypothesis, 2, 100, 139–140, 142, 264, 283, 322
Workers: research, 184, 316; social, 218; white collar, 110

Yale University, 154, 206, 219, 229, 298, 304, 321; Department of Psychology, 312; research projects, 5; Smokers' Clinic, 159, 161; Weight Reduction Clinic, 221–224, 228, 234, 251–252